ASVAB
FOR
DUMMIES®
A Wiley Brand

PREMIER PLUS

by Rod Powers

ASVAB For Dummies® Premier PLUS

Published by
John Wiley & Sons, Inc.
111 River St.
Hoboken, NJ 07030-5774
www.wiley.com

Copyright © 2013 by John Wiley & Sons, Inc., Hoboken, New Jersey

Published simultaneously in Canada

For general information on our other products and services, please contact our Customer Care Department within the U.S. at 877-762-2974, outside the U.S. at 317-572-3993, or fax 317-572-4002.

For technical support, please visit www.wiley.com/techsupport.

Wiley publishes in a variety of print and electronic formats and by print-on-demand. Some material included with standard print versions of this book may not be included in e-books or in print-on-demand. If this book refers to media such as a CD or DVD that is not included in the version you purchased, you may download this material at http://booksupport.wiley.com. For more information about Wiley products, visit www.wiley.com.

Library of Congress Control Number: 2013932931

ISBN: 978-1-118-52553-1 (pbk); ISBN 978-1-118-52550-0 (ebk); ISBN 978-1-118-52561-6 (ebk); ISBN 978-1-118-52562-3 (ebk)

Manufactured in the United States of America

10 9 8 7 6 5 4 3

About the Author

Rod Powers joined the United States Air Force in 1975 intending to become a spy. He was devastated to learn that he should've joined the CIA instead because the military doesn't have that particular enlisted job. Regardless, he fell in love with the military and made it both a passion and a career, retiring with 23 years of service. Rod spent 11 of those years as a first sergeant, helping to solve the problems of the enlisted corps.

Since his retirement from the military in 1998, Rod has become a world renowned military careers expert. Through his highly popular U.S. Military Information Website on About.com (http://usmilitary.about.com), Rod has advised thousands of troops about all aspects of U.S. Armed Forces career information.

Rod is the proud father of twin girls, both of whom enjoy successful careers in the United States Air Force. Rod currently resides in Daytona Beach, Florida, where he attempts to prove that there's no such thing as too much sunshine. Even today, Rod tries to run his life according to long-lived military ideals and standards, but he gets a bit confused about why nobody will obey his orders anymore.

Dedication

To Jeanie and Chrissy — because everything is for you. Always.

Author's Acknowledgments

I want to thank Angie Papple Johnston for reviewing the manuscript for technical accuracy.

Special thanks goes out to Tracy Boggier, my acquisitions editor; Vicki Adang, my project editor; and Amanda Langferman, my copy editor. A big thanks goes to Autumn Lindsey, who was my right-hand assistant with all the artwork and text revisions and reviews.

Finally, I send more special thanks to the recruiting commands of the United States Army, Air Force, Navy, Marine Corps, and Coast Guard for providing invaluable resource information.

Publisher's Acknowledgments

We're proud of this book; please send us your comments at http://dummies.custhelp.com. For other comments, please contact our Customer Care Department within the U.S. at 877-762-2974, outside the U.S. at 317-572-3993, or fax 317-572-4002.

Some of the people who helped bring this book to market include the following:

Acquisitions, Editorial, and Vertical Websites

Senior Project Editor: Victoria M. Adang

    (Previous Edition: Chad R. Sievers)

Acquisitions Editor: Tracy Boggier

Copy Editor: Amanda M. Langferman

Senior Copy Editor: Danielle Voirol

Assistant Editor: David Lutton

Editorial Program Coordinator: Joe Niesen

Technical Editor: Angie Papple Johnston

Vertical Websites: Laura Moss-Hollister

Editorial Manager: Michelle Hacker

Editorial Assistants: Rachelle Amick, Alexa Koschier

Art Coordinator: Alicia B. South

Cover Photo: © iStockphoto.com / mbbirdy

Cartoons: Rich Tennant (www.the5thwave.com)

Composition Services

Project Coordinator: Sheree Montgomery

Layout and Graphics: Carrie A. Cesavice, Erin Zeltner

Indexer: Sherry Massey

Special Art: Autumn Lindsey

Publishing and Editorial for Consumer Dummies

    Kathleen Nebenhaus, Vice President and Executive Publisher

    David Palmer, Associate Publisher

    Kristin Ferguson-Wagstaffe, Product Development Director

Publishing for Technology Dummies

    Andy Cummings, Vice President and Publisher

Composition Services

    Debbie Stailey, Director of Composition Services

Contents at a Glance

Table of Contents

Introduction

1 If you're reading this book, there's a good chance that you want to join the United States military. Perhaps it's been your lifelong dream to drive a tank, fire a machine gun, or blow things up (legally). Maybe you've always wanted to learn how to cook for 2,000 people at a time. Possibly you were attracted to the military because of education and training opportunities, the chance of travel, or huge enlistment bonuses. In any event, by now you've discovered that you can't just walk into a recruiter's office and say, "Hey, I'm here. Sign me up!" These days, you have to pass the ASVAB.

The ASVAB (short for Armed Services Vocational Aptitude Battery) is unlike any test you've ever taken. It covers standard academic areas, such as math and English, but it also measures your knowledge of mechanics, electronics, science, and assembling objects.

The good news is that you need to do well on some of the subtests but not all of them. The order of importance of the subtests depends on your career goals. In this book, you find out what you need to know to do well on all the subtests and then get the info to determine which subtests are important to you. I include charts and tables to help you figure out the subtest scores that individual military jobs require. In fact, this guide is the first to include this information, so you can use *ASVAB For Dummies,* Premier PLUS, to ace the subtests that make up the ASVAB and determine which subtests are important for your military-career goals.

About This Book

The paper enlistment version of the ASVAB and the computer version of the test have nine subtests, each of which is covered in its own chapter in this book. This book shows you what to expect on each subtest, offers strategies for studying each subject area, gives you test-taking (and guessing) tips, and provides three full-length sample tests that help you determine your strengths and weaknesses. These sample tests also help you prepare mentally for taking the real test — you can use them to get in the zone. I've thrown in an extra test, covering the four most important subtests of the ASVAB that make up the AFQT (Armed Forces Qualification Test) score at no extra cost.

I provide three additional computerized ASVAB-style tests at *ASVAB For Dummies Online,* which you can use to simulate taking the test in a real-life scenario. The companion website also contains the three ASVAB tests that appear in the book to give you ample opportunities to practice on your computer. You can find the computerized version of the book's AFQT on the companion CD.

Although much of the material covered on the ASVAB is taught in practically every high school in the country, you may have slept through part of the info or performed a major brain-dump as soon as the ink was dry on your report card. So you also get a basic review of the relevant subject areas to help refresh your memory, as well as some pointers on where to find more information if you need it.

Conventions Used in This Book

The following conventions are used throughout the text to help point out important concepts and make the text easier to understand:

- ✔ All Web addresses appear in monofont. *Note:* Some Web addresses may extend to two lines of text. If you use one of these addresses, just type the address exactly as you see it, pretending that the line break doesn't exist.
- ✔ New terms appear in italics and are closely followed by easy-to-understand definitions.
- ✔ Bold text highlights important points and the action parts of numbered steps, as well as correct answers.

What You're Not to Read

This book has a number of sidebars (the shaded gray boxes) sprinkled throughout. They're full of interesting information about the ASVAB and the topics you may find on it, but you don't have to read them if you don't want to — they don't contain anything you simply must know to ace the test.

If you're taking the ASVAB for the purpose of enlisting in the U.S. military, you may even want to skip entire chapters, depending on your career goals. For example, if the military careers you're interested in don't require a score on the General Science subtest, you may want to skip that chapter and concentrate your study time on chapters that are required for your particular job choices.

Foolish Assumptions

While writing and revising this book, I made a few assumptions about you — namely, who you are and why you picked up this book. I assume the following:

- ✔ You've come here for test-taking tips and other helpful information. You may be a nervous test-taker.
- ✔ You want to take a few ASVAB practice tests to measure your current knowledge in various subject areas to help you develop a study plan.
- ✔ You want the military job of your dreams, and passing the ASVAB (or certain sections of it) is of utmost importance. Or you're in a high school that takes part in the ASVAB Career Exploration Program, and you want to know what to expect on the test.

How This Book Is Organized

This book isn't organized to reflect the order in which the subtests appear on the actual ASVAB — rather, I organized it in the most logical fashion to help you study.

Part 1: Making Sense of the ASVAB

If you have no clue about how the ASVAB is organized or what it covers, turn to Part I. This part also tells you how scores are calculated and how the military bigwigs use the scores to determine whether you qualify to join the military and which jobs you qualify for. Chapter 3 also contains some great study and test-taking tips.

Part II: Words to Live By: Communication Skills

If you already know that you need help on a particular language arts–related subtest, turn to Part II, where you can pump up your vocabulary and reading comprehension skills.

Part III: Making the Most of Math: Arithmetic Skills

Maybe math wasn't your best subject in school. Maybe you love math, but you've forgotten all those equations. In either case, this section is all about math. If you know you need to bone up on your mathematical skills, flip to Part III.

Part IV: The Whole Ball of Facts: Technical Skills

If you're interested in pursuing a military job that emphasizes science and technology and you want to make sure that you're going to nail the corresponding sections of the ASVAB, turn to Part IV.

Part V: Practice ASVAB Exams

This part gives you three different tests to figure out which areas you need to brush up on. Each test is a full-length sample test. Take the first one, and after that, check your answers. Then you can determine which subtests are a piece of cake and where you need the most help. Taking this approach lets you tailor a study plan to your individual needs. This part also includes a practice Armed Services Qualification Test (AFQT), made up of the four ASVAB subtests that determine whether you get into the military branch of your choice.

Part VI: The Part of Tens

This book is a *For Dummies* book, so it's not complete without a Part of Tens. If you want to find out some of the most important information for doing well on the ASVAB and you like your info presented in easily digestible lists, turn to Part VI. This part gives you test-taking tips.

Appendixes, ASVAB For Dummies Online, and the CD

If you want to check out different military jobs and see which subtests you need to do well on, turn to Appendix A. It shows you which subtest scores different military careers require. You can also find an appendix about what appears on the CD and at *ASVAB For Dummies Online*. The companion website contains all the practice ASVAB tests that appear in the book, as well as three additional computerized ASVAB-style tests. The tests have a timer, so you can take the tests like you would take the real ASVAB. You can also find 300 flashcards to improve your vocabulary. The CD contains the AFQT that appears in the book as well as some in-depth info on scoring. You can also navigate to the website from the CD.

Before you can take the tests found on the website or practice with the flashcards posted there, you need to register. On your first visit to *ASVAB For Dummies Online,* you need to enter your PIN code. You can find your PIN in the back of the book, or you can get your PIN by registering your e-book at dummies.com/go/getaccess. (If you have trouble with the PIN or can't find it, please contact Wiley Product Technical Support at 800-762-2974 or http://support.wiley.com.)

Icons Used in This Book

Throughout this book, you find icons that help you use the material in this book. Here's a rundown of what they mean to you:

This icon alerts you to helpful hints regarding the ASVAB. Tips can help you save time and avoid frustration.

This icon reminds you of important information you should read carefully.

This icon flags actions and ideas that may prove hazardous to your plans of conquering the ASVAB. Often, this icon accompanies common mistakes or misconceptions people have about the ASVAB or questions on the test.

This icon points out information that is interesting, enlightening, or in-depth but that isn't necessary for you to read.

This icon points out sample test questions that appear in review chapters.

Where to Go from Here

You don't have to read this book from cover to cover to score well. I suggest that you begin with Chapters 1 and 2. That way, you can get a feel for how the ASVAB is organized (along with the most up-to-date changes on the test) and which subtests may be important for the military service branch and job of your choice. This plan of attack helps you set up logical and effective goals to maximize your study efforts.

You may want to start by taking one of the practice tests in Part V. By using this method, you can discover which subjects are easier and in which subjects you need help. If you choose this technique, you can use the other practice tests to measure your progress after reading through and studying the subject chapters. I wish you luck on taking this test, and if you're one of the folks who wants to join the military, I hope your journey is successful!

Part I
Making Sense of the ASVAB

The 5th Wave
By Rich Tennant

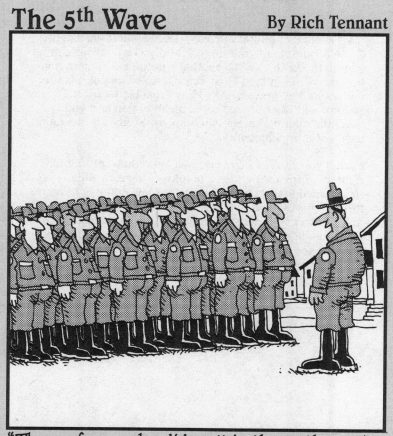

"Those of you who did well in the math portion of the ASVAB, line up in multiples of 3 to form columns which, when divided by 5, would give you a non-prime number."

In this part . . .

An ancient military proverb goes something like this: "Understand your enemy, and you will avoid getting shot in the buttocks." Okay, that's not a real ancient military proverb. (In fact, I just made it up.) The point is that understanding how the ASVAB is organized, how it's scored, and what those scores mean to you and your potential military career can help you study for this nine-part test more efficiently.

Even if you can't control yourself and you want to jump right in by reviewing the principles of algebra and memorizing word lists, chill out and take a few minutes to read through Part I. This part gives you an overview of the ASVAB, describes what each part of the exam tests, tells you when and where to take the test, and fills you in on how the scores are calculated. I even throw in some proven study techniques and test-taking strategies at no extra cost.

Chapter 1

Putting the ASVAB under a Microscope

. . . .

. . . .

The Armed Services Vocational Aptitude Battery (ASVAB) consists of nine individual tests (ten for Navy applicants who test at a Military Entrance Processing Station, or MEPS) that cover subjects ranging from general science principles to vocabulary. Your ASVAB test results determine whether you qualify for military service and, if so, which jobs you qualify for. The ASVAB isn't an IQ test. The military isn't trying to figure out how smart you are. The ASVAB specifically measures your ability to be trained to do a specific job.

The famous Chinese general Sun Tzu said, "Know your enemy." To develop an effective plan of study and score well on the ASVAB, it's important to understand how the ASVAB is organized and how the military uses the scores from the subtests. This chapter describes the different versions of the ASVAB, the organization of the subtests, how the AFQT score is calculated, and the various service policies for retaking the ASVAB.

Knowing Which Version You're Taking

The ASVAB comes in many flavors, depending on where and why you take it. You'd think that after more than 25 years in existence, the test could've been whittled down to a single version by now. But don't get too confused about the different versions. Table 1-1 boils down the choices.

Table 1-1		Versions of the ASVAB	
Version	**How You Take It**	**Format**	**Purpose**
Student	Given to juniors and seniors in high school; it's administered through a cooperative program between the Department of Education and the Department of Defense at high schools all across the United States	Paper	Its primary purpose is to provide a tool for guidance counselors to use when recommending civilian career areas to high school students (though it can be used for enlistment if taken within two years of enlistment). For example, if a student scores high in electronics, the counselor can recommend electronics career paths. If a student is interested in military service, the counselor then refers her to the local military recruiting offices.
Enlistment	Given through a military recruiter	Usually computer, may be paper	This version of the ASVAB is used by all the military branches for the purpose of enlistment qualification and to determine which military jobs a recruit can successfully be trained in.
Computer Adaptive Test (CAT) or Enlistment Screening Test (EST)	Given at the discretion of a military recruiter for a quick enlistment qualification screening	Computer	These mini-ASVABs aren't qualification tests; they're strictly recruiting tools. The EST and CAT contain questions similar but not identical to questions on the ASVAB. The tests are used to help estimate an applicant's probability of obtaining qualifying ASVAB scores.
Armed Forces Classification Test (AFCT)	Given in-house to people already in the military	Paper, though the military plans to replace it with a computerized version soon	At some point during your military career, you may want to retrain for a different job. If you need higher ASVAB scores to qualify for such retraining, you can take the AFCT. Except for the name of the exam, the AFCT is the same as the other versions of the ASVAB.

For people taking the enlistment version of the test, the vast majority of applicants are processed through a MEPS, where they take the computerized format of the ASVAB (called the CAT-ASVAB, short for *computerized-adaptive testing* ASVAB), undergo a medical physical, and run through a security screening, many times all in one trip. However, applicants may instead choose to take the paper and pencil (P&P) version, which is generally given by non-MEPS personnel at numerous Mobile Examination Test (MET) sites located throughout the United States.

Mapping Out the ASVAB Subtests

The computerized format of the ASVAB contains ten separately timed subtests, with the Auto & Shop Information subtest split in two (also, one small subtest is geared to Coding

Speed for a few Navy jobs; I don't include this subtest in the practice tests in this book because very few people test for these jobs). The paper format of the test has nine subtests. The two formats differ in the number of questions in each subtest and the amount of time you have for each one. Table 1-2 outlines the ASVAB subtests in the order that you take them in the enlistment (computerized or paper) and student (paper only) versions of the test; you can also see which chapters to turn to when you want to review that content.

Table 1-2		The ASVAB Subtests in Order		
Subtest	*Questions/Time (CAT-ASVAB)*	*Questions/Time (Paper Version)*	*Content*	*Chapter*
General Science (GS)	16 questions, 8 minutes	25 questions, 11 minutes	General principles of biological and physical sciences	Chapter 10
Arithmetic Reasoning (AR)	16 questions, 39 minutes	30 questions, 36 minutes	Simple word problems that require simple calculations	Chapter 8
Word Knowledge (WK)	16 questions, 8 minutes	35 questions, 11 minutes	Correct meaning of a word; occasionally antonyms (words with opposite meanings)	Chapter 4
Paragraph Comprehension (PC)	11 questions, 22 minutes	15 questions, 13 minutes	Questions based on several paragraphs (usually a few hundred words) that you read	Chapter 5
Mathematics Knowledge (MK)	16 questions, 20 minutes	25 questions, 24 minutes	High school math, including algebra and geometry	Chapter 7
Electronics Information (EI)	16 questions, 8 minutes	20 questions, 9 minutes	Electrical principles, basic electronic circuitry, and electronic terminology	Chapter 13
Auto & Shop Information (AS)	11 Auto Information questions, 7 minutes; 11 Shop Information questions, 6 minutes	25 questions, 11 minutes	Knowledge of automobiles, shop terminology, and tool use	Chapter 11
Mechanical Comprehension (MC)	16 questions, 20 minutes	25 questions, 19 minutes	Basic mechanical and physical principles	Chapter 12
Assembling Objects (AO)	16 questions, 15 minutes	25 questions, 15 minutes*	Spatial orientation	Chapter 14

*The Assembling Objects subtest isn't part of the student version of the test.

Deciphering ASVAB Scores

The Department of Defense is an official U.S. Government agency, so (of course) it can't keep things simple. When you receive your ASVAB score results, you don't see just one score; you see several. Figure 1-1 shows an example of an ASVAB score card used by high school guidance counselors (for people who take the student version — see "Knowing Which Version You're Taking" for details).

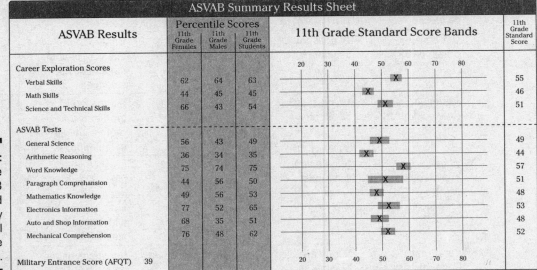

ASVAB Summary Results Sheet					
ASVAB Results	Percentile Scores			11th Grade Standard Score Bands	11th Grade Standard Score
	11th Grade Females	11th Grade Males	11th Grade Students		
Career Exploration Scores					
Verbal Skills	62	64	63		55
Math Skills	44	45	45		46
Science and Technical Skills	66	43	54		51
ASVAB Tests					
General Science	56	43	49		49
Arithmetic Reasoning	36	34	35		44
Word Knowledge	75	74	75		57
Paragraph Comprehansion	44	56	50		51
Mathematics Knowledge	49	56	53		48
Electronics Information	77	52	65		53
Auto and Shop Information	68	35	51		48
Mechanical Comprehension	76	48	62		52
Military Entrance Score (AFQT)	39				

Figure 1-1: A sample ASVAB score card used by high school guidance counselors.

Figure 1-2 depicts an example of an ASVAB score card used for military enlistment purposes.

So what do all these different scores actually mean? Check out the following sections to find out.

Defining all the scores

When you take a test in high school, you usually receive a score that's pretty easy to understand — A, B, C, D, or F. (If you do really well, the teacher may even draw a smiley face on the top of the page.) If only your ASVAB scores were as easy to understand.

In the following list, you see how your ASVAB test scores result in several different kinds of scores:

✔ **Raw score:** This score is the total number of points you receive on each subtest of the ASVAB. Although you don't see your raw scores on the ASVAB score cards, they're used to calculate the other scores.

You can't use the practice tests in this book (or any other ASVAB study guide) to calculate your probable ASVAB score. ASVAB scores are calculated by using raw scores, and raw scores aren't determined simply from the number of right or wrong answers. On the actual ASVAB, harder math questions are worth more points than easier questions.

SAMPLE CAT-ASVAB TEST SCORE REPORT

Testing Site ID: 521342   Service: AF

Testing Session: Date: 2013/05/17   Starting Time: 15:30

Applicant: Jane P. Doe   SNN: 333-33-3333

Test Form: 02E   Test Type: Initial

Standard Scores:	GS	AR	WK	PC	MK	EI	AS	MC	AO	VE
	63	59	60	52	56	81	64	62	52	58

COMPOSITE SCORES:

Army:	GT	CL	CO	EL	FA	GM	MM	OF	SC	ST
	118	121	128	130	127	132	134	129	128	125

Air Force:	M	A	G	E						
	91	76	83	96						

Navy/CG:	GT	EL	BEE	ENG	MEC	MEC2	NUC	OPS	HM	ADM
	117	259	234	120	185	173	235	225	177	114

Army:	MM	GT	EL							
	139	122	134							

SAMPLE CAT-ASVAB TEST SCORE REPORT

Figure 1-2: A sample ASVAB score card used for military enlistment purposes.

- ✔ **Standard scores:** The various subtests of the ASVAB are reported on the score cards as standard scores. A standard score is calculated by converting your raw score based on a standard distribution of scores with a mean of 50 and a standard deviation of 10.

  Don't confuse a standard score with the graded-on-a-curve score you may have seen on school tests — where the scores range from 1 to 100 with the majority of students scoring between 70 and 100. With standard scores, the majority score is between 30 and 70. That means that a standard score of 50 is an average score and that a score of 60 is an above-average score.

- ✔ **Percentile scores:** These scores range from 1 to 99. They express how well you did in comparison with another group called the *norm*. On the student version's score card, the norm is fellow students in your same grade (except for the AFQT score).

  On the enlistment and student versions' score cards, the AFQT score is presented as a percentile with the score normed using the *1997 Profile of American Youth,* a national probability sample of 18- to 23-year-olds who took the ASVAB in 1997. For example, if you receive a percentile score of 72, you can say you scored as well as or better than 72 out of 100 of the norm group who took the test. (And by the way, this statistic from 1997 isn't a typo. The ASVAB was last "re-normed" in 2004, and the sample group used for the norm was those folks who took the test in 1997.)

- ✔ **Composite scores (line scores):** Composite scores are individually computed by each service branch. Each branch has its own particular system when compiling various standard scores into individual composite scores. These scores are used by the different branches to determine job qualifications. Find out much more about this in Chapter 2.

Understanding the big four: Your AFQT scores

The ASVAB doesn't have an overall score. When you hear someone say, "I got an 80 on my ASVAB," that person is talking about the Armed Forces Qualification Test (AFQT) score, not an overall ASVAB score. The AFQT score determines whether you qualify even to enlist in the military, and only four of the subtests are used to compute it:

- Word Knowledge (WK)
- Paragraph Comprehension (PC)
- Arithmetic Reasoning (AR)
- Mathematics Knowledge (MK)

Doing well on some of the other subtests is a personal-choice type of issue. Some of the subtests are used only to determine the jobs you qualify for. (See Chapter 2 for information on how the military uses the individual subtests.)

Figure out which areas to focus on based on your career goals. If you're not interested in a job requiring a score on the Mechanical Comprehension subtest, you don't need to worry about doing well on that subtest. So as you're preparing for the ASVAB, remember to plan your study time wisely. If you don't need to worry about mechanics, don't bother with that chapter in this book. Spend the time on Word Knowledge or Arithmetic Reasoning. Keep in mind, though, if you don't have a desired job or aren't sure about your options, it's best to study this book and take the practice tests, focusing on all areas of the ASVAB. Doing well on each subtest will broaden your available job choices and make you a more desirable candidate.

Calculating the AFQT score

The military brass (or at least its computers) determines your AFQT score through a very particular process:

1. **Add the value of your Word Knowledge score to your Paragraph Comprehension score.**

2. **Convert the result of Step 1 to a scaled score, ranging from 20 to 62.**

   This score is known as your *Verbal Expression* or VE score.

3. **To get your raw AFQT score, double your VE score and then add your Arithmetic Reasoning (AR) score and your Mathematics Knowledge (MK) score to it.**

   The basic equation looks like this:

   Raw AFQT Score = 2VE + AR + MK

4. **Convert your raw score to a percentile score, which basically compares your results to the results of thousands of other ASVAB test-takers.**

   For example, a score of 50 means that you scored better than 50 percent of the individuals the military is comparing you to.

Looking at AFQT score requirements for enlistment

AFQT scores are grouped into five main categories based on the percentile score ranges in Table 1-3. Categories III and IV are divided into subgroups because the services sometimes use this chart for internal tracking purposes, enlistment limits, and enlistment incentives. Based on your scores, the military decides how trainable you may be to perform jobs in the service.

Table 1-3	AFQT Scores and Trainability	
Category	*Percentile Score*	*Trainability*
I	93–99	Outstanding
II	65–92	Excellent
III A	50–64	Above average
III B	31–49	Average
IV A	16–30	Below average
IV B	10–15	Not trainable
V	0–9	Not trainable

The U.S. Congress has directed that the military can't accept Category V recruits or more than 4 percent of recruits from Category IV. If you're in Category IV, you must have a high school diploma to be eligible for enlistment. Even so, if you're Category IV, your chances of enlistment are small and mostly limited to the Army National Guard.

Depending on whether you have a high school diploma or a GED, the military has different AFQT score requirements. Check out Table 1-4.

Table 1-4	AFQT Score Requirements		
Branch of Service	*Minimum AFQT Score with High School Diploma*	*Minimum AFQT Score with GED*	*Special Circumstances*
U.S. Air Force	36	65	In very rare cases, if the applicant possesses special skills (such as speaking a foreign language that the Air Force considers critical), the score of 36 can be waived to 31. The Air Force allows less than 1 percent of its enlistees each year to have a GED instead of a high school diploma.
Army	31	31	Occasionally, the Army approves waivers for folks with scores below 31. However, high enlistment rates and downsizing make it more competitive to get in as the Army becomes more and more selective.
Coast Guard	40	50	A waiver is possible if a recruit's ASVAB line scores qualify him or her for a specific job and the recruit is willing to enlist in that job. Very few people (about 5 percent) each year are allowed to enlist with a GED.
Marine Corps	32	50	Between 5 and 10 percent of recruits can enlist with a GED.
Navy	31	50	From 5 to 10 percent of recruits can enlist with a GED. Those with a GED must also be at least 19 and show a proven work history.

The Navy has been known to raise its minimum AFQT requirements to 50 for females (just to qualify for enlistment) when it receives too many female applicants. Because of the limited number of females that it can house on ships, the Navy restricts the number of women who can enlist each year.

Checking out the military's AFQT requirements for special programs

Achieving the minimum required AFQT score established by an individual branch gets your foot in the door, but the higher you score, the better. For example, if you need a medical or criminal history waiver in order to enlist, the military personnel who make those decisions are more likely to take a chance on you if they think you're a pretty smart cookie than if you barely made the minimum qualifying score.

Individual branches of the military tie many special enlistment programs to minimum AFQT scores:

- **Army:** The Army requires a minimum AFQT score of 50 to qualify for most of its incentive programs, such as a monetary enlistment bonus, the college-loan repayment program, and the Army College Fund.

- **Marine Corps:** Like the Army, the Marine Corps requires a minimum AFQT score of 50 for most of its incentive programs, including the Geographic Area of Choice Program, the Marine Corps College Fund, and enlistment bonuses.

- **Navy:** Applicants who want to participate in the Navy College Fund or college loan repayment program need to achieve a minimum score of 50.

Enlistment programs are subject to change without notice based on the current recruiting needs of the service. Your recruiter should be able to give you the most up-to-date information. Or visit usmilitary.about.com.

If you don't know which kind of job you want to do in the military, the ASVAB helps you and the military determine your potential ability for different types of jobs. If you're in this situation, review all the chapters in this book, brushing up on the basic principles of everything from science to electronics, but focus on the four subtests that enable you to qualify for enlistment: Word Knowledge, Paragraph Comprehension, Arithmetic Reasoning, and Mathematics Knowledge. Following this plan ensures a relatively accurate appraisal of your aptitude for various military jobs.

Do-Over: Retaking the ASVAB

An AFQT score of less than 10 is a failing score, but no branch of the service accepts that low of a score anyway. Therefore, you can fail to achieve a score high enough to enlist in the service branch you want, even if you pass the ASVAB. This means you need to work on one (or more) of the four core areas: Mathematics Knowledge, Arithmetic Reasoning, Paragraph Comprehension, and Word Knowledge. Parts II and III of this book are specifically designed to help you improve your scores on these four subtests.

When you're sure that you're ready, you can apply (through your recruiter) to take the ASVAB. After you take an initial ASVAB (taking the ASVAB in high school *does* count for retest purposes), you can retake the test after one month. After the first retest, you must again wait one month to test again. From that point on, you must wait at least six months before taking the ASVAB again.

You can't retake the ASVAB on a whim or whenever you simply feel like it. Each of the services has its own rules concerning whether it allows a retest, and I explain them in the following sections.

ASVAB tests are valid for two years, as long as you aren't in the military. In most cases, after you join the military, your ASVAB scores remain valid as long as you're in. In other words, except in a few cases, you can use your enlistment ASVAB scores to qualify for retraining years later.

U.S. Army retest policy

The Army allows a retest in one of the following instances:

- The applicant's previous ASVAB test has expired.
- The applicant failed to achieve an AFQT score high enough to qualify for enlistment.
- Unusual circumstances occur, such as if an applicant, through no fault of his own, is unable to complete the test.

 Army recruiters aren't authorized to have applicants retested for the sole purpose of increasing aptitude area scores to meet standards prescribed for enlistment options or programs.

U.S. Air Force retest policy

For the U.S. Air Force, the intent of retesting is for an applicant to improve the last ASVAB scores so the enlistment options increase. Before any retest is administered, the recruiting flight chief must interview the applicant in person or by telephone and then give approval for the retest.

Here are a few other policies to remember:

- The Air Force doesn't allow retesting for applicants after they've enlisted in the Delayed Entry Program (DEP).
- Current policy allows retesting of applicants who aren't holding a job/aptitude area reservation and/or who aren't in DEP but already have qualifying test scores.
- Retesting is authorized when the applicant's current line scores (mechanical, administrative, general, and electronic) limit the ability to match an Air Force skill with his or her qualifications.

U.S. Navy retest policy

The Navy allows retesting of applicants

- Whose previous ASVAB tests have expired
- Who fail to achieve a qualifying AFQT score for enlistment in the Navy

In most cases, individuals in the Delayed Entry Program (DEP) can't retest. One notable exception is the Navy's DEP *Enrichment Program.* This program provides for the provisional DEP enlistment of high school graduates with AFQT scores between 28 and 30. Individuals enlisted under the program are enrolled in academic enhancement training, retested with the ASVAB, and accessed to active duty, provided they score 31 or higher on the subsequent ASVAB retest.

Tracing the testing trail

In 1948, Congress made the Department of Defense develop a uniform screening test to be used by all the services. The Defense Department came up with the Armed Forces Qualification Test (AFQT). This test consisted of 100 multiple-choice questions in areas such as math, vocabulary, spatial relations, and mechanical ability. The military used this test until the mid-1970s. Each branch of the service set its own minimum qualification (AFQT) score.

When the military decides to do something, it often acts with the lightning speed of a snail carrying a backpack. So in the 1960s, the Department of Defense decided to develop a standardized military selection and classification test and to administer it in high schools. That's where your old buddy, the ASVAB, came from. The first ASVAB test was given in 1968, but the military didn't use it for recruiting purposes for several years. In 1973, the draft ended and the nation entered the contemporary period in which all military recruits are volunteers. In 1976, the ASVAB became the official entry test used by all services.

The ASVAB remained unchanged until 1980, when the ASVAB underwent its first revision. The subtest areas remained the same, but several of the questions were updated to keep up with changes in technology.

In 1993, the computerized version was released for limited operational testing, but it didn't begin to see wide-scale use until 1996. The questions on the computerized version of the ASVAB were identical to the questions on the paper version. It wasn't until the end of 2002 that the ASVAB finally underwent a major revision. Two subtests (Coding Speed and Numerical Operations) were eliminated and a new subtest (Assembling Objects) was added to the computerized version. Also during the 2002 revision, all the questions were updated, and the order of the subtests was changed. The revised ASVAB was first rolled out in the computerized format, and the paper versions of the test were updated during the next year. The most recent update occurred in 2008. The ASVAB was revised to better sync the line score with the applicants' qualified jobs.

U.S. Marine Corps retest policy

The Marine Corps authorizes a retest if the applicant's previous test is expired. Otherwise, recruiters can request a retest if the initial scores don't appear to reflect the applicant's true capability, considering the applicant's education, training, and experience.

For the Marine Corps, the retest can't be requested *solely* because the applicant's initial test scores didn't meet the standards prescribed for enlistment options or programs.

U.S. Coast Guard retest policy

For Coast Guard enlistments, six months must have elapsed since an applicant's last test before he or she may retest solely for the purpose of raising scores to qualify for a particular enlistment option.

The Coast Guard Recruiting Center may authorize retesting after one calendar month has passed from an initial ASVAB test if substantial reason exists to believe the initial test scores or subtest scores don't reflect an applicant's education, training, or experience.

Chapter 2

Knowing What It Takes to Get Your Dream Job

In This Chapter

▶ Finding out there's more to life than the AFQT score

▶ Making sense out of line scores

▶ Discovering how each military branch uses line scores

The Armed Forces Qualification Test (AFQT) portion of the ASVAB is your most important score because it determines whether you can join the service of your choice. However, qualifying to join is only part of the picture. Unless you'd be content to spend your military career painting things that don't move, you need to understand how the ASVAB relates to various military job opportunities.

Civilian employers generally use a person's education and experience level when selecting candidates for a job position, but in the military, 99 percent of all enlisted jobs are entry-level positions. The military doesn't require you to have a college degree in computer science before you're hired to become a computer programmer. You don't even have to have any previous computer experience, nor does the military care if you do. You're going to go to military school to study how to make computers stand at attention and fly right.

Sounds like a good deal, right? So what's the catch? Well, believe me — the military spends big bucks turning high school graduates into highly trained and skilled aircraft mechanics, language specialists, and electronic-doodad repair people. In an average year, the services enlist about 225,000 new recruits. Any way you look at it, that's a lot of combat boots! Each and every recruit has to be sent to a military school to train for a job. Uncle Sam needs a way to determine whether a wet-behind-the-ears high school graduate has the mental aptitude to succeed at that job — preferably before he spends your hard-earned tax dollars.

Enter the ASVAB. The services combine various ASVAB subtest scores into groupings called *composite scores* or *line scores*. Through years of trial and error, the individual military services have each determined what minimum composite scores are required to successfully complete its various job training programs. In this chapter, you discover how those test scores translate into finding the military job of your dreams.

Eyeing How ASVAB Scores Determine Military Training Programs and Jobs

Each service branch has its own system of scores. Recruiters and military job counselors use these scores, along with other factors such as job availability, security clearance eligibility, medical qualifications, and physical strength, to match up potential recruits with military jobs.

During the initial enlistment process, your service branch determines your military job or enlistment program based on established minimum *line scores:* various combinations of scores from individual subtests (see the next section for details). If you get an appropriate score in the appropriate areas, you can get the job you want — as long as that job is available and you meet other qualification factors.

For active duty, the Army is the only service that looks at the scores and offers a guaranteed job for all its new enlistees. In other words, every single Army recruit knows what his or her job is going to be before signing the enlistment contract. The other active duty services use a combination of guaranteed jobs or guaranteed aptitude/career areas:

- **Air Force:** About 40 percent of active duty Air Force recruits enlist with a guaranteed job. The majority enlists in one of four guaranteed aptitude areas, and during basic training, recruits are assigned to a job that falls into that aptitude area.

- **Coast Guard:** The Coast Guard rarely, if ever, offers a guaranteed job in its active duty enlistment contracts. Instead, new Coasties enlist as undesignated seamen and spend their first year or so of service doing general work ("Paint that ship!") before finally applying for specific job training.

- **Marine Corps:** A vast majority of Marine Corps active duty enlistees are guaranteed one of several job fields, such as infantry, avionics, logistics, vehicle maintenance, aircraft maintenance, munitions, and so on. Each of these fields is further divided into specific subjobs, called Military Occupational Specialties (MOS). Marine recruits usually don't find out their actual MOSs until about halfway through basic training.

- **Navy:** Most Navy recruits enlist with a guaranteed job, but several hundred people each year also enlist in a guaranteed career area and then *strike* (apply) for the specific job within a year of graduating boot camp.

All enlistment contracts for the reserve forces (regardless of branch) contain guarantees for a specific job. Why? Because reserve recruiters recruit for vacancies in specific reserve units, usually located within 100 miles of where a person lives.

Understanding How Each Branch Computes Line Scores

A *line score* combines various standard ASVAB scores to see which jobs or training programs you qualify for. The *standard scores* are your scores on the individual ASVAB subtests (with Word Knowledge and Paragraph Comprehension combined as a Verbal Expression score):

- General Science (GS)

- Arithmetic Reasoning (AR)

- Auto & Shop Information (AS)

- Mathematics Knowledge (MK)

- Mechanical Comprehension (MC)

- Electronics Information (EI)

- Assembling Objects (AO)

- Verbal Expression (VE), the sum of Word Knowledge (WK) and Paragraph Comprehension (PC)

Each of the military services computes its line scores differently. Some calculations even include *dummy scores* — average scores received by thousands of test takers — for Numerical Operations (NO) and Coding Speed (CS), subtests that are no longer part of the ASVAB. The following sections outline how each branch comes up with its line scores.

Line scores and the Army

To compute line scores for job qualification, the Army combines the various scores into ten separate areas by simple addition of the ASVAB standard scores. Table 2-1 shows the line scores and the ASVAB subtests that make them up.

Table 2-1	The U.S. Army's Ten Line Scores	
Line Score	*Standard Scores Used*	*Formula Used*
Clerical (CL)	Verbal Expression (VE), Arithmetic Reasoning (AR), and Mathematics Knowledge (MK)	VE + AR + MK
Combat (CO)	Arithmetic Reasoning (AR), Coding Speed (CS), Auto & Shop Information (AS), and Mechanical Comprehension (MC)	AR + CS + AS + MC
Electronics (EL)	General Science (GS), Arithmetic Reasoning (AR), Mathematics Knowledge (MK), and Electronics Information (EI)	GS + AR + MK + EI
Field Artillery (FA)	Arithmetic Reasoning (AR), Coding Speed (CS), Mathematics Knowledge (MK), and Mechanical Comprehension (MC)	AR + CS + MK + MC
General Maintenance (GM)	General Science (GS), Auto & Shop Information (AS), Mathematics Knowledge (MK), and Electronics Information (EI)	GS + AS + MK + EI
General Technical (GT)	Verbal Expression (VE) and Arithmetic Reasoning (AR)	VE + AR
Mechanical Maintenance (MM)	Numerical Operations (NO), Auto & Shop Information (AS), Mechanical Comprehension (MC), and Electronics Information (EI)	NO + AS + MC + EI
Operators and Food (OF)	Verbal Expression (VE), Numerical Operations (NO), Auto & Shop Information (AS), and Mechanical Comprehension (MC)	VE + NO + AS + MC
Surveillance and Communications (SC)	Verbal Expression (VE), Arithmetic Reasoning (AR), Auto & Shop Information (AS), and Mechanical Comprehension (MC)	VE + AR + AS + MC
Skilled Technical (ST)	General Science (GS), Verbal Expression (VE), Mathematics Knowledge (MK), and Mechanical Comprehension (MC)	GS + VE + MK + MC

Line scores and the Navy and Coast Guard

The Navy and Coast Guard use the standard scores directly from the ASVAB: the individual subtest scores and Verbal Expression (VE) score, which is the sum of Word Knowledge (WK) and Paragraph Comprehension (PC).

Although the Navy and Coast Guard don't use their line scores for officially determining jobs, the scores provide recruiters, job counselors, and recruits with a snapshot of which broad career areas recruits may qualify for. For example, the Navy regulation, which lists the qualifications to become an Air Traffic Control Specialist, states that an ASVAB score of VE + AR + MK + MC = 210 (or higher) is required for that job.

Table 2-2 shows the Navy and Coast Guard line scores that show up on the ASVAB score sheet.

Table 2-2	The U.S. Navy and Coast Guard's Line Scores	
Line Score	*Standard Scores Used*	*Formula Used*
Engineman (ENG)	Auto & Shop Information (AS) and Mathematics Knowledge (MK)	AS + MK
Administrative (ADM)	Mathematics Knowledge (MK) and Verbal Expression (VE)	MK + VE
General Technical (GT)	Arithmetic Reasoning (AR) and Verbal Expression (VE)	AR + VE
Mechanical Maintenance (MEC)	Arithmetic Reasoning (AR), Auto & Shop Information (AS), and Mechanical Comprehension (MC)	AR + AS + MC
Health (HM)	General Science (GS), Mathematics Knowledge (MK), and Verbal Expression (VE)	GS + MK + VE
Mechanical Maintenance 2 (MEC2)	Assembling Objects (AO), Arithmetic Reasoning (AR), and Mechanical Comprehension (MC)	AO + AR + MC
Electronics (EL)	Arithmetic Reasoning (AR), Electronics Information (EI), General Science (GS), and Mathematics Knowledge (MK)	AR + EI + GS + MK
Nuclear Field (NUC)	Arithmetic Reasoning (AR), Mechanical Comprehension (MC), Mathematics Knowledge (MK), and Verbal Expression (VE)	AR + MC + MK + VE
Engineering and Electronics (BEE)	Arithmetic Reasoning (AR), General Science (GS), and two times Mathematics Knowledge (MK)	AR + GS + 2MK
Operations (OPS)	Arithmetic Reasoning (AR) and Mathematics Knowledge (MK)	AR + MK

Line scores and the Marine Corps

The Marine Corps computes its three line scores for job qualification by adding scores from various ASVAB subtests, as Table 2-3 shows.

Table 2-3	The Marine Corps's Line Scores	
Line Score	**Standard Scores Used**	**Formula Used**
Mechanical Maintenance (MM)	General Science (GS), Auto & Shop Information (AS), Mathematics Knowledge (MK), and Mechanical Comprehension (MC)	GS + AS + MK + MC
General Technical (GT)	Verbal Expression (VE) and Arithmetic Reasoning (AR)	VE + AR
Electronics (EL)	General Science (GS), Arithmetic Reasoning (AR), Mathematics Knowledge (MK), and Electronics Information (EI)	GS + AR + MK + EI

Line scores and the Air Force

The U.S. Air Force uses standard scores from the ASVAB subtests to derive scaled scores in four aptitude areas called MAGE (mechanical, administrative, general, and electronics). The Air Force MAGE scores are calculated as *percentiles*, ranging from 0 to 99, which show your relationship to thousands of others who've taken the test. In other words, a percentile score of 51 indicates you scored better in this aptitude area than 50 percent of the testers who were used to establish the "norm."

Table 2-4 lays out the four areas, the subtests used, and the formula used to calculate the score for each particular area. After calculating the score for a particular area, the test-scorer converts that score to a percentile.

Table 2-4	The U.S. Air Force's MAGE Scores	
Line Score	**Standard Scores Used**	**Formula Used**
Mechanical	General Science (GS), Mechanical Comprehension (MC), and two times Auto & Shop Information (AS)	GS + MC + 2AS
Administrative	Numerical Operations (NO), Coding Speed (CS), and Verbal Expression (VE)	NO + CS + VE
General	Arithmetic Reasoning (AR) and Verbal Expression (VE)	AR + VE
Electronics	General Science (GS), Arithmetic Reasoning (AR), Mathematics Knowledge (MK), and Electronics Information (EI)	GS + AR + MK + EI

Score! Speaking the lingo

When you sit down with your recruiter to discuss your ASVAB scores and what you qualify for, you may think he suddenly decided to speak in a foreign language. For job-qualification purposes, remember three key terms and their definitions:

✔ **Standard score:** A standard score refers to individual ASVAB subtest scores (that is, Verbal Expression, Arithmetic Reasoning, Mathematics Knowledge, and so on).

✔ **Line score:** A line score combines various standard scores that the services use for job qualification purposes.

✔ **AFQT score:** Calculated from the math and English subtests of the ASVAB, the Armed Forces Qualification Test (AFQT) score is used by the military to determine overall enlistment qualification. Chapter 1 explains exactly how this critical score is computed.

Chapter 3

Getting Acquainted with Test-Taking and Study Techniques

How many times have you heard someone say (or may have even said yourself), "I just can't take tests"? Well, of course you can't do well on tests if you keep telling yourself that! In basic training, your drill sergeant (hereafter known as "Sir" or "Ma'am") will convince you that the words "I can't" simply don't exist in the military. If you don't believe me, try telling your drill sergeant, "I just can't do push-ups." You will find that with sufficient practice (and your drill sergeant will ensure you get a lot of practice), you can do push-ups just as well as the next person. (Actually, I don't recommend testing this, for reasons that should be obvious.) The truth is that those who do well on tests are those who've figured out how to study efficiently and how to use a dash of test-taking psychology.

This chapter includes information on how to prepare for the test — how you study and how and why you should take the practice exams. In addition, you get some inside info, such as secrets for guessing when you don't know the answer to a question (although if you study for the test, that will never happen, right?). The tips and techniques provided in this chapter can help you get a jump on the ASVAB and your military career.

Taking the Test: Paper or Computerized?

Many versions of the ASVAB exist (although you probably won't get a choice of which one to take), but they primarily boil down to two basic differences: the paper version and the computerized version. Each version has advantages and disadvantages, which I discuss in the following sections.

If you're taking the ASVAB as part of the student program in high school, or if you're already in the military and are retaking the ASVAB to qualify to retrain into a different job, you may take the paper version.

If you're taking the ASVAB to enlist in the military, you'll take the enlistment ASVAB. This version is available in paper format and via computer. There's a great chance that you'll take the computerized version (CAT-ASVAB), because to save time and money, the recruiting services often send applicants to the nearest Military Entrance Processing Station (MEPS) for testing, medical examination, and enlistment (one-stop shopping). MEPS only uses the computerized version, so you know you won't take the paper version if you're scheduled to take the ASVAB at MEPS.

If you have your heart set on taking the test in paper format, ask your recruiter whether a Mobile Examination Test (MET) site is nearby. Roughly 685 MET sites are located throughout the United States (generally located in National Guard Armories). Your recruiter can schedule you to take the enlistment paper version at any one of these MET sites, which may offer testing sessions anywhere from once a month to several times per week.

Writing on hard copy: The advantages and disadvantages of the paper version

Modern technology isn't always better. Taking the pencil-and-paper version of the ASVAB can provide you with certain advantages:

- ✔ **You can skip questions that you don't know the answer to and come back to them later.** This option can help when you're racing against the clock and want to get as many answers right as possible. You can change an answer on the subtest you're currently working on, but you can't change an answer on a subtest after the time for that subtest has expired.

- ✔ **You may not make any marks in the exam booklet; however, you may make notes on your scratch paper.** If you skip a question, you can lightly circle the item number on your answer sheet to remind yourself to go back to it. If you don't know the answer to a question, you can mentally cross off the answers that seem unlikely or wrong to you and then guess based on the remaining answers. Be sure to erase any stray marks you make on your answer sheet before time is called for that subtest.

Killing trees isn't the only disadvantage of the paper-based test. Other drawbacks include the following:

- ✔ **Harder questions are randomly intermingled with easier questions.** This means you can find yourself spending too much time trying to figure out the answer to a question that's too hard for you and may miss answering some easier questions at the end of the subtest, thereby lowering your overall score.

- ✔ **The paper answer sheets are scored by using an optical mark scanning machine.** The machine has a conniption when it comes across an incompletely filled-in answer circle or stray pencil marks and will often stubbornly refuse to give you credit, even if you answered correctly.

- ✔ **Getting your scores may seem like it takes forever.** The timeline varies; however, your recruiter will have access to your score no later than 72 hours (3 days) after you finish the test (not counting days the MEPS doesn't work, such as weekend days or holidays).

Going paperless: The pros and cons of the computerized test

The computerized version of the ASVAB, called *computerized-adaptive testing,* or CAT-ASVAB, contains questions similar to the ones on the paper version, but the questions are presented in a different order. The CAT-ASVAB adapts the questions it offers you based on your level of proficiency (that's why it's called *adaptive*). Translation: The first test item is of average difficulty. If you answer this question correctly, the next question will be more difficult. If you answer it incorrectly, the computer will give you an easier question. By contrast, on the paper ASVAB, hard and easy questions are presented randomly.

The CAT-ASVAB also has significantly fewer questions than the pencil-and-paper version of the test, although the questions tend to be a bit harder, which tends to result in the same scores (level of knowledge).

Maybe it's because people today are more comfortable in front of a computer than with a pencil, but military recruiters have noted that among applicants who've taken both the paper-based and computerized versions of the ASVAB, many applicants tend to score slightly higher on the computerized version of the test.

You don't have to be a computer guru to appreciate the advantages of the computerized version of the ASVAB:

- **It's impossible to record your answer in the wrong space on the answer sheet.** Questions and possible answers are presented on the screen, and you press the key that corresponds to your answer choice before moving on to the next question. Often, only the A, B, C, and D keys are activated when you take the test.

- **The difficulty of the test items presented depends on whether you answered the previous question correctly.** On the two math subtests of the ASVAB, harder questions are worth more points than easier questions, so this method helps maximize your AFQT score.

- **You get your scores right away.** The computer automatically calculates and prints your standard scores for each subtest and your line scores for each service branch. (For more on line scores, see Chapter 2.) This machine is a pretty smart cookie — it also calculates your AFQT percentile score on-the-spot. You usually know whether you qualify for military enlistment on the same day you take the test and, if so, which jobs you qualify for.

On the downside, you can't skip questions or change your answers after you enter them on the CAT-ASVAB. Instead of being able to go through and immediately answer all the questions you're sure of, you have to answer each question as it comes. This can make it difficult to judge how much time to spend on a difficult question before guessing and moving on. Also, if you have a few minutes at the end of the test, you can't go back and make sure you marked the correct answer to each question.

Tackling Multiple-Choice Questions

Both the paper-based and the computerized versions of the ASVAB are multiple-choice tests. You choose the correct (or most correct) answer from among the available (usually four) choices. Here are some tips to keep in mind as you tackle the choices:

- **Read the directions carefully.** Most ASVAB test proctors agree — the majority of the time when there's an issue with an applicant's scores, misreading directions is a prime offender. Each subtest has a paragraph or two describing what the subtest covers and instructions on how to answer the questions. If the directions on the Paragraph Comprehension subtest informs you that a paragraph applies to questions 3, 4, and 5 and you misread it as 4, 5, and 6, you're probably going to get at least one of those questions wrong.

✔ **Make sure you understand the question.** If you don't understand the question, you're naturally not going to be able to make the best decision when selecting an answer. Understanding the question requires attention to three particular points:

- **Take special care to read the questions correctly.** Most questions ask something like, "Which of the following equals 2×3?" But sometimes, a question may ask, "Which of the following does not equal 2×3?" You can easily skip right over the word *not* when you're reading, assume that the answer is 6, and get the question wrong.

- **On the math subtests, be especially careful to read the symbols.** When you're in a hurry, the + sign and the ÷ sign can look very similar. And blowing right by a negative sign or another symbol is just as easy.

- **Make sure you understand the terms being used.** When a math problem asks you to find the product of two numbers, be sure you know what finding the product means (you have to multiply the two numbers). If you add the two numbers, you arrive at the wrong answer.

✔ **Take time to review all the answer options.** On all the subtests, you almost always select the correct answer from only four possible answer options. On the ASVAB, you're supposed to choose the answer that is most correct. (Now and then you do the opposite and choose the answer that's least correct.) Sometimes several answers are reasonably correct for the question at hand, but only one of them is the best answer. If you don't stop to read and review all the answers, you may not choose the one that's most correct. Or if you review all the answer options, you may realize that you hastily decided on an incorrect answer because you misread it.

Often, a person reads a question, decides on the answer, glances at the answer options, chooses the option that agrees with his or her answer, marks it on the answer sheet, and then moves on. Although this approach usually works, it can sometimes lead you astray.

✔ **If you're taking a paper test, mark the answer carefully.** A machine scores the paper-based ASVAB answer sheets. You have to mark the answer clearly so that the machine knows which answer you've selected. This means carefully filling in the space that represents the correct letter. You've done this a million times in school, but it's worth repeating: Don't use a check mark, don't circle the answer, and don't let your mark wander into the next space. If you must erase, make sure all evidence of your prior choice is gone; otherwise, the grading machine may credit you with the wrong choice or disregard your correct answer and give you no credit at all.

Incorrectly marking the answer sheet — answering Question 11 on the line for Question 12, Question 12 on the line for Question 13, and . . . you get the idea — is a very real possibility. Be especially careful if you skip a question that you're going to return to later.

Incorrectly marking the answers can cause a real headache. If you fail to get a qualifying score, the minimum amount of time you must wait before retaking the ASVAB is one month. Even then, your journey to military glory through ASVAB torment may not be over. If within six months of a previous test, your retest AFQT score increases by 20 points or more, you'll be required by MEPCOM regulation to take an additional ASVAB test, called a *confirmation test*. (Confirmation tests can be taken only at MEPS facilities, by the way.) So if you're not careful, you'll be taking three ASVABs when all you really needed to take was one. Sound fun? Chapter 1 discusses how and when you can retake the ASVAB.

When You Don't Know an Answer: Guessing Smart

On the ASVAB, guessing is okay. In fact, it's encouraged. The reason is in the scoring of the test. Here's how the point system breaks down:

- ✔ If you choose the correct answer, you get one point (or more, depending on how the question is weighted).

- ✔ If you don't answer a question, you get nada.

- ✔ If you guess on a question and get the question wrong, you get nada — no worrying about losing points or getting any sort of penalty!

Because most questions have four possible answers, you generally have a 25 percent chance of guessing correctly, which means that you have chances to increase your score by guessing. Here are some guessing tips:

- ✔ There's always at least one answer that isn't even close to the correct answer. By using simple deduction, you can often narrow your choices down to two answers or fewer.

- ✔ Don't eliminate an answer based on how frequently that answer comes up. For example, if Choice (B) has been the correct answer for the last five questions, don't assume that it must be the wrong answer for the question you're on just because that would make it six in a row.

- ✔ Usually, an answer that has *always, all, everyone, never, none,* or *no one* is incorrect.

- ✔ The longer the answer, the more likely that it's the correct answer. The test-makers have to get all those qualifiers in there so you can't find an example to contradict the correct answer. If you see phrases like "in many cases" or "frequently," that's a clue that the test-makers are trying to make the answer most correct.

- ✔ If two choices are very similar in meaning, neither of them is probably the correct choice. On the other hand, if two answer options contradict each other, one of them is usually correct.

- ✔ Don't change an answer after you select it. If you have to guess, never, ever go back and change the answer, unless you're absolutely, 100 percent, positively convinced that you're changing it to the correct answer and you only answered incorrectly because you had sweat in your eyes and didn't read the choices properly.

- The United States Air Force Senior NCO Academy conducted an in-depth study of several Air Force multiple-choice test results, taken over several years, and found that when students changed answers on their answer sheets, they changed from a right answer to a wrong answer more than 72 percent of the time!

In each of the chapters in this book that reviews a particular subtest, you find more hints for making educated guesses that are specific to those topics.

If you guess on more than one question throughout the test, choosing the same answer for every guess is a smart way to go. For example, all your guesses could be Choice (B). This technique slightly increases your chances of getting more answers correct. However, if you can eliminate Choice (B) as a wrong answer, then, by all means, choose a different answer option for that question.

Studying and Practicing for the ASVAB

The practice tests that come with this book are valuable study aids. Before you begin studying, take one of the tests. Feel free to take a paper test in the book or hop online and go the electronic route. Either way, try to duplicate the testing environment — take the entire exam at one time, time yourself, and don't allow interruptions.

The military has a saying, "Train as you expect to fight." The same is true of the ASVAB. If you plan to take the pencil-and-paper version of the ASVAB, concentrate most of your efforts on the written practice tests in this book. If you'll be taking the CAT-ASVAB, spend most of your time practicing with the tests available online.

Get a sense of how long it takes you to complete each subtest so you know how much time you have to spend on educated guessing. After you complete the first practice test, check your answers to see where you need improvement.

When you study for the ASVAB, fall in line with these study habits to make the most of your time:

- **Focus on the subtests that matter to you.** If you have a clear interest in pursuing a career in electronics, the Electronics Information subtest should be at the top of your list to ace. Although you'll want to make sure all your line scores are good (in case you retrain or your desired job isn't available), focusing on your expertise in certain areas of interest makes you a more desirable candidate. (See Chapter 2 and Appendix A for lists of the subtests that affect your acceptance into the job areas you're pursuing.)

- **Concentrate on subject areas that need improvement.** It's human nature to find yourself spending your study time on subject areas that you have an interest in or that you're good at. If you're a whiz at fixing cars, don't waste your time studying auto information. You're already going to ace that part of the test, right? On the other hand, if you had a hard time in math during your high school years, you need to spend extra time brushing up on your arithmetic skills.

- **Be a loner.** You may want to study with a partner now and then so the two of you can brainstorm answers and quiz each other, but most of your studying should be done on your own.

- **Try to reduce distractions.** Always study in a well-lit, quiet area away from pets, screaming babies, and the TV.

- **Study in long blocks of time.** Studying for an hour or two once or twice a day is much more effective than 15 minutes six times a day.

- **Keep study breaks short.** A few minutes every hour is sufficient. Don't ignore breaks completely, however. Studies show that taking short breaks improves how well you're able to remember information.

- **Practice the actual act of test-taking.** Practice marking answers correctly on the answer key and time yourself to see how long it takes you to answer questions.

After you do some additional studying, take the second practice exam. Again, try to duplicate testing conditions. Check your answers. Compare your scores to the scores from your first test. Have you improved? If so, continue studying as you have been. If not, reconsider how you're studying or whether you're setting aside enough time to study. A school counselor or teacher can give you additional study pointers. Continue practicing with the next few tests.

A couple of weeks before the ASVAB, take the next-to-last practice test. Brush up on any of those nagging areas that still give you fits. Check to see which areas you need help with and spend more time studying those areas.

A week before your test date, take the last test. This test helps you calm your nerves before taking the ASVAB — how the test works will be fresh in your mind.

Don't waste time memorizing the practice questions in this guide or any other ASVAB study guide. You won't see the same questions on the ASVAB. Use this guide and the sample tests for two purposes:

- ✔ **To determine the subject areas in which you need to improve:** Use the tips and techniques, along with standard study materials (like high-school textbooks), to improve your knowledge of that specific subject.

- ✔ **To familiarize yourself with the types of test questions and the way they're presented on the test:** Getting a good idea of what all the subtests look like will improve your test-taking speed. You won't have to spend time trying to figure out how a question looks. You can spend your time answering the question.

Making Last-Minute Preparations: 24 Hours and Counting

You want some good advice? On the night before the test, get some sleep — at least eight hours. Don't drink alcohol the night before — headaches and the ASVAB don't work well together. And don't pull an all-night cram session. If you don't know the material the night before the test, it's too late. Staying up all night only guarantees that you'll do poorly on the test, because you'll be too tired in the morning. Here are some other suggestions:

- ✔ **On the morning of the test, eat a light meal.** Anything too heavy will make you drowsy, but not eating enough will make it hard for you to concentrate.

  Try to avoid a breakfast high in carbohydrates. Although the carbs will initially make you feel energetic, a couple of hours into the test, you may come crashing down. Select foods high in protein instead.

- ✔ **Get exercise the day before and even the morning of the test.** Doing so gets your blood pumping and helps you remain mentally sharp.

- ✔ **If you're sick, upset, or injured, consider rescheduling the test.** Right before the test starts, the proctor will ask if there's anything, such as sickness or injury, that may affect your test performance. After the test actually starts, it's considered an "official test," and you'll have to wait a certain time period before any possibility of a retest. See Chapter 1 for details.

- ✔ **Don't bring personal supplies to the test.** Your test administrator will provide you with pencils and scratch paper. Don't bring calculators, personal CD players, backpacks, or a cooler of munchies to the testing site. You won't be allowed to have them with you. (But if you wear eyeglasses, bring them. If you wear contacts, bring your glasses as a backup.)

- ✔ **Bring a watch to help you keep track of time if you're taking the paper version.** The computerized version has a clock on the screen.

- ✔ **Don't drink a lot of liquids just before the test.** You don't want to waste valuable test time in the bathroom!

- ✔ **Make sure you arrive at the test site with plenty of time to spare.** In the military, arriving on time means that you're five minutes too late. You should plan to be in your seat at least 15 minutes before the scheduled testing time. Unless your recruiter is driving you (which is often the case), you may want to do a test run a day or two before your testing date to make sure you know where the test is, the availability of parking, and how to find the testing room.

Part II

Words to Live By: Communication Skills

The 5th Wave   By Rich Tennant

"I guessed my way to a perfect score on the ASVAB, then I guessed my way through basic training and several military jobs. So — would you like me to guess your weight?"

In this part . . .

The ASVAB measures your communication skills through two subtests: Word Knowledge and Paragraph Comprehension. Together, these two subtests make up one-half of your Armed Forces Qualification Test (AFQT) score, which the military uses to predict whether you're teachable. If you don't achieve a qualifying score on the AFQT, you're not allowed to play alongside the other soldiers.

In this part, you discover why it's important to do well on the ASVAB vocabulary and reading subtests, and you find some useful tools to accomplish the mission. You review basic vocabulary and reading skills and find rock-solid advice, such as how to find the main idea of a paragraph, and see quick tips for defining a vocabulary word based on context, roots, prefixes, and suffixes.

Chapter 4

Word Knowledge

To make it to basic combat training, you'd better know how to spell it (along with an army of other words) to score well on the Word Knowledge subtest of the ASVAB. Not only do you have to know how to spell to some degree (so you can differentiate among words), but you also need to know what the words on the test mean. Word Knowledge just means *vocabulary,* which means *hard words no one uses in ordinary conversation.* (Well, not really.) If you're on a military base and you're hungry, don't bother looking for a sign that says Chow Hall. Instead, you need to find the Enlisted Personnel Dining Facility. If you want to work out after your big lunch, forget about the Base Gym. You're looking for the Fitness and Wellness Center.

So what if you don't know the difference between a *carbine* and a *carbon?* Never fear — I'm here to give you a helping hand (bestow upon you inestimable guidance and encouragement — that's Word Knowledge speak). With the help of this chapter and a little brow-sweat on your part, your word-knowledge skills will whip right into shape. And then in Chapter 6, you can check out the practice questions to test your word-knowledge skills.

Grasping the Importance of Word Knowledge

Word Knowledge isn't part of the ASVAB just because the military likes to use big words. It's included because words stand for ideas, and the more words you understand, the more ideas you can understand (and the better you can communicate with others). A decent vocabulary is essential in the military if you want to get ahead. The military operates on paperwork, and whether you're trying to get more supplies (submit necessary logistical requisitions) or get the assignment you want (via application for personnel career-enhancement programs), you need to develop a good vocabulary. The military considers clear communication so important that it's taught and graded at all levels of leadership training, including at the Army, Navy, and Air Force War Colleges, which are requirements to be promoted to General officer equivalent rank (Admiral in the Navy).

The Word Knowledge subtest is one of the four most important subtests on the ASVAB (along with the Paragraph Comprehension, Mathematics Knowledge, and Arithmetic Reasoning). This subtest comprises a significant portion of the AFQT score — the score that determines your eligibility for military service. You also need to do well on the Word Knowledge subtest to qualify for many military jobs, such as air traffic controller, military intelligence, and even firefighting.

Table 4-1 shows the military job qualification line scores that are calculated by using your Word Knowledge subtest score.

Table 4-1	Military Line Scores that Use the Word Knowledge Score
Branch of Service	**Line Score**
U.S. Army	Clerical, General Technical, Operators and Food, Surveillance and Communications, and Skilled Technical
U.S. Air Force	Administrative and General
U.S. Navy/Coast Guard	Administrative, General Technical, Health, and Nuclear
U.S. Marine Corps	General Technical

Chapter 2 has more information about military line scores. Check out Appendix A for more information on the scores you need to get the job you want.

Checking Out the Word Knowledge Question Format

The Word Knowledge portion of the ASVAB measures your vocabulary. The questions usually come in one of two flavors:

✔ The first type asks for a straight definition.

✔ The second type gives you an underlined word used in the context of a sentence.

When you're asked for a straight definition, your task is quite simple: Choose the answer closest in meaning to the underlined word. Look at the following example:

Abate most nearly means

(A) encourage.

(B) relax.

(C) obstruct.

(D) terminate.

Abate means to suppress or terminate. In this case, the correct answer is Choice (D).

When you see an underlined word in a sentence, your goal is to choose the answer closest in meaning to the underlined word. ***Remember:*** Closest in meaning doesn't mean the exact same thing. You're looking for similar or related words. For example:

His house was derelict.

(A) solid.

(B) run-down.

(C) clean.

(D) inexpensive.

Here, the answer is Choice (B).

When you take the Word Knowledge subtest on the paper version of the ASVAB, you have 11 minutes to answer the 35 questions, which means that you have slightly less than 20 seconds to answer each question. On the computerized version, you luck out. You have 8 minutes to answer only 16 questions (or 30 seconds for each question). These days most candidates take the computerized version of the ASVAB. Either way, it's plenty of time, as long as you stay focused and don't waste time thinking about last night's date (sorry, I mean social encounter).

Keep in mind that although you may know the word in the question, you may not know one or more of the words in the multiple-choice answers. If this is the case, use the process of elimination to help you narrow down your choices. Eliminate the words that you know aren't correct and guess which of the remaining words is most likely correct.

Building Words from Scratch: Strategies to Help You Decipher Word Meanings

Webster's New World Dictionary lists more than 170,000 primary English words, and who knows how many derivatives of those words? Wow! Any way you look at it, that's a lot of memorization. Fortunately, you don't need to study all those words. It's possible to decipher English word meanings, even if you've never heard a particular word before.

Developing a large vocabulary takes time — often years. However, just because you have a limited amount of time to study doesn't mean you should give up hope. Instead, focus on the tips throughout this section to help you improve your Word Knowledge score.

From beginning to end: Knowing prefixes and suffixes

Prefixes, roots, and suffixes are the main parts that make up words. Not every word has all three, but most have at least one. *Prefixes* are the parts that come at the front of a word, *suffixes* are the parts that come at the end of a word, and *roots* are the parts that lie in the middle of a word. Think of roots as the base of the word and prefixes and suffixes as word parts that are attached to the base. (Check out the section "Determining the root of the problem" later in this chapter for more info on — you guessed it — roots.)

These basic word parts generally have the same meaning in whatever word they're used. For instance, *pro-* means something along the lines of *in favor of, forward,* or *positive,* whether you use it in the word *pro*ton or the word *pro*ceed.

Tables 4-2 and 4-3 list some common prefixes and suffixes. Each list has the word part, its meaning, and one word that uses each word part. Write down additional words that use each word part to help you memorize the list.

If you memorize prefixes, suffixes, and roots, you have a better chance of figuring out the meaning of an unfamiliar word when you see it on the ASVAB. Figuring out the meaning of unfamiliar words is how people with large vocabularies make them even larger. (They look up words in the dictionary, too.)

Table 4-2	Prefixes	
Prefix	*Meaning*	*Sample Word*
a-	no, not	atheist
ab- or abs-	away, from	absent
anti-	against	antibody
bi-	two	bilateral
circum-	around	circumnavigate
com- or con-	with, together	conform
contra- or counter-	against	contradict
de-	away from	detour
deca-	ten	decade
extra-	outside, beyond	extracurricular, extraordinary
fore-	in front of	foreman
geo-	earth	geology
hyper-	above, over	hyperactive
il-	not	illogical
mal- or male-	evil, bad	malediction
multi-	many	multiply
ob-	blocking	obscure
omni-	all	omnibus
out-	external	outside
que-, quer-, or ques-	ask	question, query
re-	back, again	return
semi-	half	semisweet
super-	over, more	superior
tele-	far	telephone
trans-	across	transatlantic
un-	not	uninformed

Table 4-3	Suffixes	
Suffix	*Meaning*	*Original Word: Suffixed Word*
-able or -ible	capable of	agree: agreeable
-age	act of	break: breakage
-al	relating to	function: functional
-ance or -ence	instance of an action	perform: performance
-ation	action, process	liberate: liberation
-en	made from	silk: silken
-ful	full of	help: helpful
-ic	relating to, like	alcohol: alcoholic

Suffix	Meaning	Original Word: Suffixed Word
-ical	possessing a quality of	magic: magical
-ion	result of, act of	legislate: legislation
-ish	resembling	child: childish
-ism	belief in	Buddha: Buddhism
-ist	one who characterizes	elite: elitist
-ity	quality of	specific: specificity
-less	not having	child: childless
-let	small one	book: booklet
-man	relating to humans	gentle: gentleman
-ment	act or process of	establish: establishment
-ness	possessing a quality	good: goodness
-or, -er	one who does a thing	orate: orator
-ous	state of	danger: dangerous
-y	quality of	taste: tasty

Determining the root of the problem

Root words are word parts that serve as the base of a word. In English, one root word can be changed slightly to perform all sorts of roles — it can act as a noun, a verb, an adjective, or an adverb with just a little modification. If you recognize a root, you can generally get an idea of what the word means, even if you're not familiar with it. For example, if you know what the root word *attach* means, you can figure out what the word *attachment* means. If you know *adherent,* you can deduce what *adherence* means.

Table 4-4 lists some common roots. Memorize them. When you sit down to take the ASVAB, you'll be glad you did.

When you see an unfamiliar word, try dropping a couple of letters from the beginning and/or the end of the word to see whether you recognize what's left — the root. If so, you can make a good guess about the meaning of the word.

Table 4-4	Roots	
Root	**Meaning**	**Sample Word**
anthro or anthrop	relating to humans	anthropology
bibl	relating to books	bibliography
brev	short	abbreviate
cede or ceed	go, yield	recede
chrom	color	monochrome
cogn	know	cognizant
corp	body	corporate
dict	speak	diction

(continued)

Table 4-4 *(continued)*

Root	Meaning	Sample Word
domin	rule	dominate
flu or fluc	flow	influx
form	shape	formulate
fract or frag	break	fragment
graph	writing	biography
junct	join	juncture
liber	free	liberate
lum or lumen	light	illuminate
oper	work	cooperate
path or pathy	suffer, feeling	pathology
port	carry	portable
press	squeeze	repress
scrib or script	write	describe
sens or sent	feel	sentient
tract	pull	traction
voc or vok	call	revoke

Word families: Finding related words

When you see an unfamiliar word on the Word Knowledge section, don't get upset and pound on the computer (they make you pay for those things if you break them). You may know the word after all . . . just in a different form. Suppose you run across the word *beneficent* on the Word Knowledge portion:

<u>Beneficent</u> most nearly means

(A) kind.

(B) beautiful.

(C) unhappy.

(D) troubled.

You sit there in the school-cafeteria chair and begin to sweat. You've never seen the word before, and it's all over for you, right? Well, maybe not. Take a closer look. What other word starting with the letters *benefi* do you know? How about the word *benefit*? A benefit is something that helps or aids. It'd be a good bet that the word *beneficent* is related to helping or aiding. So when you look over the possible choices, you can choose the one that has something to do with helping.

But wait! None of the answers state help or aid. Now what? Just use the process of elimination. If something is helpful (beneficent), it probably isn't troubled or unhappy. It may be beautiful, but more likely, it's kind. So the best answer would be Choice (A).

Remember when your high-school guidance counselor recommended that you take French or Spanish? You should thank her when you score well on this subtest. Why? Because knowledge of other languages can help you puzzle out the meaning of many English words. For example, if you know that *salud* means *health* in Spanish, you may be able to puzzle out the meaning of the English word *salutary* (favorable to or promoting health). Knowing that *sang* means *blood* in French may help you figure out what the English word *sanguine* means (try to puzzle this one out on your own; then check a dictionary to see how close you are).

Ying and Yang: Understanding Synonyms and Antonyms

A *synonym* is a word that has the same meaning as or a very similar meaning to another word. *Smile* and *grin* are synonyms. They may not mean exactly the same thing, but their meanings are very similar. An *antonym* is a word that has an opposite or nearly opposite meaning as another word. *Smile* and *frown* are antonyms.

To help remember the definitions of *synonym* and *antonym,* think of a synonym as the same (both also start with an *s*) and an antonym as the enemy.

The ASVAB may ask you to find the word that most nearly means the same thing as a given word, which is a synonym. Or you may be asked to find the word that most nearly means the opposite of a given word, which is an antonym. Most of the questions on the Word Knowledge subtest ask you to find synonyms, although a few may ask you to find antonyms.

How can you study and find the synonym of a word (or the antonym, for that matter)? Take a look at these suggestions:

- ✔ **Start in the dictionary.** Many dictionary entries include the abbreviation *syn.,* which means synonym. The words that follow this abbreviation are synonyms of the entry word. You may also see the abbreviation *ant.,* which stands for antonym; the word or words that follow it mean the opposite of the entry word.

- ✔ **Make a list of synonyms and antonyms of the words you learn.** As you study vocabulary words for the Word Knowledge subtest, add them to your list.

- ✔ **Use the root-word list from Table 4-4 (in the preceding section).** Using a dictionary and/or thesaurus, come up with a list of synonyms and antonyms for each word listed in the Sample Word column. (Of course, not every word has synonyms and antonyms, but many do.)

Many of the ASVAB Word Knowledge questions require you to know a one-word definition for another word. There's no better study aid for this concept than a thesaurus, a book of synonyms.

You Are What You Speak: Improving Your Vocabulary, Improving Yourself

Having an extensive vocabulary can help you do well on the Word Knowledge subtest. But even if you don't have a huge vocabulary, the strategies in this section can help you make up for that.

You can acquire vocabulary words in the short term as well as over a long period of time. Combining both approaches is best, but if you're pressed for time, focus on short-term memorization and test-taking skills.

Reading your way to a larger vocabulary

In a world of DVDs, video games, and 17 billion channels on TV, the pastime of reading for enjoyment is quickly fading. To build your vocabulary, you have to read — it's that simple. Studies consistently show that those who read for enjoyment have a much larger vocabulary than those who dislike reading. You have to see the words in print, not just hear someone say them. Besides, people can read and understand many more words than they could ever use in conversation.

That doesn't mean you have to start with *Advanced Astrophysics*. In fact, if you don't read much, you can start with your daily newspaper, a news magazine, or any type of reading material that's just a notch or two above what you ordinarily read. Choose topics that interest you. If you're interested in the subject matter, you'll enjoy reading more. Plus, you may just learn something new!

When you encounter a word you don't know, try to understand what it means by looking at the context in which the word is used. For example, if you read, "The scientist extrapolated from the data," and you don't know what *extrapolated* means, you can try substituting words you do know to see whether they'd make sense. For example, the scientist probably didn't hide from the data. She probably used the data to make some sort of decision, judgment, or guess. To confirm your understanding of the word, check your dictionary. Making predictions like this can help you remember a definition for the long term.

You may even consider keeping a running list of terms you come across as you read, along with their definitions (see the following section). On the Word Knowledge subtest of the ASVAB, you often won't be able to guess what a word means from its context (in many cases, there's no context in the test because the words aren't used in sentences). You also won't be able to look the word up in the dictionary. But considering context and consulting a dictionary are two great ways to discover vocabulary words during your test preparation.

Keeping a list and checking it twice

Not long ago, an 11-year-old girl went through the entire dictionary and made a list of all the words she didn't know. (The process took several months.) She then studied the list faithfully for a year and went on to win first place in the National Spelling Bee finals. You don't have to go to this extent, but even putting in a tenth of her effort can dramatically improve your scores on the Word Knowledge subtest.

One way to improve your vocabulary is to keep a word list. Here's how that list works:

1. **When you hear or read a word that you don't understand, jot it down.**

2. **When you have a chance, look up the word in the dictionary and then write the meaning on your list.**

3. **Use the word in a sentence that you make up.**

   Write the sentence down, too.

4. **Use your new word in everyday conversation.**

   Finding a way to work the word *zenith* into a description of last night's basketball game requires creativity, but you won't forget what the word means.

Arrange your list by related items so that the words are easier to remember. For example, list the words having to do with your work on one page, words related to mechanical knowledge on another page, and so on.

You can also find web sites that offer lists of words if you spend a few minutes surfing. Try using search phrases such as "vocabulary words" and "SAT words." Here are a few resources:

- ✔ **Free Vocabulary:** This site (www.freevocabulary.com) offers a free list of more than 5,000 collegiate words, along with brief definitions.
- ✔ **Dictionary.com:** Dictionary.com (www.dictionary.com) includes a great online dictionary, thesaurus, and word of the day.
- ✔ **Merriam-Webster online:** Merriam-Webster online (www.m-w.com) is another useful site with a free online dictionary, thesaurus, and word of the day.

A ton of books exist to help build your vocabulary. Try *Vocabulary For Dummies* by Laurie E. Rozakis or *SAT Vocabulary For Dummies* by Suzee Vlk, both published by Wiley. These books are great resources designed to help you improve your word-knowledge skills.

Crosswords: Making vocabulary fun

Before she passed away, my mom was a walking dictionary. It seemed like she could give you a single-word definition for almost any English word, which was quite a feat for a woman who only made it to the ninth grade. What was her secret? Early in life, she fell in love with crossword puzzles.

One of the great things about crossword puzzles (other than fun) is that you can find them at all levels of difficulty. Start with one that has a difficulty consistent with your word-knowledge ability and then work your way up to more difficult puzzles. Before you know it, you'll be a lean, mean word machine and have loads of fun in the process.

Sounding off by sounding it out

Sometimes you actually know a word because you've heard it in conversation, but you don't recognize it when you see it written down. For instance, a student who'd heard the word *placebo* (pronounced "plah-*see*-bow") knew that it meant an inactive substance, like a sugar pill. But when she came across it in writing, she didn't recognize it. She thought it was a word pronounced "plah-*chee*-bow," which she'd never heard before.

When you see a word on the ASVAB that you don't recognize, try pronouncing it (not out loud, please) a couple of different ways. The following pronunciation rules can help you out:

- ✔ Sometimes letters are silent, like the *b* in *subtle* or the *k* in *knight.* A letter at the end of a word may be silent, especially if the word is French; for instance, *coup* is pronounced *coo.*
- ✔ Some sounds have unusual pronunciations in certain contexts. Think of the *l* in *colonel,* which is pronounced like *kernel.*
- ✔ The letter *c* can sound like *s (lice)* or *k (despicable).*
- ✔ The letter *i* after a *t* can form a sound like *she.* Think of the word *initiate.*
- ✔ The letter *x* at the beginning of a word is generally pronounced like *z (Xerox).*

✔ A vowel at the end of a word can change the pronunciation of letters in the word. The word *wag* has a different *g* sound than the word *wage*.

✔ When several vowels are right next to each other, they can be pronounced many different ways (consider *boo, boa,* and *bout*). Try a couple of different possibilities. For instance, if you see the word *feint,* you may think that it should be pronounced *feent* or *fiynt,* but it in fact sounds like *faint.* It means *fake* or *pretend.*

Chapter 5

Paragraph Comprehension

- -

- -

Any other organization would call this section of the ASVAB the *Reading Comprehension* subtest, but the Department of Defense is a stickler for precision. You'll be reading paragraphs, darn it, so you're being tested on how well you understand paragraphs! Not words, not sentences, not essays, but paragraphs! Don't you just love the military way?

One thing you get from basic training is that comprehending the drill sergeant's orders and the information in your instruction manuals is important. The ability to read and understand the written directions in your basic training manual can save you and your buddies hundreds of push-ups. Trust me on this one. The Paragraph Comprehension subtest measures your ability to understand what you read and draw conclusions from that material. It contains a number of reading passages and questions about those passages.

After you enlist, you discover that the military runs on paperwork. If you can't read and understand a regulation that's buried within a pile of papers, how are you going to obey it?

The Importance of Paragraph Comprehension for Military Jobs

The Paragraph Comprehension subtest is an important part of your AFQT score, which is the most important score because it determines whether a particular branch of service lets you join. The score is so important that I plan to keep on repeating it until you're mumbling, "The AFQT is the most important score," in your sleep.

You'd be surprised at how many diverse military jobs require a decent score on the Paragraph Comprehension subtest. But think about it for a moment: If the directions in a military recipe make you rub your eyes and mumble to yourself, how are you going to cook a meal for 2,000 troops? (Assuming you want to become a military cook, that is.) Table 5-1 shows the military job qualification line scores that are calculated by using your Paragraph Comprehension subtest score.

Table 5-1	Military Line Scores that Use the Paragraph Comprehension Score
Branch of Service	**Line Score**
U.S. Army	Clerical, General Technical, Operators and Food, Surveillance and Communications, and Skilled Technical
U.S. Air Force	Administrative and General
U.S. Navy and Coast Guard	Administrative, General Technical, Health, and Nuclear
U.S. Marine Corps	General Technical and Clerical

Chapter 2 has more information about military line scores. See Appendix A for more information on the scores you need to get the job you want.

Eyeing the Physique of the Paragraph Comprehension Subtest

When you get to the Paragraph Comprehension subtest, you have several passages to read. Most passages are only one paragraph long, and rarely are they longer than two paragraphs. Each passage contains between 50 and 200 words. (Look at it this way: At least you won't be required to read *War and Peace*!)

The ASVAB test-makers may ask you to answer only one question about a given reading passage, or they may ask you to answer as many as five questions about one passage. Unfortunately, this subtest doesn't consist of the most interesting passages you'll ever read. (You won't find paragraphs from your favorite spy or romance novel here.) So it's important that you set your attention span dial all the way to the maximum setting. If you're taking the paper-and-pencil version of the ASVAB, you have 13 minutes to read the passages and answer 15 questions. On the computer version, you have 22 minutes to answer 11 questions.

In order to understand what you read — which is what the Paragraph Comprehension subtest is all about — you need to develop several abilities, which I cover later in this chapter:

- Finding the main idea or argument that the author is making
- Remembering specific details about the reading
- Drawing conclusions from what you've read
- Understanding relationships between ideas
- Paraphrasing or summarizing what you've read

Trying the Four Flavors of Comprehension Questions

The Paragraph Comprehension questions on the ASVAB usually take one of four forms:

- Finding specific information
- Recognizing the main idea

✔ Determining word meaning in context

✔ Drawing an implication from a stated idea

Each type of question asks you to perform a different kind of analysis of the reading passage. If a passage has more than one question associated with it, chances are each question falls under a different category. The following sections spell out the differences among these four types of questions.

Treasure hunt: Finding specific information

This type of Paragraph Comprehension question asks you to pick out (you guessed it) specific information from a passage. Sounds easy, right? Take a look at the following passage, which clearly states the answer to the question that directly follows it:

> An industry trade association found that more than 13,000 martial arts schools exist in the United States with nearly 6 million active members. Of the 13,000 schools, nearly 7,000 offered tae kwon do lessons.

According to this passage, how many people actively participated in martial arts lessons?

(A) 13,000

(B) 7,000

(C) 6 million

(D) It can't be determined.

The correct answer is Choice (C).

At times, the information that a question asks about isn't directly stated in the question, but you can infer the information from the text. Remember, in the military, the only easy day was yesterday.

When questions are phrased in the negative, you may be easily confused about what the question is asking. (This fact is especially true when the information being sought isn't directly stated in the passage.) Misreading a negative question is also easy. Research has shown that people often skip over a negative word, such as *not*, when they read. Be aware that questions on the Paragraph Comprehension portion of the ASVAB are frequently stated in the negative. When you see a negative word, an alarm should go off in your head to remind you to read the question more carefully.

Cutting to the chase: Recognizing the main idea

Sometimes the Paragraph Comprehension questions ask you to identify the main point of a passage. The main point can be directly stated, or it can be implied.

If you're not sure what the main point of a paragraph is, reread the first sentence and the last sentence. Chances are one of these two sentences contains the main point. (Flip to "What's the big idea? Determining the main idea in a paragraph," later in this chapter, for more information on identifying main ideas.)

If the shoe fits: Determining word meaning in context

Sometimes the Paragraph Comprehension subtest asks you to determine the meaning of a word when it's used in a passage. The correct definition that the question is looking for can be the most common meaning of the word, or it can be a less well-known meaning of the word. In either case, you have to read the passage, make sure you understand how the word is being used, and select the answer option that's closest in meaning to the word as it's used in the passage. Consider this example:

> In the 18th century, it was common for sailors to be pressed into service in Britain. Young men found near seaports could be kidnapped, drugged, or otherwise hauled aboard a ship and made to work doing menial chores. They weren't paid for their service, and they were given just enough food to keep them alive.

In this passage, *pressed* means

(A) hired.

(B) ironed.

(C) enticed.

(D) forced.

The descriptions of the conditions these sailors found themselves in should help you decide that they weren't hired or enticed; *ironed* is one meaning of the word *pressed,* but it isn't correct in this context. The correct answer is Choice (D). Here's another example:

> Since the 1980s, computers have become an indispensable part of American business. Computers can be used for thousands of applications from word processing and running spreadsheets to keeping one's checkbook updated.

In this passage, *applications* means

(A) functions.

(B) sizes.

(C) requests.

(D) types.

Try putting the answer choices in this sentence: "Computers can be used for thousands of applications." You can see that *functions* is closest in meaning to *applications,* although in a different context, some of the other answer choices may be correct. The correct answer is Choice (A).

Reading between the lines: Understanding implications

Some Paragraph Comprehension questions ask you to draw an inference from a stated idea. This simply means that you may need to draw a conclusion from what you've read. This conclusion should always be based on the reading, not your own particular opinions about a subject.

The conclusion — which may be called an *inference* or *implication* — must be reasonably based on what the passage says. You have to use good judgment when deciding which conclusions can be logically drawn from what you've read. Give it a shot:

> Twenty-five percent of all automobile thefts occur when the doors of a car are left unlocked. People often forget to lock their doors, find it inconvenient, or tell themselves, "I'll only be a minute." But it only takes a minute for an accomplished car thief to steal a car. And thieves are always alert to the opportunities that distracted or rushed people present them with.

To prevent auto theft, it's a person's responsibility to

(A) leave the doors unlocked.

(B) never be in a rush.

(C) prevent the opportunity.

(D) be willing to perform a citizen's arrest.

Although the paragraph doesn't state, "To prevent auto theft, it's a person's responsibility to prevent the opportunity," this idea is certainly implied. The correct answer is Choice (C). There's no implication that people should be willing to (or can) perform a citizen's arrest. Leaving the doors unlocked is the opposite of what one should do, and never being in a rush is probably impossible.

An example of an unreasonable conclusion drawn from the passage would be something like "if everyone locked their doors, there would be no crime" or "all car thieves should be sentenced to 30 years in prison." Nothing in this particular passage supports such a conclusion.

One way to help determine whether you've drawn a reasonable conclusion is to ask yourself, "Based on what I've just read, would the author agree with the conclusion I've reached?" If the answer is yes, your conclusion is probably reasonable. If the answer is no, it's time to think up a new conclusion.

Check out another example:

> Boiler technicians operate main and auxiliary boilers. They maintain and repair all parts, including pressure fittings, valves, pumps, and forced-air blowers. Technicians may have to lift or move heavy equipment. They may have to stoop and kneel and work in awkward positions.

According to this job description, a good candidate for this job would be

(A) a person with joint problems.

(B) an individual unaccustomed to heavy lifting.

(C) a person who isn't mechanically minded.

(D) a person who's physically fit.

Although the passage doesn't state, "This job requires a physically fit person," the duties listed imply that this is so. The correct answer is (D). A person with joint problems may not be able to stoop or kneel or work in awkward positions. A person who's unaccustomed to heavy lifting may not be able to lift or move the heavy equipment as needed. A person who isn't mechanically minded may not have the knowledge necessary to maintain and repair boilers and all their parts. This leaves Choice (D) as the answer, and it's true that a person who's physically fit would be a good choice for the job.

Do You Get My Point?

All good writing has a point. Some writing has more than one point. Points are ideas that the writer is trying to convey to the reader. The primary purpose of the writing is known as the *main point* or *main idea*. Points used to support or clarify the main point are called *subpoints* or *supporting points*. You should know how to identify main points and subpoints when you practice reading.

What's the big idea? Determining the main idea in a paragraph

Questions on the Paragraph Comprehension subtest frequently ask you to identify the main point of a reading passage. How do you get better at identifying main ideas? Practice. The *main idea,* which is the most important point the author is making, is sometimes stated and sometimes implied in a piece of writing.

Finding a topic sentence

Often, the author begins or ends a paragraph or passage with the main idea, which is located in what's called a *topic sentence.* A topic sentence, reasonably enough, describes the topic that the author's writing about.

If you're looking for the main idea, start off by checking the first and last sentence of the passage. (No, this doesn't mean that you should skip the rest of the passage.) For example, suppose you read the following paragraph:

> The local school district is facing a serious budgetary crisis. The state, suffering a revenue shortfall of more than $600 million, has cut funding to the district by $18.7 million. Already, 65 teachers have been laid off, and more layoffs are expected.

No, the primary theme of this passage isn't "schools in our area suck." The main point of this paragraph can be found in the opening sentence, "The local school district is facing a serious budgetary crisis." What follows are details regarding the budget crisis.

Sometimes a passage builds up to its main idea, and sometimes the main idea is implied instead of stated. Consider the following paragraph:

> The farmers' market reopened on the second weekend of May. Amid the asparagus and flowers, shoppers chatted about the return of temperatures in the 70s. Across the street, children (and their dogs) played Frisbee in the park. Finally, spring has come to town.

In this paragraph, you may think that the farmers' market's reopening is the main point, but the other information about the temperature and the kids' playing Frisbee tells you that the main idea is something a bit broader than the market's opening. The main idea is stated in the last sentence: "Finally, spring has come to town."

In boot camp, your drill instructor may say, "Some of you better check to see that your bunks are properly made." Or he may rip your bunk bed apart and say, "Now make this $%*& bunk the right way, you moron!" Both comments mean the same thing. In the first statement, the drill instructor implies the meaning; the second statement is a bit more direct.

In other words: Rephrasing passages

One of the best ways to identify the main point of a paragraph is to put the paragraph into your own words (*paraphrase* it) or to sum up the basic idea of the paragraph (*summarize* it). By quickly doing this when you take the Paragraph Comprehension portion of the ASVAB, you can be confident that you're answering the question correctly. In other words (to paraphrase), you'll know you understand what the paragraph is talking about.

You likely won't have time to write down the main point or to jot down your paraphrase or summary. Instead, as you're reading, simply try to mentally keep track of what's being said by putting it into your own words.

Look at the following paragraph:

> The local school district is facing a serious budgetary crisis. The state, suffering a revenue shortfall of more than $600 million, has cut funding to the district by $18.7 million. Already, 65 teachers have been laid off, and more layoffs are expected.

Now close this book and spend a few moments paraphrasing the previous paragraph. Come on. Pick up that pencil and get those brain cells firing. When you're done, reopen to this page and compare your ideas to the passage. If you wrote something like the following, you're right on track:

> The school district has a budget crunch because the state has a budget crunch. The state cut funding to the school district. Some teachers have been laid off already. More may be laid off soon.

Now if you wrote something like, "It's finally May, and shoppers and kids-at-play are out and about, enjoying the warmer temperatures of spring," then you're not paying attention. Turn off the TV and give it another try.

As you study for the ASVAB, practice paraphrasing reading passages. You can paraphrase or summarize any short passage you read — a few sentences or a paragraph or two. Read different passages from a book or magazine and then close the pages. Get out a pencil and jot down your paraphrases. (Remember, you won't have time to do this on the test itself, but the practice helps you mentally prepare for when you take the test.)

Extra, extra! Identifying subpoints

If a writer stuck to just one point, the Paragraph Comprehension subtest would be a breeze. However, an author usually doesn't make just one point in a piece of writing, so you also need to understand the other points the author makes. These details, or *subpoints,* may include facts or statistics, or they may be descriptions that support the main point of the passage. Subpoints help you see what the author's saying. For instance, look at this passage (from the previous section):

> The local school district is facing a serious budgetary crisis. The state, suffering a revenue shortfall of more than $600 million, has cut funding to the district by $18.7 million. Already, 65 teachers have been laid off, and more layoffs are expected.

The subpoints help you understand the main point, which is that the school district is facing a severe budgetary crisis. The subpoints help you understand why: "The state, suffering a revenue shortfall of more than $600 million, has cut funding to the district by $18.7 million."

You can see that the budgetary crisis is part of a larger problem, which is the state's suffering a severe revenue shortfall. The subpoints also help you understand what this crisis means: "Already, 65 teachers have been laid off, and more layoffs are expected." By using these facts and figures, the author helps you grasp not only the main point but also the implications of that main point.

Analyzing What You've Read: Guessing at What the Writer Really Means

The Paragraph Comprehension subtest of the ASVAB also requires you to analyze what you've read. Analysis is more than simply picking out the point of text. *Analyzing* a passage requires you to draw conclusions from what you've read and understand relationships among the ideas presented in the text.

By drawing conclusions about the meaning of a passage, you reach new ideas that the author implies but doesn't come right out and state. You must analyze the information the author presents in order to make inferences from what you've read. For instance, look at the following paragraph:

> The local school district is facing a serious budgetary crisis. The state, suffering a revenue shortfall of more than $600 million, has cut funding to the district by $18.7 million. Already, 65 teachers have been laid off, and more layoffs are expected.

Although the author doesn't say so, you can draw the conclusion that if the state revenue shortfall could somehow be corrected — by increasing state sales tax or income tax, for example — the local school district's budgetary crisis could be resolved. The $18.7 million cut from the school budget could be restored. The author never actually makes this point in the paragraph, but by using logic, you can draw this conclusion from the facts presented.

Making inferences and drawing conclusions requires you to use your judgment. You don't want to read too much into a passage. For example, nothing in the example paragraph suggests that electing a new governor is necessary or that increasing federal income taxes would help the problem.

Look at the next paragraph:

> The farmers' market reopened on the second weekend of May. Amid the asparagus and flowers, shoppers chatted about the return of temperatures in the 70s. Across the street, children (and their dogs) played Frisbee in the park. Finally, spring has come to town.

Suppose you're asked the following question about this paragraph:

It can be inferred from the passage that

(A) Frisbee playing in the park doesn't happen in winter.

(B) the warm weather is unusual for this time of year.

(C) the shoppers were disappointed in the farmers' market produce.

(D) rain is imminent.

If the point of the passage is that spring has come to town and the author uses Frisbee playing as evidence of the arrival of spring, then it's likely that Frisbee playing doesn't occur in the winter but does begin again in spring. The answer is Choice (A).

Faster than a Speeding Turtle: Tips for Slow Readers

Today's military is much more complex than attending basic training, learning how to shoot a gun, and shipping off to war. After boot camp, you attend intensive classroom training to learn your military job. If you can't read well, you're going to have a very hard time. But the good news is that it's never too late to work on improving your reading skills.

For many people, 13 or 22 minutes is enough time to read all the passages, understand the questions, and choose the correct answers. But slow readers may have more difficulty getting all the questions answered before time is up. Don't despair: Take the suggestions in this section to help you build your reading speed. Of course, they require work, but you knew the mission came with its challenges, right?

Read more, watch less

If you're a slow reader, chances are you don't do a lot of reading. If you have plenty of time before you're due to take the ASVAB, start reading more — right now. It's in your best interest.

You don't have to pick up *A Tale of Two Cities* or *War and Peace;* you can start with the newspaper, a biography of a person you admire, or magazines you find at the library. (Sorry, but the instruction guide to your favorite video game doesn't count.) You don't need to enroll in a speed-reading course. If you devote at least one hour a day simply to reading, you'll see your reading comprehension and speed increase within a month or so.

Several studies have shown that folks who enjoy reading as a pleasurable pastime score better on reading comprehension tests than individuals who dislike reading. Sounds obvious, right? So why study it? The idea is if you grow to enjoy reading, you'll want to read more. You'll become a better reader and thereby score better on reading comprehension tests. How do you discover an enjoyment of reading? Simple — choose reading material in subject areas that interest you.

Become a lean, mean word machine

People sometimes read slowly because they don't have a large vocabulary and don't understand everything they read. If you can identify with this situation, improving your vocabulary is your first step toward increasing your reading comprehension and your reading speed. (Chapter 4 gives you info on building your word knowledge. Check it out.)

Keep a pocket dictionary handy while reading so you can look up words you don't know. If you're reading articles on the Internet, keep a window open to one of the online dictionaries (such as www.dictionary.com, www.yourdictionary.com, or www.m-w.com) so you can quickly find the definition of words you find confusing. Your reading will become more enjoyable, and you'll be adding to your vocabulary knowledge to boot.

Build your confidence

Another reason people read slowly is that they don't have confidence in themselves. They're not convinced that they understand what they're reading, so they read a passage several times, trying to make sure they haven't missed anything. But just like people who check that the front door is locked 15 times before leaving for vacation and still lie awake at night wondering whether they locked the door, reading and rereading a passage doesn't give you confidence that you understand the text. You get confidence from proving that you understand it.

How do you prove to yourself that you understand what you're reading? Here are a couple of tips:

- ✔ Get out a textbook or even an encyclopedia (preferably a volume that contains some subject matter that interests you) and read one or two paragraphs straight through without going back and rereading anything. Then close the book (keeping your place marked) and write, in your own words, a brief description of what you've read. Finally, turn back to the passage and compare your description to the information on the page.

- ✔ Play the 20-questions game. Read an article from a magazine, encyclopedia, or textbook. Then ask someone to pick out facts from the article and ask you questions.

- ✔ Create motivation and interest by reading the daily newspaper or news magazines. Discuss the news events with your classmates, friends, or co-workers. Stronger interest equals greater comprehension.

Is your written version of the article close in meaning to the original? Are you getting most of the 20 questions correct? Do you feel comfortable discussing current events with others? If so, you understand what you're reading, and that should build your confidence. If not, don't toss the book or magazine aside in frustration or go ballistic on your mom for asking you tough questions. Keep working on it, and your comprehension will improve. Do the preceding confidence-building drills a few times a day until you feel like you can read any paragraph or two and understand the content without having to reread the information.

The Paragraph Comprehension subtest tests your ability to understand what you read, not how quickly you can read it. When you sit down to take this subtest, try to go as quickly as you can without sacrificing accuracy. Being methodical in your reading isn't a bad thing as long as you're getting the answers right. Just try to read a little faster than normal without panicking or missing the point. It's better to read the paragraphs carefully and answer the questions correctly on half of the questions and guess on the other half of the questions than it is to speed through all the reading and get none of the answers right.

Test-Taking Tips for Reading and Gleaning

Although no shortcuts exist for improving your reading comprehension skills (besides practice), you can do a few things on test day to make sure that you score as high as possible on this part of the ASVAB.

If you're running out of time on this subtest or you're not sure whether you can identify the main idea of a passage, take a guess. If you think that's a good piece of advice, check out these tried-and-true tactics for test day:

- ✔ **Read first, ask questions later.** Read the passage all the way through before glancing at the question and answer options.

- ✔ **Take it one question at a time.** Some passages have more than one question associated with them, but look at only one question at a time.

✔ **Understand each question.** What's the question asking you to do? Are you supposed to find the main point? Draw a conclusion? Find a word that's nearest in meaning? Make sure you know what the question is asking before you choose among the answer options. This tip may seem obvious, but when you're in a hurry, you can make mistakes by misunderstanding the questions.

✔ **Read each answer option carefully.** Don't just select the first answer that seems right. Remember, on the Paragraph Comprehension subtest, one answer is often most right and others are almost right. You want to choose the most right answer, not the almost right answer. And to do that, you have to read all the answers.

✔ **Check your feelings at the door.** Answer each question based on the passage, not your own opinions or views on the topic.

✔ **Don't choose vague answer options.** They're incorrect 99.99 times out of 100. (Oh heck, call it 100 times out of 100.) If an answer strikes you as not quite true but not totally false, that answer is incorrect. Those nasty ASVAB test-makers have put those answers in there to throw you off. Don't give them the satisfaction of falling for their trap!

✔ **(Almost) never select *never*.** For the most part, answer options that are absolutes are incorrect. *Never, always,* and related words are often a sign that you should select a different answer. Words like *generally* and *usually* are more likely to be correct.

Chapter 6

All's Well That Tests Well: Communication Practice Questions

· ·

In This Chapter

▶ Proving your knowledge of word meanings

▶ Demonstrating that you can retain what you read

· ·

To help you hone your communication skills a little further, this chapter contains some Word Knowledge and Paragraph Comprehension practice questions to get you rolling. Don't sweat. This test is just for practice, and it doesn't count for a score. (Plus, sweating makes your answer sheet soggy so it's harder to mark.)

The communication subtests of the ASVAB are very important because they comprise a significant portion of your AFQT score. (I promised I'd keep pounding this concept into your head — and I wouldn't lie to you, ever!)

On the paper version of the ASVAB (and on the full-length practice tests later in this book), you see 35 Word Knowledge questions and 15 questions about Paragraph Comprehension. The CAT-ASVAB has 16 Word Knowledge questions and 11 Paragraph Comprehension questions. In this chapter, you get 25 total questions just to help you warm up for the practice tests later on in this book.

Word Knowledge Practice Questions

In the stem of each of the following Word Knowledge practice questions, you see an underlined word. Select the choice that best answers the question in relation to the underlined word.

Pay attention to the wording of each question. Some questions ask you to select the choice closest in meaning to the underlined word. Some questions may ask you to select the word most opposite in meaning. On other questions, you see the underlined word used in a sentence. In that case, your task is to select the choice most similar in meaning to the underlined word as it is used in the context of the sentence.

1. <u>Acclaim</u> most nearly means

   (A) enthusiastic approval.

   (B) religion.

   (C) help.

   (D) program.

Used as a noun, *acclaim* means a shout of approval, so the answer is Choice (A).

2. The college student met with the <u>bursar</u> to discuss tuition payment options.

   (A) planner

   (B) treasurer

   (C) politician

   (D) ghost

   Bursar is similar to the word *reimburse*. The question gives context clues about tuition payment, and that should give you enough clues to select the correct answer, Choice (B).

3. <u>Estrange</u> most nearly means

   (A) sharp.

   (B) small.

   (C) alienate.

   (D) shiny.

   Estrange means to alienate, Choice (C). Note that *estrange* is a verb, and the only answer choice that's also a verb is Choice (C); the others are adjectives.

4. <u>Momentous</u> most nearly means

   (A) significant.

   (B) small.

   (C) reality.

   (D) postpone.

   Momentous is an adjective and means very significant, Choice (A).

5. The mother <u>chastised</u> her child.

   (A) comforted

   (B) carried

   (C) lectured

   (D) supervised

   Chastised means disciplined or punished, so Choice (C) is the most correct choice. Choices (A), (B), and (D) are unrelated.

6. <u>Obtrude</u> most nearly means

   (A) condition.

   (B) absorb.

   (C) prepare.

   (D) impose.

   The correct answer is Choice (D). *Obtrude* means to intrude or to impose oneself on another. The other choices are unrelated.

7. We often wondered why Daniel lived in such an <u>opulent</u> apartment.

    (A) run-down

    (B) lavish

    (C) far away

    (D) hideous

    Opulent is an adjective that means wealthy, rich, or affluent. Choice (B) is the answer closest in meaning. The other choices are unrelated or opposite of the meaning.

8. Now that you've read through it once, it's time to <u>recapitulate</u> the Word Knowledge chapter.

    (A) discuss

    (B) summarize

    (C) test

    (D) reread

    Recapitulate is a verb that means to summarize. It's also the longer version of the word *recap*. The correct answer is Choice (B). Choice (A) is somewhat close, but Choice (B) is the closest in meaning.

9. <u>Clemency</u> most nearly means

    (A) mercy.

    (B) force.

    (C) imprisonment.

    (D) compliment.

    Clemency means forgiveness or leniency in punishing a person. Choice (A) is the correct answer. The other choices are unrelated.

Knowing prefixes can be useful when determining the definitions of many words. For example, you may have heard the word *inclement* used to describe stormy, severe weather. If you know that the prefix *in-* can mean *not,* you can conclude that *clement* is likely to be mild or gentle, traits related to mercy. (See Chapter 4 for more info on using prefixes and word families to guess what words mean.)

10. This year the Paris fashion industry has decided to <u>eschew</u> short skirts and high heels.

    (A) favor

    (B) manufacture

    (C) shun

    (D) sell

    Eschew is a verb that means to avoid or keep away from. Choice (C) is the correct answer, and the other answers are unrelated.

11. <u>Pollute</u> most nearly means

    (A) eliminate.

    (B) contaminate.

    (C) clean.

    (D) confuse.

    Pollute means to contaminate, Choice (B).

12. <u>Latent</u> most nearly means

    (A) hidden

    (B) dull

    (C) pretentious

    (D) active

    Latent means present but not visible or noticeable, so Choice (A) is the correct answer. *Latent* can also mean dormant, but none of the answer choices relate to that definition.

13. Paul sent all of his friends a <u>salutary</u> message on the Internet.

    (A) beneficial

    (B) profane

    (C) funny

    (D) interesting

    Salutary is an adjective meaning beneficial, so Choice (A) is correct. If you took Spanish in high school, you may remember that a related word, *salud,* relates to health and well-being, making (A) a good guess.

Paragraph Comprehension Practice Questions

The last half of the questions in this chapter is designed to present you with an opportunity to practice your Paragraph Comprehension skills. Read each short paragraph, followed by one or more questions regarding information contained in that passage. Make sure to read the paragraph carefully before selecting the choice that *most correctly* answers the question.

Passage one

Mrs. Berry's was my first *coup de main.* The house was at the top of a high hill with more steps to climb to reach the porch which spanned a plain but scrupulously neat living room. The floor was freshly scrubbed with white sand, there was a deal table also scrubbed to snowy whiteness and a few splint bottomed chairs scrubbed likewise. All this I noticed standing on the threshold of the front door which stood wide open from habit, one could see, rather than with any notion of inviting wayfarers to enter. I knocked on the floor with the point of my umbrella and after some minutes a comely little black woman appeared in the doorway just opposite and stood with hands crossed in front of her waiting to learn the cause of the intrusion.

14. When the narrator arrives at the house, she

    (A) knocks on the door.

    (B) knocks on the floor.

    (C) opens the door.

    (D) rings the doorbell.

The correct answer is Choice (B) — she knocks on the floor using her umbrella. If you missed this one, read the passage more carefully.

15. The woman's crossed hands imply that she's

    (A) bothered.

    (B) excited.

    (C) afraid.

    (D) bored.

The correct answer is Choice (A). The passage states that the woman is waiting to see "the cause of the intrusion," which indicates she is bothered or annoyed.

Passage two

Some people argue that baking is an art, but Chef Debra Dearhorn says that baking is a science. She says that if you follow a recipe carefully, assembling the ingredients accurately, cooking at the specified temperature for the specified period of time, your cookies will always turn out right. Chef Dearborn says the best baking is like the best experiment — anyone can duplicate it.

16. In this passage, the word *assembling* most nearly means

    (A) measuring.

    (B) putting together.

    (C) buying.

    (D) storing.

Although *measuring* is something you do when baking, it doesn't most nearly mean the same thing as *assembling*. *Putting together* does. Therefore, Choice (B) is the correct answer.

17. According to the passage, a person who's all thumbs in the kitchen

    (A) should get out of the kitchen.

    (B) is an artist.

    (C) isn't following the recipe carefully.

    (D) is Chef Dearborn.

The passage states that if you follow a recipe carefully, "your cookies will always turn out right." The correct answer is Choice (C).

Passage three

At dinner-time tonight I was feverish to do three things at once: write out my day's journal, eat my food, and read *The Journal of Marie Bashkirtseff.* Did all three—but unfortunately not at once, so that when I was occupied with one I would surreptitiously cast a glance sideways at the other—and repined.

18. Which of the following was the author NOT planning to do?

    (A) go shopping

    (B) eat food

    (C) write a journal

    (D) read a journal

The passage's first sentence tells you everything you need to know — it mentions writing and reading journals and eating food. Shopping isn't mentioned, so the correct answer is Choice (A).

Passage four

To motivate your people, give them tasks that challenge them. Get to know your people and their capabilities, so you can tell just how far to push each one. Give them as much responsibility as they can handle and then let them do the work without looking over their shoulders and nagging them. When they succeed, praise them. When they fall short, give them credit for what they've done and coach or counsel them on how to do better next time.

19. According to the above paragraph, if your subordinates fail to adequately perform their tasks, you should

    (A) punish them.

    (B) praise them.

    (C) counsel them.

    (D) both B and C.

If you didn't read the passage, praising someone who didn't measure up may seem like a bad idea. However, the last sentence states you should give your subordinates credit for the parts of the task they performed correctly and counsel them how to do better the next time. Although that sentence doesn't use the word *praise,* you can infer that giving someone credit means the same thing. The correct answer is Choice (D).

20. After assigning responsibility for the tasks at hand to your subordinates, you should

    (A) supervise them closely to ensure the tasks are performed correctly.

    (B) let them do the work on their own.

    (C) check their progress at the end of each day.

    (D) schedule sufficient work-breaks to avoid job burnout.

Choices (C) and (D) sound like good ideas, but they aren't suggestions discussed in the paragraph. Remember to avoid the trap of answering based on your personal feelings. Choice (A) is the opposite of what the passage suggests — the writer says to "let [employees] do the work without looking over their shoulders." Choice (B) is the correct answer.

Passage five

Approximately 15,000 years ago the first Native Americans may have appeared in Colorado. The earliest inhabitants were hunters and nomadic foragers on the plains, as well as the western plateau. Agricultural settlements began appearing along river valleys in the eastern part of Colorado from approximately 5,000 B.C. as people learned farming techniques from the Mississippi River Native Americans.

21. The first Native Americans in Colorado were

    (A) farmers.

    (B) traders.

    (C) hunters and gatherers.

    (D) originally from the Mississippi River region.

The second sentence states that the original inhabitants "were hunters and nomadic foragers," and because none of the other answer options include hunters, you can deduce that *nomadic foragers* means gatherers. The correct answer is Choice (C).

Passage six

Organizational leaders influence several hundred to several thousand people. They do this indirectly, generally through more levels of subordinates than do direct leaders. The additional levels of subordinates can make it more difficult for them to see results. Organizational leaders have staffs to help them lead their people and manage their organizations' resources. They establish policies and the organizational climate that support their subordinate leaders.

22. Organizational leaders provide

    (A) direct leadership.

    (B) general policies.

    (C) organizational budgets.

    (D) daily work schedules.

The passage mentions direct leaders but only to contrast them with organizational leaders, so (A) is wrong. According to the passage, organizational leaders "establish policies and the organizational climate that support their subordinate leaders." The correct answer is Choice (B).

23. In order to become more efficient, organizational leaders make significant use of

    (A) computer technology.

    (B) rules and regulations.

    (C) efficiency and management reports.

    (D) staffs.

Organizational leaders have staffs to help them efficiently lead their subordinates and manage the organization. Therefore, Choice (D) is the correct answer.

Passage seven

His name is Frank Clarke, but his real name isn't really as real as the one the children gave him — The Toyman — because he's always making the kids things, such as kites and tops, sleds and boats, jokes and happiness and laughter. His face is as brown as saddle leather, with a touch of apple red in it from the sun. His face is creased, too, because he laughs and jokes so much. Sometimes when The Toyman appears to be solemn you want to laugh most, for he's only pretending to be solemn. And, best of all, if you hurt yourself or if your pet doggie hurts himself, The Toyman knows how to fix it to make it all well again.

24. Frank Clarke's face could best be described as

   (A) rugged.

   (B) pink and smooth.

   (C) fair.

   (D) feminine.

According to the passage, Frank's face is "brown as saddle leather," and he has wrinkles from laughing often. Choice (A) is the correct answer.

25. Clarke received his nickname because he was always

   (A) fixing toys.

   (B) making toys for the children.

   (C) telling stories about toys.

   (D) playing with toys.

The first sentence in the passage explains why the children gave Frank the nickname of The Toyman. Frank knows how to fix things, but that's not how he got his name. The correct answer is Choice (B).

Part III
Making the Most of Math: Arithmetic Skills

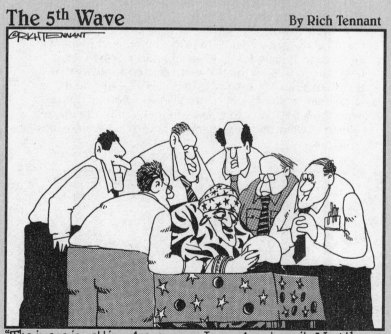

The 5th Wave   By Rich Tennant

"The image is getting clearer now...I can almost see it...Yes! there it is. The answer is $3ab^2 \times 7d^3 - \sqrt{19L} + U\frac{9}{m^4} \div \pm 100.(15)7\frac{9}{5} \phi Q69$."

In this part . . .

Many military careers require a solid understanding of math principles. Even though the military will spring for a calculator, you're expected to know how to add and subtract before you hit boot camp. And you can't use a calculator on the ASVAB.

Part III gives you a chance to brush up on your numbers knowledge. It includes all kinds of information that can help you do well on the two math-related subtests that the ASVAB throws at you: Arithmetic Reasoning and Mathematics Knowledge. I also give you a ton of tips on everything from how to guess whether you're running out of time to what to do if you forget how to solve a quadratic equation.

Chapter 7

Mathematics Knowledge and Operations

Albert Einstein once said, "Do not worry about your problems with mathematics. I assure you mine are far greater." The good professor obviously never faced an upcoming ASVAB exam! Okay, just kidding. You don't have to be a mathematical theoretician to score well on the Mathematics Knowledge subtest. This subtest asks questions about basic high school mathematics. No college or graduate degrees needed.

On the paper version of the ASVAB, the Mathematics Knowledge subtest consists of 25 questions, and you have 24 minutes to complete the subtest. The CAT-ASVAB offers 16 questions in 20 minutes. You don't necessarily have to rush through each calculation, but the pace you need to set doesn't exactly give you time to daydream. You have to focus and concentrate to solve each problem quickly and accurately. And no calculators allowed!

Most of the time, the Mathematics Knowledge subtest contains only one or two questions testing each specific mathematical concept. For example, one question may ask you to multiply fractions, the next may ask you to solve a mathematical inequality, and the question after that may ask you to find the value of an exponent. (If you're freaked out by the last sentence, calm down. I cover these concepts in this chapter.)

All this variety forces you to shift your mental gears quickly to deal with different concepts. You can look at this situation from two perspectives. These mental gymnastics can be difficult and frustrating, especially if you know everything about solving for x but nothing about finding a square root. But variety can also be the spice of life. If you don't know how to solve a specific type of problem, any oversight may only cause you to get one or two questions wrong.

To qualify for certain jobs in the military, you have to score well on the Mathematics Knowledge subtest. You also have to do well on this subtest, which is part of the AFQT discussed in Chapter 1, in order to enlist. Turn to Appendix A to find out more about the subtest scores needed for specific military jobs.

In this chapter, I go over the basic arithmetic, algebra, and geometry you need to know. This info also comes in handy when solving word problems on the Arithmetic Reasoning subtest, which I cover in Chapter 8.

Just When You Thought You Were Done with Vocab: Math Terminology

Math has its own vocabulary. In order to understand what each problem on the Mathematical Knowledge subtest asks, you need to understand certain mathematical terms:

- **Integer:** An integer is any positive or negative whole number or zero. The ASVAB often requires you to work with integers, such as –6, 0, or 27.

- **Factors:** Factors are integers (whole numbers) that can be divided evenly into another integer. To *factor* a number, you simply determine the numbers that you can divide into it. For example, 8 can be divided by the numbers 2 and 4 (in addition to 1 and 8), so 2 and 4 are factors of 8.

  Numbers may be either composite or prime, depending on how many factors they have:

  - **Composite number:** A composite number is a whole number that can be divided evenly by itself and by 1, as well as by one or more other whole numbers; in other words, it has more than two factors. Examples of composite numbers are 6 (whose factors are 1, 2, 3, and 6), 9 (whose factors are 1, 3, and 9), and 12 (whose factors are 1, 2, 3, 4, 6, and 12).

  - **Prime number:** A prime number is a whole number that can be divided evenly by itself and by 1 but not by any other number, which means that it has exactly two factors. Examples of prime numbers are 2 (whose factors are 1 and 2), 5 (whose factors are 1 and 5), and 11 (whose factors are 1 and 11).

- **Exponent:** An exponent is a shorthand method of indicating repeated multiplication. For example, 15×15 can also be expressed as 15^2, which is also known as "15 squared" or "15 to the second power." The small number written slightly above and to the right of a number is the *exponent,* and it indicates the number of times you multiply the number it accompanies *by itself.* Note that 15^2 (15×15, which equals 225) isn't the same as 15×2 (which equals 30).

  To express $15 \times 15 \times 15$ using this shorthand method, simply write it as 15^3, which is also called "15 cubed" or "15 to the third power." Again, 15^3 (which equals 3,375) isn't the same as 15×3 (which equals 45).

- **Base:** A base is a number that's used as a factor at least two times — it's a number raised to an exponent. For instance, the term 4^3 (which can be written $4 \times 4 \times 4$, and in which 4 is a factor three times) has a base of 4.

- **Square root:** The square root of a number is the number that, when multiplied by itself (in other words, *squared*), equals the original number. For example, the square root of 36 is 6. If you square 6, or multiply it by itself, you produce 36. (Check out "Getting to the Root of the Problem" later in this chapter.)

- **Factorial:** A factorial is represented by an exclamation point (!). You calculate a factorial by finding the product of (multiplying) a whole number and all the whole numbers less than it down to 1. So 6 factorial (6!) is $6 \times 5 \times 4 \times 3 \times 2 \times 1 = 720$.

  A factorial helps you determine *permutations* — all the different possible ways an event may turn out. For example, if you want to know how many different ways six runners could finish a race (permutation), you would solve for 6! — $6 \times 5 \times 4 \times 3 \times 2 \times 1$.

- **Reciprocal:** A reciprocal is the number by which another number can be multiplied to produce 1; if you have a fraction, its reciprocal is that fraction turned upside down. For example, the reciprocal of 3 is $\frac{1}{3}$. If you multiply 3 times $\frac{1}{3}$, you get 1. The reciprocal of $\frac{1}{6}$ is $\frac{6}{1}$ (which is the same thing as 6); $\frac{1}{6} \times 6 = 1$. The reciprocal of $\frac{2}{3}$ is $\frac{3}{2}$. Get the idea?

✔ **Rounding:** Rounding is limiting a number to a few (or no) decimal places. You perform rounding operations all the time — often without even thinking about it. If you have $1.97 in change in your pocket, you may say, "I have about two dollars." The rounding process simplifies mathematical operations.

Often, numbers are rounded to the nearest tenth. The ASVAB may ask you to do this. For any number that ends in 5 and over, round up; for any number under 5, round down. For example, 1.55 can be rounded up to 1.6, and 1.34 can be rounded down to 1.3.

Many math problems require rounding — especially when you're doing all this without a calculator. For example, pi (π) represents a number approximately equal to 3.1415926535897932384626433383 (and on and on and on). However, in mathematical operations, it's common to round π to 3.14.

Operations: What You Do to Numbers

When you toss numbers together (mathematically speaking), you perform an *operation*. When you add or multiply, you perform a *basic operation*. But because math functions according to yin-yang-like principles, each of these basic operations also has an opposite operation called an *inverse operation*. Thus, the inverse of addition is subtraction, and the inverse of multiplication is division. And of course, the inverse of subtraction is — you got it — addition. The inverse of division is multiplication.

Don't confuse *opposite* with *inverse*. When you're doing mathematical operations, such as adding and multiplying, the inverse operation is the opposite operation. But when you're talking numbers, *opposite* and *inverse* don't mean the same thing. The opposite of a positive number is a negative number, so the opposite of x is $-x$. But the inverse of a number is its reciprocal — that number turned on its head! The inverse of x is $\frac{1}{x}$. The inverse of $\frac{1}{5}$ is $\frac{5}{1}$ (or just 5).

First things first: Following the order of operations

Operations must be performed in a certain order. For example, when you have parentheses in a math problem, the calculation in the parentheses must be done before any calculations outside of the parentheses. In the equation $2 \times (16 + 5) = ?$, you first add 16 to 5 to arrive at 21, and then you multiply by 2 to come up with a total of 42. You get a different (and wrong) answer if you simply calculate from left to right: $2 \times 16 = 32$, and $32 + 5 = 37$. And you better believe that both results will be choices on the test!

Naming the answers

The result of each operation — addition, subtraction, multiplication, or division — goes by a different name:

✔ When you add two numbers together, you arrive at a *sum*.

✔ When you subtract, all that remains is a *difference*.

✔ When you multiply, you come up with a *product*.

✔ When you divide, you're left with a *quotient*.

To figure out which mathematical operation you should perform first, second, third, and so on, follow these rules, otherwise known as the *order of operations:*

1. **Parentheses take precedence.**

   You should do everything contained in parentheses first. In cases where parentheses are contained within parentheses, do the innermost parentheses first.

   Note: If you're dealing with a fraction, treat the top as though it were in parentheses and the bottom as though it were in parentheses, even if the parentheses aren't written in the original state. Suppose you have the problem: $\frac{3}{1+2} = ?$ Add the numbers below the fraction bar before dividing. The answer is $\frac{3}{3} = 1$. (For more on fractions, see the later section "Working on Both Sides of the Line: Fractions.") The square root sign ($\sqrt{\ }$) is also a grouping symbol, so you solve for whatever's under the top bar of the square root sign before doing any other operation in the problem.

2. **Exponents come next.**

   Remember that the exponent goes with the number or variable that it's closest to. If it's closest to a parenthesis, then you already should've performed the calculation inside the parentheses in Step 1. For example, $(5 \times 2)^2 = 10^2 = 100$. The square root sign ($\sqrt{\ }$) is also treated as an exponent, so you take the square root during this step.

3. **Multiplication and division are next.**

   Do these operations in left-to-right order (just like you read).

4. **Addition and subtraction are last.**

   Perform these operations from left to right as well.

Check out the following example for a little practice with order of operations:

$(15 \div 5) \times 3 + (18 - 7) = ?$

Do the work in parentheses:

$3 \times 3 + 11 = ?$

No exponents are present, so division and multiplication come next (in this problem, only multiplication is needed):

$9 + 11 = ?$

Finally, do the addition and subtraction (in this problem, only addition is needed). Your final answer is 20.

Completing a number sequence

The Arithmetic Reasoning (AR) subtest often includes questions that test your ability to name what comes next in a sequence of numbers. Generally, these problems are the only AR questions that aren't word problems (which I cover in Chapter 8). However, sequence questions do test your ability to do arithmetic and to reason, because you have to determine how the numbers relate to each other. And to do this, you must be able to perform mathematical operations quickly.

Suppose you have a sequence of numbers that looks like this: 1, 4, 7, 10, ?

Each new number is reached by adding 3 to the previous number: 1 + 3 = 4, 4 + 3 = 7, and so on. So the next number in the sequence is 10 + 3, or 13. But of course, the questions on the ASVAB aren't quite this simple. More likely, you'll see something like this: 2, 4, 16, 256, ?

In this case, each number is being multiplied by itself, so 2 × 2 = 4, 4 × 4 = 16, and so on. The next number in the sequence is 256 × 256, which equals 65,536 — the correct answer. You may also see sequences like this: 1, 2, 3, 6, 12, ?

In this sequence, the numbers are being added together: 1 + 2 = 3, and 1 + 2 + 3 = 6. The next number is 1 + 2 + 3 + 6 = 12. So the next number would be 24.

Finding the pattern

To answer sequence questions correctly, you need to figure out the pattern as quickly as possible. Some people, blessed with superior sequencing genes, can figure out patterns instinctively. The rest of the population has to rely on a more difficult, manual effort.

Finding a pattern in a sequence of numbers requires you to think about how numbers work. For instance, seeing the number 256 after 2, 4, 16 should alert you that multiplication is the operation, because 256 is so much larger than the other numbers. On the other hand, because the values in 1, 2, 3, 6, 12 don't increase by much, you can guess that the pattern requires addition.

Dealing with more than one operation in a sequence

Don't forget that more than one operation can occur in a sequence. For example, a sequence may be "add 1, subtract 1, add 2, subtract 2." That would look something like this: 2, 3, 2, 4, ?

Because the numbers in the sequence both increase and decrease as the sequence continues, you should suspect that something tricky is going on.

Make sure to use your scratch paper! Jot down notes while you're trying to find the pattern in a sequence. Writing your work down helps you keep track of which operations you've tried.

Working on Both Sides of the Line: Fractions

I don't know why, but it seems almost all math textbooks explain fractions in terms of pies. (I think most mathematicians must have a sweet tooth.) But I like pizza, so I'm going to use pizza instead. If a *whole number* is a pizza, a *fraction* is a slice of pizza. A fraction also illustrates the slice's relationship to the whole pizza. For example, consider the fraction $\frac{3}{5}$. If you accuse your cousin of eating $\frac{3}{5}$ of the pizza when he comes over for movie night, you're saying that the pizza is divided into five equal-sized slices — fifths — and your cousin ate three of those five slices. Can anyone say *pig*?

The number above the fraction bar — the three slices your cousin ate — is called the *numerator.* The number written below the fraction bar — the total number of slices the pizza is divided into — is called the *denominator.*

Common denominators: Preparing to add and subtract fractions

To add and subtract fractions, the fractions must have the same denominator (bottom number), which is called a *common denominator.* If the fractions don't have a common denominator, you have to find one. There are two basic methods to use. Sound fun? Read on.

Method one

Finding a common denominator can be easy, or it can be as hard as picking off all the anchovies. Suppose you want to add $\frac{3}{5}$ and $\frac{3}{10}$. Getting a common denominator is easy here, and you use this process whenever you can evenly divide one denominator by another. Follow these steps:

1. **Divide the larger denominator by the smaller denominator.**

   If there's a remainder, then you can't use this method, and you have to use method two (see the next section). In this case, 10 can be divided evenly by 5. The quotient (answer) that results is 2.

2. **Take the fraction with the smaller denominator** $\left(\frac{3}{5}\right)$; **multiply both the numerator (top number) and the denominator (bottom number) by the answer that resulted in Step 1.**

   Multiply 3 by 2, and the result is 6 — that's your new numerator. Multiply 5 by 2, and the result is 10 — that's your new denominator.

3. **Replace the numerator and denominator with the numbers from Step 2.**

   You can also express $\frac{3}{5}$ as $\frac{6}{10}$. (If you cut the pizza into 10 slices instead of 5 and your cousin eats 6 slices instead of 3, he's eaten exactly the same amount of pizza.)

After you've found a common denominator, you add the two fractions by simply adding the numerators together: $\frac{6}{10} + \frac{3}{10} = \frac{9}{10}$. Think of it this way: If your cousin eats $\frac{6}{10}$ of the pizza (which is just another way of saying $\frac{3}{5}$) and you eat $\frac{3}{10}$ of the pizza, together you've eaten $\frac{9}{10}$ of the pizza.

Method two

Suppose your cousin eats $\frac{3}{5}$ of one pizza and your sister eats $\frac{1}{6}$ of another pizza (one that was cut into 6 slices instead of 5), and you want to know how much pizza has been eaten. In this case, you need to add $\frac{3}{5}$ and $\frac{1}{6}$.

Adding these fractions is a bit more difficult because you can't divide either denominator by the other. You have to find a common denominator that both 5 and 6 divide into evenly. Here's how:

1. **Multiply the denominator of the first fraction by the denominator of the second fraction.**

   In the preceding example, $5 \times 6 = 30$. The common denominator for both fractions is 30.

2. **Express the first fraction in terms of the new common denominator.**

   $$\frac{3}{5} = \frac{?}{30}$$

3. **Multiply the numerator by the number that you multiplied by to result in the new denominator.**

   To convert the denominator (5) to 30, you multiply by 6, so multiply the numerator (3) by 6. The result is 18. Therefore, the fraction $\frac{3}{5}$ can be expressed as $\frac{18}{30}$.

   When you're trying to find the common denominator for a fraction, always multiply the numerator and the denominator by the same number. Otherwise, you change the value of the fraction.

   With this example, you multiply the numerator and the denominator by 6, discovering that $\frac{3}{5}$ is the same thing as $\frac{18}{30}$. But if you were to multiply only the denominator by 6, you'd have a new number — $\frac{3}{5}$ and $\frac{3}{30}$ don't have the same value.

4. **Next, express the second fraction in terms of the new common denominator.**

   $$\frac{1}{6} = \frac{?}{30}$$

5. **Multiply the numerator of the second fraction by the number you used to result in the denominator.**

   To get 30, you have to multiply 6 by 5. Multiply the numerator by the same number: You find that $1 \times 5 = 5$, so the fraction $\frac{1}{6}$ can be expressed as $\frac{5}{30}$.

After all that work, you can finally add the fractions: $\frac{18}{30} + \frac{5}{30} = \frac{23}{30}$. Now pause and take a bite of pizza.

Finding common denominators for three or more fractions

If you have more than two fractions with different denominators, you have to find a common denominator that all the denominators divide into. Suppose you need to add $\frac{1}{2} + \frac{2}{3} + \frac{3}{5}$.

A simple way to find a common denominator is to take the largest denominator (in this case 5) and multiply it by whole numbers, starting with 1, 2, 3, 4, and so on until you find a denominator that the other denominators also divide into evenly.

If you multiply 5 by 2, you get 10, but 3 doesn't divide evenly into 10. So keep going: $5 \times 3 = 15$, $5 \times 4 = 20$, and so on until you find a number that 2, 3, and 5 can divide into evenly. In this case, 30 is the first number you can find that 2, 3, and 5 can divide into evenly, so 30 is your common denominator.

Multiplying and reducing fractions

Multiplying fractions is easy. You just multiply the numerators and then multiply the denominators. So look at the following equation: $\frac{1}{2} \times \frac{3}{4} \times \frac{3}{5} = ?$. You multiply $1 \times 3 \times 3 = 9$ (the numerators) and then $2 \times 4 \times 5 = 40$ (the denominators) to result in $\frac{9}{40}$.

Occasionally, when you multiply fractions, you end up with an extremely large fraction that can be simplified or reduced. To express a fraction in its *lowest terms* means to put it in such a way that you can't evenly divide the numerator and the denominator by the same number (other than 1).

A number that you can divide into both the numerator and the denominator is called a *common factor*. If you have the fraction $\frac{6}{10}$, both the numerator (6) and the denominator (10) can be divided by the same number, 2. If you do the division, $6 \div 2 = 3$ and $10 \div 2 = 5$, you find that $\frac{6}{10}$ can be expressed in the simpler terms of $\frac{3}{5}$. You can't reduce (simplify) $\frac{3}{5}$ any further; the only other number that both the numerator and denominator can be divided by is 1, so the result would be the same, $\frac{3}{5}$.

Remember, you can't use a calculator on the ASVAB, so multiplying large numbers can take extra steps and valuable time. You can make your work easier by *canceling out* common factors before multiplying. For example, suppose you have the problem $\frac{20}{21} \times \frac{14}{25}$. Multiplying the numerators ($20 \times 14 = 280$), then multiplying the denominators ($21 \times 25 = 525$), and finally reducing the fraction $\left(\frac{280}{525} = \frac{8}{15}\right)$ may require you to write out three or more separate multiplication/division problems. But you can save time if a numerator and denominator have common factors. Here, the numerator of the first fraction (20) and the denominator of the second (25) have a common factor of 5, so you can divide both of those numbers by 5: Your problem becomes $\frac{4}{21} \times \frac{14}{5}$. The numerator of the second fraction (14) and the denominator of the first fraction (21) are both divisible by 7, so you can cancel out a 7: Divide 14 and 21 by 7. This changes the equation to $\frac{4}{3} \times \frac{2}{5} = \frac{8}{15}$, a much simpler math problem.

Dividing fractions

Dividing fractions is simple if you remember this rule: Dividing a fraction by a number is the same as multiplying it by the inverse (reciprocal) of that number. Of course, there are always exceptions. You can't use this operation on zero. Zero has no inverse. No one knows why — it just is.

The inverse of a number is obtained by reversing the number. That means that if you want to divide a fraction by 5, you simply multiply the fraction by the inverse of 5, which is $\frac{1}{5}$.

You can understand this process more easily if you remember that 5 is the same thing as $\frac{5}{1}$. In other words, 5 divided by 1 equals 5 (that is, $5 \div 1 = 5$). And the inverse of $\frac{5}{1}$ is $\frac{1}{5}$. To come up with the inverse of a number, simply stand the number on its head.

So to divide a fraction, use the inverse of the number that follows the division symbol ($\div$) and substitute a multiplication symbol ($\times$) for the division symbol. Therefore, $\frac{1}{3} \div 2$ is expressed as $\frac{1}{3} \times \frac{1}{2}$, and you already know how to multiply fractions. (If not, check out the "Multiplying and reducing fractions" section earlier in the chapter.) $1 \times 1 = 1$ and $3 \times 2 = 6$, so the product of $\frac{1}{3} \times \frac{1}{2} = \frac{1}{6}$. Therefore, $\frac{1}{3} \div 2 = \frac{1}{6}$.

Converting improper fractions to mixed numbers . . . and back again

If you have a fraction with a numerator larger than its denominator, you have an *improper fraction*. For example, $\frac{7}{3}$ is an improper fraction. To put an improper fraction into simpler (proper) terms, you can change $\frac{7}{3}$ into a *mixed number* (a number that includes a whole number and a fraction). Simply divide the numerator by the denominator: 7 divided by 3 gives you a quotient of 2 with a remainder of 1. There's something left over because 3 doesn't divide evenly into 7. The remainder becomes a numerator over the original denominator, so $\frac{1}{3}$ is left over. Therefore, $\frac{7}{3}$ is the same as $2\frac{1}{3}$.

If you want to multiply or divide a mixed number, you need to convert it into a fraction — an improper fraction. To make the change, convert the whole number into a fraction and add it to the fraction you already have. Here's how:

1. **Multiply the whole number by the denominator (bottom number) of the existing fraction to arrive at a new numerator.**

   Suppose you have $7\frac{2}{3}$. Multiply 7 by 3: $7 \times 3 = 21$

2. **Place this new numerator over the existing denominator.**

   $\frac{21}{3}$

3. **Add that fraction to the original fraction to get the final answer.**

   $\frac{21}{3} + \frac{2}{3} = \frac{23}{3}$

   Check out the "Common denominators: Preparing to add and subtract fractions" section earlier in this chapter for the complete scoop on adding fractions.

Or if you want to get technical, you can look at the whole process this way, too:

$7\frac{2}{3} = \frac{7 \times 3 + 2}{3} = \frac{23}{3}$

Expressing a fraction in other forms: Decimals and percents

A fraction can also be expressed as a decimal and as a percent. Here's how to convert between forms:

- **To change a fraction into a decimal:** Divide the numerator (top number) by the denominator (bottom number). Given that handy explanation, $\frac{3}{5}$ (or $3 \div 5$) converted into decimal form is 0.6.

  Some fractions convert to *repeating decimals* — a decimal in which one digit is repeated infinitely. For instance, $\frac{2}{3}$ is the same as 0.66666... (with the sixes never stopping).

  Repeating decimals are often rounded to the nearest hundredth; therefore, $\frac{2}{3}$ rounds to 0.67. (**Remember:** The first space to the right of the decimal is the *tenths* place, the second space is the *hundredths* place, and the third is the *thousandths,* and so on.)

- **To make a decimal into a percent:** Move the decimal point two spaces to the right and add a percent sign. For example, 0.6 becomes 60%.

See the following sections for more thorough discussions of decimals and percents.

Adding and subtracting decimals

To add and subtract decimals, put the numbers in a column and line up the decimal points. Then add or subtract as if the decimals were whole numbers, keeping the decimal point in the same position in your answer.

Here are two examples:

$$\begin{array}{r} 1.4583 \\ +0.55 \\ \hline 2.0083 \end{array} \qquad \begin{array}{r} 1.4583 \\ -0.55 \\ \hline 0.9083 \end{array}$$

You can add zeros to the end of a decimal if performing the calculations this way is easier for you. So 0.1 can be 0.100 without changing its value. In the preceding problems, 0.55 can be 0.5500 to help you line up the decimal points and perform the operation.

Multiplying decimals

Multiplying a decimal is like multiplying a regular, everyday whole number, except that you have to place the decimal point in the correct position after you reach an answer.

1. **Multiply as though you were multiplying whole numbers, without the decimal points.**

   Suppose you're multiplying 3.77×2.8. In this example, $377 \times 28 = 10556$.

2. **Count and add the number of decimal places (to the right of the decimal point) in the numbers being multiplied.**

   If one of the numbers you're multiplying is 3.77, you have two decimal places. If the other number you're multiplying is 2.8, you have one more decimal place, so the total number of decimal places in your answer will be three.

   If you're multiplying a number that has only zeros to the right of the decimal point, then those decimals don't count. For instance, 3 can also be expressed as 3.0, but you wouldn't count the 0 as a decimal place. All the zeros to the right of the decimal point don't count unless a number other than zero comes after them. For instance, 3.000007 has six decimal spaces, 3.0070 has three decimal spaces, and 3.000 has none, at least not for the purpose of multiplying.

3. **In the answer, move the decimal point back to the left the number of places you counted in Step 2.**

   This time, zeros do count. You counted three total decimal places in 3.77 and 2.8, so you move the decimal point in 10566 back to the left three places. The resulting product is 10.556.

   If your answer doesn't include enough numbers for the decimal spaces you need, then add as many zeros as necessary to the left of the answer. Suppose your answer is 50, and you have to move the decimal point to the left three spaces. There aren't three spaces in 50, so you add a zero to the left to make 050 and put the decimal point in its proper position: 0.050 is your answer.

Here's another example: 0.04×0.25. Multiply the decimals as if they were whole numbers: $4 \times 25 = 100$. Count and add the number of decimal places in the original two numbers; there are four. Then put the decimal point in the correct place in the answer. For 100, count from right to left four places, and put the decimal point there: 0.0100, or 0.01. Here's the method behind the madness:

$$\frac{4}{100} \times \frac{25}{100} = \frac{100}{10,000} = \frac{1}{100} = 0.01 \ (\text{or } 0.0100)$$

Dividing decimals

Decimals are divided according to slightly different rules, depending on whether both numbers in the problem are decimals.

Dividing decimals by whole numbers

Here's how to divide a decimal by a whole number:

1. **Move the decimal point over to the right until the decimal is a whole number, counting the number of decimal places.**

   For example, if you want to find $1.25 \div 4$, change 1.25 to 125 by moving the decimal two decimal places to the right. Remember how many places you moved the decimal — you need that info later.

2. **Perform the division operation on the whole number.**

   $125 \div 4 = 31.25$

3. **In your answer, move the decimal point to the left the number of places you moved it in Step 1.**

To make up for moving the decimal point two places to the right when you made 1.25 into a whole number, move the decimal point two places to the left in 31.25. Your answer is 0.3125.

Dividing decimals by decimals

Here's how to divide a decimal by another decimal in which there are the same number of places after the decimal point:

1. **Make the *divisor* (the decimal going into the other number) into a whole number: Move the decimal point all the way to the right, counting the number of places you move it.**

   Suppose you want to divide 0.15 by 0.25 (that is, 0.15 ÷ 0.25). Move the decimal point in 0.25 two places to the right: It then becomes 25.

2. **Move the decimal in the dividend (the number being divided) the same number of decimal places.**

   Move the decimal point in 0.15 two places: 0.15 becomes 15.

3. **Divide.**

   When you divide 15 by 25, the result is 0.60. You don't need to move any more decimals around — 0.60 is your final answer.

If the dividend is a longer decimal than the divisor, you follow the same steps, but you have to do an extra step at the end. So if your problem is 0.125 ÷ 0.50, first move the decimal point in the divisor (0.5) one place to the right so that you have the whole number 5. Then move the decimal point in the dividend one place to come up with 1.25.

Now the problem looks like this: 1.25 ÷ 5. Convert the first number (1.25) to a whole number by moving the decimal point two places to the right. Now perform the division operation on the whole numbers: 125 ÷ 5 = 25. Move the decimal point two places to the left (to make up for moving it two places to the right when you converted 1.25 to a whole number). The answer is 0.25.

When the divisor is a longer decimal than the dividend, such as 0.50 ÷ 0.125, move the decimal point in the divisor all the way to the right, in this case making 0.125 into 125, counting places. Then move the decimal the same number of places in the dividend, adding zeros as needed: 0.5 then becomes 500. Then 500 ÷ 125 = 4, which is the correct answer (0.50 ÷ 0.125 = 4).

Playing with percents

A percent is a fraction based on one-hundredths. Five percent (5%) is the same as $\frac{5}{100}$ or 0.05. The ASVAB often asks you to calculate "10% off" or "an increase of 15%" on the Arithmetic Reasoning subtest. You need to be able to convert percents to fractions or decimals to answer these questions correctly.

To add, subtract, multiply, or divide using percents, change the percent to a fraction or a decimal. Here are some helpful hints for figuring percents:

- Remember, a percent is just hundredths, so 3% is $\frac{3}{100}$ or 0.03, 22% is $\frac{22}{100}$ or 0.22, and 110% is $\frac{110}{100}$ or 1.10.

- To convert a percent to a decimal, just drop the percent sign and move the decimal point two places to the left, adding zeros as needed.

- The decimal point always starts to the right of a whole number, so 60 is the same thing as 60.0. Moving the decimal point two spaces to the left leaves you with 0.6.

After you do the conversion, follow the rules outlined in the earlier sections for performing specific operations on fractions or decimals.

Showing comparisons with ratios

A *ratio* shows a relationship between two things. For example, if Margaret invested in her tattoo parlor at a 2:1 (or 2 to 1) ratio to her business partner Julie, then Margaret put in $2 for every $1 that Julie put in. You can express a ratio as a fraction, so 2:1 is the same as $\frac{2}{1}$.

Or suppose you fill up your brand-new, shiny SUV, and you want to compute your gas mileage — miles per gallon. You drive for 240 miles and then refill the tank with 15 gallons of gas, so the ratio of miles to gallons is 240:15. You can compute your gas mileage by dividing the number of miles by the number of gallons: 240 miles ÷ 15 gallons. You're getting 16 miles per gallon. Time for a tune up!

In this section, I cover some uses for ratios, including scale drawings and rates such as speed.

Navigating scale drawings

Scale, particularly when used on the ASVAB, relates to scale drawings. For example, a map drawn to scale may have a 1-inch drawing of a road that represents 1 mile of physical road in the real world. The Arithmetic Reasoning portion of the ASVAB often asks you to calculate a problem based on scale, which can be represented as a standard ratio (1 inch:1 mile) or a fraction $\left(\frac{1\ \text{inch}}{1\ \text{mile}}\right)$.

On a map with a scale of 1 inch to 1 mile, the ratio of the scale is represented as 1:1. But questions are never this easy on the ASVAB. You're more likely to see something like, "If a map has a scale of 1 inch to every 4 miles. . . ." That scale is expressed as the ratio 1:4, or $\frac{1}{4}$.

Try your hand with the following common scale problem:

If the scale on a road map is 1 inch = 250 miles, how many inches would represent 1,250 miles?

The problem wants you to determine how many inches on the map represent 1,250 miles if 1 inch is equal to 250 miles. You know that 1 inch = 250 miles, and you also know that some unknown number of inches, which you can call *x,* equals 1,250 miles. The problem can be expressed as two ratios set equal to each other, known as a *proportion*: $\frac{1}{250} = \frac{x}{1,250}$. Now all you have to do is solve for *x:*

$$\frac{1}{250} = \frac{x}{1,250}$$

$$\frac{1}{250} \times 1,250 = \frac{x}{1,250} \times 1,250$$

$$\frac{1,250}{250} = x$$

$$x = 5$$

So if 1 inch is equal to 250 miles, then 5 inches would be equal to 1,250 miles. If this problem causes you to scratch your head, check out the upcoming section "An Unknown Quantity: Reviewing Algebra" for info on solving for *x.*

Almost every military job makes use of scales, which is why scale-related questions are so common on the ASVAB. Whether you're reading maps at Mountain Warfare School or organizing trash pickup around the base, you need to use and interpret scales frequently.

Remembering important rates

A *rate* is a fixed quantity — a 5% interest rate, for example. It can mean the speed at which one works (John reads at the rate of one page per minute). Or it can mean an amount of money paid based on another amount (life insurance may be purchased at a rate of $1 per $100 of coverage). A rate is often a speed, something per a unit of time.

Word problems often ask you to solve problems that involve speed or simple interest rates. Here are two rate formulas you should commit to memory:

- **Simple interest:** $I = Prt$, where I represents the amount of interest, P is the principal (the initial amount invested), r is the interest rate, and t is the length of time the money is invested.

- **Distance:** $d = rt$, where d represents the distance traveled, r is the rate (speed) of travel, and t is the amount of time traveled.

In a rate, you can generally think of the word *per* as a division sign. For instance, suppose someone drives 141 miles in 3 hours, and you have to find the average speed. You want the rate of speed in *miles per hour,* so you take *miles* (distance) divided by *hours* (time): 141 miles ÷ 3 hours = 47 miles/hour. Using algebra, you can rearrange the distance formula to say the same thing: $d \div t = r$.

A Powerful Shorthand: Writing in Scientific Notation

Scientific notation is a compact format for writing very large or very small numbers. Although it's most often used in scientific fields, you may find a question or two on the Mathematics Knowledge subtest of the ASVAB, asking you to covert a number to or from scientific notation.

Scientific notation separates a number into two parts: a number between 1 and 10 and a power of ten (such as 10^7, 10^{21}, or 10^{-18}; see the earlier section "Just When You Thought You Were Done with Vocab: Math Terminology" for info on powers and exponents). Therefore, 1.25×10^4 means 1.25×10 to the fourth power, or 12,500; 5.79×10^{-8} means $5.79 \div 10$ to the eighth power, or 0.0000000579. The exponent tells you how many places to move the decimal point and whether to move it left or right (depending on whether it's positive or negative).

Getting to the Root of the Problem

A *square root* is the factor of a number that, when multiplied by itself, produces the number. Take the number 36, for example. One of the factors of 36 is 6. If you multiply 6 by itself (6×6), you come up with 36, so 6 is the square root of 36. The number 36 has other factors, such as 18. But if you multiply 18 by itself (18×18), you get 324, not 36. So 18 isn't the square root of 36.

All whole numbers are grouped into one of two camps when it comes to roots:

- **Perfect squares:** Only a few whole numbers, called *perfect squares,* have exact square roots. For example, the square root of 25 is 5.

- **Irrational numbers:** Other whole numbers have square roots that are decimals that go on forever and have no pattern that repeats (nonrepeating, nonterminating decimals), so they're called *irrational numbers.* The square root of 30 is 5.4772255 with no end to the decimal places, so the square root of 30 is an irrational number.

The sign for a square root is called the *radical sign.* It looks like this: $\sqrt{}$. Here's how you use it: $\sqrt{36}$ means "the square root of 36" — in other words, 6.

Perfect squares

Square roots can be difficult to find at times without a calculator, but because you can't use a calculator during the test, you're going to have to use your mind and some guessing methods. To find the square root of a number without a calculator, make an educated guess and then verify your results.

To use the educated-guess method (see the next section), you have to know the square roots of a few perfect squares. One good way to do this is to memorize the squares of the square roots 1 through 12:

- ✔ 1 is the square root of 1 ($1 \times 1 = 1$)
- ✔ 2 is the square root of 4 ($2 \times 2 = 4$)
- ✔ 3 is the square root of 9 ($3 \times 3 = 9$)
- ✔ 4 is the square root of 16 ($4 \times 4 = 16$)
- ✔ 5 is the square root of 25 ($5 \times 5 = 25$)
- ✔ 6 is the square root of 36 ($6 \times 6 = 36$)
- ✔ 7 is the square root of 49 ($7 \times 7 = 49$)
- ✔ 8 is the square root of 64 ($8 \times 8 = 64$)
- ✔ 9 is the square root of 81 ($9 \times 9 = 81$)
- ✔ 10 is the square root of 100 ($10 \times 10 = 100$)
- ✔ 11 is the square root of 121 ($11 \times 11 = 121$)
- ✔ 12 is the square root of 144 ($12 \times 12 = 144$)

Irrational numbers

When the ASVAB asks you to figure square roots of numbers that aren't perfect squares, the task gets a bit more difficult. In this case, the ASVAB usually asks you to find the square root to the nearest tenth.

Suppose you run across this problem:

$$\sqrt{54}$$

Think about what you know: You know that the square root of 49 is 7, and 54 is slightly greater than 49. You also know that the square root of 64 is 8, and 54 is slightly less than 64. So if the number 54 is somewhere between 49 and 64, the square root of 54 is somewhere between 7 and 8. Because 54 is closer to 49 than to 64, the square root will be closer to 7 than to 8, so you can try 7.3 as the square root of 54.

Multiply 7.3 by itself: $7.3 \times 7.3 = 53.29$, which is very close to 54. Now try multiplying 7.4 by itself to see if it's any closer to 54: $7.4 \times 7.4 = 54.76$, which isn't as close to 54 as 53.29. Therefore, 7.3 is the square root of 54 to the nearest tenth without going over.

Other roots

The wonderful world of math is also home to concepts like cube roots, fourth roots, fifth roots, and so on. A *root* is a factor of a number that when cubed (multiplied by itself three times), taken to the fourth power (multiplied by itself four times), and so on produces the original number. A couple of examples seem to be in order:

- ✔ The cube root of 27 is 3. If you cube 3 (also known as raising it to the third power or multiplying $3 \times 3 \times 3$), the product is 27.

- ✔ The fourth root of 16 is the number that, when multiplied by itself four times, equals 16. Any guesses? Drumroll, please: 2 is the fourth root of 16 because $2 \times 2 \times 2 \times 2 = 16$.

An Unknown Quantity: Reviewing Algebra

Some people freak out just hearing the word *algebra*. But algebra is just a way to put problems into mathematical language using the simplest mathematical terms possible. In fact, it's almost impossible to solve most word problems without some use of algebra.

The letters in an algebra problem are called *variables*. In an algebra equation, if the same letter is used more than once, it stands for the same number. In $3x + 2x = 10$, the first x will *never* be a different number from the second x. In this case, $x = 2$ (both times).

Solving for x

In algebra, you often hear about "solving for x" or "solving for the unknown," but what's the unknown? The *unknown* is the answer you want find. Check out this example:

Rod's mom has worked up a powerful thirst solving a ton of math problems and asked Rod to run to the corner store and get her one of those super-duper gigantic nuclear soft drinks. If a regular-sized soft drink costs $0.50 and the super-duper gigantic nuclear size costs three times the cost of the regular size, how much will Rod have to spend?

You can express this problem in terms of x, with x being the cost of the super-duper-sized drink: x equals 3 (the price difference) $\times$ 50 cents. Written a bit more formally, the equation looks like this: $x = 3(0.50)$ or $3(0.50) = x$.

What if you don't know how much the regular-sized soft drink costs? You can express this missing piece of information in an equation as well: x (how much it will cost to buy a super-duper size) equals 3 (the cost increase) times p (the price of one regular-sized drink). Once again, written a bit more formally, the equation looks like this: $x = 3p$ or $x = 3 \cdot p$.

You can remove the multiplication symbol in algebraic expressions when using a combination of letters and numbers. Therefore, the equation $x = 3 \times p$ can also be written $x = 3p$. The multiplication symbol is implied. It's also common to use parentheses or the dot multiplication symbol, $\cdot$, to indicate multiplication. Most people avoid using the $\times$ because it looks so close to the letter x.

When all things are equal: Keeping an algebra equation balanced

Algebra problems are equations, which means that the quantities on both sides of the equal sign are equal — they're the same. For instance, $2 = 2$, $1 + 1 = 2$, and $3 - 1 = 2$. In all these cases, the quantities are the same on both sides of the equal sign. To solve an algebra equation, you find out what the variable equals by getting it by itself on one side of the equal sign. So if $x = 2$, then x is 2 because the equal sign says so.

You can perform any calculation on either side of an equation as long as you do it to both sides of the equation. That keeps the equation equal.

You can also combine *like terms* — terms that have matching variables — when operating on algebraic expressions: $3x + 3x = (3 + 3)x = 6x$. However, $3x + 3y$ doesn't equal $6xy$, nor does $x^2 + x^3 = x^5$ (see the section "Explaining exponents in algebra" later in this chapter, to find out more about algebra involving exponents).

Solving one-step equations involving addition and subtraction

If $x + 1 = 2$, then x must be 1, because only 1 added to 1 is 2. So far, so simple, so good. But what if the equation is a little more complicated?

$$x + 47{,}432 = 50{,}000$$

To solve the problem, you need to isolate x on one side of the equal sign. To get that job done, move any other numbers on the x side of the equal sign to the other side of the equal sign.

By looking at the x side of the equation, you can see that it's an addition problem. To move the number on the x side to the opposite side, you have to perform the inverse operation. The inverse operation of addition is subtraction. (For a full rundown on inverse operations, check out the earlier section "Operations: What You Do to Numbers.") So to move 47,432 from the x side to the non-x side of the equation, simply subtract that number from both sides:

$$x + 47{,}432 - 47{,}432 = 50{,}000 - 47{,}432$$

Performing these operations removes the 47,432 from the x side of the equation (47,432 – 47,432 = 0, so that side of the equation is $x + 0$ or simply x) and gives you 2,568 on the non-x side of the equation (50,000 – 47,432 = 2,568). You're left with the final answer: $x = 2{,}568$

To double-check that this answer is correct, you can plug your answer into the original problem:

$$x + 47{,}432 = 50{,}000$$
$$2{,}568 + 47{,}432 = 50{,}000$$

If you plug the answer in and it doesn't work, you've made an error in your calculations. Start again; remember that you're trying to isolate x on one side of the equation.

Multiplying and dividing

In multiplication and division, if the two terms being operated on (on either side of the equal sign) are both positive numbers or both negative numbers, the answer will be a positive number. If one number is negative and the other is positive, the answer will be negative.

To solve the problem $-6x = 36$ (don't forget, $6x$ is the same thing as $6 \times x$), you need to isolate x. So perform an inverse operation; the inverse operation of multiplication is division. Division in algebra is usually represented with a fraction bar:

$$\frac{-6x}{-6} = \frac{36}{-6}$$
$$x = -6$$

The answer is a negative number because the two terms, 36 and –6, have different signs.

Solving multistep equations

Not all algebra problems have one-step solutions. (That would be too easy, and you wouldn't sweat nearly as much.) Solving algebra problems on the ASVAB often requires you to perform several steps.

An example of a multistep equation is one in which x shows up on both sides of the equal sign. Then you have to get rid of x on one side of the equation by moving x terms from one side to the other. You do this by performing the inverse operation.

Suppose you want to solve this equation: $3x + 3 = 9 + x$. To remove the x from one side of the equation, perform the inverse operation. The right side of the equation adds an x, so subtract x from both sides of the equation:

$$3x + 3 - x = 9 + x - x$$
$$3x + 3 - 1x = 9 + 0$$
$$2x + 3 = 9$$

To get the x term, $2x$, by itself, subtract 3 from each side of the equation:

$$2x + 3 - 3 = 9 - 3$$
$$2x = 6$$

Divide both sides of the equation by 2 to isolate x:

$$\frac{2x}{2} = \frac{6}{2}$$
$$x = 3$$

When you have a variable by itself, such as x, it's always equal to 1 times that variable (or one of that variable), like $1x$, even if the 1 isn't written out. In fact, any number is equal to 1 times itself, so you could also say $2 = 2 \times 1$.

Explaining exponents in algebra

Exponents are an easy way to show that a number is to be multiplied by itself a certain number of times. For example, 5^2 is the same as 5×5, and y^3 is the same as $y \times y \times y$. The number or variable that's multiplied by itself is called the *base,* and the number or variable showing how many times it is to be multiplied by itself is called the *exponent* or *power*.

Here are important rules when working with exponents in algebra:

- ✔ Any base raised to the power of one equals itself: $x^1 = x$
- ✔ Any base raised to the zero power (except 0) equals 1: $x^0 = 1$
- ✔ To multiply terms with the same base, add the exponents: $x^2(x^3) = x^{2+3} = x^5$

  So if $x = 2$, then $2^2 = 4$ and $2^3 = 8$, and $4(8) = 32$. That's the same as $2^5 = 32$, which equals $2 \times 2 \times 2 \times 2 \times 2$.

- ✔ To divide terms with the same base, subtract the exponents: $x^5 \div x^2 = x^{5-2} = x^3$
- ✔ If a base has a negative exponent, it's equal to its reciprocal (inverse) with a positive exponent: $x^{-3} = \frac{1}{x^3}$
- ✔ When a product has an exponent, each factor is raised to that power: $(xy)^3 = x^3 y^3$

A step back: Factoring algebra expressions to find original numbers

Now and then, the ASVAB gives you a *product* (the answer to a multiplication problem), and you have to find the original numbers that were multiplied together to produce that product. This process is called *factoring*. You use factors when you combine like terms and add fractions.

Pulling out the greatest common factor

Your task may be to pull out the greatest common factor from two or more terms. Take, for example, this product: $4xy + 2x^2$. To factor this product, follow these steps:

1. **Find the *greatest common factor* — the highest number that evenly divides all the terms in the expression.**

   Look at both the constants (numbers) and variables. In this case, the highest number that divides into 4 and 2 is 2. And the highest variable that divides into both xy and x^2 is x. Take what you know to this point, and you can see that the greatest common factor is $2x$.

2. **Divide both terms in the expression by the greatest common factor.**

   When you divide $4xy$ and $2x^2$ by $2x$, the resulting terms are $2y + x$.

3. **Multiply the entire expression (from Step 2) by the greatest common factor (from Step 1) to set the expression equal to its original value.**

   Doing so produces $2x(2y + x)$.

Factoring a three-term equation ($x^2 + bx + c$)

Time to try something a little more complicated: factoring a trinomial (an expression with three terms). Suppose you start with $x^2 - 12x + 20$. Follow these steps:

1. **Find the factors of the first term of the trinomial.**

   The factors of the first term, x^2, are x and x ($x \cdot x = x^2$). Put those factors (x and x) on the left side of two sets of parentheses: $(x\ )(x\ )$.

2. **Determine whether the parentheses will contain positive or negative signs.**

   You can see that the last term in the trinomial (+20) has a plus sign. That means the signs in the parentheses must be either both plus signs or both minus signs. (Why? Because two positive numbers multiplied equals a positive number, and two negative numbers multiplied equals a positive number, but a negative number times a positive number equals a negative number.)

   Because the second term ($-12x$) is a negative number, both of the factors must be negative: $(x -)(x -)$.

3. **Find the two numbers that go into the right sides of the parentheses.**

   This part can be tricky. The factors of the third term, when added or subtracted together, must equal the second term of the trinomial.

   In this example, the third term is 20 and the second term is $-12x$. You need to find the factors of 20 (the third term) that add to give you -12. The two factors you want are -2 and -10, because $-2 \times -10 = 20$ (the third term) and $-2 + -10 = -12$ (the second term). Plug in these numbers: $(x - 2)(x - 10)$

   Thus, the factors of $x^2 - 12x + 20$ are $(x - 2)$ and $(x - 10)$.

Making alphabet soup: Solving quadratic equations

So what's a quadratic equation? Sounds a little scary, huh? The Mathematics Knowledge subtest may ask you to solve one of these equations, but have no fear. You've come to the right place.

A *quadratic equation* is an equation that includes the square of a variable. The exponent in these equations is never higher than 2 (because it would then no longer be the square of an unknown but a cube or something else). Here are some examples of quadratic equations:

- ✔ $x^2 - 4x = -4$
- ✔ $2x^2 = x + 6$
- ✔ $x^2 = 36$

Simple quadratic equations (those that consist of just one squared term and a number) can be solved by using the square root rule:

If $x^2 = k$, then $x = \pm\sqrt{k}$, as long as k isn't a negative number.

Remember to include the $\pm$ sign, which indicates the answer is a positive or negative number. Take the following simple quadratic equation: $7y^2 = 28$.

First get rid of the pesky 7 by dividing both sides by 7: $y^2 = 4$. Using the square root rule, take the square root of both sides of the equation. You know that $\sqrt{y^2} = y$ and $\sqrt{4} = \pm 2$, so $y = \pm 2$.

When you're solving a complex quadratic equation, you put all the terms on one side of the equal sign, making the equation equal zero. In other words, get the quadratic equation into this form: $ax^2 + bx + c = 0$, where a, b, and c are numbers and x is unknown. Take a look at the following equation: $x^2 - 2x = 15$. You can convert this equation to standard form by subtracting 15 from both sides of the equation: $x^2 - 2x - 15 = 0$.

The most efficient way to solve most quadratic equations is by factoring the equation and then setting each separate factor equal to zero. See the section "A step back: Factoring algebra expressions to find original numbers" earlier in this chapter for info on factoring.

Look at the factored equation:

$$x^2 - 2x - 15 = 0$$
$$(x - 5)(x + 3) = 0$$

For the left side of the equation to equal zero, one of the quantities in parentheses has to equal zero (because zero times any number equals zero). That means you can split the equation in two, setting each factor equal to zero:

$$x - 5 = 0 \qquad \text{or} \qquad x + 3 = 0$$
$$x = 5 \qquad\qquad\qquad x = -3$$

The solution for $x^2 - 2x - 15$ is $x = 5$ or -3.

All math isn't created equal: Solving inequalities

Some algebra problems state that two quantities aren't equal to each other; thus, they're *inequalities*. In an inequality, the first number is either greater than or less than the second.

Just like with equations, the solution to an inequality is a value that makes the inequality true. For the most part, you solve inequalities the same as you would solve a normal equation. There are some facts of inequality life you need to keep in mind, however. Short and sweet, here they are:

- Negative numbers are less than zero.
- Zero is less than positive numbers but greater than negative numbers.
- Positive numbers are greater than zero.

A regular algebraic equation includes the equal sign (=), because the very basis of the equation is that one side of the equation must equal the other. Quite the opposite is true with inequalities, and they have their own special symbols, used to express the differences:

- $\neq$ means *does not equal* in the way that 3 does not equal 4, or $3 \neq 4$.
- $>$ means greater *than* in the way that 4 is greater than 3, or $4 > 3$.
- $<$ means *less than* in the way that 3 is less than 4, or $3 < 4$.
- $\leq$ means *less than or equal to* in the way that x may be less than or equal to 4, or $x \leq 4$.
- $\geq$ means *greater than or equal to* in the way that x may be greater than or equal to 3, or $x \geq 3$.

To solve an inequality, you follow the same rules as you would for solving any other equation. For example, check out this inequality: $3 + x \geq 4$

To solve it, simply isolate x by subtracting 3 from both sides of the equation:

$$3 + x - 3 \geq 4 - 3$$
$$x \geq 1$$

Therefore, 1 or any number greater than 1 makes this inequality true.

The only special rule for inequalities takes effect when you multiply or divide both sides of the inequality by a negative number. In that case, the inequality sign is reversed. So if you multiply both sides of the inequality $3 < 4$ by -4, your answer is $-12 > -16$. And if you divide both sides of $-2x < 14$ by -2, your answer is $x > -7$.

Looking at Math from a Different Angle: Geometry Review

Geometry is the branch of mathematics that makes grown adults cry — end of discussion. What? You want a more specific explanation of geometry than that? Okay, *geometry* is the branch of mathematics concerned with measuring things and defining the properties of and relationships among shapes, lines, points, angles, and other such objects. Hey, don't blame me; you asked for it.

Before you read any further, you should note a few things:

- Arcs of a circle and angles are measured in *degrees* and (not very often) in *minutes* or even *seconds;* 1 degree equals 60 minutes, and 1 minute equals 60 seconds.

- A *circle* has 360 degrees (360°). Any arc that isn't a complete circle measures less than 360°.

- A *quadrilateral* (a shape with four sides, such as a square or rectangle) has angles that add up to 360°.

Outlining angles

Angles are formed when two lines intersect (cross) at a point. Angles are measured in degrees. The greater the number of degrees, the wider the angle is:

- A *straight line* is 180°.

- A *right angle* is exactly 90°.

- An *acute angle* is more than 0° but less than 90°.

- An *obtuse angle* is more than 90° but less than 180°.

- *Complementary angles* are two angles that equal 90° when added together.

- *Supplementary angles* are two angles that equal 180° when added together.

Take a look at the different types of angles in Figure 7-1.

Figure 7-1: Types of angles.

Pointing out triangle types

A *triangle* consists of three straight sides whose three angles always add up to 180°. Triangles can be classified according to the relationship among their angles or the relationship among their sides:

- **Isosceles triangle:** An isosceles triangle has two equal sides; the angles opposite the equal sides are also equal.

- **Equilateral triangle:** An equilateral triangle has three equal sides; each of the angles measures 60°.

✔ **Right triangle:** A right triangle has one right angle (90°); therefore, the remaining two angles are complementary (add up to 90°). The side opposite the right angle is called the *hypotenuse,* which is the longest side of a right triangle. The other two sides are called *legs.*

The *Pythagorean theorem* states that if you know the lengths of two sides of a right triangle, you can determine the length of the third side using the formula $a^2 + b^2 = c^2$, where a and b represent the legs and c is the hypotenuse.

Check out Figure 7-2 to see what these triangles look like.

Figure 7-2:
Isosceles,
equilateral,
and right
triangles.

Isosceles Triangle

If sides *a* and *c* are equal,
then angles 1 and 2 are equal.

Equilateral Triangle

Sides *a, b, c* are equal.
Angles 1, 2, 3 are equal.

Right Triangle

$a^2 + b^2 = c^2$

You can find the *perimeter* — the distance around a shape — of a triangle by adding together the lengths of the three sides. The *area* — the space within a shape — of a triangle is one-half the product of the base (*b*, the bottom or the length) and the height (*h*, the tallest point of the triangle), or $A = \frac{1}{2}bh$.

Back to square one: Quadrilaterals

Quadrilaterals — shapes with four sides — all contain angles totaling 360°. Many types of quadrilaterals exist (see Figure 7-3):

✔ *Squares* have four sides of equal length, and all the angles are right angles.

✔ *Rectangles* have all (four) right angles.

✔ *Parallelograms* have opposite sides that are parallel, and their opposite sides and angles are equal. The angles don't have to be right angles.

✔ *Rhombuses* have four sides of equal length, but the angles don't have to be right angles.

✔ *Trapezoids* have exactly two sides that are parallel.

Figure 7-3:
Types of
quadri-
laterals.

Square Rectangle Parallelogram Rhombus Trapezoid

To determine the perimeter of a quadrilateral, simply add the lengths of all the sides. You can write the formula for the perimeter of a rectangle as $P = 2(l + w)$ or $P = 2l + 2w$, where l is length and w is width. And to figure the area of a rectangle, including squares, multiply length times width: $A = lw$.

Going around in circles

A circle is formed when the points of a closed line are all located an equal distance from its center. A circle always has 360°. Here are some key circle terms (see Figure 7-4, which shows the parts of a circle):

- ✔ **Circumference (C):** The closed line of a circle — that is, the distance around the circle — is called its *circumference.*

- ✔ **Radius (r):** The *radius* of a circle is the measurement from the center of the circle to any point on the circumference of the circle.

- ✔ **Diameter (d):** The *diameter* of the circle is measured as a line passing through the center of the circle, from a point on one side of the circle all the way to a point on the other side of the circle.

    The diameter of a circle is always twice as long as the radius of a circle: $d = 2r$.

Figure 7-4:
The parts of a circle.

Navigating the circumference

To measure the circumference of a circle, use the number pi (π). Although π is a lengthy number, it's generally rounded to 3.14 or $\frac{22}{7}$. If you round π so you can solve a problem, the equal sign isn't used because the answer isn't equal to the actual length. The approximation symbol ($\approx$) is used.

The formula for circumference is circumference = $\pi \times$ diameter, or $C = \pi d$. Because the radius of a circle is half its diameter, you can also use the radius to determine the circumference of a circle. Here's the formula: $C = 2\pi r$.

Suppose that you know that the pie you just baked has a diameter of 9 inches. You can determine its circumference by using the circumference formula:

$C = \pi d$

$C \approx 3.14 \times 9$

$C \approx 28.26$ inches

Mapping out the area

Determining the area of a circle also requires the use of π. Area = $\pi \times$ the square of the circle's radius, or $A = \pi r^2$.

To determine the area of a 9-inch-diameter pie, multiply π by the square of 4.5. Why 4.5 and not 9? Remember, the radius is always half the diameter, and the diameter is 9 inches.

$A = \pi r^2$

$A \approx 3.14 \times 4.5^2$

$A \approx 3.14 \times (4.5 \times 4.5)$

$A \approx 3.14 \times 20.25$

$A \approx 63.585$ inches

Filling 'er up: Calculating volume

Volume is the space a solid (three-dimensional) shape takes up. You can think of volume as how much a shape would hold if you poured water into it. Volume is measured in cubic units. The formula for finding volume depends on the object:

✔ **Boxes:** For rectangular objects, you multiply length × width (depth) × height. This is possible because the length, width, and height of a rectangle are consistent throughout the whole shape. The formula looks like this: $V = lwh$.

For a box that measures 5 feet long, 6 feet deep, and 2 feet tall, you simply multiply $5 \times 6 \times 2$ to arrive at a volume of 60 cubic feet, or 60 ft.[3]

✔ **Cylinders:** A cylinder has two circles for its bases. The volume equals π × the radius squared × height, or $V = \pi r^2 h$.

Basically, you're multiplying the area of the cylinder's circular base ($A = \pi r^2$) times the height *(h)* of the cylinder. For a cylinder that has a radius of 2 inches and a height of 10 inches, here's the deal: Multiply the value of π (approximately 3.14) times 4 (which is the radius squared) times 10, or $3.14 \times 4 \times 10 = 125.6$ cubic inches.

Test-Taking Techniques for Your Mathematical Journey

As with all of the other subtests on the ASVAB, guessing on the Mathematics Knowledge subtest doesn't count against you. So scribble in an answer, any answer, on your answer sheet because, if you don't, your chances of getting that answer right are zero. But if you take a shot at it, your chances increase to 25%, or 1 in 4. In the following sections, you find some tips that can help you improve those odds, even when you don't know how to solve the problem.

If you're not confident in your math skills, you may want to invest some extra study time. Check out *Algebra I For Dummies* by Mary Jane Sterling, *Geometry For Dummies* by Mark Ryan, and *SAT Math For Dummies* by Mark Zegarelli — all published by Wiley.

Knowing what the question is asking

The Mathematics Knowledge subtest presents the questions as straightforward math problems, not word problems, so knowing what the question is asking you to do is relatively easy. However, reading each question carefully, paying particular attention to plus (+) and minus (–) signs (which can really change the answer) is still important. Finally, make sure you do *all* the calculations needed to produce the correct answer. Check out this example:

Find the value of $\sqrt{81^2}$.

(A) 9

(B) 18

(C) 81

(D) 6,561

If you're in a hurry, you may put 9 down as an answer because you remember that the square root of 81 is 9. Or in a rush, you could multiply 9 (the square root of 81) by 2 instead of squaring it, as the exponent indicates you should. Or you may just multiply 81 by 81 to get 6,561 without remembering that you also need to then find the square root, which gives you the correct answer, Choice (C). So make sure you perform all the operations needed (and that you perform the *correct* operations) to find the right answer. Here, noticing that you're both squaring 81 and taking the square root of 81^2 should make it easy for you to recognize that the answer is actually just 81, without having to work out the multiplication.

Figuring out what you're solving for

Right out of the gate, read the question carefully. Some questions can seem out of your league at first glance, but if you look at them again, a light may go on in your brain. Suppose you get this question:

Solve for s: $s = \frac{2}{5} \times \frac{1}{2}$.

(A) $2\frac{1}{2}$

(B) 2

(C) $\frac{1}{5}$

(D) $\frac{1}{10}$

At first glance, you may think, "Oh, no! Solve for an unknown, s. I don't remember how to do that!" But if you look at the question again, you may see that you're not solving for s at all. You're simply multiplying a fraction. So you take $\frac{2}{5}$ times $\frac{1}{2}$ and arrive at $\frac{2}{10}$, but you should reduce that fraction to get $\frac{1}{5}$. The correct answer is Choice (C).

Solving what you can and guessing the rest

Sometimes a problem requires multiple operations for you to arrive at the correct answer. If you don't know how to do all of the operations, don't give up. You can still narrow down your choices by doing what you can.

Suppose this question confronts you:

What's the value of $(0.03)^3$?

(A) 0.0027

(B) 0.06

(C) 0.000027

(D) 0.0009

Say you don't remember how to multiply decimals. All isn't lost! If you remember how to use exponents, you know that you have to multiply $0.03 \times 0.03 \times 0.03$. So if you simplify the problem and just multiply $3 \times 3 \times 3$, without worrying about those pesky zeros, your answer will have a 27 in it. With this pearl of wisdom in mind, you can see that Choice (B), which adds 0.03 to 0.03, is wrong. It also means that Choice (D), which multiplies 0.03 and 0.03, is wrong. Now you have two possible answers, and you've improved your chances of guessing the right one to 50 percent! Multiply $3 \times 3 \times 3$ to get 27, and don't forget to put the decimal points back in. You have six places to make up, so move the decimal from 27 six places to the left to get 0.000027. The correct answer is Choice (C).

Using the process of elimination

Another method for when you run into questions and draw a total blank is to plug the possible answers into the equation and see which one works. Say the following problem is staring you right in the eyes:

Solve for x: $x - 5 = 32$

(A) $x = 5$

(B) $x = 32$

(C) $x = -32$

(D) $x = 37$

If you're totally stumped and can't think of any possible way of approaching this problem, simply plugging in each of the four answers to see which one is correct is your best bet.

- **Answer (A):** $5 - 5 = 32$, which you know is wrong
- **Answer (B):** $32 - 5 = 32$, which is wrong
- **Answer (C):** $-32 - 5 = 32$, which is wrong
- **Answer (D):** $37 - 5 = 32$, which is correct

Don't forget that plugging in all the answers is time-consuming, so save this procedure until you've answered all the problems you can answer. If you're taking the computer version, you can't skip a question, so remember to budget your time wisely. If you don't have much time, just make a guess and move on. You may be able to solve the next question easily.

Chapter 8

Reasoning with Arithmetic: Math Word Problems

• •

In This Chapter

▶ Solving life's little (math) problems

▶ Multiplying your chances for a better score

• •

How many miles per gallon does your brand-new SUV get? How long does it take to go over the river and through the woods to Grandmother's house? How much wood could a woodchuck chuck? These are examples of everyday questions that can be answered by arithmetic reasoning. (Okay, maybe the woodchuck situation doesn't happen every day.)

The rest of the world calls this type of question math *word problems*. The ASVAB calls them *Arithmetic Reasoning*. No matter what they're called, these problems help you apply mathematical principles to the real world (at least the real world according to the people who think up word problems). Your job is to read a word problem, determine what the question asks, and select the correct answer.

Arithmetic Reasoning is an important part of the Armed Forces Qualification Test (AFQT) score, which is used to determine your general qualification for enlistment in all the service branches (see Chapter 1 for more information). Also, certain military jobs require that you score well on this subtest (see Appendix A).

The test administrator will supply you with scratch paper and a trusty number two pencil, but one thing he or she *won't* give you (or even let you bring) is a calculator. You can use your paper and lead to clarify the data, write formulas, and mathematically solve the problem. You can even use them to draw pretty pictures to help you understand the problem. Don't get too artistic, though — you have only 36 minutes to answer 30 questions if you're taking the paper version and 39 minutes to answer 16 questions if you're taking the CAT-ASVAB.

To do well on the Arithmetic Reasoning subtest, you have to remember that there are two parts: arithmetic and reasoning. You usually have to use both of these skills for each problem. The arithmetic part comes in when you have to perform mathematical operations such as addition, subtraction, multiplication, and division. The reasoning comes in when you figure out which numbers to use in your calculations. In other words, Arithmetic Reasoning tests how you apply your ability to perform calculations to real-life problems. If you slept through high school math, don't worry. This chapter helps you decipher these math problems, focusing on the reasoning part. For additional info on the arithmetic, flip to Chapter 7.

Tackling the Real World of Word Problems

Test-takers often waste a lot of time reading and rereading word problems as if the answer might reveal itself to them by some miracle; however, correctly solving math word problems requires you to perform a series of organized steps:

1. **Read the problem completely.**

2. **Figure out what the question is asking.**

3. **Dig out the relevant facts.**

4. **Set up one or more equations to arrive at a solution and then solve the problem.**

5. **Review your answer.**

I cover these steps in detail throughout this section.

Reading the entire problem

The first step in solving a word problem is reading the entire problem to discover what it's all about. Try forming a picture about the problem in your mind or — better yet — draw a sketch of the problem on your scratch paper. Ask yourself whether you've ever seen a problem like this before. If so, what's similar about it, and what did you do to solve it in the past?

As plain as the nose on a fly: Figuring out what the question is asking

The second and most important step in solving a word problem is to determine exactly what the question is asking. Sometimes the question is asked directly. At other times, identifying the actual question may be a little more difficult. Suppose you're asked the following question:

What's the volume of a cardboard box measuring 12 inches long by 14 inches wide by 10 inches tall?

(A) 52 cubic inches

(B) 88 cubic inches

(C) 120 cubic inches

(D) 1,680 cubic inches

The problem directly asks you to determine the volume of a cardboard box. Recall from your high school algebra and geometry classes that the volume of a rectangular container is length × width × height, or $V = lwh$. So $12 \times 14 \times 10 = 1,680$. The correct answer is Choice (D).

Now take a look at the next example:

How many cubic inches of sand can a cardboard box measuring 12 inches long by 14 inches wide by 10 inches tall contain?

(A) 52 cubic inches

(B) 88 cubic inches

(C) 120 cubic inches

(D) 1,680 cubic inches

This is the same problem, but the question you need to answer isn't as directly stated. Therefore, you have to use clues embedded in the problem to figure out what the actual question is. Would figuring out the perimeter of the box help you with this question? Nope. Would figuring out the area of one side of the box help you? Nope — you're not painting the box; you're filling it. The question wants you to determine the volume of the container.

Clue words can be a big help when trying to figure out which question is being asked. Look for the following clue words:

- **Addition:** Sum, total, in all, perimeter, increased by, combined, added
- **Division:** Share, distribute, ratio, quotient, average, per, out of, percent
- **Equals:** Is, was, are, were, amounts to
- **Multiplication:** Product, total, area, cubic, times, multiplied by, of
- **Subtraction:** Difference, how much more, exceed, less than, fewer than, decreased

Digging for the facts

After you figure out which question you're answering in the first place, the next step is to figure out which data is necessary to solve the problem and which data is extra. Start by identifying all the information and variables in the problem and listing them on your scratch paper. Make sure you attach units of measurement contained in the problem (miles, feet, inches, gallons, quarts, and so on). After you've made a list of the facts, try to eliminate those facts that aren't relevant to the question. Look at the following example:

To raise money for the school yearbook project, Tom sold 15 candy bars, Becky sold 12 candy bars, Debbie sold 17 candy bars, and Jane sold the most at 50. How many candy bars were sold by the girls?

The list of facts may look something like this:

> Tom = 15 bars
>
> Becky = 12 bars
>
> Debbie = 17 bars
>
> Jane = 50 bars
>
> ? = total sold by the girls

Because the question is the total number of candy bars sold by the girls, the number of bars sold by Tom isn't relevant to the problem and can be scratched off the list. Just add the remaining bars from your list. The answer is 79.

Setting up the problem and working your way to the answer

You need to decide how the problem can be solved and then use your math skills to arrive at a solution. For instance, a question may ask the following:

Joan just turned 37. For 12 years, she's dreamed of traveling to Key West to become a beach bum. To finance this dream, she needs to save a total of $15,000. How much does Joan need to save each year if she wants to become a beach bum by her 40th birthday?

Write down, in mathematical terms, what the question is asking you to determine. Because the question is asking how much money Joan needs to save per year to reach $15,000, you can say y (years Joan has to save) × m (money she needs to save each year) = $15,000. Or to put it more mathematically,

$$ym = \$15,000$$

You don't know the value of m (yet) — that's the unknown you're asked to find. But you can find out the value of y — the number of years Joan has to save. If she's 37 and wants to be a beach bum by the time she's 40, she has 3 years to save. So now the formula looks like this:

$$3m = 15,000$$

To isolate the unknown on one side of the equation, you simply divide each side by 3, so $3m \div 3 = 15,000 \div 3$. (If you don't remember how to isolate unknowns, flip to Chapter 7.) Therefore, your answer is

$$m = 5,000$$

Joan needs to save $5,000 each year for 3 years to reach her goal of $15,000 by the time she's 40. You may be tempted to include the 12 years Joan has been dreaming of this trip in your formula. This number was put into the problem as a distraction. It has no bearing on solving the problem.

Reviewing your answer

Before marking your answer sheet or punching in that choice on the computer, review your answer to make sure it makes sense. Review by asking yourself the following questions:

- ✔ **Does your solution seem probable?** Use your common sense. If you determine that a 12- x 16-foot roof is covered in only 12 shingles, you've probably made a mistake in your calculations.

- ✔ **Does it answer the question asked?** Reread the problem. For example, if a question asks you to calculate the number of trees *remaining* after 10 percent of the total was cut down, the correct answer wouldn't be 10 percent of the trees but rather the 90 percent still standing.

- ✔ **Are you sure?** Double-check your answer. Those tricky test-makers often supply false answers, which are very, very close to the correct answer.

- ✔ **Is your answer expressed using the same units of measurement as used in the problem?** A question may ask how many cubic feet of concrete is required to cover a driveway. Your answer in cubic yards would have to be converted to cubic feet so you can select the correct answer choice.

Although you may have been taught in school to round 5 or above up and below 5 down, rounding real-world problems requires a different mindset. For example, if someone needs 2.2 cans of paint for a particular job, she really needs 3 cans of paint to make sure she has enough, even though you'd generally round down. And if someone gets a 15-minute break for every 4 hours of work but works only 7 hours, he'd get only one break, even though 7 divided by 4 equals 1.75, which is generally rounded up to 2.

You may find that the solution you arrived at doesn't fit the facts presented in the problem. If this is the case, back up and go through the steps again until you arrive at an answer that seems probable.

The Guessing Game: Putting Reason in Your Guessing Strategy

Guessing wrong on any of the ASVAB subtests doesn't count against you. If you don't guess, your chances of getting that answer right are zero, but if you take a shot at it, your chances increase to 25%, or 1 in 4. Eliminate two wrong answers, and you have a 50-50 shot.

If you're taking the paper version of the ASVAB, you can always skip the tough questions and come back to them after you've finished the easier ones. If you're taking the computerized version of the ASVAB, the software won't let you skip questions, so you need to make your guess right then and there.

If you're taking the paper version of the test and elect to skip questions until later, make sure you mark the next answer in the correct space on the answer sheet. Otherwise, you may wind up wearing out the eraser on your pencil when you discover your error at the end of the test. Or even worse, you may not notice the error and wind up getting several answers wrong because you mismarked your answer sheet.

Using the process of elimination

Guessing doesn't always mean "pick an answer, any answer." You can increase your chances of picking the right answer by eliminating answers that can't be right. To eliminate some obvious wrong answers, you can do the following:

- ✓ **Make sure the answer is realistic in relation to the question asked.** For example, if a question asks you how much water would be required to fill a child's wading pool, 17,000 gallons isn't a realistic answer. You can save time by eliminating this potential answer choice immediately.

- ✓ **Pay attention to units of measurement.** If a question asks how many feet of rope you'll need, answer choices listed in inches or cubic feet are probably incorrect.

- ✓ **Consider easier answer choices first.** Remember, you're not allowed to use a calculator on the ASVAB, so math answers that you'd arrive at by using complicated formulas are probably not correct.

Solving what you can and guessing the rest

Sometimes you may know how to solve part of a problem but not all of it. If you don't know how to do all the calculations — or don't have time for them — don't give up. You can still narrow down your choices by doing what you can. Here's how partially solving problems can help:

- ✓ When adding mixed numbers (a whole number and a fraction), add the whole-number parts first; then immediately eliminate answer choices that are too low. Or when adding lengths, add full feet first and cross off choices that are too small, even before considering the inches.

- ✓ Multiply just the last digits and cross off all answers that don't end in the right numbers (assuming the answers aren't rounded).

Making use of the answer choices

If you're stuck on a particular problem, sometimes plugging possible answers into an equation can help you find the right answer. Here's how using the answer choices can improve your guessing:

- ✓ **Plug in each remaining answer choice until you get the right answer.** Plugging in all the answer choices is time-consuming, so make sure you eliminate obviously wrong choices first.

- ✓ **Estimate and plug in numbers that involve easy mental calculations.** For instance, if Choice (A) is 9 and Choice (B) is 12, plug in 10 and solve the equation in your head. Think about whether the right answer has to be higher or lower than 10, and choose from there.

- ✓ **Using a little logic, do calculations with an obviously wrong answer choice.** Sometimes a wrong answer choice — especially one that differs drastically from the other answers — represents an intermediate step in the calculations, so you can use it to solve the problem. For instance, take this example:

A security guard walks the equivalent of six city blocks when he makes a circuit around the building. If he walks at a pace of eight city blocks every 30 minutes, how long will it take him to complete a circuit around the building, assuming he doesn't run into any thieves?

(A) 20.00 minutes

(B) 3.75 minutes

(C) 22.50 minutes

(D) 24.00 minutes

Choice (B) is obviously way too low to be the right answer, but it would be a logical guess for the security guard's rate for a single lap. Multiply 3.75 minutes/block by 6 blocks, and you probably have a good candidate for the right answer — 22.50 minutes, Choice (C).

Chapter 9

Brother, Can You Spare an Equation? Arithmetic Practice Questions

- -

In This Chapter
▶ Putting your mathematical reasoning to the test
▶ Practicing your arithmetic skills

- -

*1*t's time to put those calculators, pocket computers, and abacuses away — the actual ASVAB doesn't allow you to use anything except paper, pencil, and a winning personality to solve the math problems. You should use the old-fashioned way on these practice questions, too. Tell you what: Instead of a number two pencil, you can use a number three or four instead. Heck, you can even use a pen. See? I'm easy. No pressure here!

You may be tired of hearing this by now (if you've taken any of the tests in this book), but the math subtests of the ASVAB are very important because they're used in calculating your Armed Forces Qualification Test (AFQT) score, which makes or breaks you as far as your eligibility to join the military. Additionally, every technical-oriented job in the military requires good to excellent math scores. Chapter 1 explains the AFQT in more detail.

On the paper version of the ASVAB (and on the full-length practice tests later in this book), you see 30 Arithmetic Reasoning questions and 25 Mathematics Knowledge questions. On the CAT-ASVAB, you get 16 questions on each math subtest. In this chapter, you only have to sweat through 25 total questions.

Arithmetic Reasoning (Math Word Problems) Practice Questions

Arithmetic Reasoning questions are math problems expressed in a story format. Your goal is to determine what the question is asking by picking out the relevant factors needed to solve the problem, set up mathematical equations as needed, and arrive at the correct solution. Sounds easy, right? Check out Chapter 8 for more help with Arithmetic Reasoning.

1. If apples are on sale at 15 for $3, what's the cost of each apple?

   (A) 50 cents

   (B) 25 cents

   (C) 20 cents

   (D) 30 cents

Divide $3 by 15. The answer is $0.20, so the correct answer is Choice (C).

2. A noncommissioned officer challenged her platoon of 11 enlisted women to beat her record of performing a 26-mile training run in 4 hours. If all the enlisted women match her record, how many miles will they have run?

   (A) 71.5 miles

   (B) 6.5 miles

   (C) 286 miles

   (D) 312 miles

   Multiply 26×11. The other information in the question is irrelevant — it's there to throw you off. The correct answer is Choice (C). You can immediately eliminate Choice (B) because it isn't a reasonable answer. Identifying unreasonable answers (through the process of elimination) can help you choose the correct answer choice faster.

3. Margaret gets her hair cut and colored at an expensive salon in town. She's expected to leave a 15% tip for services. If a haircut is $45 and a color treatment is $150, how much of a tip should Margaret leave?

   (A) $22.50

   (B) $29.25

   (C) $20.00

   (D) $224.25

   Add 45 and 150 to get the cost of the services ($45 + $150 = $195); then multiply the answer by 0.15 (15%) to find the tip. The question asks for the amount of the tip, so the correct answer is Choice (B), $29.25. You can immediately eliminate Choice (D), because the amount is far too high to make sense.

4. A bag of sand holds 1 cubic foot of sand. How many bags of sand are needed to fill a square sandbox measuring 5 feet long and 1 foot high?

   (A) 25 bags

   (B) 5 bags

   (C) 10 bags

   (D) 15 bags

   To find the volume of the sandbox, you take length times width times height ($V = lwh$). Don't forget that the measurements are for a *square* sandbox, so you can assume that if the box is 5 feet long, then it's also 5 feet wide. So $5 \times 5 \times 1$ is 25 cubic feet. Each bag holds 1 cubic foot of sand, and $25 \div 1 = 25$. Choice (A) is the correct answer. If you were thinking answer Choice (B) sounded good, remember that the answer should make sense. Five cubic feet of sand would not fill a very large sandbox, would it?

5. The day Samantha arrived at boot camp, the temperature reached a high of 90 degrees in the shade and a low of –20 at night in the barracks. What was the average temperature for the day?

   (A) 35 degrees

   (B) 45 degrees

   (C) 55 degrees

   (D) 62 degrees

   Add the two temperatures: 90 + (–20) = 70. Divide 70 by 2 to reach the average temperature, 35. Choice (A) is the correct answer.

6. Farmer Beth has received an offer to sell her 320-acre farm for $3,000 per acre. She agrees to give the buyer $96,000 worth of land. What fraction of Farmer Beth's land is the buyer getting?

   (A) $\frac{1}{4}$

   (B) $\frac{1}{10}$

   (C) $\frac{1}{5}$

   (D) $\frac{2}{3}$

   The buyer's price, $96,000, divided by $3,000 (price per acre) equals 32 acres. Thirty-two acres divided by 320 acres (total of the farm) equals 10%, or $\frac{1}{10}$, of the land. The correct answer is Choice (B).

7. A large wall map is drawn so that 1 inch equals 3 miles. On the map, the distance from Kansas City to Denver is $192\frac{1}{2}$ inches. How far is the round trip from Kansas City to Denver in miles?

   (A) $192\frac{1}{2}$ miles

   (B) $577\frac{1}{5}$ miles

   (C) 385 miles

   (D) 1,155 miles

   Multiply 192.5×3 to get the distance in miles, and then double the answer to account for both legs of the trip. Choice (D) is the correct answer. ***Note:*** A quick approach here involves rounding. The distance is about 200 inches, or 400 inches round trip. Multiply that by 3, and you get 1,200 miles. The only choice that comes close is (D).

8. Margaret and Julie can sell their tattoo parlor for $150,000. They plan to divide the proceeds according to the ratio of the money they each invested in the business. Margaret put in the most money at a 3:2 ratio to Julie's contribution. How much money should Julie get from the sale?

   (A) $50,000

   (B) $30,000

   (C) $60,000

   (D) $90,000

   According to the ratio, Margaret should get $\frac{3}{5}$ of the money and Julie should get $\frac{2}{5}$ of the money. You calculate the fractions by adding both sides of the ratio together ($3 + 2 = 5$) to determine the denominator — Margaret gets 3 parts of the total, and Julie gets 2 parts, so there are 5 total parts. Each side of the ratio then becomes a numerator. Multiply the total amount of money by the fraction representing Julie's share: Multiply $150,000 by 2, and then divide the answer by 5 to determine Julie's share of the money. The correct answer is Choice (C).

9. What is the fifth number in the series 4, 8, 16, 32?

   (A) 48

   (B) 64

   (C) 96

   (D) 8

   The pattern is to double each number: $4 + 4 = 8$; $8 + 8 = 16$; $16 + 16 = 32$; so $32 + 32 = 64$. The correct answer is Choice (B).

10. In the military, $\frac{1}{4}$ of an enlisted person's time is spent sleeping and eating, $\frac{1}{12}$ is spent standing at attention, $\frac{1}{6}$ is spent staying fit, and $\frac{2}{5}$ is spent working. The rest of the time is spent at the enlisted person's own discretion. How many hours per day does this discretionary time amount to?

    (A) 6.0 hours

    (B) 1.6 hours

    (C) 2.4 hours

    (D) 3.2 hours

    Calculate this answer by first assigning a common denominator of 60 to all the fractions and adjusting the numerators accordingly: $\frac{15}{60}, \frac{5}{60}, \frac{10}{60}$, and $\frac{24}{60}$. Add the fractions to find out how much time is allotted to all of these tasks. The total time is $\frac{54}{60}$, which leaves $\frac{6}{60}$ or $\frac{1}{10}$ of the day to the enlisted person's discretion. One-tenth of 24 hours is 2.4 hours. Therefore, Choice (C) is the correct answer.

11. A designer sells a square yard of carpet for $15.00. The same carpet can be purchased at the carpet outlet store for $12.50. As a percentage, how much more expensive is the designer's carpet?

    (A) The designer's carpet costs about 17% more than the outlet-store carpet.

    (B) The designer's carpet costs about 20% more than the outlet-store carpet.

    (C) The designer's carpet costs about 25% more than the outlet-store carpet.

    (D) The designer's carpet costs about 12% more than the outlet-store carpet.

    You want the cost of the designer's carpet in terms of the outlet-store carpet, so divide the difference in costs by the lower price: $15.00 − $12.50 = $2.50, and $2.50 ÷ $12.50 = 0.20 = 20%. The correct answer is Choice (B) — the designer's carpet is 20% more expensive.

12. Terry got a haircut for $32.50, a hair color for $112.20, and a manicure for $17.25. How much total money did she spend at the salon?

    (A) $167.45

    (B) $144.70

    (C) $161.95

    (D) $156.95

    Simply add the amounts together: $32.50 + $112.20 + $17.25 = $161.95. Choice (C) is the correct answer.

13. Mailing the first ounce of a letter costs $0.39, and it costs $0.24 to mail each additional ounce. How much does it cost to mail a 5-ounce letter?

    (A) $1.85

    (B) $1.16

    (C) $1.45

    (D) $1.35

    The first ounce costs $0.39. The next 4 ounces cost $0.24 each. Multiply $0.24 × 4 and then add $0.39 to determine how much mailing a 5-ounce letter costs: $0.24 × 4 = $0.96, and $0.96 + $0.39 = $1.35, the cost of mailing a 5-ounce letter. Choice (D) is the correct answer.

Math Knowledge Practice Questions

The remaining practice questions are straightforward math. You won't have to wonder how Terry got so much money to spend at the salon in the first place (like in the previous section). Remember, these questions are designed for high school level and below. You won't be solving equations to calculate the orbit of Mars around the sun here.

14. Which of the following fractions is the largest?

    (A) $\frac{2}{3}$

    (B) $\frac{5}{8}$

    (C) $\frac{11}{16}$

    (D) $\frac{3}{4}$

    To arrive at the answer, find a common denominator that all the denominators divide into evenly. In this case, the common denominator is 48. Next, convert all fractions to 48ths. In the case of Choice (A), multiply $\frac{2}{3} \times \frac{16}{16}$ to reach $\frac{32}{48}$. Perform the same type of calculation for all the other fractions, figuring out what number times the denominator gives you 48, and then multiplying each numerator by that number; then compare numerators. The largest numerator is the largest fraction. The other fractions are equal to $\frac{30}{48}$, $\frac{33}{48}$, and $\frac{36}{48}$. Choice (D) is the correct answer.

15. What's the product of $\sqrt{36}$ and $\sqrt{49}$?

    (A) 1,764

    (B) 42

    (C) 13

    (D) 6

    The square root of 36 is 6, and the square root of 49 is 7. The product of those two numbers (6 × 7) is 42. The correct answer is Choice (B).

16. Solve for x: $2x - 3 = x + 7$.

    (A) 10

    (B) 6

    (C) 21

    (D) −10

    Isolate the x's on the left side of the equation by subtracting x from both sides: $2x - 3 - x = x + 7 - x$, or $x - 3 = 7$. Continue to perform operations to isolate x: Add 3 to both sides of the equation to get rid of the −3 on the left: $x - 3 + 3 = 7 + 3$, or $x = 10$. The correct answer is Choice (A).

17. A circle has a radius of 15 feet. What's most nearly its circumference?

    (A) 30 feet

    (B) 225 feet

    (C) 94 feet

    (D) 150 feet

    The circumference of a circle is π times the diameter; the diameter equals two times the radius. Therefore, 3.14×30 feet = 94.2 feet. The correct answer is Choice (C).

18. At 3:00 p.m., the angle between the hands of the clock is

    (A) 90 degrees

    (B) 180 degrees

    (C) 120 degrees

    (D) 360 degrees

    At 3:00 p.m., one hand is on the 12, and the other is on the 3. This creates a right angle — a 90-degree angle. The correct answer is Choice (A).

19. $2^3 \times 2^4 =$

    (A) 16

    (B) 108

    (C) 128

    (D) 148

    $2^3 \times 2^4 = 2^7 = 2 \times 2 \times 2 \times 2 \times 2 \times 2 \times 2 = 128$. Choice (C) is the correct answer.

20. Express 403,000,000,000,000 in scientific notation.

    (A) 4.03×10^{14}

    (B) 4.03×10^{-14}

    (C) 4.03×10

    (D) 0.43×10

    The correct way to write the number in scientific notation is 4.03×10^{14}. When the exponent is positive, the decimal point moves said number of places to the right. When the exponent is negative, the decimal point moves said places to the left. The exponent in Choice (A) is a positive 14, which means you move the decimal point 14 places to the right. Choice (A) is the correct answer.

21. Simplify $8x^2 - 3x + 4xy - 9x^2 - 5x - 20xy$.

    (A) $5x^2 + 9xy$

    (B) $8x - 9x^2$

    (C) $-x^2 - 8x - 16xy$

    (D) $8x + 9x^2$

    $8x^2 - 3x + 4xy - 9x^2 - 5x - 20xy = (8x^2 - 9x^2) + (-3x - 5x) + (4xy - 20xy) = -x^2 - 8x - 16xy$. The correct answer is Choice (C).

22. What's the prime factorization of 90?

    (A) $2 \times 3 \times 5$

    (B) $2 \times 3^2 \times 5$

    (C) $2^2 \times 3^2$

    (D) $2 \times 3 \times 5^2$

    When you figure which prime numbers you need to multiply together to get the original number, you're using *prime factorization*. Here, $90 = 9 \times 10 = 3 \times 3 \times 2 \times 5 = 2 \times 3^2 \times 5$. The correct answer is Choice (B). If you don't know how to solve this problem, you can guess by finding the value of each answer choice. Choice (A) is 30, (B) is 90, (C) is 36, and (D) is 150.

23. $\frac{1}{4} \times \frac{2}{3}$

    (A) $\frac{3}{4}$

    (B) $\frac{1}{4}$

    (C) $\frac{1}{6}$

    (D) $\frac{1}{3}$

    $\frac{1}{4} \times \frac{2}{3} = \frac{2}{12} = \frac{1}{6}$. The correct answer is Choice (C).

24. A baker has s pounds of sugar to use in baking. After she uses 50 pounds to make donuts, how much sugar does she have left?

    (A) $s + 50$

    (B) $50 - s$

    (C) $s - 50$

    (D) $s \div 50$

    The variable s stands for the amount of sugar the baker had before she made the donuts. Taking away 50 pounds, the amount of sugar used, gives you $s - 50$. Choice (C) is the correct answer.

25. Six pizzas are pepperoni, seven are hamburger, four are cheese, and three are "with every-thing." What's the probability that a randomly selected pizza is pepperoni?

(A) $\frac{1}{2}$

(B) $\frac{2}{5}$

(C) $\frac{3}{10}$

(D) $\frac{2}{3}$

There are 20 total pizzas (6 + 7 + 4 + 3). The probability that the one chosen is a pepperoni pizza is $\frac{6}{20}$, or $\frac{3}{10}$. The correct answer is Choice (C).

Part IV
The Whole Ball of Facts: Technical Skills

The 5th Wave   By Rich Tennant

"Sure I work on diesels. Bring her around and we'll put her on the lift."

In this part . . .

To get into the military, you have to know how to read and how to add. But to qualify for certain military jobs, you also have to understand how the world works. Several ASVAB subtests test your knowledge of science and mechanics. Don't worry — I've got you covered.

Part IV helps you review principles of science, auto and shop information, mechanical comprehension, principles of electronics, and spatial relationships. Even if you're not interested in jobs that require this type of background (for a list of jobs that do, see Appendix A), you'll want to do your best on these tests because they contribute to your overall score. But if you've set your heart on working on Humvees or F-18 Super Hornets, focus your efforts on this part to get you started.

Chapter 10

General Science

As you study for this subtest, you may feel overwhelmed by facts and figures. General Science requires a lot of straight-up memorization. You're presented with questions about facts you probably learned in high school in various science classes, such as health, Earth science, biology, and chemistry. If you don't know that Earth is the third planet from the sun, then all the other science knowledge you have won't help you one bit when the question asks, "What is the third planet from the sun?"

Instead of trying to remember nine million individual facts, spend some time reviewing the general principles behind the facts. Think about how the facts relate to each other. Looking at the big picture is an effective learning technique.

You have 11 minutes to answer 25 questions on the paper version of the General Science subtest, or you have 8 minutes to answer 16 General Science questions on the CAT-ASVAB. That comes out to about 26 or 30 seconds per question, so there's no time to dilly-dally. For the most part, you either know the answer or you don't. If you don't know the answer, you can always guess (check out Chapter 3 for tips on guessing on the ASVAB).

You can relax this time around . . . well, just a little. The General Science subtest has no bearing on your Armed Forces Qualification Test (AFQT) score. On the other hand, your score on this subtest is used to calculate some of the military composite scores that are used for job qualification purposes (see Appendix A for more information).

Take some time to review the facts in this chapter as a mini science lesson. If the job you want requires a good score on this subtest, dedicate yourself to the information in this chapter to boost your General Science score. You may also want to seek additional study time in these references to boost your science knowledge: *Chemistry For Dummies* by John T. Moore, *Biology For Dummies* by Donna Rae Siegfried, *Astronomy For Dummies* by Stephen P. Maran, *Weather For Dummies* by John D. Cox, and *Physics I For Dummies* and *Physics II For Dummies* by Steven Holzner, Ph.D. (all from Wiley).

There's a Scientific Method to the Madness

Scientists are pretty skeptical. They don't necessarily believe anything said by anyone else unless it's been shown to be true (time after time after time) using a process called the scientific method. Scientists know that personal and cultural biases may influence perceptions and interpretations of data, so they've derived a standard set of procedures and criteria to minimize those influences when developing a theory. Because the scientific method is prevalent in all fields of science, you can expect to see a few questions about the process on the General Science subtest.

Here are the usual steps to solving a problem using the scientific method:

1. **Observe some aspect of the universe.**

2. **Make an educated guess** *(hypothesis)* **about why this is happening.**

3. **Make predictions based on the hypothesis.**

4. **Experiment and observe to test the predictions.**

   If the results don't match the predictions, modify the hypothesis.

5. **Keep repeating Steps 3 and 4 until there are no discrepancies in experimentation and observation in relation to the hypothesis.**

When developing and testing a hypothesis, scientists are guided by a principle known as *Ockham's razor* (sometimes spelled *Occam's razor*). This rule states, "When given two equally valid explanations for a phenomenon, one should embrace the less complicated formulation." In other words, all things being equal, the simplest solution tends to be the best one. At this point, if a hypothesis holds up to repeated testing, it becomes a theory. When a theory is supported consistently over time, scientists may then consider it as a law, fact, or principle.

Understanding Forms of Measurement

Because science is based on developing objective facts — evidence and results that are measurable and experiments that can be reproduced — measurements are an important part of science. And because this subtest is all about science, you can expect to run into a few questions about measuring scientifically on the ASVAB.

Doing the metric thing

The metric system (or SI, the International System of Units) is based on a decimal system of multiples (and fractions) of ten. Scientists almost always use the metric system for precise measurement. No, they don't use it just to make the ASVAB harder for you; they use this system so a standard exists among scientists around the world. In fact, the majority of countries around the globe use the metric system — the United States is in its own world when it comes to the Imperial (non-metric) system.

Here are some units of measurement you need to know for the General Science subtest of the ASVAB:

- ✔ The *meter* (m) is the unit of length.
- ✔ The *liter* (L) is the unit of volume.
- ✔ The *gram* (g) is the unit of mass (similar to weight).

You can attach prefixes to these base units to indicate units that are larger or smaller. Check out Table 10-1 for metric prefixes and Table 10-2 for some abbreviations of common metric measurements.

Table 10-1	Metric Prefixes	
Prefix	*Symbol*	*What It Means*
milli-	m	One-thousandth (0.001)
centi-	c	One-hundredth (0.01)
deci-	d	One-tenth (0.1)
deca-	da	10
hecto-	h	100
kilo-	k	1,000
mega-	M	1,000,000

Table 10-2	Common Metric Units and Their Abbreviations	
Length	*Liquid Volume*	*Mass*
millimeter (mm)	milliliter (mL)	milligram (mg)
centimeter (cm)	centiliter (cL)	centigram (cg)
meter (m)	liter (L)	gram (g)
kilometer (km)	kiloliter (kL)	kilogram (kg)

Figuring temperature conversions

When you think of temperature, you may think of the Fahrenheit and Celsius scales, which measure temperatures in degrees. Scientists actually use three different scales to report temperature:

- **Fahrenheit (°F):** This scale is more common in the United States. On the Fahrenheit scale, water freezes at 32°F and boils at 212°F.

- **Celsius or Centigrade (°C):** This scale is the metric standard worldwide. On the Celsius scale, the freezing point for water is 0°C, and the boiling point for water is 100°C.

- **Kelvin (K):** Scientists have theorized that the coldest anything can get is –273.15°C. They believe that at this temperature, molecular motion would stop. That's pretty darn cold! This temperature, often called *absolute zero,* is assigned to be 0 on the Kelvin scale (with the units the same size as degrees on the Celsius scale). On this scale, the freezing point of water is 273.15 K, and the boiling point is 373.15 K.

The word *degrees* isn't used when stating temperature in kelvins. Scientists who work with thermodynamics, such as physicists and astronomers, measure temperature using kelvins. For instance, the surface temperature of planets is always stated in kelvins.

An ASVAB question may ask you to convert temperatures from one scale to another, so here are some formulas to commit to memory (*C* stands for the temperature in degrees Celsius, and *F* is the temperature in degrees Fahrenheit):

- To convert from Celsius to Fahrenheit, use this formula:

$$F = \frac{9}{5}C + 32$$

✔ To convert from Fahrenheit to Celsius, use the following formula:

$$C = \frac{5}{9}(F - 32)$$

✔ To get temperatures in the kelvin scale, add 273.15 degrees to the Celsius temperature:

$$K = C + 273.15$$

To go from kelvins to degrees Celsius, do the opposite: Subtract 273.15 from the kelvin temperature. Then you can convert the Celsius temperature to Fahrenheit if you like.

Here's a quick temperature conversion system that may be easier to remember. (**Note:** This process only works with Celsius and Fahrenheit.)

1. **Add 40 to the temperature you want to convert.**

2. **Multiply this sum by $\frac{5}{9}$ if converting from Fahrenheit to Celsius or $\frac{9}{5}$ if converting from Celsius to Fahrenheit.**

3. **Subtract the 40 you added at the beginning to yield the result.**

An easy way to remember whether to use $\frac{9}{5}$ or $\frac{5}{9}$ in the conversion is to associate the *f* in *F*ahrenheit with *F*raction ($\frac{5}{9}$ is a proper fraction); similarly, $\frac{9}{5}$ can be *C*onverted to a mixed number ($1\frac{4}{5}$) — *c* is for *C*onvert and *C*elsius.

Another Day, Another Science: Scientific Disciplines You Should Know

Science is divided into areas of study called *disciplines,* and most of these disciplines have subdisciplines. When you take the ASVAB, the General Science subtest may ask you some definitions of these disciplines. I couldn't possibly list all the scientific disciplines, but here's a handy list for you to start looking over.

First, here are some popular Earth and space sciences (see the later sections "Where Few Have Gone Before: Astronomy" and "Down to Earth: Rocking Out with Geology and Meteorology" for more info on these disciplines):

✔ **Astronomy:** Astronomers (not to be confused with *astrologists*) study outer space. They get their jollies examining the existence, locations, orbits, energy, and compositions of planets and other celestial matter.

✔ **Geology:** Is it a real diamond or just a piece of glass? A geologist can tell you. These scientists study the dynamics and physical history of the Earth, the rocks of which it's composed, and the physical, chemical, and biological changes that the Earth has undergone or is undergoing.

✔ **Meteorology:** You know that person who gets on the TV each day and tells you whether your planned outing to the beach is going to be ruined by rain? Meteorologists study the weather and attempt to predict it.

✔ **Paleontology:** Paleontologists study prehistoric life, including dinosaurs. How cool is that? The science involves the examination of fossils, including those of plants, animals, and other organisms.

Biologists love everything to do with living organisms and life sciences. There are more subdisciplines of biology than you can shake a stick at. And yes, some biologists study sticks.

Other biologists specialize in fish, trees, snakes, insects . . . you get the picture. Here are some subdisciplines of biology (for further info, check out the next section):

- ✔ **Agriculture:** An agriculturalist studies farming. This discipline includes studying methods of cultivating soil, producing crops, and managing livestock.
- ✔ **Botany:** A botanist studies plant life. This includes everything from flowers to the moss that grows on the north side of the tree.
- ✔ **Ecology:** Ecologists do more than just warn people that they're destroying the ozone layer. They study all aspects of the environment and how organisms (such as people) interact with it.
- ✔ **Entomology:** Entomologists like bugs. Specifically, they like insects (bugs with six legs). This position isn't to be confused with an arachnologist, who studies spiders and other critters with eight legs.
- ✔ **Genetics:** Geneticists study heredity, especially the aspect that deals with inherited characteristics, such as eye color. (For details, see the later section "Swimming in the gene pool: Genetics.")
- ✔ **Ichthyology:** This discipline is the branch of *zoology* (the study of animals) dealing with fish.

Here are a couple of social sciences:

- ✔ **Archeology:** For an archeologist, the older, the better. Archeologists study past human life and culture. The job requires recovery and examination of material evidence, such as graves, tools, pottery, and buildings.
- ✔ **Genealogy:** If you want to find out where your great, great, great, great, great grandfather was born and what he did for a living, ask a genealogist. These specialists study ancestry and family history.

Another large discipline is chemistry, in which people mix things together to see what happens. These scientists study the structure, properties, composition, and reactions of matter. I discuss chemistry later in "Chemistry: Not Blowing Up the Lab."

Lastly, don't forget physics. *Physics* involves the study of matter and its movement. This includes concepts such as energy, force, and motion. In short, physics is concerned with the study of the universe's behavior and, in general, how things work in nature. *Mechanics,* which plays a big role in the ASVAB's Mechanical Comprehension subtest (see Chapter 12), is a major topic in physics.

If the ASVAB only asked questions like "What does a chemist do?" the test would be a piece of organic matter (cake). Unfortunately, it's not that easy. The ASVAB writers expect you to know a little more than just the definitions of various scientific disciplines. The following sections detail a few of the main branches of science you see on the ASVAB.

Uncovering Biology, from Big to Small

It would be impossible to cover all the areas of biology in this book, and I'm not going to try. Luckily, the General Science subtest of the ASVAB measures your knowledge of scientific disciplines at the average high school level. You remember studying about the Animal Kingdom and the human body and cell structures in high school, right? If not, the following sections can serve as a short refresher course.

Relating to your world through ecology

Ecology is the study of the environment — more specifically, the relationship between organisms and the world around them. All plants and animals are part of an *ecosystem* (a community including living things and their environment). Like the economy, an ecosystem includes *producers* (which make their own food) and *consumers* (which eat other things). An ecosystem also has *decomposers,* such as bacteria, which break down dead plants, animals, and the waste of all organisms.

Animals can't produce their own food, so they're consumers, which are classified in three categories:

- **Carnivores eat only meat.** A few examples include lions, tigers, polar bears, snakes, crocodiles, hawks, and eagles.
- **Herbivores eat only plants.** Cows, moose, giraffes, and elk are herbivores.
- **Omnivores eat both plants and other animals.** People are omnivores, and so are pigs, mice, raccoons, chickens, crows, and foxes.

Conditions in the world either encourage or prevent the establishment of individual ecosystems. For plants (producers) to grow, adequate sunlight, good soil, moderate temperatures, and water must be part of the environment. If plants aren't around, plant-eating consumers can't be sustained, which means predators (who eat other animals) can't be sustained, either. For consumers, mates are as essential as a food supply. Diseases and enemies can prevent an animal from establishing itself in an ecosystem.

Human actions, such as wasting natural resources and polluting the air, water, or soil, can disrupt an entire ecosystem.

Categorizing Mother Nature

A long time ago, scientists looked at the world, noticed the hundreds of thousands of plants and animals around them, and decided that all these organisms (living things) needed to be labeled and grouped. To effectively study and discuss plants, animals, and other living creatures, all scientists needed to use the same names. Thus, a system of scientific classification was developed.

The most common classification system was created by Swedish botanist Carl Linnaeus, who published ten editions of his works from 1753–1758. Scientists often refer to this system as *taxonomy.* Not only does taxonomy provide official names for every plant and animal, but it also helps scientists understand how living creatures are related to one another. Modern day taxonomy has its roots in the Linnaean taxonomic system.

No one is privy to the actual questions asked on the ASVAB (test materials are considered "controlled items" and are locked up in safes when not in actual use). In this category, questions can range anywhere from "How many kingdoms are there?" to "What's the genus for *Canis familiaris?*"

Counting down the classification system

The scientific classification system notes the relationships and similarities among organisms. It consists of seven main levels:

- **Kingdom:** A kingdom is the broadest level, so it contains the most kinds of organisms. The relationship between organisms in a kingdom is extremely loose, so members share only a few key characteristics.

- ✔ **Phylum:** Phylum (plural *phyla*) is the next major taxonomic group. Within the kingdoms, organisms are divided into phyla by general characteristics. For example, in the Animal Kingdom, animals with backbones (vertebrates) are placed in a separate phylum from animals without backbones.

- ✔ **Class:** Organisms in a phylum are divided into classes. In the Animal Kingdom, for example, birds, mammals, and fish all go in their own classes. Among plants, all flowering plants comprise the *angiosperm* class, and all conifers, such as pines and spruces, comprise the *conifer* class.

- ✔ **Order:** Scientific groupings don't follow hard and fast rules, so when you get to the order of a living thing, there's disagreement about where it belongs. You may find that different scientific organizations group creatures in different orders or families.

- ✔ **Family:** Families further divide organisms of the same class by similar characteristics. Sometimes, not all scientific organizations agree to the exact family an organism should be classified in.

- ✔ **Genus:** Two or more species that share unique body structures or other characteristics are closely related enough to be placed in a single genus. A genus may include only a single species if no other organism has characteristics similar enough for it to be considered the same genus.

- ✔ **Species:** A species is the most specific level, so it contains the fewest types of organisms. Organisms of the same species have very similar characteristics.

To get a better idea of how the scientific classification system works, consider how a lion is classified:

Kingdom *Animalia:* This kingdom includes all animals.

Phylum *Chordata:* All vertebrate animals belong to the phylum *Chordata.*

Class *Mammalia:* All mammals belong to this class.

Order *Carnivora:* All mammals that eat meat belong to the order *Carnivora.*

Family *Felidae:* The family *Felidae* includes all cats.

Genus *Panthera:* This genus includes all the roaring cats, such as lions, tigers, jaguars, and leopards.

Species *leo:* This is just a lion.

Humans belong to the kingdom *Animalia,* the phylum *Chordata,* the class *Mammalia,* the order *Primata,* the family *Hominidae,* the genus *Homo,* and the species *sapiens.* You know, just in case you were wondering.

Visiting the kingdoms

Not every scientist agrees (scientists rarely agree on any subject), but in general, most lab-coated individuals settle on five as the number of kingdoms. Check out the kinds of organisms that comprise the five kingdoms:

- ✔ **Animals:** This is one of the two largest kingdoms, and it includes many-celled organisms that, unlike plants, don't have cell walls, chlorophyll, or the capacity to use light to make energy (photosynthesis). Members of this kingdom can move. The Animal Kingdom includes more than 1,000,000 species.

- ✔ **Plants:** Plants are also one of the two largest kingdoms. This kingdom includes organisms that can't move, don't have obvious nervous or sensory systems (the Venus flytrap is one exception), and possess cell walls made of cellulose. More than 250,000 species belong to the Plant Kingdom.

✔ **Monerans:** This kingdom includes bacteria and cyanobacteria (blue-green algae) — one-celled organisms that don't have a nucleus (see the later section "Thinking small: Looking at cells"). More than 10,000 species have been discovered and classified in the Monera Kingdom.

✔ **Protists:** Protists include one-celled organisms that do have a nucleus, such as the protozoan, which you may remember from biology class. This kingdom consists of more than 250,000 species.

✔ **Fungi:** Examples of common fungi are mushrooms and yeast. Fungi don't *photosynthesize* (use light to create energy) like plants, but they do have cell walls made of a carbohydrate called chitin. More than 100,000 species belong to the Fungi Kingdom.

Thirty-three phyla make up the Animal Kingdom, and 12 main phyla comprise the Plant Kingdom. Monerans consist of two phyla; protists have seven phyla, and fungi are made up of four phyla. Numerous classes, orders, families, genera, and species fall under each phylum.

Just name it: Showing off your genius about the species

Each organism is given a scientific name that consists of two words (usually derived from Latin) — the genus and the species of the organism. The genus is the first word, and the species is the second. Thus, *Homo sapiens* refers to humans. *Canis familiaris* is the family dog, and *Canis lupus* is the family wolf. Because wolves and dogs share many similarities, they share the same genus (no, no, not the same *genes,* the same *genus*).

When writing a scientific name, the genus name is capitalized, and the species name is all lowercase. Both names are italicized.

Perusing the human body systems

Your body consists of major systems that work together to keep you alive. (And staying alive is a good thing, so be sure to thank your circulatory system and all the rest!) These systems include the ones listed in Table 10-3.

Table 10-3	Five Major Human Body Systems	
System	**Components**	**What the System Does**
Central nervous system	Brain, spinal cord, and nerves	Receives, processes, and responds to all physical stimuli; for example, if you burn your hand on the stove, this system prompts you to remove your hand from the stove
Circulatory system	Heart, blood, and blood vessels	Delivers oxygenated blood from the heart to the rest of the body and returns the blood to the heart to be oxygenated again
Digestive system	Mouth, esophagus, stomach, small and large intestines, rectum, and anus	Breaks down food into smaller substances that the body can absorb and process into energy and eliminates the resulting waste

System	Components	What the System Does
Musculoskeletal system	Bones, joints, voluntary and involuntary muscles	Bones support the body's muscles and organs; joints allow bones to move; voluntary muscles work in pairs to move joints; involuntary muscles, which you can't control, are found in organs such as the heart
Respiratory system	Nose, nasal cavity, trachea, lungs, and blood	Inhales air, uses the oxygen in the air to release energy, and exhales the carbon dioxide that results from this process

Thinking small: A look at cells

Living things are made up of cells that share certain characteristics. Cells come in different sizes and shapes, depending on what they do. In the human body, a muscle cell looks very different from a brain cell. (Has all this talk of cells caused your brain cells to hurt yet?) Cells combine to create *tissues,* which form structures like bones and skin.

Looking at cell structure

A cell has three main parts — the nucleus, the cytoplasm, and the cell membrane:

- **Nucleus:** The nucleus controls cellular activity. It's like the brains behind the cell, and it holds the cell's genetic material, such as DNA.

   Bacteria are *prokaryotes,* which means their cells don't have nuclei. Their genetic material floats in the cytoplasm instead of being held inside a membrane *(nuclear envelope).*

- **Cytoplasm:** The cytoplasm is a gel-like substance, composed mostly of water, that's inside the cell membrane and outside the nucleus. Cytoplasm contains many chemicals that carry out the life processes in the cell.

- **Cell membrane (plasma membrane):** This thin membrane holds the cell together, protecting the nucleus and cytoplasm.

See Figure 10-1 for a description of other cell structures.

Plant cells differ from animal cells in a number of ways:

- Plant cells have a firm *cell wall* that supports and protects the cell. Animal cells don't have such a structure.

- Plant cells have larger *vacuoles* (storage areas) than those found in animal cells.

- Unlike animal cells, many plant cells contain *chloroplasts,* which contain *chlorophyll,* a chemical that helps plants create food with the help of sunlight.

- Animal cells contain *centrioles* (cylindrical structures involved in cell division). Most plant and fungi cells don't.

- Animal cells have *lysosomes* (sacs of enzymes), which aren't found in plant cells.

Plant Cell

1. Chloroplast: Contains chlorophyll, which produces food
2. Cell wall: Protects the cell
3. Nucleus: The "brain" of the cell
4. Chromatin: Thin fibers containing genes
5. Nucleoplasm: Protoplasm (living material) in the nucleus
6. Ribosome: Combines amino acids into proteins
7. Cytoplasm: The cell's factory
8. Mitochondria: Produce the energy for cellular activity
9. Cell membrane: Contains the cellular material within it
10. Vacuole: Storage area

Animal Cell

1. Nucleus
2. Chromatin
3. Nucleoplasm
4. Ribosome
5. Cytoplasm
6. Mitochondria
7. Cell membrane
8. Vacuole

Figure 10-1: Basic structures of plant and animal cells.

Profiting from cell processes

Cells perform various processes in order to function at an optimum level. Here are a few of these processes:

- **Metabolism:** Chemical processes within a cell that are necessary for life to be maintained

- **Osmosis:** Movement of water through the cell membrane

- **Phagocytosis:** Acquisition of particles of material from outside of the cell; it's accomplished by surrounding the particles and passing them through the cell membrane

- **Photosynthesis:** Conversion of carbon dioxide and water into glucose and oxygen (in plants); in other words, sunlight is used to create energy

- **Cellular respiration:** Process in which food is broken down, producing energy

Swimming in the gene pool: Genetics

Someday you're going to find yourself acting like your mother or father. Whether you like it or not, it happens because parents pass their traits on to their offspring. Understanding *genetics* — how traits are physically passed from parents to offspring and what happens when the process goes wrong — helps scientists pinpoint the causes of diseases and disorders and can help them develop treatments and cures.

In human genetics, a healthy person contains 23 pairs of *chromosomes* (the structure that contains the genes). The mother and the father each supply one chromosome per pair. Genes contained in the chromosomes determine many characteristics of the resulting child.

Copying genes

When body cells multiply to produce tissues and organs (and eventually a complete living thing), they reproduce their genetic material. Most cells reproduce by *mitosis,* in which the nucleus of a cell divides, forming two cells and two identical sets of chromosomes.

However, sex cells (eggs and sperm) reproduce differently. Through *meiosis,* each cell divides into four cells, each containing only half the number of chromosomes as a nonsex cell. This process takes place so that the sex cells of one person (with 23 chromosomes) can hook up with the sex cells of another person (with 23 chromosomes) to produce 46 chromosomes, or 23 pairs. Otherwise, way too many chromosomes would be floating around.

Sometimes cells don't copy themselves and divide perfectly, and a genetic mistake is made. This frequently results in a fetus who doesn't live or in a fetus with a genetic disease or disorder. For example, Down Syndrome is the result of a fetus's having 47 instead of 46 chromosomes.

Determining your gender with two little letters

The genes on one pair of chromosomes, called the *sex chromosomes,* determine whether a child will be male or female. In females, the two sex chromosomes are alike, and they're labeled XX. In males, the chromosomes are different and are labeled XY.

The child always receives an X chromosome from the mother (who only has XX chromosomes). The father (who has XY chromosomes) can contribute either an X or a Y chromosome, so Papa actually determines the sex of the child.

Knowing which genes get passed down the family line

Many characteristics that you possess (from the way your nose turns up at the end to the color of your eyes) are determined by a pair of genes (or multiple pairs of genes). These two genes may be alike, or they may not.

Some genes are dominant, and some genes are recessive. If you have two unalike genes, the characteristic that they produce comes from the *dominant* gene; the gene that doesn't overshadow the other is called the *recessive* gene. If each parent has two unalike genes, both parents will have the dominant trait, but they can have a child with the recessive trait — because each parent contributes a gene to the offspring, each parent may contribute a recessive gene to the child. Whew!

Chemistry: Not Blowing Up the Lab

Chemists study matter, and everything that has mass and takes up space — including your old Chevy that's up on blocks and the mosquito buzzing around the room — is *matter.* All matter is made up of basic substances (building blocks) called *elements.*

Mass isn't the same thing as weight. *Weight* has to do with the force that gravity exerts on mass. If you were in a gravity-free zone, you wouldn't weigh anything, but you'd still be there, so you'd still exist and have mass.

Those mad scientists in the movies always seem to be chemists, but chemistry shouldn't drive you crazy. Here's a straightforward review of the chemistry you need to know for the General Science subtest.

Understanding the elements, my dear Watson

The *atom* is the smallest part of an element that still retains the characteristics of that element. Every atom has particles — pieces of matter that are very, very small. *Electrons* are negatively charged particles that float around the atom's *nucleus,* or core, which is made up of *neutrons* (particles with no charge) and *protons* (positively charged particles).

Each element has its own atomic number that's equal to the number of protons. If an atom has one proton in its nucleus, it has the atomic number 1. Hydrogen is the only element with just one proton in its nucleus. Magnesium, which has 12 protons in its nucleus, is given the atomic number 12.

Atoms can combine with each other to form *molecules.* If those atoms are of two or more different elements, the molecule is called a *compound.* A compound can have very different properties from the elements that make it up. For example, table salt, which is mostly harmless, consists of two lethal elements — sodium and chlorine. But when combined, these elements make a compound that people ingest every day.

Sitting down at the periodic table

The *periodic table* (also known as the table of elements) classifies all elements, because scientists love to classify things. Elements are listed according to their atomic numbers (number of protons) and are arranged into *families* of similar elements.

The periodic table lists the atomic number, the abbreviation for each element, and its *atomic weight,* which is the average mass of one atom of the element. Looking at Figure 10-2, you can see that copper (Cu, atomic number 29) has an atomic weight of 63.546, which means that copper is much, much heavier than helium (He, atomic number 2), which has an atomic weight of 4.0026.

You don't have to memorize these charts to do well on the ASVAB, but you should know the atomic numbers for common elements such as hydrogen (1), helium (2), carbon (6), nitrogen (7), oxygen (8), sodium (11), iron (26), copper (29), gold (79), mercury (80), lead (82), uranium (92), and plutonium (94).

Getting physical: Changing states

Particles of matter are always in motion. How much *kinetic energy* (motion energy) a particle has determines whether the matter is a solid, liquid, or gas in its normal state. Gas particles move around very quickly, liquid particles move more slowly, and solid particles move much more slowly than either of the other two.

When heat or cold is applied to matter, the kinetic energy of the matter changes; therefore, the nature of the substance can change. Heat applied to water changes the water from a liquid to a gas (steam), and cold applied to water changes it from a liquid to a solid (ice). When physical changes occur, the molecule itself remains the same. For example, water is still made of hydrogen and oxygen, no matter which state it's in.

Figure 10-2: The periodic table.

Causing a chemical reaction

Unlike physical changes, *chemical reactions* create new molecules. For example, when iron rusts, a chemical change occurs. The rust isn't the same molecule as the iron.

In a chemical reaction, two kinds of substances are present:

- ✔ **Reactants:** The elements or molecules involved in the reaction
- ✔ **Products:** The elements or molecules that result from the chemical reaction

Where Few Have Gone Before: Astronomy

Earth's solar system consists of the sun and a number of smaller bodies (such as planets, the planets' moons, and asteroids) that the sun's mass holds in orbit. The sun's mass creates gravity, and this gravity controls the movements of the smaller bodies.

Taking a quick glimpse at the sun

The sun is the largest and most important object in the solar system. It contains 99.8 percent of the solar system's mass (quantity of matter). The sun provides most of the heat, light, and other energy that makes life possible.

Is Pluto really a planet?

Pluto was referred to as the ninth planet since its discovery in the 1930s. But in August 2006, the International Astronomical Union (IAU) established a new definition for the word *planet*. Pluto has so many unusual features that it was reclassified as a *dwarf planet*. For example, it travels around the sun in an elongated oval path much different from the nearly circular orbits of the other planets. And unlike the other outer planets, Pluto is small and solid and contains only $\frac{1}{500}$ of the mass of Earth.

Under the new standards, Pluto is no longer considered a planet but instead is classified as a dwarf planet. According to the planet definition, the solar system consists of eight planets and three dwarf planets. The definition doesn't apply outside the solar system and doesn't include provisions for extra-solar planets. The definition was a controversial one; it has been both criticized and supported by different astronomers.

The sun's outer layers are hot and stormy. The hot gases and electrically charged particles in those layers continually stream into space and often burst out in solar eruptions. This flow of gases and particles forms the *solar wind,* which bathes everything in the solar system.

The sun is much larger than Earth. The distance from the sun's center to its surface (the sun's radius) is about 109 times the radius of Earth. Some of the streams of gas rising from the solar surface are even larger than the Earth's diameter.

Knowing the planets

A *planet* is a nonluminous celestial body larger than an asteroid or comet, illuminated by light from a star that the planet revolves around. The solar system consists of eight known planets: Mercury, Venus, Earth, Mars, Jupiter, Saturn, Uranus, and Neptune. Pluto is no longer classified as a planet by most scientists. (See the sidebar "Is Pluto really a planet?" for details.)

The Earth revolves around the sun in an oval-shaped pattern called an *ellipse.* Every 365¼ days, the Earth completes its orbit around the sun and starts again. The Earth rotates (spins) on its axis, completing a rotation every 24 hours, but because of the tilt of the Earth, hours of daylight and darkness aren't equal, except for on two days a year.

The inner four planets consist chiefly of iron and rock. They're known as the *terrestrial* (earthlike) planets because they're somewhat similar in size and composition. The outer planets are giant worlds with thick, gaseous outer layers. Almost all their mass consists of hydrogen and helium, giving them compositions more like that of the sun than of Earth. Beneath their outer layers, the giant planets have no known solid surfaces. The pressure of their thick atmospheres turns their insides liquid, though they may have rocky cores.

Rings of dust, rock, and ice chunks encircle all the giant planets. Saturn's rings are the most familiar, but thin rings also surround Jupiter, Uranus, and Neptune.

Shooting for the moons

Moons (sometimes called *satellites*) orbit all the planets except Mercury and Venus. The moon you refer to as *the moon* revolves around the Earth. It makes a complete revolution every 27⅓ days. When the moon moves into the Earth's shadow, a *lunar eclipse* results — the

Earth is positioned between the sun and the moon. When the Earth moves into the moon's shadow, a *solar eclipse* results — the moon is positioned between the Earth and the sun.

The inner planets have few moons. The giant planets probably have more small moons not yet discovered. See Table 10-4 for a lineup of the planets and their moons. Although Pluto is no longer officially considered a planet, you never know what those rascally ASVAB test-writers will ask, so I've included Pluto in the table.

Table 10-4	The Number of Moons per Planet in Earth's Solar System
Planet	*Number of Moons*
Mercury	0
Venus	0
Earth	1
Mars	2 tiny satellites
Jupiter	63
Saturn	61
Uranus	27
Neptune	13
Pluto (dwarf planet)	3

 Jupiter's four largest moons are known as the *Galilean satellites* because the Italian astronomer Galileo Galilei discovered them in 1610 with one of the first telescopes. The largest Galilean satellite — and the largest satellite in the solar system — is Ganymede, which is even bigger than Mercury and Pluto. The largest of Saturn's moons, Titan, has an atmosphere thicker than Earth's and a diameter larger than that of Mercury or Pluto. Pluto's largest moon, Charon, is more than half the size of Pluto.

Watching for meteors, comets, and asteroids

A *meteor* is a rock from space that hits Earth's atmosphere and glows as it heats up, resulting in a brief streak of light. It's often called a *shooting star*. When a meteor enters the Earth's atmosphere, it usually burns up (and that's a good thing). If a meteor actually strikes the Earth, it's called a *meteorite*.

Comets are snowballs composed mainly of ice and rock. When a comet approaches the sun, some of the ice in its nucleus (center) turns into gas. The gas shoots out of the sunlit side of the comet. The solar wind then carries the gas outward, forming it into a long tail. Astronomers divide comets into two main types:

- Long-period comets, which take 200 years or more to orbit the sun.
- Short-period comets, which complete their orbits in fewer than 200 years.

 The most famous of all comets, Halley's Comet — also referred to as Comet Halley after Edmond Halley — is a comet that can be seen every 75 to 76 years, making it a short-period comet. Halley is the only short-period comet that is visible to the naked eye and will return within a human lifetime. Its many appearances over the centuries have had a notable effect on human history. Halley's Comet last appeared in the inner solar system in 1986 and will next appear in mid-2061.

Asteroids are sometimes called *minor planets* because they're small bodies that orbit the sun. Some have elliptical orbits that pass inside the orbit of Earth or even that of Mercury. Others travel on a circular path among the outer planets. Most asteroids circle the sun in a region called the *asteroid belt,* between the orbits of Mars and Jupiter. The belt contains more than 200 asteroids larger than 60 miles (100 kilometers) in diameter. Scientists estimate that more than 750,000 asteroids with diameters larger than ⅗ mile (1 kilometer) exist in the belt. There are millions of smaller asteroids, and astronomers have even found several large asteroids with smaller asteroids orbiting them.

Down to Earth: Rocking Out with Geology and Meteorology

The study of the physical makeup of the Earth is often called *Earth science. Geology* describes the Earth's physical appearance, and *meteorology* explains the Earth's atmosphere.

Peeling back the layers of the planet

The Earth is like an onion in that it consists of several layers. The *crust* is the Earth's surface, and it varies in depth from a few miles to 30 miles. The *mantle* (including the mantle and an upper mantle) is the solid rock below the crust, and it makes up most of the mass of the Earth. The *core* (including the inner and outer cores) is the Earth's fiery center, with a temperature estimated to reach as hot as 4,300 degrees Celsius (to see what that is in Fahrenheit, use the conversion equations in "Figuring temperature conversions" earlier in this chapter). The mantle accounts for about two-thirds of the Earth's mass.

Sometimes cracks in the Earth's crust, called *faults,* appear. When the land shifts along these faults, earthquakes result. Molten rock trapped between the crust and the mantle is called *magma.* Magma collects in pockets called *magma chambers* and forms volcanoes. When volcanoes erupt, the magma is spewed out as *lava.*

Outta this world: Checking the atmosphere

The atmosphere contains many layers of air surrounding the Earth's surface. Starting with the layer closest to the Earth and extending outward, Table 10-5 names those layers.

Table 10-5		Layers of Earth's Atmosphere
Layer Name	*Location*	*Details*
Troposphere	Extends about 8 miles above the Earth	This layer is where the jet stream is located and where almost all weather changes occur.
Stratosphere	Extends about 30 miles	A major reported cause of ozone depletion is the presence of chlorofluorocarbons (CFCs) in the Earth's stratosphere. CFCs undergo a series of chain reactions, which ultimately leads to the destruction of the ozone layer.

Layer Name	Location	Details
Mesosphere	Extends about 50 miles	Millions of meteors burn up daily in the mesosphere as a result of collisions with the gas particles contained there.
Ionosphere	Extends about 70 miles	This layer reflects most radio waves, making it important to communications. **Note:** Scientists disagree among themselves as to whether the ionosphere is a separate atmospheric layer or whether it's part of the thermosphere.
Thermosphere	Extends about 350 miles	The International Space Station has a stable orbit within the upper part of the thermosphere, between 208 and 285 miles.
Exosphere	Extends about 6,200 miles	It's only from the exosphere that atmospheric gases, atoms, and molecules can escape into outer space. No boundary exists between the exosphere and space; therefore, *exosphere* is sometimes used synonymously with *outer space*.

Warming up to cold fronts

Temperature affects *air density* (how closely packed the air molecules are). When the sun shines, land and water absorb its warmth. Land warms up more quickly than water, so air over land is warmer than air over water during most of the day. At night, the air over land cools more quickly than air over water. The angle of the sun also affects air density (the sun shines directly over the Equator but not the poles).

Cold air is denser than warm air. Because it's denser, cold air has high pressure, compared to warm air's low pressure. (A *barometer* measures atmospheric pressure.) Air moves from areas of high pressure to areas of low pressure, creating wind.

Air masses have certain characteristics depending on where they form:

- If an air mass forms over land, it's dry, and if it forms over water, it's wet.
- Air masses formed in Earth's northern and southern regions are cold, and those formed at the Equator are warm.

When two different air masses meet, they don't mix. They form a boundary called a *front*. When cold air meets warm air, a *cold front* develops. The warm air may be pushed up to form clouds, causing heavy rain. When a warm air mass meets a cold air mass, a *warm front* develops. The warm air passes over the cold air, forming a different kind of cloud, which causes light rain.

Classifying clouds

Clouds are made of small droplets of water or bits of ice that are spread out from each other. Rain (or snow) falls when the drops get too big and heavy to stay in the cloud. Clouds have three main types, and the ASVAB may ask you a question or two about their characteristics, which are detailed in Table 10-6.

Table 10-6	Types of Clouds	
Cloud Type	**Description**	**What It Forecasts**
Cirrus	Thin, wispy, high clouds	Generally indicate rain or snow
Cumulus	White, puffy pillows, often flat-bottomed with rounded tops	Common during fair weather, but when they gather, they cause heavy rains
Stratus	Broad, flat, and low-hanging (gray blanket)	If close to the ground, they may produce drizzle

Additionally, a prefix or suffix is frequently given to the cloud name to indicate which level of the atmosphere it's in or whether it's producing precipitation (rain, sleet, snow, and the like):

- *Cirro-* is the prefix given to high clouds (base above 20,000 feet).

- *Alto-* is the prefix given to mid-level clouds (base between 6,000 and 20,000 feet).

- *Nimbo-* added to the beginning of a cloud name or *-nimbus* added to the end means the cloud is producing precipitation.

Therefore, a *cirrocumulus* cloud is a white, puffy, flat-bottomed, rounded-topped cloud at high altitude. *Altostratus* clouds are gray, broad, flat clouds at mid altitude.

Improving Your Chances on the General Science Subtest

Even if you study hard for the General Science subtest, chances are you may come across at least a couple of questions that you can't answer. That's the nature of this subtest — it pretty much asks you to know all there is to know about the universe. However, you can use several strategies to improve your chances of selecting the correct answer.

Using common sense to make educated guesses

If you don't know the answer to a question right off the bat, don't panic. You can often eliminate a few incorrect choices simply by using common sense. Even if you can't determine the answer, keep in mind that this subtest doesn't penalize you for guessing, so guessing makes sense — you have a 25 percent chance of guessing the right answer even if you can't eliminate any obviously wrong answers. If you can eliminate just one wrong answer, you improve your chances to 33 percent.

Most people don't have to rush to finish the General Science subtest, but then again, you don't have much leisure time to stop and think about all the questions at length, either. So if you don't know the answer to a question right away, do your best to eliminate wrong answers quickly, mark your best guess, and move along. (For help on making these eliminating decisions, check out Chapter 3.)

Try the process of elimination on the following question:

The knee joint is known as a

(A) pivot joint.

(B) fixed joint.

(C) ball-and-socket joint.

(D) hinge joint.

Looking at the choices, you can eliminate Choice (B), fixed joint, because your knee isn't fixed, or not moveable (or if it is, it shouldn't be). Your skull is an example of a fixed joint, but that's irrelevant to this question. Is your knee a pivot joint? If you think of something that pivots, you think of it moving in a circular or at least a semi-circular manner. Your knee doesn't do that either; therefore, you can safely eliminate Choice (A). A ball-and-socket joint is one that permits limited movement in any direction (your shoulder joint is a ball-and-socket joint). Your knee doesn't do that, so you can strike off Choice (C) and choose Choice (D), hinge joint, as the most likely answer. Your knee moves like a door on a hinge.

Now suppose you have a question like this:

The most common gas found in Earth's atmosphere is

(A) oxygen.

(B) nitrogen.

(C) calcium.

(D) helium.

Eliminate Choice (C) because calcium isn't a gas. You can also cross out Choice (D) because if helium were the most common gas, everyone would be talking in squeaky voices (you know, like after sucking helium from a balloon). Eliminating these two answers leaves you with just two choices, and if you simply guessed, you'd have a 50 percent chance of being right. Unfortunately, most people would guess that oxygen is the most common gas in Earth's atmosphere, but they'd be wrong. Nitrogen — Choice (B) — tops the list, making up 78 percent of the atmosphere.

Getting back to your Latin roots

Just when you thought vocabulary study was over, leave it to me to bring it up again. Many scientific words come from Latin or Greek. If you know the meaning of the Latin or Greek word, you can often figure out the meaning of the scientific word. Often, a Latin or Greek root word is used to create a longer, more specific word. (For common word roots, see Chapter 4.)

For example, the Latin root *homo* means *human being,* and the Greek root *homo* means *same.* So *Homo sapiens* refers to members of the human species, but *homogeneous* means "of the same kind." So if you were to run across the word *homologous* on the General

Science subtest, you'd know that it has something to do with humans or with things that are the same.

 Take a look at the following example question:

Which of the following instruments might an oceanographer be expected to use?

(A) aspirator

(B) hydrophone

(C) calorimeter

(D) centrifuge

Even if you don't have a clue about what any of these instruments do, if you know that *hydro* relates to water, you've significantly increased your chances of getting the right answer, Choice (B).

Chapter 11

Auto & Shop Information

. . . .

In This Chapter

▶ Looking under the hood of vehicles

▶ Knowing the tools of the trade

▶ Checking out the many uses of fasteners

▶ Driving up your test score

. . . .

*E*ver wonder why automobile mechanics and carpenters charge you about a billion dollars an hour when you need to hire their services? Because if the jobs were easy, everyone would do them.

Fortunately, to do well on the Auto & Shop Information (AS) subtest of the ASVAB, you don't have to get your hands greasy or chance hitting your thumb with a hammer. The questions on this subtest are pretty basic. Automotive questions usually ask about basic automotive systems and malfunctions. The shop questions generally ask you to identify a tool or fastener or the purpose of such.

The Auto & Shop Information subtest consists of 25 questions on the paper and pencil version. Happily, the ASVAB gurus give you 26.4 seconds to answer each question (11 minutes total). About half of the questions measure your basic knowledge of automotive principles and half query you about shop tools and basic shop principles. On the CAT-ASVAB, you have 7 minutes to answer 11 questions on Auto Information and 6 minutes to answer 11 questions on Shop Information. Your scores on these subtests are combined to give you a single Auto & Shop score.

The military uses the Auto & Shop Information subtest only to determine your qualifications for certain jobs. It's not used in the calculation of your AFQT score. Turn to Appendix A at the back of this book to find the jobs that require a good score on this subtest. If you don't need to do well on this subtest to qualify for the kind of job you want, you may be better off studying for a different part of the ASVAB, but it is better to try to get the best possible score on every subtest. Doing so will make you a more desirable candidate and may open the door for more job opportunities if your choice doesn't work out.

Checking under the Hood

Contrary to what you may think, an automobile is much more than the mechanical monster you park in your driveway each night. It's actually a complex machine that has undergone more than a century of evolution. Henry Ford would probably have a stroke if he could see what his simple horseless carriage evolved into.

The modern car is divided into several primary and secondary systems. I cover these systems in the next few sections.

The engine: Different strokes

How does an engine work? You turn the key, and if it doesn't start, you call your mechanic or your dad, right? Well, not quite. The internal combustion engine burns a mixture of gas and air. Burning the gas and air (the fuel mixture) makes it expand quickly (explode). The pressure from this explosion is transferred (via additional systems) to the wheels to make the car move.

The movement is brought about by a cycle, which your car's engine repeats a zillion and one times. Here are the four strokes that make up a cycle (Figure 11-1 illustrates how this process works):

1. **Intake:** The intake valve opens as the connecting rod pulls the piston down, drawing the gas/air mix into the cylinder.

2. **Compression:** The valves are closed. The connecting rod pushes the piston up, compressing the gas/air mix.

3. **Power:** The spark plug ignites the gas/air mix, forcing the piston down. That pushes down on the connecting rod, turning the crankshaft; the crankshaft turns the flywheel, which keeps the engine going.

4. **Exhaust:** The exhaust valve opens as the connecting rod moves the piston back up, pushing out the exploded gases. The valves are timed, of course, using push rods attached to the camshaft.

Figure 11-1:
A four-stroke engine.

Generally cars have an even number of cylinders — four, six, or eight. These cylinders are arranged in a row or rows, which are called *inline* (one row) or *V* (two rows), depending on the arrangement.

Most people refer to their engines as *four-cycle* engines. This isn't really true. It is a *four-stroke,* one-cycle engine. The intake stroke, compression stroke, power stroke, and exhaust stroke are one engine cycle. When the fourth stroke is completed, the cycle begins again. Automobile engines do this very fast. When the *tachometer* (an instrument measuring revolutions per minute [rpm]) on your dashboard shows 4,800 rpm, for example, that means the engine is performing 4,800 of these cycles every minute.

In order for the cycle to happen at all, fuel must be properly mixed with air and transported within the cylinder at the proper time. Various components perform this function. Depending on how old a car is, it may use a carburetor or fuel injectors:

- **Carburetors:** Carburetors are used on most older cars (pre-1990) to mix the fuel and air mechanically. As air moves quickly through the carburetor, it creates a vacuum, which draws more and more fuel into the mixture.

- **Fuel injectors:** Fuel injectors have replaced carburetors on newer cars to perform the air/fuel mixture function. (Actually, fuel injectors have been around since the late 1950s, but they weren't widely introduced until the late 80s and early 90s.) The fuel injector acts as the fuel-dispensing nozzle. It injects liquid fuel directly into the engine's air stream. In almost all cases, this requires an external pump.

  A doodad called the *EFI computer* (electronic fuel injection computer) determines the amount of fuel entering the engine. The EFI computer receives information from the sensors in the fuel, air, and exhaust system, and from that information, it determines how much fuel the engine needs to operate at optimum levels.

A *throttle* is mechanically connected to the carburetor or electronically connected to the EFI computer. Advancing (opening) the throttle causes more fuel to be transferred to the carburetor or the fuel injectors. The accelerator (the gas pedal) is connected to the throttle by mechanical linkages. The harder you push on the gas pedal, the farther the throttle is advanced (opened). Thus, more fuel is transported to the carburetor or fuel injectors.

Cooling system: Acting cool, staying smooth

Because of the high temperature at which the fuel burns, the engine has a cooling system (otherwise, the engine would melt). In this system, *water jackets* surround the parts that reach the highest temperatures. A *water pump* circulates water through the jackets. While the water circulates, it absorbs heat from the engine and then passes through the *radiator,* where outside air cools the water.

The water in the system is usually mixed with coolant (antifreeze), which raises the boiling point of the water (which keeps the water from boiling away) and lowers its freezing point (which keeps the system from freezing up during cold weather).

In addition, the engine parts must be lubricated to prevent them from breaking down, which occurs if the metal parts are allowed to rub against each other. An oil pump circulates oil through the engine; oil flows through the crankshaft and connecting rods, lubricating as it goes. Lubrication reduces friction, which in turn reduces heat.

Electrical and ignition systems: Starting up

Your car requires more than just gasoline to operate. It also needs a supply of electricity. In the old days, automotive electrical systems operated on 6 volts. Shortly after World War II, as electrical accessories became more prevalent in automobiles, 12 volts became the standard.

An electric motor powered by the battery starts the engine when you turn the key. This motor is called a *starter* (for obvious reasons). A gizmo called an *alternator* sends an electric current back to the battery to keep the battery charged and also powers the other electronic gadgets on your car when the engine is running.

The *ignition system* supplies a high-voltage current to the spark plugs to ignite the fuel mixture in the cylinders. (See the section titled "The engine: Different strokes," earlier in this chapter.) The system takes the 12-volt current from the battery, steps it up to about 20,000 volts, and then sends the current to the spark plugs.

In older cars, this increase of voltage is accomplished by means of a device called a *coil,* which uses electromagnetic induction to step up the voltage. The current then passes through an electrical/mechanical switching device called a *distributor.* A rotating shaft and a switch within the distributor, called *breaker points,* route the current through wires to the spark plugs. A *condenser* absorbs excess current and protects the breaker points from damage by the high-voltage surge. The distributor and other devices control the timing of the spark-plug discharges.

In the 1970s, the electronic ignition systems were introduced. In modern ignition systems, the distributor, coil, points, and condenser have been replaced by solid-state electronics controlled by a computer. A computer controls the ignition system and adjusts it to provide maximum efficiency in a variety of driving conditions.

Drive system: Taking it for a spin

Having a working engine is all fine and dandy, but the power of the engine still has to be transferred to the wheels to make them move. This is the job of the *drive system.* Cars have drive systems that run on axles. The *axle* is the shaft on which the wheels revolve. The *universal joint* allows the axle to move up and down without breaking the drive shaft. The *drive shaft* is the connecting component that carries torque and transmits rotation. Gears on the axle allow the vehicle to make turns. Axle shafts turn the wheels. The wheels on vehicles turn in three different ways:

- ✔ **Rear-wheel drive:** The rear wheels push the car. The drive shaft extends from the transmission to the rear axle.

- ✔ **Front-wheel drive:** The front wheels pull the car. The drive shaft extends from the transmission to the front axle.

- ✔ **All-wheel drive (four-wheel drive):** All wheels push and pull the car at the same time. The drive shaft extends from the transmission to both axles.

Cars also have transmissions. The *transmission* changes the speed of the engine in relation to the speed of the rear wheels (in rear-wheel drive), the front wheels (in front-wheel drive), or all the wheels (in four-wheel or all-wheel drive). Vehicles have two types of transmissions: automatic or manual (stick shift).

The transmission consists of gears in several combinations so that the amount of torque used can vary according to needs. When the terrain is difficult (as in snow), the wheels need more torque (the force that produces rotation) in order to move. The transmission increases torque as needed. In an automatic transmission, this variation is done automatically by the *torque converter.* In a manual transmission, the driver shifts the gears by hand. The *clutch* is used to facilitate this process by disconnecting the engine from the drive shaft. It's necessary to temporarily disconnect the engine in order to change to a different gear (torque). The clutch also allows the engine to run when the car isn't moving.

Brake system: Pulling out all the stops

When a vehicle is in motion, you apply brakes to stop that car from moving (a long way from the time when Fred and Barney stopped their car by dragging their heels). Each wheel has a brake that applies friction to the wheel to stop its rotation.

A brake system consists of a master cylinder that has *brake lines* (filled with *brake fluid*) running from it. The brake pedal applies pressure to the master cylinder, which sends pressure (and brake fluid) through the lines. What happens next depends on the type of brakes:

- **Drum brakes:** In a drum brake, the lines are connected to a *hydraulic cylinder* on each wheel. This cylinder contains pistons that move outward and force two *brake shoes* against the metal drum that rotates the wheel.

- **Disc brakes:** In a *disc-brake system,* the master cylinder forces a *caliper,* containing a piston, with brake shoes on each side, to squeeze against a rotating disc in each wheel, thus stopping your car by using fluid and releasing hot air.

Most modern cars use both drum brakes and disc brakes. Drum brakes are usually installed on the rear wheels, and disc brakes are generally installed on the front wheels. A drum brake system usually consists of a rotating drum with shoes that expand to rub the inside of a drum. This differs from the disc brake, which uses pads that pinch a rotating disc.

Emissions-control systems: In layman's terms, filters

Think of the engine as a giant cigarette and the emissions-control system as a filter. The exhaust from automobiles emits pollutants, including carbon monoxide. These pollutants are a result of the combustion process (or they're partially combusted fuel or unburned fuel). To prevent these pollutants from poisoning the atmosphere, manufacturers place emissions-control systems on cars. These systems include the following:

- **Positive-crankcase ventilation:** An old method (still in use) that forces unburned or partially burned fuel back into the cylinder so the fuel can be burned

- **Air-injection system:** System that forces air into the engine's exhaust system to burn unburned or partially burned fuel before the fuel comes out the exhaust pipe

- **Catalytic converter:** Oxidizes hydrocarbons and carbon monoxide into water vapor and carbon dioxide (the same thing people exhale); this system doesn't control other types of pollutants such as nitrogen oxides

- **Exhaust-gas-recirculation system:** Helps control nitrogen-oxide emissions by forcing some of the gases back into the cylinders

Picking Up the Tools of the Trade

You've probably heard the phrase "the right tool for the right job." This comment is what Dad used to yell at you when you'd use a Phillips screwdriver to punch holes in oil cans (thereby getting oil on your shirt). The ASVAB folks also believe in using the right tool for the right job, and many of the questions on the Auto & Shop Information subtest ask you to identify the best tool for certain tasks.

Tools are easiest to understand when you classify them by their function, so the following sections are divided by function. See Figure 11-2 for an illustration of the various types of tools covered.

Figure 11-2: Various tools you need to know for the ASVAB.

Striking tools

Striking tools apply driving force to an object. (Watch your fingers!) These tools include hammers, sledges, and mallets. Here's a brief explanation of the three:

✔ **Hammer:** A hammer is generally made of metal or plastic and consists of a handle, a head, a face (the part of the hammer that touches the nail or other fastener), a claw (to pull nails), and a wedge that attaches the head to the handle. The face of a hammer may be made of steel, brass, or lead.

✔ **Mallet:** A mallet is generally made of metal or plastic but may be made of wood, rubber, or rawhide. It's used to strike another tool or to strike a surface without damaging it. A mallet doesn't have a claw like its friend, the hammer.

✔ **Sledge:** A sledge is generally made of metal. People use it to drive bolts and chisels and to break rock. A sledge doesn't have a claw, either.

Fastening tools

Fastening tools apply fasteners, such as screws, to objects. (For more info on fasteners, check out "Sticking Materials Together with Fasteners," later in this chapter.) Numerous tools make up the fastening category:

✔ **Stapler:** A stapler is a fastening tool. Heavy-duty staplers can staple roofing felt to a roof, for instance.

✔ **Wrenches:** Wrenches turn nuts and bolts. The bolt or nut fits between the jaws of the wrench, and the wrench turns the bolt. Some wrenches have adjustable jaws. Not only can wrenches be used to turn nuts and bolts, but they may also be used to keep nuts and bolts stationary.

  • **Open-end wrenches:** These wrenches have open jaws.

  • **Box wrenches:** Box wrenches are closed. Some wrenches have open-end jaws on one end and a box wrench on the other.

  • **Socket wrenches:** Socket wrenches have box-type sockets of varying sizes that can be attached to a handle, which in turn can be attached to an extension.

    Note: Socket, box, and open-ended wrenches come in set, standard sizes — either in inches or in millimeters. They're not interchangeable. (Selecting the wrong socket wrench is how mechanics learn to use cuss words.)

  • **Torque wrenches:** These wrenches apply additional leverage to a fastener. A torque wrench looks much like a socket wrench but has additional internal mechanisms designed to measure and limit the amount of torque (force) being applied.

  • **Pipe wrenches:** Pipe wrenches have serrated jaws and grip round objects.

✔ **Screwdrivers:** A screwdriver, in the shop world, turns screws. (In the civilian world, it's a yummy drink!) Some special screwdrivers have different blades to fit different types of screws:

  • **Standard screwdriver:** A standard screwdriver has a flat blade at one end of the shank (the other end of the shank goes into a handle).

  • **Phillips screwdriver:** Phillips screwdrivers have a blade that is shaped like a cross; this blade fits into a cross-shaped Phillips screw head.

  • **Allen wrench:** An Allen wrench fits hexagonal screw heads. Nobody knows why this tool is called an *Allen wrench* instead of an *Allen screwdriver;* after all, it's used on hexagonal screws. That's just one of the mysteries of the shop world.

The Allen wrench, which was designed in 1943, gets its name from the Allen Manufacturing Company of Hartford, Connecticut.

- **Offset screwdriver:** Offset screwdrivers have the shank set at an angle to the blade to allow the tool to be used in cramped spaces. Offset screwdrivers can have a standard blade, Phillips blade, or any number of other blades.

✔ **Pliers:** Pliers can be used to fasten and unfasten fasteners, hold objects, and cut material. When you squeeze the handles, the jaws of the pliers come together.

- **Long-nosed or needle-nosed:** Long-nosed pliers, also called *needle-nosed pliers,* have tapered jaws that can hold small objects or fit into small spaces.

- **Curved-nose:** These pliers have curved jaws.

- **Slip-joint:** These pliers can be adjusted so the handles lock in a certain position.

- **Wrench or vise-grip:** Wrench pliers, or vise-grip pliers, have serrated jaws that clamp onto and hold objects of all shapes.

- **Cutting:** These pliers are used to cut wire.

Cutting tools

Cutting tools use sharp blades to cut through metal, wood, or other materials. Cutting tools have teeth. The number of teeth per inch (or points per inch) gives an indication of the type of work the saw can do. Because of the way points and teeth are counted, a saw always has one more point per inch than tooth per inch. A saw with fewer teeth is used for rough work, like cutting wood to size. A saw with more teeth cuts more finely and is used for more delicate work, like sawing joints and lightweight pieces of wood. Check out Table 11-1 for a breakdown of the different cutting tools that may be covered on the ASVAB.

Table 11-1	Cutting Tools
Cutting Tool	*Description/Function*
Bolt cutters	Heavy-duty shears that produce enough force when the handles are closed to slice through metal bolts or rods
Circle snips	Used to cut curves
Crosscut saw	A type of handsaw that cuts against the grain of the wood; the shape of the teeth and the angle in which they're set are the main differences in this type of saw
Coping saw	A type of handsaw that's used to cut curved lines or shapes
Hacksaw	A type of handsaw that's used to cut metal; a hacksaw has an adjustable frame that holds thin blades of varying length in place; a handle is set in one end
Pipe cutters and tube cutters	Used to score and cut metal pipes and tubes
Ripsaw	A type of handsaw that cuts with the grain of the wood; the shape of the teeth and the angle in which they're set are the main differences in this type of saw
Snips and shears	Snips and shears have two cutting blades that scissor together when the handles close; the blades can be curved or straight

Drilling, punching, and gouging tools

No, this section isn't about hand-to-hand combat training from basic training. Masters in the art of shop often make holes in the material they're working with in order to build that perfect birdhouse (or whatever else they're working on). These holes can be made with a variety of tools, which I cover in the following sections.

Drills and bits

Twist drills use *drill bits,* which are round pieces of steel shaped in a spiral, to create holes. Drill bits are attached to a drill (usually a power drill but sometimes a hand drill operated by manually turning a crank). The point of the drill bit is sharpened, and the shank is smooth and fits into the drill.

A *countersink* is a drill bit that enlarges just the surface of a hole so that a screw head can be accommodated. A countersink is used to allow the top of the fastener to be set exactly even with the material to which it's attached. Without a countersink, the fastener slightly protrudes from the material to which it's been attached.

Auger bits bore larger holes. They're shaped differently from drill bits. They have a long deep spiral flute for easy chip removal. They're also much larger. Auger bits are most commonly used with a brace for drilling holes in wood. Their length varies from 7 to 10 inches.

Punches

Punches have a sharp end that's placed against the material to be punctured; the other end is struck with a hammer. A center punch is used to mark where a drilled hole is to be placed; this keeps the drill bit in position and prevents the drill from jumping to another part of the material.

Using a Phillips screwdriver as a punch is bad form in the shop world because hitting the handle of a screwdriver with a hammer can damage it (and then you'll get talked about in serious shop circles).

Chisels

Chisels are made of steel and have a sharp cutting edge. They're used to chip or cut metal or wood:

- **Metal-cutting chisels:** Chisels that cut metal are usually struck with a mallet to make the cut. These chisels have different shapes depending on how they'll be used; *cold chisels* are flat, and they're used for cutting metals without using heating torches or forges, whereas *round chisels* make circular cuts.

- **Wood-cutting chisels:** Some wood chisels, called *socket chisels,* are also struck with a mallet. Other wood chisels require only the pressure of your hands.

  Wood chisels also come in different shapes, depending on what they're used for. A *butt chisel* has a short blade and is used for in-close work. A *mortising chisel* has a narrow blade made for chiseling out the narrow mortises in joints. A *framing chisel* has a heavy, strong blade meant for rough work.

Because you use chisels with other tools and the pressure of your hands, there's a little bit of a risk involved with this tool. One slip and these instruments can easily cut large chunks out of your skin, so be careful.

Finishing tools

Filing and finishing shop tools are used to sharpen the blades of other tools and to smooth the edges of cut metal objects. Files come in a range of fineness, and the blades can be cut in different patterns. Files also come in different shapes to finish different kinds of objects. Here are the different kinds of files:

- **Single-cut:** Single-cut files are used for finishing work and sharpening blades.

- **Double-cut:** Double-cut files are used for rough work.

- **Flat files and half-round:** These files are for general purposes.

- **Square and round:** These files fit square and round openings.

Planes are a type of finishing tool used to prepare wood for final finishing and to fit doors and trim. Planes consist of a handle to push with, a knob to guide with, a frame, a sole, and a mouth (where the blade is). *Bench planes* are used to smooth surfaces. Longer planes give a more uniform surface by shaving off a portion of the wood.

Clamping tools

A clamping tool is a device used to hold or fasten objects securely so they won't move while you're working on them. There are several types of clamping tools available for many different purposes:

- **Pliers:** Pliers (discussed in the "Fastening tools" section earlier in the chapter) can be used to hold objects while you're working on them.

- **Vises:** Vises hold material while it's being sawed, drilled, or glued. Here are some different types of vises:

  - **Bench vise:** A bench vise has large, rough jaws that keep the material from slipping.

  - **Pipe vise:** Pipe vises hold round trim or pipes.

  - **Handscrew vise:** A handscrew vise has two hard, wooden jaws connected by two long screws. The screws are tightened to bring the jaws of the handscrew vise together.

- **Clamps:** Clamps are used when a vise won't work. Vises generally attach to a work-bench, while clamps generally connect only to the items being worked with. C-clamps consist of a stationary frame and a screw that moves back and forth to open and shut the clamp.

Measuring tools

As any shop enthusiast will tell you, the golden rule of shop is to "measure twice and cut once." It's frustrating to cut a piece of material only to find it's just a little bit too short to fit in the place you intended. Using measuring tools helps you avoid this embarrassing situation.

Tape rules, rigid steel rules, steel (or fiberglass) tape rules, and folding rules are all used to measure material. *Calipers* are also used for very exact and small measurements. Calipers can be used with a rule to measure diameter; the legs of a set of calipers curve in to measure outside curves and curve out to measure inside curves. Slide calipers have the rule built in.

Depth gauges measure the depth of holes. Thickness gauges measure the thickness of small openings. *Thread gauges* measure the number of threads per inch in threaded fasteners. *Wire gauges* measure the thickness of wire.

Leveling and squaring tools

A *square* is used to check the trueness (accuracy) of an angle. Because most squares have a rule, they can also be used for measuring (see the preceding section). Squares have two arms, called the *blade* and the *tongue,* that meet at a right angle. A square can be set against any angle that is supposed to be a 90-degree angle. If a gap exists between the square and the material, the material isn't true — that is, it's not at the specified angle. A sliding T-bevel has an adjustable blade so that different angles can be checked.

Levels show whether a surface is true. A basic level has one or more small tubes filled with a liquid (like alcohol) and an air bubble. If the level is placed on a surface and the bubble remains exactly in the center of the tube, the surface is level. (This method can't be used to see if your recruiter is on the level. I tried it. Recruiters simply won't hold still long enough.)

A *plumb bob* is a heavy weight that's suspended from a line. It indicates vertical trueness.

Sticking Materials Together with Fasteners

Although wood and metal (and other materials) can be held together with glue, straps, duct tape, and other brilliant fastening methods, people usually fasten these types of materials with nails, screws, bolts, and rivets. These fasteners offer more strength and stability than the white glue that you used to fasten painted macaroni noodles onto construction paper in the first grade.

Nails

Nails are used to hold pieces of wood together. The nail head is flat, and the shank is usually round. Nail length is designated by the *penny system,* which is abbreviated with a *d*. A ten-penny nail is a 10d nail. Length and thickness generally correspond. Nails that are larger than 20-penny are called *spikes* and are measured in inches.

The penny system is used in the United States. Penny size indicates the nail's length. The higher the penny size, the longer the nail. The penny system is derived from the price of 100 nails in the 15th century in England.

Other type of nails include the following:

- **Brads and finishing nails:** They have heads that are made to fit flush with or slightly below the surface of the wood.

- **Common nails:** These nails are the most commonly used nails. (How about that for a truly difficult vocab word?)

- **Double-headed nails:** These have two heads, one lower than the other, and a point on the other end. The nail is driven to the lower head but can be pulled out of the material because of the remaining higher head. These nails are used for temporary construction that will be taken apart.

The magic of ABS

In the modern world of cars, most vehicles are equipped with an *antilock brake system* (ABS). The ABS is a four-wheel system (usually) that prevents the wheels from locking up. The system does this by automatically adjusting the brake pressure during an emergency stop. This enables the driver to maintain steering control and to stop in the shortest possible distance under most conditions.

The theory behind ABS is simple. If your car isn't equipped with ABS and you have to stop quickly, your wheels simply stop turning when you hit the brakes. If your tires don't have much traction on the road, your car may continue forward in a skid, even though the wheels are locked. You don't stop as quickly as you would with ABS, and you won't be able to steer. However, with ABS, your wheels are slowed to a stop as quickly as possible, without locking up, which gives the driver much better control during an emergency stop situation.

Screws and bolts

Unlike nails, you can easily take screws and bolts out of the wood without causing additional damage to the wood (unless, of course, the threads are stripped). These fasteners also hold more tightly than nails. Screws have flat heads, round heads, or oval heads; and in addition to this classification, they also have standard heads (for standard slotted screwdrivers) or Phillips heads (with cross-shape slots). Screw sizes are based on length and the diameter of the unthreaded part of the screw.

Here's the lowdown on these types of fasteners:

- **Wood screws:** Wood screws are used to fasten wood. (Hmm, ingenious!)
- **Lag screws:** Lag screws have square- or hexagon-shaped heads.
- **Bolts:** Bolts don't thread into wood. They have flat ends (as opposed to the pointed ends of screws). They're held in place by a nut (which is what actually screws into the threads) and washer. The body of the bolt may have few threads or many.
- **Machine screws:** Machine screws are used to fasten metal parts. Machine screws are sometimes used with nuts. They come in various lengths and widths and have a wide variety of heads.

Nuts and washers

Nuts can be square or hexagonal. *Cap nuts* are rounded and smooth; *stop nuts* prevent the screw or bolt from coming loose. *Wing nuts* have flanges on each side so they can be tightened by hand.

Washers prevent damage to the surface of material by preventing the bolt head from digging into the material. They also help keep the bolt (or screw) in place. *Flat washers*, a simple ring of flat metal, are the most common type of washer. *Shake-proof washers* have teeth to prevent them from skipping, while *split-lock washers* have two ends that dig into the nut and the material to keep the screw from slipping out.

Rivets

Rivets are commonly used to fasten metal parts together, especially when a weld is insufficient. Standard rivets are driven using a *bucking bar*. Rivets come in a wide variety of lengths, diameters, and head shapes. The rivet material should match the material being fastened. *Pop rivets* can be driven when only one side of a joint is accessible.

Building a Better Score

If you haven't picked up auto and shop knowledge by this point in your life and want to do well on this subtest, one thing you can do is get an automotive manual and take your car apart (hoping that you can get it back together again). Then get a woodworking book and build some furniture for your mom. (Even if you mess it up, Mom always likes gifts from the heart.)

Or you can check out your local community college, which may be a more practical solution. Many community colleges offer basic Auto and Shop classes. You may also want to take a gander at the following books, all published by Wiley:

- *Auto Repair For Dummies* by Deanna Sclar

- *Woodworking For Dummies* by Jeff Strong

- *Home Improvement All-in-One For Dummies* by Roy Barnhart, James Carey, Morris Carey, Gene Hamilton, Katie Hamilton, Donald R. Prestly, and Jeff Strong

On this subtest, you usually either know the answer or you say, "Huh?" However, some questions you run into can be answered by using the common sense approach. For example, say you run into a question on the ASVAB that reads something like the following:

When attaching two pieces of wood together, the most secure bond would be formed by using:

(A) wood screws

(B) nails

(C) wood glue

(D) both A and C

If you think about it, screws have threads, which are likely to "grab" wood more securely than a nail would. Glue would likely strengthen that bond even more. It's obvious that the common sense answer would be Choice (D).

Try a variation of the same question:

The best fastening method to use when attaching pieces of wood together when time is of the essence would be

(A) wood screws

(B) nails

(C) wood glue

(D) both A and C

Making the grade: Octane ratings

Octane ratings measure gasoline's ability to resist *engine knock,* a rattling or pinging sound that results from premature ignition of the compressed fuel-air mixture in one or more cylinders. Most gas stations offer three octane grades: regular (usually 87 octane), midgrade (usually 89 octane) and premium (usually 92 or 93). By federal law, the ratings must be posted on bright yellow stickers on each gasoline pump.

The octane rating correlates to how much the gasoline can be compressed before it ignites spontaneously. When gasoline ignites this way, instead of by the spark of a spark plug, the engine begins knocking. That's not a good thing because early ignition can cause engine damage over time.

But don't be fooled — that doesn't mean using higher octane gas is better. In most cases, using a higher octane gasoline than your owner's manual recommends offers absolutely no benefit. It won't make your car perform better, go faster, get better mileage, or run cleaner. The only time you may need to switch to a higher octane level is if your car engine knocks when you use the recommended fuel. This happens to a small percentage of cars. Buying higher octane gasoline is a waste of money, too. Premium gas costs 15 to 20 cents or more per gallon more than regular. That can add up to hundreds of dollars a year in unnecessary costs.

How can you tell if you're using the right octane level? Listen to your car's engine. If it doesn't knock when you use the recommended octane, you're using the right grade of gasoline.

In this case, the best answer would be Choice (B), because pounding a nail in with a hammer is generally faster than waiting for glue to dry or screwing a screw in with a screwdriver (even in these days of electric screwdrivers).

When all else fails, guessing is okay. If you guess, you have a 25 percent chance of guessing the right answer. If you leave the answer blank, you have a 0 percent chance. If you're taking the computerized version of the ASVAB, you don't have a choice, of course, because you must provide an answer before you're presented with the next question. For general guessing hints, check out Chapter 3.

Chapter 12

Mechanical Comprehension

. . . .

In This Chapter

▶ Using the forces of physics

▶ Figuring out the principles of work

▶ Manipulating machines to help you work

▶ Jacking up your test score

. . . .

*1*f your M-16A2 .223 caliber rifle jams on the firing range, knowing how to take it apart and put it back together will benefit you. Of course, your drill sergeant in basic training will be more than happy to teach you this, but how easily you grasp such tasks depends greatly on your aptitude for understanding simple mechanical operations. That's the purpose of the Mechanical Comprehension (MC) subtest of the ASVAB.

The questions on this subtest measure your understanding of simple machines and mechanisms. Many of the questions on this subtest display a diagram, such as a series of gears, followed by a question, such as which direction the gears turn or how fast they revolve. This subtest is almost all about mechanical physics, so you may want to review some basic physics textbooks from your local library.

Only some military jobs require a good score on this subtest. Turn to Appendix A for information about the subtest scores you need to qualify for specific military jobs. If you have no interest in taking apart a fighter aircraft or rebuilding a tank, you're better off reviewing for the Word Knowledge or Arithmetic Reasoning subtests, which make up part of the core exam (the AFQT; see Chapter 1) that you must do well on to even qualify for enlistment. Remember, though, it doesn't hurt to understand mechanical operations. You never know when you'll be offered an interesting job opportunity that requires a good score in this area.

To ace this subtest, you also have to bone up on your mathematical skills. The Mechanical Comprehension subtest often asks you to make calculations based on formulas to explain mechanical principles. Don't panic; the formulas are easy to understand, but you do have to use math to come up with a final answer. See Chapters 7 and 8 for more information on math. In this chapter, you get the mathematical formulas for commonly asked questions on the ASVAB, so pay especially close attention to these little beauties. (If the information probably isn't on the ASVAB, I don't burden you with it here.)

The CAT-ASVAB (computerized test) has 16 Mechanical Comprehension questions that you're supposed to answer in 20 minutes. For the paper version of the ASVAB, this subtest has 25 questions. You have 19 minutes to answer the questions, which is enough time for a mechanically oriented individual to tackle this subtest and put a broken clock back together. Well, maybe not the whole clock.

Understanding the Forces of the Universe

By applying *force* (a push or pull), you can open the door or close it, speed it up (slam it) or slow it down (catch it before it slams), or make it change direction (push it shut when the wind blows it open).

In physics, applying force allows changes in the *velocity* (the speed and direction) of an object. A change in velocity is known as *acceleration*. Here's the mathematical formula to determine force:

Force = Mass × Acceleration

Martial artists use this concept all the time. Although a larger fighter may have more size (mass), a smaller fighter can usually speed up more quickly (have more acceleration), possibly resulting in both fighters' applying the same amount of force. This concept is why 110-pound martial artists can break boards and bricks just as well as 200-pound martial artists.

This section gives you the basics of force that you need to know for the ASVAB.

He hit me first! The basics of action and reaction

Sir Isaac Newton sure was one of the sharpest crayons in the box. His third law of motion states that for every action (force) in nature, there's an equal and opposite reaction. In other words, if object A exerts a force on object B, then object B also exerts an equal and opposite force on object A. Notice that the forces are exerted on different objects.

Take a look at Figure 12-1. As you sit in your chair, your body exerts a downward force on the chair, and the chair exerts an upward force on your body. There are two forces resulting from this interaction: a force on the chair and a force on your body. These two forces are called *action* and *reaction forces*.

Figure 12-1:
An example of action and reaction forces.

This force can also be used to describe how a motorboat moves through the water. As the propellers turn, they push the water behind the boat (action). The water reacts by pushing the boat forward (reaction).

Equilibrium: Finding a balance

Forces are *vector* quantities. That means that they have both a magnitude (size) and a direction associated with them. Forces applied in the same direction as other forces increase the total force, and forces that move in opposite directions reduce the total force. In general, an object can be acted on by several different forces at any one time.

A very basic concept when dealing with forces is the idea of *equilibrium* or balance. When two or more forces interact so that their combination cancels the other(s) out, a state of equilibrium occurs. In this state, the velocity of an object doesn't change. The forces are considered to be balanced if the rightward forces are balanced by the leftward forces and the upward forces are balanced by the downward forces.

If an object is at rest and is in a state of equilibrium, then it's at *static equilibrium. Static* means being stationary or at rest. For example, a glass of water sitting on a table is at static equilibrium. The table exerts an upward force on the glass to counteract the force of gravity.

Under pressure: Spreading out the force

Pressure is a measurement of force over an area. Pressure is usually measured in pounds per square inch (psi). The formula for deriving pressure is

$$\text{Pressure} = \frac{\text{Force (in pounds)}}{\text{Area (in inches)}}$$

If 50 pounds of force is exerted on 10 square inches of surface, the amount of pressure is 5 pounds per square inch (5 = 50 ÷ 10).

Consider this: If you're sleeping in bed, the amount of pressure being exerted per square inch is much less than when you're standing on your feet. The surface area of the bottoms of your feet (supporting all that weight) is much less than the surface area of all your body parts that touch the mattress.

Ever wonder how a person can lie on a bed of nails? The answer involves elementary physics. His or her body rests evenly on hundreds of nails; therefore, no individual nail exerts a great amount of pressure against the skin. Have you ever seen someone stand on a bed of nails? It's unlikely because more pressure is on the feet, and the nails would puncture the feet.

A *barometer* is a gauge that measures atmospheric pressure. Normal atmospheric pressure is 14.7 psi. A change in air pressure means the weather is about to change. For more information on science and barometric pressure, see Chapter 10.

Looking at kinds of forces

Here are some of the forces that act on objects:

- ✔ **Friction:** Resistance to the motion of two objects or surfaces that touch
- ✔ **Gravity:** The physical property that draws objects toward the center of the Earth (and other objects that have mass)
- ✔ **Magnetism:** The property of attracting iron or steel
- ✔ **Recoil:** The property of kicking back when released
- ✔ **Static electricity:** The production of stationary electrical charges, often the result of friction

In this section, I explain a few of these forces in detail.

Friction: Resisting the urge to move

When one surface (such as a floor) resists the movement of another surface (the bottom of a piano), the result is *frictional* resistance. (This friction isn't like resisting orders to cut the grass. That type of resistance may cause friction between you and your dad, but I'm talking about a different kind of resistance here.)

In order to perform work — that is, to get an object to move in the direction you're pushing or pulling — sometimes you have to overcome friction by applying more force. For example, when you're moving a piano across a smooth, vinyl floor, little friction is produced, so the amount of force required to push the piano comes from the piano's weight and the very minor friction produced by the smooth floor. But when you're moving a piano across a carpeted floor, more friction is produced, so you have to push harder to move the same piano the same distance. (See the later section "You Call That Work?!" for more information on what's considered work in physics terms.)

Rolling friction (like the friction that occurs when you roll a wheel along the pavement) is always less than sliding friction (which occurs when you shove a piano along the floor). If you put wheels on a piano, it's much easier to push!

You can decrease friction by using a lubricant. Oil, grease, and similar materials reduce friction between two surfaces. So theoretically, if you oil the bottom of a piano, it's easier to move! *Note:* Oiling the bottom of your piano isn't recommended (for reasons involving the appearance of your floor and piano).

Gravity: What goes up must come down

Sir Isaac Newton invented gravity in 1687 when he failed to pay attention while sitting under a tree and got bonked on the noggin by an apple. Before that, gravity didn't exist, and everyone just floated around. Okay, I'm kidding. Isaac Newton didn't invent gravity. But the famous mathematician was the first to study gravity seriously, and he came up with the theory (now a scientific law) of how gravity works.

Newton's *law of universal gravitation* states that every object in the universe attracts every other object in the universe. The Earth produces gravity, and so do the sun, other planets, your car, your house, and your body. Even this book you're reading produces gravity. The amount (force) of the attraction depends on the following:

✔ **Mass:** The force of gravity depends on the *mass* of (amount of matter in) the object. If you're sitting in front of your television, you may be surprised to know that the television set is attracting you. However, because the mass of the TV is so small compared to the mass of the Earth, you don't notice the physical "pull" toward the television set.

   Note that the force of gravity acting on an object is equal to the weight of the object. Of course, other planets have lesser or greater masses than the Earth, so the weight of objects on those planets will be different.

✔ **Distance:** Newton's law also says that the greater the distance is between two objects, the less the objects will attract each other. In other words, the farther away an object is from the Earth (or any large body), the less it will weigh. If you stand at the top of a high mountain, you will weigh less than you will at sea level. Don't get too excited about this weight-loss technique. Gravitational pull isn't the next big diet craze. The difference is incredibly small. Sorry!

   For an object to really lose weight, it must be far away from the Earth (or any other large body). When an object is far enough away from these bodies that it experiences practically no gravitational pull from them, it is said to experience weightlessness — just like the astronauts you see on TV.

Gravity pulls objects downward toward the center of the Earth, so the old saying "what goes up must come down" is appropriate when discussing gravity. If you fire a bullet straight up into the air, it will travel (overcoming the force of gravity) until it reaches its furthest or highest point, and then it will fall.

Centrifugal force: False gravity

An object traveling in a circle appears to experience a gravitational force. This isn't really gravity, but instead it's a concept known as *centrifugal force.* The amount of force depends on the mass of the object, the speed of rotation, and the distance from the center:

✔ The more massive the object, the greater the force.

✔ The greater the speed of the object, the greater the force.

✔ The greater the distance from the center, the greater the force.

The centrifugal force, or effect, on an object is actually a fictitious outward force on an object moving along a curved path, which can be equal to the centripetal force on an object. *Centripetal force* points toward the center of an object's circular path, perpendicular to the direction of motion of an object.

If you're riding on a merry-go-round on the playground (wee!), you have to exert a constant force to keep from flying off. This feeling of being pushed outward isn't due to something actually pushing you in that direction but to your body's inertia trying to keep you moving in a straight line. Because one of Newton's laws states that moving objects tend to want to travel in one direction, as the merry-go-round turns, your body wants to keep traveling in one direction (*tangent* to the circle, if you like math), so you feel you're being pushed outward.

Applying force to two ends: Tension

Tension force is the force transmitted through a rope, string, or wire when force is applied to both ends. The force is the amount of tension directed along the rope, string, or wire and pulls equally on the objects at both ends. Tension force is usually measured in either pounds-force or newtons (N); 4.45 newtons equal 1 pound-force. See Figure 12-2.

Elastic recoil: The trampoline of physics

Liquids and gasses don't have a specific shape, but solid matter does. Solids are perfectly happy with the way they look and resist changes in shape. If you exert a force on a solid shape, it responds by exerting a force in the opposite direction. This force is called *elastic recoil.*

Take a look at Figure 12-3. The cat is standing on a board suspended on two blocks. While the board bends, the cat can feel the force of the board trying to regain its original shape. If the cat steps off the board, the board will spring back to its normal state.

Force = 150 pounds-force

Tension = 150 pounds-force

Weight = 150 pounds

Figure 12-2: An example of tension force.

Figure 12-3:
The concept
of elastic
recoil.

Force

Recoil

You Call That Work?!

Mechanically speaking, *work* happens when a force (usually measured in pounds) moving over a measurable distance (usually measured in feet) overcomes a resistance. In the United States, the unit of measure for work is often called a *foot-pound*. One foot-pound of work occurs when a 1-pound weight is lifted to a height of 1 foot. You can represent this concept in equation form:

Work = Force × Distance

Work is different from effort; *work* is the result of effort. You can think of *effort* as being force and of *work* as being what you produce with that force.

Overcoming resistance

The resistance that the work overcomes isn't the same thing as the weight of the object. (If you've ever tried to put your freaked-out cat in a cat carrier to go to the vet, you know what I mean.) In other words, if you try to move a 1,200-pound piano, you'll probably notice a measurable difference between the amount of work it takes to shove it along the floor and the amount of work it takes to carry it up the stairs. But don't take my word for it — you can demonstrate this concept at home. First, find a 1,200-pound piano and push it across the floor. Next, put it on your back and carry it up the stairs. See the difference? (Really, don't put the piano on your back. I'm just trying to make a point here.)

When you move the piano across the floor, you're really working (pushing) against the frictional resistance (the force that's produced when two surfaces rub together) of the piano rather than its full weight. Under these circumstances, the frictional resistance of the piano offers less resistance than its full weight. There are times when an object's full weight is less than its frictional resistance. Consider trying to push a textbook across a deep-pile carpet. Picking the book up and carrying it is easier. (For more about friction, see the earlier section "Friction: Resisting the urge to move.")

Gaining power by working more quickly

Power is the rate of work. If Mary Lou is able to lift more 50-pound sacks of potatoes onto the truck bed in ten minutes than Joe is, Mary Lou is more powerful than Joe. Mathematically speaking,

$$Power = \frac{Work}{Time}$$

In this formula, work is usually measured in foot-pounds, time is measured in minutes, and power is measured in foot-pounds per minute. However, the unit of measure for power is commonly put in terms of horsepower (hp).

Horsepower is derived from the estimate that an average horse can do 33,000 foot-pounds of work in one minute (according to James Watt). Therefore, 1 horsepower = 33,000 foot-pounds per minute. One horsepower is also the same as 550 foot-pounds per second.

Relying on Machines to Help You Work

Ever since Zog crawled out of his cave and invented the wheel to help him carry fur coats to his girlfriend, mankind has made use of machines that help him to make work easier.

In addition to increasing efficiency, machines are also used to help with work that couldn't be done otherwise. Think of the mechanisms and machines you use everyday — from the simple (like the hinge that allows a door to move easily when you push it open) to the more complex (like the hydraulic lift that allows you to lift a car up to check its underside). You could move most doors out of the way without hinges, but you couldn't lift a car over your head without some help.

Machines give you the ability to magnify and change the direction of forces. When a machine multiplies the force you use, it gives you a *mechanical advantage*. This concept can be stated as

$$\text{Mechanical Advantage} = \frac{\text{Resistance}}{\text{Effort}} = \frac{\text{Output Force}}{\text{Input Force}}$$

Some simple machines may give you a mechanical advantage of only 1 or 2. This means that they enable you to do one or two times the amount of work by expending the same effort. But those simple machines are still worth using! Often, even if a machine doesn't multiply your effort (or doesn't multiply your effort by much), it can at least spread your effort out and make it more effective.

Machines make work easier by providing some trade-off between the force applied and the distance over which it's applied. Keep reading to find out more on some basic types of machines.

Using levers to your advantage

You may not think of the seesaw at the neighborhood park as a machine, but it is. It's a lever. Levers are among the simplest machines used to help increase force.

All levers work by using a *fulcrum* (point of support) to reduce resistance and multiply the effect of effort. Resistance is exerted at one end of the lever (the *resistance arm*) and effort is exerted at the other (the *effort arm*). The effort arm moves the resistance arm. See Figure 12-4.

Figure 12-4: A simple lever.

To determine how much a lever reduces the amount of effort needed to do work, use the following formula:

$$\frac{\text{Length of Effort Arm}}{\text{Length of Resistance Arm}} = \frac{\text{Resistance Force}}{\text{Effort Force}}$$

As you can see, the amount of effort needed to move the lever varies depending on how long the effort arm is and how long the resistance arm is. Keep in mind that a short resistance arm, although easier to move, can't move an object as far through space as a longer resistance arm can.

The mechanical advantage of using a lever can be stated as

$$\text{Mechanical Advantage} = \frac{\text{Effort Arm}}{\text{Resistance Arm}}$$

If the effort arm is 6 inches and the resistance arm is 3 inches, the mechanical advantage is 2. If the effort arm is 6 feet and the resistance arm is 3 feet, the mechanical advantage is still 2.

Ramping up the inclined plane

The *inclined plane,* also called a *ramp,* is another very simple machine that makes moving an object from one point to another easier. The ramp spreads your work out over a longer distance, so less force is needed to do the work.

For instance, suppose you have to lift a 50-pound barrel to a truck bed that's 3 feet off the ground. You would have to use 50 pounds of force for 3 feet to move the barrel. But if you put a 6-foot ramp in place and push the barrel up the ramp, you'd only use half as much force to get the barrel in the truck (assuming there's no friction) because the mechanical advantage of such a ramp is 2.

The advantage of using a ramp can be expressed as

$$\frac{\text{Length of Ramp}}{\text{Height of Ramp}} = \frac{\text{Weight of Object Being Moved}}{\text{Force Required to Move Object}}$$

Wedges are a form of inclined plane and can multiply your effort in much the same way as a ramp can. Screws are also inclined planes, only in spiral form. Screw jacks, which you can use to lift your house up to build a new foundation, are a combination of a lever and an inclined plane.

Easing your effort: Pulleys and gears

Pulleys and gears are simple machines that can be used to change the magnitude (size) and direction of force. When you ride in an elevator, step onto an escalator, drive your car, or wind up your watch, you're using pulleys and gears.

Block and tackle systems

When used in a *block and tackle* arrangement (see Figure 12-5), pulleys make lifting heavy objects easier. In block and tackle systems, pulleys can also be used to change the direction of your pull. If you tie a 200-pound crate to one end of a rope, run the rope through a pulley, and grab the other end of the rope, you can pull down on the rope to lift the crate up. Without a pulley, you could pull down on the crate all day, and it wouldn't go up. In this case, using a simple pulley, the force of your pull must equal the weight of the object being lifted. The regular pulley doesn't multiply your force, but it makes the process of lifting easier.

Using a block and tackle allows you to distribute your force more effectively. Instead of hoisting that entire 200-pound crate in one try, you can pull on a rope to lift it a few inches, pull on the rope some more to lift it a few more inches, and so on. This makes the work easier to perform.

A block and tackle system can also be used to reduce effort by magnifying force. To help understand how this works, look at Figure 12-6:

- Example 1 shows a 100-pound box secured to the ceiling by a single line. The weight supported by the line is equal to the weight of the box.

- In Example 2, the box is secured to the ceiling by using two lines. Each line is supporting one-half the weight of the box.

- In Example 3, a single line is threaded through a pulley. Although the line (as a whole) is supporting the entire weight of the box, each section of the line is supporting only one-half of the box's weight, just as in Example 2.

- In Example 4, a man is using this principle to lift the 100-pound box by applying only 50 pounds of force. In short, this block and tackle system provides the man with a mechanical advantage of 2. In receiving a mechanical advantage of force, the man must pull the rope farther than if he weren't using a pulley. In this example, the man would have to pull 2 feet of rope to raise the box 1 foot.

Additional pulleys can be added to a block and tackle arrangement to further increase the mechanical advantage. Figure 12-7 shows a couple of examples:

- In Example 1, three sections of rope produce a mechanical advantage of 3. Lifting a weight with this pulley arrangement requires only ⅓ of the effort required to lift the weight directly. However, in order to lift the crate 1 foot, you have to pull 3 feet of rope.

- Example 2 illustrates a block and tackle system with six sections of rope. Using this arrangement provides you with a mechanical advantage of 6, but you have to pull the rope 6 feet for every foot you want to raise the box.

Figure 12-5: A pulley used in a block and tackle system.

HOOK

SWALLOW

CHEEK (EITHER FACE)

SHEAVE

STRAP

PIN

BREECH

SHELL (ENTIRE OUTER PART)

Block and tackle (pulley)

EFFORT

200-pound crate

Figure 12-6:
Reducing
effort by
using a
block and
tackle.

Figure 12-7:
Two
examples
of a block
and tackle
arrange-
ment.

Understanding how gears work

Machines often use gears to transmit motion from one place to another. An additional advantage of using gears is that they can be used to change direction, increase or decrease speed, or increase or decrease force.

Gears arranged in a series turn in the opposite direction of each other. If you have an even number of gears connected in a series, the first and last gear turn in opposite directions. If you have an odd number of gears aligned in a series, the first and last gear spin in the same direction. Look at Figure 12-8. Gear 1 is rotating counterclockwise, which causes Gear 2 to turn clockwise, resulting in Gear 3's spinning counterclockwise, with Gear 4 turning clockwise.

Figure 12-8:
The motion
of gears
with an
even num-
ber of gears
aligned in a
series.

The speed at which a gear rotates (in relation to the driving gear connected to it) depends on the number of teeth. In Figure 12-9, Gear 1 has six teeth, and Gear 2 has eight teeth. This relation of teeth can be expressed as a ratio of 6:8, which can be further reduced to 3:4. That means that Gear 1 has to rotate four times in order for Gear 2 to make three revolutions. Or expressed another way, for each rotation made by Gear 1, Gear 2 will make three-quarters of a revolution.

Figure 12-9:
The ratio
of teeth
between
two gears
affects
rotational
speed.

When gear shafts aren't parallel to one another, *bevel gears* can be used to connect gears that have shafts at different angles. The principles of gear rotation remain the same. Figure 12-10 shows an example of bevel gears designed to connect shafts having a 90-degree angle to the other.

Figure 12-10:
Two bevel
gears meet
at a right
angle.

Pulley and belt arrangements

In addition to magnifying force as part of a block and tackle system, pulleys have another use. When connected by a system of belts, pulleys can drive other pulleys.

Like gears, pulleys are used to transmit motion from one location to another. However, the physical properties of pulleys are different from those of gears:

- **Turning direction:** Unless the driving belt is reversed (twisted), pulleys connected in series rotate in the same direction. Figure 12-11 illustrates this concept with two sets of pulleys. In the first set of pulleys, all the pulleys turn in the same direction (counter-clockwise) as the driving pulley. However, in the second set of pulleys, the driving pulley and the lower pulley are rotating counterclockwise, but the right-hand pulley is rotating in a clockwise direction because the belt is twisted.

Driving Pulley

Driving Pulley

Figure 12-11: Pulleys rotate in the same direction unless the belt is reversed.

- **Speed of rotation:** Although the speed of gear rotation is determined by the number of teeth, how fast a pulley rotates depends on the diameter of the pulley in relation to the diameter of the pulley that's driving it. Have a look at Figure 12-12. Pulley A has a diameter of 1 inch, Pulley B has a diameter of 2 inches, and Pulley C measures 4 inches in diameter. The ratio among the three pulleys is 1:2:4. For every complete revolution made by Pulley A, Pulley B makes half of a revolution. Each time Pulley B makes a full revolution, Pulley C makes half of a revolution. Thus, for every full revolution of Pulley A, Pulley C makes a quarter of a revolution.

Multiplying your effort: Wheels and axles

The *wheel-and-axle* machine multiplies the effort you use, producing a greater force. When you steer a car by using a steering wheel (which is a wheel-and-axle device), a little effort exerted on the steering wheel turns the wheels of the car in the direction you desire. Turning your car wheels would be a lot more complicated if you didn't have the steering wheel.

In true wheel-and-axle machines, the wheel and the axle are fixed together and turn at the same time. This arrangement multiplies the amount of force you can exert by a considerable amount.

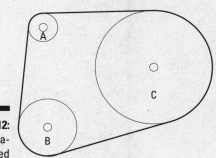

Figure 12-12:
Pulley rotation speed
is based on
the pulley's
diameter.

Pulley A Diameter = 1 inch
Pulley B Diameter = 2 inches
Pulley C Diameter = 4 inches

The relationship between the radius of the wheel and the radius of the area to which force is being applied determines the mechanical advantage you receive by using this piece of equipment. (Remember, the radius of a circle equals half the diameter; a straight line extending from the center of the circle to the edge is the *radius* of a circle.) A hand drill may apply 200 pounds of force for your 10 pounds of effort. (A hand drill uses a gear to convert the direction of the force.) See Figure 12-13.

Force required
to turn handle
(E)

Radius of
wheel's circle
(R)

Mechanical advantage of
wheel and axle =

$$\frac{R}{\frac{1}{2}W} = \frac{S}{E}$$

Resistance
offered by
material **(S)**

Figure 12-13:
A hand drill.

Width of
drill tip **(W)**

Getting a grip on things with vises

Although many mechanisms are designed to transmit motion, some machines have the purpose of keeping things motionless. Vises are very useful because they can close around items and hold them with great force (much greater force than you could do by holding the item in your hands). Figure 12-14 shows an illustration of a standard shop vise.

Figure 12-14:
A standard
shop vise.

Rotating the handle on the vise causes a screw to turn, which either tightens or loosens the vise. A *screw* is a cylinder wrapped in a continuous spiral. The distance between the ridges of the spiral is called the *pitch* of the thread. The greater the pitch of the thread, the farther the jaws of the vice move for each revolution of the handle. However, there's a trade-off. Larger pitches require more force to rotate the handle than screws with smaller pitches do.

Magnifying your force with liquid: Hydraulic jacks

A *hydraulic jack* uses a nearly incompressible liquid, such as oil, to exert force in order to move an object (see Figure 12-15). As the handle moves, it applies pressure to the oil. Because the oil doesn't compress, the oil transmits whatever force is applied to it to the work cylinder with no (or little) loss in efficiency. The mechanical advantage is the ratio between the diameters of the two cylinders.

In the figure, the small cylinder has a diameter of 1 inch and the large cylinder has a diameter of 4 inches. This difference in diameter results in a mechanical advantage of 4. If the rocks weigh a total of 100 pounds, only 25 pounds of force has to be applied to the piston in the small cylinder in order to lift the load. However, although the force required is reduced by a factor of 4, the smaller piston has to move 4 feet for every foot the piston in the larger cylinder moves.

Figure 12-15:
A hydraulic
jack.

Working Your Way to a Better Test Score

When you take the Mechanical Comprehension subtest, you may not know the correct answer to a question, or you may not know the mechanical principle involved. You may know the mechanical principle but not remember the formula you need to come up with the right answer. Never fear — you can still stumble through this test without totally flaming out.

Using your observations and common sense

Questions on this subtest often include illustrations. The ASVAB test-makers expect you to look at the illustrated device and guess how it operates. When you run across these types of questions, make sure that you understand the illustration. Often, parts of the device are labeled. Make certain you read and understand these labels before you try to answer a question about the illustration.

Also, try to use a common-sense approach. You may see the following question:

Which of the following controls an automatic sump pump?

(A) mechanical switch

(B) manual switch

(C) pneumatic valve

(D) float

You may not know the answer to this question, but you can rule out Choice (B), manual switch, because the question asks you about an automatic sump pump, and anything manual isn't automatic. Eliminating one choice narrows your chances from one in four to one in three. Not a bad start, huh?

A *sump pump* is used to drain water from an area, and if you know that, you have an even better shot at getting this question right. Think about what type of device detects the presence of water, and you may guess correctly that Choice (D), float, is the right answer.

You can answer a lot of the questions correctly if you just think about what you've observed in the world around you. Remember, the Mechanical Comprehension subtest also tests your knowledge of physical principles of the world around you — questions you may expect to find on the General Science subtest. For example, a question may ask something like this:

If all the following objects are the same temperature, which one will feel coldest on a cool day?

(A) a wooden spoon

(B) a plastic spoon

(C) a metal spoon

(D) a fiberglass spoon

You don't need to know mechanical or scientific principles to know that a metal spoon will feel colder than the other spoons. So it makes sense to select Choice (C) as your answer, even if you can't explain the science behind this correct answer.

The nerve endings in your skin detect the difference between your inside body temperature and your outside skin temperature. Metal is an excellent conductor of heat, so heat readily flows from your hand into the metal. The heat is conducted rapidly away into the bulk of the metal, leaving your skin surface relatively cool. That's why metal feels cooler than other, less efficient conductors of heat, such as wood, plastic, or fiberglass.

Using the mathematics of mechanics

Mechanical principles are based on mathematical principles. Therefore, a screw making a complete revolution turns 360 degrees, because a mathematical principle states that 360 degrees are in a circle, a complete revolution. If you have to know the surface area of a floor in order to determine the pounds per square inch that a ton of tile would put on the floor, that's a mathematical principle, too (Area = Length × Width).

Suppose you run across this question:

A 3-inch-diameter flanged pipe with six holes is being fitted to a base with six holes. What's the maximum number of degrees the pipe must be rotated in order to line up the holes?

(A) 120 degrees

(B) 180 degrees

(C) 60 degrees

(D) 360 degrees

This isn't really a Mechanical Comprehension question at all — it's a math question. The only part that requires mechanical knowledge is knowing that the holes are spaced equally distant from one another on a flanged pipe. The answer is 360 degrees ÷ 6 = 60 degrees, Choice (C).

Guessing with a mechanical mind

Like most of the other subtests on the ASVAB, you can and should guess on the Mechanical Comprehension subtest when you don't know the answer. Check out these tips to help you narrow the field:

- ✔ The amount of force needed to move an object (not including friction resistance) is never greater than the weight of the object. Any answer that includes a force that's greater than the weight of the object being moved is probably wrong.

- ✔ The correct answer is a mechanical answer. For example, if the question asks, "What's the purpose of lubricating oil in an engine?" the correct answer won't be "to make the parts look shiny." The answer may be "to reduce friction between moving parts."

- ✔ Any change in a mechanical operation almost always has pluses and minuses associated with it. So when a question proposes a change, the correct answer is probably the one that specifies the good, the bad, and the ugly. For instance, suppose the question says, "Enlarging the wheel on a hand drill will . . . ?" The correct answer is the one that says something like "increase the mechanical advantage and decrease the amount of effort needed to operate the drill."

For more general tips on guessing on the ASVAB, flip to Chapter 3.

Chapter 13

Electronics Information

• •

In This Chapter

▶ Understanding current, voltage, power, and more

▶ Comprehending electrical flow

▶ Deciphering circuit diagrams

▶ Amplifying your test score

• •

When I was around 12 years old, I impressed my parents by taking an old television set apart and putting it back together. I impressed them right up to the point where I plugged it in and blew up the garage. But the world of electronics is a bit more complex than simply plugging something in and seeing whether it works. I (and the garage) learned this lesson the hard way.

Six years later, when I took the ASVAB, I scored very well on the Electronics Information subtest. (Go figure!) This subtest is designed to measure your knowledge of the principles of electricity and how these principles are applied in the real world. You may see questions about transistors, magnets, engines and motors, and radio and television. (Curiously, there are no questions on this subtest concerning the impromptu demolition of garages.)

You don't have to be an electronics whiz to score well on this subtest. If you're not familiar with this information and you want to pursue a military career that requires you to do well on this subtest, this chapter is calling your name. You also need to have some familiarity with basic mathematical and algebraic principles (see Chapters 7 and 8 for more information).

Not every military career requires a good score on this subtest. (Turn to Appendix A to find out which military jobs require a score on this — and other — subtests.) If the military feels that the Electronics Information subtest is important to your desired career, study intensively for this test. You can even take a course or two at the local community college if you don't have a strong enough background in this area.

You have 9 minutes to answer 20 questions on this subtest on the paper version of the ASVAB and 8 minutes to answer 16 questions on the computerized ASVAB. Although 8 or 9 minutes is sufficient time to answer the questions, it doesn't provide much time for anything else — if you don't know an answer, guess and go.

Uncovering the Secrets of Electricity

One day in 1752, Benjamin Franklin was minding his own business, flying a kite in a storm. A key was tied to the kite string and when lightning struck the metal key, Ben was struck by the notion that lightning must be electrified air (well, it happened something like that).

Although electricity was just a hobby for Ben Franklin, he made many important contributions. As a result of his famous kite flight, he created many of the terms used today when folks talk about electricity: battery, conductor, condenser, charge, discharge, uncharged, negative, minus, plus, electric shock, and electrician.

Electricity is a general term for the variety of phenomena resulting from the presence and flow of electric current. You can't see electricity running through a wire (but you can certainly feel it). You only know electricity is there when you flip on the light switch and the light turns on. Even though electricity appears to be pretty mysterious at first glance, scientists understand a great deal about its properties and how it works.

Electricity is measured in three different ways:

- ✔ **Volts:** Volts measure the difference of potential between two points.

- ✔ **Amperes (amps):** Amps measure the number of electrons that move past a specific point in 1 second.

- ✔ **Ohms:** Ohms measure resistance, including anything that could limit the flow of electrons.

Here are some other electricity terms that are important for you to know for the ASVAB:

- ✔ **Current:** Electricity is like water — it flows. Electrical current occurs when electrons move from one place to another. The use of *conductors,* such as copper and water, allows the electrons to move freely. *Insulators,* such as rubber and wood, discourage the electric current.

- ✔ **Watt:** A watt measures *power,* the rate at which electrical energy is consumed or transformed into another type of energy, such as light or heat.

- ✔ **Watt-hour:** A *watt-hour* is the amount of energy used in 1 hour at a rate of 1 watt. Most electricity is measured in *kilowatt-hours,* which is how much energy you'd use if you ran a 1,000-watt (1-kilowatt) device for an hour. For example, 10 kilowatt-hours is enough energy to run a 10,000-watt speaker system for an hour-long outdoor concert, or it could run a 5,000-watt air conditioner for 2 hours or a 1,000-watt waffle iron for 10 hours. You find watt-hours by multiplying wattage by time (expressed in hours).

The following sections explain electricity in more detail.

Measuring voltage: Do you have the potential?

A *circuit* is just the path of an electrical current. A very simple circuit consists of several components. For example, it may consist of a battery, one side *(terminal)* of which is connected by a conductor (a wire) to an on/off switch, which is connected to a lamp (a light bulb) by another wire, which is then connected back to the other side of the battery. As long as the switch is off — which means it's set to a position so that there's an *open* (literally an open space) in the circuit — current cannot flow. When you flip the switch, there's a *short* (meaning the open space has been closed), and current can flow from one side of the battery, through the closed switch, through the light bulb, and back to the other terminal of the battery, all by way of the wires connecting the components.

Voltage, which is supplied by the battery in this circuit, is the difference of the pressure between two points in a circuit. It is sometimes called the *voltage drop* or *difference of potential.* So, for instance, a 9-volt battery supplies 9 volts of electricity. To see what the voltage is anywhere in a circuit, you have to compare the voltage at that point to ground. *Ground* is any part of a circuit (or other object that has electricity running through it) that measures

0 volts, such as the case of your radio, the base of a lamp, or the chassis of your car. The negative terminal of a 9-volt battery is at ground potential, so the voltage from the negative terminal to ground will measure 0 volts. The voltage from the positive terminal to either ground or the negative terminal of the battery will measure 9 volts.

To measure voltage in a circuit, you use a *voltmeter* or a *multimeter,* which has several meters in one instrument. A voltmeter has two leads. To measure voltage, you place one lead somewhere in the circuit and one lead at another location in the circuit. The voltmeter tells you what the voltage is between those two points.

A cell (a storage compartment for electricity in a battery) has a specific voltage. For example, in a particular battery, cells may be 1.5 volts. Therefore, you can figure out the number of cells a battery has by dividing the voltage of the battery by 1.5. Pretty handy stuff, huh?

Examining the current of the electrical river

Electrons are negatively charged, and they attempt to shift from one atom to the next, to the next, trying to get to a positive charge, such as the positive side of a battery. They're able to shift if the material is a conductor. But if the material is an insulator, the electrons will be much, much less able to shift because of the insulating material's molecular structure.

Electrical current is the flow — or, more precisely, the rate of flow — of electrons in a conductor. Current flow can be expressed in terms of coulombs (abbreviated C), which measure charge. A *coulomb* is the amount of electricity provided by a current of 1 ampere flowing for 1 second. It's called a coulomb because a guy named Charles de Coulomb discovered it in the late nineteenth century, and the rules say that if you discover something, someone will stick your name on it (not sure who made up those rules, though).

If 1 coulomb (about 6,241,500,000,000,000,000 electrons) flows past a specified point in 1 second, that's a flow rate of 1 *ampere* (amp, abbreviated A). An ampere represents the strength of a current. For the sake of convenience, electrical currents are measured in amps. Typically current is tiny, so small that it's measured in milliamperes; 1 *milliampere* is one-thousandth of an ampere. Current meters, called *ammeters,* measure the flow of current through a circuit.

The amount of voltage (the difference in potential) and the resistance in a circuit determine the number of amperes along a wire — or whatever you're using to conduct the electricity from one place to another. More voltage (for instance, a higher-voltage battery) means that more amps flow in a wire (or conductor). You can read more about this relationship in the next section, which discusses Ohm's law.

Resistance: Slowing the electrical river

Current doesn't just flow in any properly working circuit unimpeded. Resistance pops up along the way. If the flow of electricity needs to be regulated, resistance is deliberately set up in a circuit. If the flow weren't regulated, the motors powering devices like can openers and microwave ovens would quickly overheat and melt. (But before that happens, hopefully a fuse would blow or a circuit breaker would trip, halting current flow and saving the equipment.) In a sense, even a wire, such as a filament in a light bulb, is a type of resistance and is a way to deliberately create circuit resistance.

Adding or removing resistance

Sometimes a circuit must be opened in order to add or remove resistance. In other words, the flow of the electricity must be interrupted in order to physically change the resistance. Using a *circuit breaker,* which is a device that automatically interrupts the electrical current, is an example of opening a circuit to control the current. When the circuit breaker *trips,* the electrical device can no longer operate.

Some devices use a *rheostat,* which can vary the resistance without opening the circuit — the device can continue to work even as the resistance is altered. If an application doesn't use all the electricity, the rheostat absorbs it. A dimmer switch on a light is an example of a rheostat. You increase the amount of resistance to dim the light and decrease the resistance to brighten the light.

Ohm's law: Relating resistance to current and voltage

The amount of resistance that interferes with the flow is measured in *ohms* (pronounced just like those yoga chants). The symbol for ohm is the Greek letter omega, which looks like an upside-down horseshoe: Ω. Resistance can be measured by dividing the voltage measured at any given point (the voltmeter reading) by the amount of current at the same point in a circuit (the ammeter reading). Or you can measure the resistance directly by an ohmmeter.

If you have a current flowing through a wire, three influences are present:

- The amount of voltage, measured in volts
- The resistance to the current, measured in ohms
- The amount of current, measured in amps

These three units are always present in a specific relationship to each other. If you know the value of any two of the influences, you can find the value of the third. (Yes, this requires more math. Sorry.)

Ohm's law, which was first stated by Georg Simon Ohm, reads, "The current in a circuit is directly proportional to the applied voltage and inversely proportional to the circuit resistance," but it's actually easier to understand in mathematical terms. When stating the relationship mathematically, abbreviations are used, where I is current, E is voltage, and R is resistance:

$$\text{Current (amperes)} = \frac{\text{Voltage (volts)}}{\text{Resistance (ohms)}}, \text{ or } I = \frac{E}{R}$$

This essentially means that current in a basic circuit is always dependent on the voltage and resistance in the circuit. If you use a higher-voltage battery (increase E), the resistance doesn't change, but current in the circuit increases. By the same token, if you leave the same battery in the circuit but increase the resistance (increase R), current decreases.

Here are two other ways to write the same formula, solved for voltage and resistance:

- Voltage = Current $\times$ Resistance, or $E = IR$
- Resistance $= \dfrac{\text{Voltage}}{\text{Current}}$, or $R = \dfrac{E}{I}$

Ohm's law works exactly the same, no matter which format you use.

Measuring power

Power is measured in *watts*. One watt is a very small amount of power. It would require nearly 750 watts to equal 1 horsepower. One kilowatt represents 1,000 watts.

A *kilowatt-hour* (kWh) — the amount of electricity a power plant generates or a customer uses — is equal to the energy of 1,000 watts working for one hour. Kilowatt-hours are determined by multiplying the number of kilowatts (kW) required by the number of hours of use. For example, if you use a 40-watt light bulb 5 hours a day, you've used 200 watt-hours, or 0.2 kilowatt-hours of electrical energy.

The term *watt* was named to honor James Watt, the inventor of the steam engine.

Getting around to circuits

Although this section suggests that electricity flows like water, it actually flows more like NASCAR. Electricity must be sent along the path of a closed circle (a circuit), just like all those NASCAR speedsters roaring around the track. The drivers never actually get anywhere; they just keep driving in circles. Electrical charges are a lot like that.

However, electricity does flow like a river in one respect. In general, electricity follows the path of least resistance. The conventional way in thinking about the electrical flow of current is based on that the vacancies left by electrical particles "moving" from the positive (+) terminal to the negative (–) terminal of a battery. This concept is called *conventional current*. However, the military teaches current flow based on the flow of the electrons, and electrons, no matter how you look at them, flow from the negative terminal to the positive terminal (see Figure 13-1).

Figure 13-1:
A simple electric current.

Terminal

If any of the wires leading from one terminal to the other is broken, the circuit is shot — no more current. Current can't flow because under most circumstances, the electrons can't bridge the open gap in a conductor (the open gap is basically air, and air is an insulator).

In some cases, current does flow through an insulator — if there's enough difference of potential (voltage). When lightning bridges an expanse of air from a cloud to ground (or a tree or a golfer), it's because there is a huge amount of voltage, on the order of 100 million volts between the source of the lightning and (literally) ground.

Here's another circuit problem that may come up: A *short circuit* occurs when any wire accidentally crosses over another wire, causing the electricity to bypass the rest of the circuit and not follow the intended path.

Magnetic, electric: No, not your personality

Certain magnetic effects always accompany an electric current, and these effects follow definite laws. In a wire, the *magnetic lines of force* (imaginary lines used to explain magnetic effects) are perpendicular to the conductor and parallel to each other.

But when you wrap a wire around a core and pass current through it, the wire forms a coil. As the lines of force around the core take on a different shape, the field around each turn of wire links with the fields from the other turns of wire around it. The combined influence of all the turns of wire produce a two-pole magnetic field, very much like the magnetic field of a simple bar magnet — one end of the coil is a *north pole;* the other end is a *south pole.*

The strength of the magnetic field depends on several factors. Here are the main ones:

✔ **Number of turns:** If you increase the number of turns, you increase the field strength.

✔ **Closeness of the turns:** The closer the turns, the stronger the field.

✔ **Amount of current:** If you increase current, you increase field strength.

✔ **Material in the core:** Most coils are classified as either air or soft iron, based on their cores. *Air coils* are usually wrapped around a piece of cardboard; *soft-iron coils* are wrapped around a piece of iron. Soft iron offers a better path for magnetic lines of force because its high permeability offers less reluctance to magnetic flux, resulting in more lines of force. (Think of *magnetic flux* as a measurement of magnetic strength located on a two-dimensional surface. A good example of magnetic flux would be the magnetic strength of one side of a magnet.) The more lines of force, the stronger the magnetic field.

Passing a suspended loop of conductive material (wire) through a magnetic field creates *electromagnetic induction,* which is the basic principle behind the electric generator. When the conductor is standing still, current doesn't flow through it. But when the loop starts to rotate clockwise through the lines of force of the magnets, the lines of force induce free electrons to move through the wire.

Producing electrical effects

Electric currents can produce different effects. These effects are packaged and sold commercially. The following is a description of effects produced by current and some of their commercial applications:

✔ **Chemical effect:** Current produces this effect when it passes through a chemical compound and breaks that compound up. Also called *electrolytic decomposition,* this phenomenon is used in *electroplating,* a process used to cover objects with a very thin coating of metal.

✔ **Heat effect:** Conducting electricity causes wires to become heated. Heat develops because the current must overcome the resistance of the wire. This heat energy can be quite obvious or hardly noticeable to touch, depending on the size of the wire and the amount of current.

✔ **Magnetic effect:** When a wire is introduced into a magnetic field, electricity flows through the wire and creates a magnetic field that repels a magnet. This effect is used to create energy through *electromagnetic induction,* the basic principle behind the electric generator. If the wire is wrapped around an iron core and a current is sent through the wire, the iron becomes magnetized. (See the nearby sidebar for more on the magnetic effect.)

✔ **Physiological effect:** Current produces this effect when it passes through your bicep (or any of your muscles for that matter) and causes the muscle to contract. This effect is used in medicine.

Switching Things Up with Alternating and Direct Current

A current doesn't always flow in one direction. A *direct current* (DC) does — it only and always flows in one direction. An *alternating current* (AC), however, constantly changes direction in a regular pattern. Higher voltages are easier to obtain with alternating current, and transferring high voltage down a power line is ultimately cheaper than transferring low voltage, so most electricity comes in the form of AC. The following sections cover some important points about alternating and direct current.

Figuring out frequency

The number of times an alternating current changes direction per second is known as its *frequency.* Hertz (Hz) is the unit of measurement for frequency. One hertz (Hz) equals one complete cycle per second. In other words, the current makes two complete alternations of direction.

The AC (alternating current, not the air conditioner) in your house probably completes 60 alternating cycles per second. Therefore, the AC in your house has a frequency of 60 Hz. Most electronic devices operate at higher frequencies; therefore, frequencies may be measured in kilohertz (kHz, 1,000 hertz), megahertz (MHz, 1 million hertz) or even gigahertz (GHz, 1 billion hertz).

AM radio stations often broadcast in the 530–1,700 kHz range. Television stations may broadcast at as low as 7 to as high as 1,002 MHz. Radar operates in the 1–40 GHz range.

Impedance: Join the resistance!

Resistance interferes with the flow of current in a circuit. But the flow of current is also impeded by two properties of alternating currents:

- **Capacitive reactance (capacitance):** Capacitance is the storage of energy that occurs in a nonconductor. This property resists any change in voltage in a circuit.

- **Inductive reactance (inductance):** Inductance is the property that causes an electromotive force (another way of saying *voltage*) to be induced in a circuit.

These two types of reactance combine to impede the flow of current. Impedance can be expressed as the ratio of electromotive force to the current:

$$\text{Impedance} = \frac{\text{Electromotive force}}{\text{Current}}$$

Electronic devices often require a specific capacitive or inductive reactance to work. *Capacitors* and *inductors* are devices used in circuits to provide the type of reactance needed. Capacitors are rated in microfarads (μF), and inductors are rated in millihenries (mH).

You can relate impedance to Ohm's law in reference to AC circuits. Simply substitute resistance in Ohm's law with impedance and voltage with electromotive force.

Sorting out capacitors and inductors

Capacitors store or hold a charge of electrons. In an AC circuit, because AC voltage goes positive and negative in each cycle, the capacitor is constantly charging and discharging. The rate of the charging and discharging acts as opposition to the changing AC voltage — as a resistive effect called *capacitive reactance.*

Inductors are coils of wire that make use of the properties of a magnetic field. The property specifically desired is the flow of current through the wire. With full current, the magnetic field is at its maximum. However, if you take away the current, the field doesn't disappear immediately. It decays gradually, and the decay continues to push electrons in the path they were going. But in an AC circuit, the current constantly reverses. The rate of changing current flow and the resulting collapse and regeneration of the magnetic field in the coil act as opposition to changing AC current — a resistive effect called *inductive reactance.*

Rectifying the situation: Going direct

Certain electronic circuits are engineered to change alternating current to direct current. The process of making the change is called *rectification,* and the circuits that perform the rectification are called *rectifiers.*

Rectifiers contain *semiconductor diodes,* a component made of a material with conductivity somewhere between that of a conductor and an insulator. *Diodes* conduct electricity in only one direction. Rectification also often requires inductors and capacitors (see the preceding section).

Rectification helps appliances run at cooler temperatures and allows them to run at variable speeds. Devices typically need direct current to run properly. The process of rectification changes the incoming AC to DC.

Turning up the old transistor radio

A transistor is a *semiconductor* (an object that conducts electricity poorly at low temperatures) that controls the flow of electricity in a circuit. It's usually made of germanium or silicon. This electrical device can amplify a signal, which is why it's used in transistor radios. Transistors have many properties:

✔ Unlike rectifier diodes (see the preceding section), a transistor doesn't require a vacuum to operate.

✔ Transistors are small, require little power, and last a long time.

✔ A transistor contains at least three terminals:

- The *emitter* is the voltage output.

- The *base* acts like a gate, and the voltage at the base controls the flow of current through the transistor (and therefore the voltage).

- The *collector* is the voltage input.

Picture It: Decoding Electrical Circuit Codes

Electronic circuits can be combined to create *complex systems,* such as those required to operate a stereo system. *Block diagrams* are used to show the various combined circuits that form a complex system.

Many of the questions on the Electronics Information subtest require you to identify an electronic component symbol and know what that component does in an electronic circuit. Figure 13-2 shows the most common component symbols. The figure's items are grouped based on similarity of functions. For example, cells, batteries, DC power supplies, and AC power supplies all have similar functions (they supply power to the circuit).

So, what do all these electronic doodads do when connected in a circuit? I cover each item in the following list:

- **Wires:** Wires are used to pass current from one part of the component to another. Wires that are connected to each other are indicated by a dark circle and are called *joined wires.* Sometimes in complex circuit diagrams, it's necessary to draw wires crossing even though they aren't connected. In this case, the dark circle is omitted, or a hump symbol is drawn to make it clear the wires aren't connected — this is called *unjoined wires.*

- **Cell:** A cell supplies electrical current. Some call this a battery, but technically a battery is more than one cell. The large terminal (on the left side of the cell image in Figure 13-2) is positive.

- **Battery:** A battery is two or more cells. The large terminal is positive.

- **DC power supply:** A DC power supply provides direct current. Direct current always flows in one direction.

- **AC power supply:** An AC power supply provides alternating current. Alternating current constantly changes direction at a specific frequency.

- **Fuse:** A fuse is a safety device that *blows* (melts) if the current flowing through it exceeds a specified value.

- **Transformer:** A transformer consists of two coils of wire linked by an iron core. Transformers are used to step up (increase) and step down (decrease) AC voltages. No electrical connection exists between the coils. Energy is transferred between the coils by the magnetic field in the core.

- **Ground:** A ground is a connection to the earth.

- **Transducer:** A transducer is a device that converts energy from one form to another. Here are various types of transducers:

  - **Lighting lamp:** Converts electrical energy to light, such as in a light bulb or automobile headlight

  - **Indicator lamp:** Converts electrical energy to light for such uses as a warning light on a car's dashboard

  - **Motor:** Converts electrical energy to kinetic energy (motion)

  - **Heater:** Converts electrical energy to heat

  - **Bells and buzzers:** Convert electrical energy to sound

  - **Microphone:** Converts sound to electrical energy

  - **Earphones and speakers:** Convert electrical energy to sound

Figure 13-2:
Symbols in
electronic
circuit
diagrams.

✔ **Inductor:** An *inductor* is a coil of wire that creates a magnetic field when current passes through it.

✔ **Switch:** Here are several types of switches:

- **Push switch:** A push switch allows current to flow only when the button is pressed, such as in a doorbell.

- **Push-to-break switch:** With this switch, the circuit is normally closed (the device is on), and the circuit is open (device is off) only when the button is pressed.

- **On/off switch:** An on/off switch allows current to flow only when it's in the closed (on) position.

- **Two-way switch:** A two-way switch directs the flow of current to one of two routes, according to its position.

- **Dual on/off switch:** This type is often used to switch main electricity because it can isolate both the live and neutral connections.

- **Relay (relay switch):** A relay is an electrically operated switch that may operate multiple switches at one time. Current flowing through a coil sets up a magnetic field, which causes the lever(s) to move, effectively changing the (relay) switch's position(s).

✔ **Resistor (nonvariable):** There are two different versions of the basic resistor symbol. Resistors restrict the flow of electric current. Resistors are rated in ohms and have a color code on them to indicate their value, tolerance, and sometimes quality. The band code is as follows:

- Black is 0
- Brown is 1
- Red is 2
- Orange is 3
- Yellow is 4
- Green is 5
- Blue is 6
- Violet is 7
- Gray is 8
- White is 9

The first and second bands on the resistor are the first two digits in the resistor's value. The next band indicates the multiplier (number of zeros after the first two numbers). So if the first band is red, the second is yellow, and the third band is orange, the resistor's value is 24,000 ohms. A gold or silver band after the first bands indicates tolerance, and a quality band may follow the tolerance band.

✔ **Variable resistor:** Variable resistors also restrict the flow of electric current. There are several symbols in use in circuit diagrams for standard variable and preset variable resistors. Types of variable resistors include the following:

- **Rheostat:** A type of variable resistor with two contacts, usually used to control current; examples of controlling current would be adjusting lamp brightness or adjusting motor speed

- **Potentiometer:** A type of variable resistor with three contacts that's used to control voltage

- **Preset variable resistor:** A device that operates with a small screwdriver or similar tool; it's designed to be set when the circuit is made and then left without further adjustment

✔ **Capacitor:** Capacitors store electric charge. They're used with resistors in timing circuits because it takes time for a capacitor to fill with charge. They're also used in filter circuits because capacitors easily pass AC (changing voltage) signals but they block DC (constant voltage) signals. Two types of capacitors include the following:

- Polarized capacitors must be connected the correct way in circuit.

- Variable capacitors are used most often in radio tuning circuits.

✔ **Diode:** Diodes allow electricity to flow in only one direction. The arrow of the circuit symbol shows the direction in which the current can flow. Diodes are the electrical version of a valve, and early diodes were actually called *valves.* Light-emitting diodes (LEDs) emit light when an electric current passes through them. Specialized diodes, called *Zener diodes,* do allow current in the opposite direction after a threshold is met.

✓ **Transistor:** Transistors amplify current. For example, they can be used to amplify the small output current from a logic chip so it can operate a lamp, relay, or other high-current device.

✓ **Amplifier:** An amplifier isn't actually an electronic component but instead is a complex circuit. The block diagram symbol shows where an amplifier circuit would be connected. Amplifier circuits are used to magnify power, current, or voltage.

✓ **Antenna:** An antenna is a device designed to receive and/or transmit radio signals.

Circuit diagrams show how electronic components are connected together. These diagrams show the connections as clearly as possible with all wires drawn neatly as straight lines. The actual layout of the components is usually quite different from the circuit diagram, however. Circuit diagrams are useful when testing a circuit and for understanding how it works. Figure 13-3 shows a diagram of an adjustable timer circuit. See how many components you can identify.

Adjustable Timer Circuit

Figure 13-3:
An adjustable timer circuit.

Eyeing Some Electronic Information Test Tips

When it comes to the electronics test, don't feel like you have to know as much as Ben Franklin to get a passing score. Just use your common sense. If a question asks, "What's the safest way to run an extension cord to a reading light?" the answer "across the middle of the floor" is probably going to be wrong.

You can also figure out quite a few answers if you remember these units of measure:

✓ **Current:** Amperes (or amps)

✓ **Voltage:** Volts

✓ **Resistance:** Ohms

✓ **Power:** Watts

✓ **Energy:** Watt-hours

Memorizing simple principles

If you commit the following principles to memory, you'll have an easier time succeeding on the Electronics Information subtest:

- Ohm's law: $\text{Current} = \dfrac{\text{Voltage}}{\text{Resistance}}$

- Power (watts) = Voltage (volts) × Current (amperes), or $P = EI$

- Current flows from a negative pole to a positive pole.

- A closed circuit must exist for electricity to flow. (Think NASCAR.)

- Alternating current (AC) changes direction constantly at a constant rate. The number of times a current completes two alternations of direction per second is known as its *frequency;* the unit of measurement for frequency is the hertz (Hz).

- Electronic devices operate at very high frequencies.

- Electronic devices often require a specific capacitive or inductive reactance to work. Capacitors and inductors are devices used in circuits to provide the type of reactance needed.

- Devices that change alternating current to direct current are called *rectifiers.*

- A *transistor* can amplify a signal.

If you need a good score on this subtest to get your military dream job or you want to rebuild that old television set without sacrificing your garage, you may want to check out *Electronics For Dummies* by Gordon McComb and Earl Boysen (Wiley) for additional help.

Playing the guessing game

The Electronics Information subtest is the type of test where you either know the answer or you don't. But if you don't know the answer, you should still guess. Remember, you don't have a lot of time to ponder the answer choices. Guess and move on. To increase your chances of guessing correctly, you can often eliminate an incorrect answer.

Sometimes one answer is obviously wrong, or one answer is more obviously right than another. The electronics answer is usually the right answer. Therefore, an answer that has to do with how much something costs or how pretty it looks will probably be wrong.

Not all questions are specifically electronics questions. You may be asked, "A mil measures what quantity?" Think about how you've seen that prefix used before, such as in the word *millimeter.* A millimeter, you may remember, is one-thousandth of a meter. So you may be safe in assuming that a mil is one-thousandth of an inch. For additional guessing help, flip back to Chapter 3.

Chapter 14

Assembling Objects

· ·

In This Chapter

▶ Checking out the newest ASVAB subtest

▶ Connecting the dots and putting the pieces together

▶ Getting your test score into shape

· ·

Although much of the ASVAB measures academic knowledge at the high school level, Assembling Objects is a subtest that probably doesn't resemble any of your high school classes (unless your high school offered a course in Jigsaw Puzzles 101).

The Assembling Objects subtest is designed to measure your ability to look at pieces of an object and determine how those pieces should fit together (technically called *visualizing spatial relationships*). Spatial skills, which help people figure out maps and interpret technical drawings, are important to everyday living as well as for performing well in school and on the job. Society today places greater demands on spatial skills, such as interpretation of graphs, maps, architectural drawings, and X-rays.

The Assembling Objects subtest of the CAT-ASVAB consists of 16 graphical problems that must be solved in 15 minutes; the paper version of the ASVAB has 25 questions to be solved in 15 minutes. That gives you a little less than a minute for each question (not counting any time you take out to scratch your head). That's plenty of time to finish if you're good at jigsaw puzzles.

Getting the Picture about Assembling Objects

The Assembling Objects subtest is relatively new to the ASVAB. It was added when the ASVAB was revised in 2005, when the Numerical Operations and Coding Speed subtests were deleted. First it was added only to the computerized version of the ASVAB, and then it was added to the paper enlistment version about a year later. If you're taking the high school version of the ASVAB or the in-service version (Armed Forces Classification Test), you won't see this subtest.

At the time of this writing, only the Navy uses the score from the Assembling Objects subtest for job qualification purposes. Additionally, only a handful of ratings (what the Navy calls *jobs*) require a score in this area. The other branches don't use the results of this subtest at all, but they may in the future. For details about which Navy enlisted jobs require a score in this area, see Appendix A.

The upshot is that unless you're planning to join the Navy, in one of only a handful of Navy enlisted jobs, you can safely ignore this entire chapter. Don't say I never gave you a gift.

Adopting the AO subtest

It's interesting that the Navy is the only service to use scores from the Assembling Objects subtest, because it was an Army study that brought this subtest to life. Way back in 1994, the Army concluded a study called *Project A.* (Kind of makes you wonder if the people in charge of naming military projects were on vacation that week, doesn't it?) Project A was all about trying to improve the selection and classification of enlisted personnel. The Assembling Objects subtest was a major product of this effort. The U.S. Army Research Institute for the Behavioral and Social Sciences found Assembling

Objects questions to be an excellent measure of both overall spatial ability and complex problem-solving skills.

The Army developed two types of Assembling Objects questions and tested them under field conditions for a few years. A mere ten years later, the Department of Defense incorporated the subtests into the ASVAB. (You just got to love the speed at which the military makes changes.) By that time, the Army had decided that they really didn't need to use this new subtest at all. But the Navy said, "Hey, that looks pretty cool . . . let's give it a try!"

Two Types of Questions for the Price of One

The Assembling Objects subtest has two types of questions, both of which consist of five separate drawings. In the first drawing, you see a picture with various disassembled parts, followed by four drawings that show the parts assembled or connected. Your task is to choose the drawing that shows what the parts may actually look like after they're assembled or connected properly.

Both types of Assembling Objects problems require you to perform *mental rotation* — a process through which you predict what an array of objects would look like if they were rotated or turned by some number of degrees.

Putting slot A into tab B: Connectors

The first type of problem presents you with simple geometric figures such as stars, cloud shapes, letter shapes, circles, and triangles. In the first drawing, you can see shapes and lines labeled with dots and the letters *A* and *B.* These letters and dots indicate points of attachment.

The next four drawings show possible solutions of what the shapes would look like if connected at designated points by the line. The shapes may be reoriented or rotated from what you observe in the first drawing. The correct solution shows the line connected correctly to reflect the points shown in the first drawing.

Look at Figure 14-1 and see whether you can solve it. In the first drawing, you see a star and a sort of lopsided T. There's a small dot on the short appendage of the T, labeled *A,* and a dot on one of the points of the star, labeled *B.*

Figure 14-1:
Identifying
points and
shapes.

In Figure 14-1, Choice (A) is the correct solution. Choices (B) and (C) include shapes that aren't included in the first drawing, so they're obviously incorrect. Although Choice (D) has the correct shapes, they aren't connected at the same points depicted in the first drawing.

Okay that sounds simple, doesn't it? Don't worry; it gets more complicated (sorry to burst your bubble). Figure 14-2 shows the same problem but with a different twist.

Figure 14-2:
Rotated shapes make the problem harder.

Choice (A) is the correct solution for the problem in Figure 14-2. In this case, the two shapes have been repositioned and rotated.

On the flip side: Avoiding mirrors

Mirroring (or flipping or reflecting) isn't the same as rotation, as Figure 14-3 illustrates. The shape in Box B isn't the same as the shape in Box A. It's a mirror image. No matter how you rotate the shape in Box A, it will never look like the shape in Box B. Think of it this way — although you can turn a jigsaw puzzle piece upside down so the picture side is facing the table, it may fit, but that's not the proper method of putting the puzzle together. (It wouldn't look very pretty, either.) The Assembling Objects subtest is the same way. The possible solutions may include shapes that are reflections of a shape shown in the first drawing, but they'll never be the correct solution.

Figure 14-3:
Figuring out mirrored shapes (A and B) and rotated shapes.

Crossing over the right places

If a shape in the first drawing shows a line that goes through any part of the shape, the correct solution must also reflect the same line-shape relationship. Check out Figure 14-4. In the first drawing, Point B is in the center of the star. But note the line intersects the star at one of its indentations and not one of its points. That means the correct solution shows the same intersection.

Figure 14-4:
Line-shape relation-ships.

In this example, Choice (B) is the correct solution. At first glance, Choice (C) looks like it could be correct. Can you spot the reason it's not the correct solution? Right! The lopsided T shape in the image is a reflection of the shape shown in the first drawing.

Putting it all together

You're starting to see the shape of things! (I'm sorry, but these little zingers just keep popping out.) Try a couple more, just to get into shape. Look at Figure 14-5.

Figure 14-5:
Another example of spatial relationships.

In Figure 14-5, did you select Choice (C) as the correct answer? If so, good job! Choice (A) is incorrect because the line intersects the triangle at the wrong point and conection point A is misplaced. Choice (B) is incorrect because the weird shape is actually a mirror image of the shape shown in the first drawing. Choice (D) is incorrect because the points don't correlate to the points depicted in the first drawing.

Now try Figure 14-6. The first drawing includes a shape that kind of looks like a Y and a shape that looks like the letter C.

Figure 14-6:
More shapes to test your spatial skills.

The correct answer for the problem shown in Figure 14-6 is Choice (B). Choice (A) is incorrect because the Y shape is a mirror image of the shape shown in the first drawing, and the connection points don't correspond to the first drawing's points. Choice (C) is incorrect because the Y shape is a mirror image of the shape shown in the first drawing. Choice (D) is incorrect because the Y shape is a different shape (the stem is much shorter) than the shape shown in the first drawing and because the connection dot on the C shape is in the wrong location.

Solving the jigsaw puzzle: Shapes

Many people may find the second type of Assembling Objects problem easier than the connection problems. This type of problem is very much like a jigsaw puzzle, except it doesn't result in a picture of the Statue of Liberty or a map of the United States. Also, there's a heck of a lot fewer pieces than that 1,000-piece puzzle your parents kept insisting on buying you. The difficulty lies in the fact that you can't use your hands to twist the pieces around on the table in order to see how they fit. You have to rotate and move the pieces mentally.

In Figure 14-7, the solution is pretty straightforward.

Figure 14-7:
A simple jigsaw example.

By mentally sliding the shapes in the first drawing together, it's easy to see that they fit together to form the picture shown in Choice (A). Look at Figure 14-8.

Figure 14-8:
Putting the pieces together with rotation.

Choice (A) is the correct answer. The figure shown in Choice (A) is the same as the figure depicted in Choice (A) of Figure 14-7, except it's been rotated.

The previous two figures were warm-up exercises — the questions on the ASVAB are harder. Check out Figure 14-9 for a better representation of the types of questions on the ASVAB.

Figure 14-9:
A harder example of spatial problems.

Pay attention to the curve of the leaf shape inside the square. It's not bowed out as in Choice (B) — the edges have more of a wave shape. Choice (C) has that shape too thin. If you selected Choice (D) as the correct solution, give yourself a pat on the back. Examining spatial relationships can help locate the correct answer with ease. Try a couple more examples to see if you've gotten the hang of it. Check out Figure 14-10.

Figure 14-10:
Practice mentally rotating and relocating pieces of puzzles.

In Figure 14-10, Choice (B) is the correct answer. Mentally rotate and relocate the pieces in the first picture until you can see how they fit together to form the shape in Choice (B). In the puzzle, three pieces have both a curved edge and a single straight edge. Practice eliminating choices that lack these characteristics. Choice (A) lacks these shapes, so you can discount it right away. Notice the curved pieces are all different sizes. Visualize fitting these pieces of the puzzle in your mind and compare the sizes and differences. Now try Figure 14-11.

Figure 14-11:
Putting the pieces of the puzzle together with your mental spatial skills.

In Figure 14-11, Choice (A) is the correct answer. If you didn't get this one quite right, head to Chapter 15 for additional practice and Chapters 16, 18, and 20 for practice examinations.

Tips for the Assembling Objects Subtest

In the following sections, I offer some tips for improving your score on the Assembling Objects subtest. I offer strategies for eliminating wrong answers during the test, and I name some ways you can improve your spatial skills in general (which may come in handy the next time you have to read a map, too).

Comparing one piece or point at a time

On the Assembling Objects subtest, you can sometimes improve your odds of getting the answer right if you select just one shape from the first drawing and then quickly look at each of the choices to see whether that shape is represented there but in a different orientation. This process can help you quickly eliminate answer choices that are obviously wrong.

On connection-type problems, note the position of the dot on one of the shapes in the first drawing and then quickly scan the possible answers, eliminating any choice that depicts the dot in a different location or that shows the line passing through the shape at a different point than shown in the first drawing.

Remember to be aware of mirror images — shapes that are reflected (instead of rotated) from the image shown in the first drawing. The tricky test-makers often make use of such mirror representations to see whether they can trick your eyes.

Visualizing success: Practicing spatial skills ahead of time

Researchers at the University of Chicago have determined that your basic foundation for spatial skills is established at a very early age, perhaps as young as age 4 or 5. But don't worry. That doesn't mean all is lost if your parents never got you that model rocket kit you wanted. The same research has concluded that you can still improve spatial skills by engaging in activities that are spatially orientated. Some of those activities include the following:

- **Practicing reading maps:** Map reading can help you develop the ability to gauge scales of size and direction between related objects (roads, rivers, towns, cities, and so on).

- **Putting together jigsaw puzzles:** This way is an obvious form of practice for improving your spatial perceptions.

- **Playing puzzle games online:** Many puzzle games at free online game sites exercise the skill of identifying spatial relationships and visual similarities.

- **Playing graphical computer games:** Computer games may help you to improve your spatial skills. A study conducted in the United Kingdom showed that children who played computer games consistently scored higher on spatial aptitude tests than children who didn't play the games.

- **Sketching:** Look at an object or a picture and attempt to sketch it as viewed from a different view. This exercise can help you to improve your ability to mentally visualize angles.

Chapter 15

Facing the Facts: Technical Skills Practice Questions

··

In This Chapter

▶ Taking a stab at General Science questions

▶ Getting a handle on Auto & Shop Information

▶ Practicing your Mechanical Comprehension knowledge

▶ Tuning in to the Electronics Information section of the ASVAB

▶ Building a better score on an Assembling Objects practice test

··

It's time to see a few examples of what the ASVAB technical skills questions look like. None of these subtests are used in calculating your AFQT score (the score used to determine your general qualification to join the military), but they may be used in computing the line score you need to get the military job you want. See Appendix A to determine whether you need to do well on any of these subtest areas for the job that you want.

On the actual paper version of the ASVAB (and on the full-length practice tests in Part V of this book), you get 25 General Science questions, 25 Auto & Shop questions, 25 Mechanical Comprehension questions, 20 Electronics Information questions, and 25 Assembling Objects graphical problems. The CAT-ASVAB gives you 16 General Science questions, 16 Electronics Information questions, 11 Auto Information questions, 11 Shop Information questions, 16 Mechanical Comprehension Questions, and 16 Assembling Objects questions. I don't want you to tire out too quickly, so in this chapter, you get only eight sample questions in each area.

General Science Practice Questions

General science is a hard topic to study for because the field is so broad. To score well on this subtest, you pretty much have to wade through the textbooks and memorize the facts. You can also check out Chapter 10 for additional help. See how well you do on the following eight practice questions.

1. If the temperature in Fahrenheit is 212 degrees, the temperature in Celsius is

   (A) 0 degrees.

   (B) 32 degrees.

   (C) 100 degrees.

   (D) 106 degrees.

   Measured in Celsius, the boiling point of water is 100 degrees. If you don't have this memorized, you can calculate it. To convert from Fahrenheit to Celsius, use the formula $C = \frac{5}{9}(F - 32)$. The correct answer is Choice (C).

2. A cell nucleus is often referred to as the

   (A) control center.

   (B) cytoskeleton.

   (C) cell membrane.

   (D) chromosome.

   The nucleus contains most of the cell's genetic material and is often referred to as the *control center* of the cell, so the correct answer is (A).

3. The human circulatory system

   (A) uses air to release energy.

   (B) processes food and eliminates waste.

   (C) moves oxygenated blood throughout the body.

   (D) controls movement of joints.

   The *respiratory system* uses air to release energy, the *digestive system* processes food and eliminates waste, and the *musculoskeletal system* controls the movement of joints. The correct answer is Choice (C).

4. Compasses work by

   (A) measuring heat in the air.

   (B) reacting to magnetic fields.

   (C) repulsing wave currents.

   (D) magic.

   A compass is a device that takes advantage of the Earth's magnetic field. Choice (B) is the correct answer.

5. If an atom has one proton and one electron, the atomic number is

   (A) 2

   (B) 10

   (C) 5

   (D) 1

   The *atomic number* refers to the number of protons an atom has in its nucleus. Choice (D) is the correct answer.

6. The element with the lowest atomic number is

   (A) hydrogen.

   (B) helium.

   (C) lithium.

   (D) uranium.

   Hydrogen has an atomic number of 1. The atomic numbers for the other elements listed are 2 (helium), 3 (lithium), and 92 (uranium). The correct answer is Choice (A).

7. Absolute zero is equivalent to

   (A) 0 degrees Kelvin.

   (B) 0 kelvins.

   (C) –273.15 degrees Kelvin.

   (D) –273.15 kelvins.

   Absolute zero is –273.15 degrees Celsius, which is equivalent to 0 kelvins. Temperatures stated in the Kelvin scale are measured by using units of kelvins, not degrees. The correct answer is Choice (B).

8. A comet's tail is visible when

   (A) the metal alloys react to the atmospheric change.

   (B) the ice and rock collide.

   (C) the comet is close enough to the sun.

   (D) the comet passes the Kuiper Belt.

   Comets are balls composed mainly of ice and rock. The comet's tail is formed when the ice turns into gas from the heat of the sun; therefore, the comet must be closer to the sun for the tail to be visible. The correct answer is Choice (C).

Auto & Shop Information Practice Questions

If you like to tinker with cars and your idea of a fun weekend is to rebuild the engine, you should do well on this subtest without too much additional study. If your idea of fixing your car involves calling that guy down the street, a little extra study may be in order. Check out Chapter 11 for help with this area.

9. A two-penny nail is

   (A) thicker than a 10d nail.

   (B) shorter than a 10d nail.

   (C) the same thing as a 10d nail.

   (D) harder than a 10d nail.

   Penny, abbreviated *d* (for the ancient Roman *denarius* coin), indicates length; a 2d nail is shorter than a 10d nail. Choice (B) is the correct answer.

10. A carburetor has the same function as a/an

   (A) distributor.

   (B) fuel-injection system.

   (C) alternator.

   (D) exhaust system.

   The alternator, exhaust system, and distributor all have very different purposes from the carburetor, which combines the fuel and air mixture and sends it to the engine, just as the fuel-injection system does. Therefore, Choice (B) is the correct answer.

11. An engine's rotational energy is stored by using which mechanical device?

    (A) connecting rod

    (B) rear axle

    (C) flywheel

    (D) cylinder

    The flywheel accelerates a rotor to a high speed and uses rotational energy to maintain and store the energy to keep the engine speed constant as the flywheel and rotor work together. The correct answer is Choice (C). As for the other devices, the drive shaft turns the rear axle. The cylinder contains the piston that moves the connecting rod that's connected to the crankshaft, which turns the flywheel.

12. A *hacksaw* is used to cut

    (A) with the grain of wood.

    (B) against the grain of wood.

    (C) round stock.

    (D) metal.

    The hacksaw has a blade specifically designed to cut metal, not wood. Choice (D) is the correct answer.

13. To drive a cold chisel, the best object to use would be

    (A) a frozen hammer.

    (B) a warm sledge.

    (C) a mallet.

    (D) your foot.

    A hammer has a smaller, harder striking surface than a mallet. A mallet won't damage the chisel (or the object being chiseled, should the mallet slip off the chisel). A sledge is exceptionally large and heavy and is therefore inappropriate for this use. Temperature of the striking object is irrelevant. Choice (C) is the correct answer.

14. Which of the following is NOT normally part of an automotive tune-up?

    (A) Replace the air filter.

    (B) Replace the spark plugs.

    (C) Replace the CV axles.

    (D) Check the fluids.

    A general automotive tune-up consists of checking/replacing the following: air and fuel filter, belts, spark plugs, distributor cap, battery, clutch (if it's manual), engine timing, fluids, ignition timing, and valves. You can also change the positive crankcase ventilation valve and change the points and condenser if you have an older vehicle. Replacing the CV (constant velocity) axles is something that is accomplished when they become worn. Choice (C) is the correct answer.

15. Antifreeze is used to

    (A) prevent the engine from overheating.

    (B) prevent water in the cooling system from freezing.

    (C) prevent damage to the engine block.

    (D) all of the above

    Antifreeze raises the boiling point of water and lowers the freezing point. This process keeps the water in the cooling system from boiling away or freezing. Either condition can cause damage to the engine. The correct answer is Choice (D).

16. The best tool for cutting curves or shapes in wood is a

    (A) ripsaw.

    (B) crosscut saw.

    (C) coping saw.

    (D) pliant saw.

    Coping saws have thin blades with many teeth and are specifically designed to cut curves and shapes in wood. The correct answer is Choice (C).

Mechanical Comprehension Practice Questions

Mechanical comprehension is all about figuring out how machines and mechanical mechanisms operate. A solid background in mechanical physics is a big advantage in scoring well in this area. You can flip back to Chapter 12 if you need additional help with mechanical info. Basic math skills are also a plus in this area. Test yourself with the next several questions.

17. The moisture that forms on the inside of a window on a cold day is called

    (A) condensation.

    (B) distillation.

    (C) evaporation.

    (D) tarnation.

    Distillation is the process of extracting or refining a substance using both boiling and condensation. *Evaporation* is the process of removing moisture from the surface of a liquid — the water molecules escape the surface and assume gas form. *Tarnation* is an interjection used to express anger. The correct answer is Choice (A), condensation.

18. If a 200-pound barrel must be lifted 4 feet to the bed of a box truck, an inclined plane will reduce the amount of effort required to move the barrel by half if the inclined plane is

    (A) 2 feet long.

    (B) 6 feet long.

    (C) 8 feet long.

    (D) 9 feet long.

    The formula used for determining how an inclined plane reduces effort is Length of Ramp ÷ Height of Ramp = Weight of the Object ÷ Force, or $x \div 4 = 200 \div 100$. The amount of force needed to lift the object is equivalent to the object's weight, but the question wants to reduce that amount of force to half, so half of the object's weight is 100. Now do the math: $x \div 4 \times 4 = 2 \times 4$; $x = 8$. The correct answer is Choice (C).

19. Two people are carrying a 100-pound crate on a 2- x 8- x 12-foot board. To distribute the load evenly between the two people, the crate should be placed

    (A) 2 feet from the end of the board.

    (B) in the middle of the board.

    (C) 3 feet from the end of the board.

    (D) The load can't be evenly distributed.

    If the weight is placed closer to one person or the other, that person would carry more of the load, so the weight should be placed in the middle. Choice (B) is the correct answer.

20. Wheel A has a diameter of 9 feet. Wheel B has a diameter of 12 feet. If both wheels revolve at the same rate, Wheel B will cover a linear distance of 24 feet

    (A) at the same speed as Wheel A.

    (B) more slowly than Wheel A.

    (C) in half the time of Wheel A.

    (D) more quickly than Wheel A.

    Because Wheel A has a smaller circumference, it covers a shorter linear distance than Wheel B when turning at the same rate. Thus, Wheel B covers the distance of 24 feet faster than Wheel A. Choice (C) is inaccurate because the diameter of Wheel A is not exactly half the diameter of Wheel B. If both wheels revolve at the same rate, then Wheel A turns 25% more slowly than Wheel B, because Wheel A's diameter is three-quarters of Wheel B's. Choice (D) is the correct answer.

21. Not including friction, a stationary single pulley gives a mechanical advantage of

    (A) 2.

    (B) 4.

    (C) 3.

    (D) 1.

    A stationary single pulley allows you to change the direction of force but doesn't result in an increased mechanical advantage. The correct answer is Choice (D).

22. Four gears are connected in a series. If Gear #1 is turning clockwise, Gear #4 will turn

    (A) clockwise.

    (B) counterclockwise.

    (C) more quickly than Gear #1.

    (D) more slowly than Gear #1.

    Gears connected in series turn in opposite directions of each other. Gears 1 and 3 rotate clockwise, and Gears 2 and 4 rotate counterclockwise. The size of gears is unknown, so there isn't enough information to determine whether (C) or (D) is correct. The correct answer is Choice (B).

23. The sideways force one feels when a car turns sharply is often called

    A) thrust force.

    (B) angle force.

    (C) centrifugal force.

    (D) positive force.

    Although commonly referred to as *centrifugal force,* this property isn't actually a force at all but is rather a property of inertia, one of Newton's laws of motion. As the car turns, your body is trying to continue traveling in a straight line. The correct answer is Choice (C).

24. When two or more forces act to balance each other out, the condition is called

    (A) equilibrium.

    (B) static recoil.

    (C) gravitational balance.

    (D) concurrent forces.

    When two or more forces interact so that their combination cancels the other(s) out, there's a state of equilibrium. In this state, the velocity (speed and direction) of an object doesn't change. Choice (A) is the correct answer.

Electronics Information Practice Questions

The questions in this section measure your knowledge of basic electronics principles. Chapter 13 contains a more in-depth discussion of electronics if you need some help. For now, give these questions a try.

25. What does the abbreviation DC stand for?

    (A) duplicate charge

    (B) direct charge

    (C) direct current

    (D) diode current

    DC stands for *direct current.* I made up the other choices. The correct answer is Choice (C).

26. Which of the following is the ohm symbol?

    (A) Σ

    (B) Δ

    (C) Φ

    (D) Ω

    Remember, the upside-down horseshoe (the Greek letter omega) is the symbol for ohm, the measure of electrical resistance. The correct answer is Choice (D).

27. Which of the following has the least resistance?

    (A) iron

    (B) rubber

    (C) silver

    (D) wood

    Silver is the best conductor of electricity of those listed here. Therefore, it offers the least resistance to an electric current. The correct answer is Choice (C).

28. What is the point at which electrical connections (such as two wires) are made?

    (A) terminal

    (B) trigger

    (C) transmitter

    (D) transformer

    A *terminal* is a device that connects electrical circuits together, a *trigger* initiates a circuit action, a *transmitter* is a device used to achieve transmission, and a *transformer* is an inductor with two or more windings. *Windings* are magnetic wires that are coated with enamel and wrapped around the core of a transformer. The primary winding is driven by transistors, and the secondary winding is driven by the core's magnetic field, produced by the primary winding. Choice (B) is the correct answer.

29. A device used to amplify a signal is called a

    (A) diode.

    (B) transformer.

    (C) rectifier.

    (D) transistor.

    A *diode* is a semiconductor that conducts electricity in one direction only; a *transformer* is a device that changes voltage (either "transforming" low voltage to high voltage or high voltage to low voltage); a *rectifier* is a circuit that changes alternating current to direct current. Choice (D) is the correct answer.

30. The amount of electrical power is measured in units called

    (A) volts.

    (B) amperes.

    (C) watts.

    (D) ohms.

    A *watt* measures the amount of power, the rate at which energy is produced or used. The correct answer is Choice (C).

31. Components designed to store electrical charge are called

    (A) capacitors.

    (B) transformers.

    (C) resistors.

    (D) transistors.

    Capacitors store electric charge. They're used with resistors in timing circuits because it takes time for a capacitor to store voltage (to become charged). The correct answer is Choice (A).

32. In an electronic circuit diagram, the symbol used to show wires' connecting is a/an

    (A) X symbol.

    (B) dot.

    (C) dark square.

    (D) T symbol.

    Wires connected to each other are indicated by a darkened circle. The correct answer is Choice (B).

Assembling Objects Practice Questions

Assembling Objects questions measure your spatial skills. There are two types of questions: connecting questions and putting-pieces-together questions. The first type presents you with simple geometric figures such as stars, cloud shapes, letter shapes, circles, and triangles. Your task is to choose the answer that shows the shapes properly connected together at the designated points. The second type of question is similar to putting a jigsaw puzzle together. Choose the answer that best shows what the shapes in the first drawing would look like if assembled together. See Chapter 14 for a complete explanation and illustrated examples.

33.

Note that the bottom figure in the first drawing has a line that intersects the short side of the trapezoid shape, so (C) and (D) are wrong. Connection point A is at the tip of the mitten shape, so (A) is wrong as well. The correct answer is Choice (B).

34.

Mentally rotate and reposition the shapes in the first drawing until you can see how they fit together to form the shape shown in Choice (C) — the correct answer. In the first drawing, notice that the shape at the upper right resembles a shark fin — it has two sharp points, and the third point is curved. Choice (C) is the only image that contains this shape (it's at the bottom).

35.

If you selected Choice (A), you were fooled. The arrow shape shown in Choice (A) is a mirror of the shape depicted in the first drawing. The correct answer is Choice (D).

36.

Mentally rotate and reposition the shapes in the first drawing until you can see how they fit together to form the shape shown in Choice (A) — the correct answer. If you had trouble with this one, notice that the piece in the center of the upside-down heart should have a corner that dips a bit on the left. Choice (C) has the dip in the center, and Choice (D) has it on the right, so these answers are wrong. Choice (B) has only three pieces.

37.

Note that both shapes in the first drawing have lines that intersect the shapes at designated points. If you selected Choice (B), your eyes were fooled by mirror images. The correct answer is Choice (D).

38.

Mentally rotate and reposition the shapes in the first drawing until you can see how they fit together to form the shape shown in Choice (B) — the correct answer. Here, you can take a mental snapshot of the largest shape and look for it in the answers — (B) is the only choice that has it. Verify that this is the right answer by recognizing that (B) is also the only answer that contains a segment of a circle, at the top.

39.

Don't be fooled by the mirror shape in Choice (B), because the correct answer is Choice (A).

40.

Mentally rotate and reposition the shapes in the first drawing until you can see how they fit together to form the shape shown in Choice (C), which is the correct answer. Here, you may note that the first drawing contains two shapes that resemble triangles with one side curved inward. Choice (C) is the only image that contains those shapes.

Part V
Practice ASVAB Exams

The 5th Wave   By Rich Tennant

"Excuse me. I'm a dog. Can I still take the CAT-ASVAB?"

In this part . . .

Doing well on the ASVAB requires an effective study plan. You want to concentrate your study time on subject areas you may be having problems with. The practice examinations in this part are great tools to enhance and plan your study program.

Take the first test in this section to determine your strengths and weaknesses. Concentrate most of your study efforts on subject areas that are hard for you. When you think you've got it down, take the second test to measure your improvement. Take the third test right before you're ready to take the actual ASVAB to brush up on your test-taking skills.

In this part, you also find a bonus Armed Forces Qualification Test (AFQT) practice exam. This practice test includes only the four ASVAB subtests that are used to make up your AFQT score — the score that determines whether you can even join the military branch of your choice.

Not only does taking the sample tests help you understand what you need to study, but it also gets you into the test-taking mindset. By taking the tests, you get used to the format of each subtest. Trust me — these sample tests will give you confidence on test day.

Chapter 16

Practice Exam 1

• •

*T*his sample test features nine subtests, just like the ASVAB. As you may have guessed, the sample tests in this book are paper-based tests. (Yes, I'm a master of the obvious.) When you take the actual ASVAB, it may be a paper-based or computer-based exam. The computer version has the same subtests as the paper version, but it follows a different time format and has a different number of questions.

Another difference with the computer-based test is that you can't skip a question and go back to it, and you can't change an answer after you enter it into the computer. Check out the computer-based test in greater detail in Chapter 3, and experience computer-based practice tests at *ASVAB For Dummies Online.*

To get the most out of this sample test, take it under the same conditions as the real ASVAB:

- ✔ Allow yourself about 3 hours to take the entire exam, and take the whole thing at one time.

- ✔ Find a quiet place where you won't be interrupted.

- ✔ Bring a timer that you can set for various lengths of time, some scratch paper (you get two pieces during the exam, but you can get more; just ask for it as needed), and a pencil.

- ✔ At the start of each subtest, set your timer for the specified period of time. Don't go on to the next section until the timer has gone off, and don't go back to a previous section. If you finish early, check your work for that section only.

- ✔ Use the answer sheet that's provided.

- ✔ Don't take a break during any subtest. You can take a short one- or two-minute break between subtests if you need it.

After you complete the entire sample test, check your answers against the answers and explanations in Chapter 17.

Your primary goal with this sample test is to determine your strengths and weaknesses. If you miss only one question on the Word Knowledge subtest but you miss 15 on Arithmetic Reasoning, you know where to spend your study time. If you're not going to pursue a career that requires a score on a particular subtest or the type of knowledge a subtest covers, don't worry about your score there. (See Appendix A for information on the subtests that various careers require good scores on.)

Answer Sheet for Practice Exam 1

Subtest 1: General Science

1 Ⓐ Ⓑ Ⓒ Ⓓ	6 Ⓐ Ⓑ Ⓒ Ⓓ	11 Ⓐ Ⓑ Ⓒ Ⓓ	16 Ⓐ Ⓑ Ⓒ Ⓓ	21 Ⓐ Ⓑ Ⓒ Ⓓ
2 Ⓐ Ⓑ Ⓒ Ⓓ	7 Ⓐ Ⓑ Ⓒ Ⓓ	12 Ⓐ Ⓑ Ⓒ Ⓓ	17 Ⓐ Ⓑ Ⓒ Ⓓ	22 Ⓐ Ⓑ Ⓒ Ⓓ
3 Ⓐ Ⓑ Ⓒ Ⓓ	8 Ⓐ Ⓑ Ⓒ Ⓓ	13 Ⓐ Ⓑ Ⓒ Ⓓ	18 Ⓐ Ⓑ Ⓒ Ⓓ	23 Ⓐ Ⓑ Ⓒ Ⓓ
4 Ⓐ Ⓑ Ⓒ Ⓓ	9 Ⓐ Ⓑ Ⓒ Ⓓ	14 Ⓐ Ⓑ Ⓒ Ⓓ	19 Ⓐ Ⓑ Ⓒ Ⓓ	24 Ⓐ Ⓑ Ⓒ Ⓓ
5 Ⓐ Ⓑ Ⓒ Ⓓ	10 Ⓐ Ⓑ Ⓒ Ⓓ	15 Ⓐ Ⓑ Ⓒ Ⓓ	20 Ⓐ Ⓑ Ⓒ Ⓓ	25 Ⓐ Ⓑ Ⓒ Ⓓ

Subtest 2: Arithmetic Reasoning

1 Ⓐ Ⓑ Ⓒ Ⓓ	7 Ⓐ Ⓑ Ⓒ Ⓓ	13 Ⓐ Ⓑ Ⓒ Ⓓ	19 Ⓐ Ⓑ Ⓒ Ⓓ	25 Ⓐ Ⓑ Ⓒ Ⓓ
2 Ⓐ Ⓑ Ⓒ Ⓓ	8 Ⓐ Ⓑ Ⓒ Ⓓ	14 Ⓐ Ⓑ Ⓒ Ⓓ	20 Ⓐ Ⓑ Ⓒ Ⓓ	26 Ⓐ Ⓑ Ⓒ Ⓓ
3 Ⓐ Ⓑ Ⓒ Ⓓ	9 Ⓐ Ⓑ Ⓒ Ⓓ	15 Ⓐ Ⓑ Ⓒ Ⓓ	21 Ⓐ Ⓑ Ⓒ Ⓓ	27 Ⓐ Ⓑ Ⓒ Ⓓ
4 Ⓐ Ⓑ Ⓒ Ⓓ	10 Ⓐ Ⓑ Ⓒ Ⓓ	16 Ⓐ Ⓑ Ⓒ Ⓓ	22 Ⓐ Ⓑ Ⓒ Ⓓ	28 Ⓐ Ⓑ Ⓒ Ⓓ
5 Ⓐ Ⓑ Ⓒ Ⓓ	11 Ⓐ Ⓑ Ⓒ Ⓓ	17 Ⓐ Ⓑ Ⓒ Ⓓ	23 Ⓐ Ⓑ Ⓒ Ⓓ	29 Ⓐ Ⓑ Ⓒ Ⓓ
6 Ⓐ Ⓑ Ⓒ Ⓓ	12 Ⓐ Ⓑ Ⓒ Ⓓ	18 Ⓐ Ⓑ Ⓒ Ⓓ	24 Ⓐ Ⓑ Ⓒ Ⓓ	30 Ⓐ Ⓑ Ⓒ Ⓓ

Subtest 3: Word Knowledge

1 Ⓐ Ⓑ Ⓒ Ⓓ	8 Ⓐ Ⓑ Ⓒ Ⓓ	15 Ⓐ Ⓑ Ⓒ Ⓓ	22 Ⓐ Ⓑ Ⓒ Ⓓ	29 Ⓐ Ⓑ Ⓒ Ⓓ
2 Ⓐ Ⓑ Ⓒ Ⓓ	9 Ⓐ Ⓑ Ⓒ Ⓓ	16 Ⓐ Ⓑ Ⓒ Ⓓ	23 Ⓐ Ⓑ Ⓒ Ⓓ	30 Ⓐ Ⓑ Ⓒ Ⓓ
3 Ⓐ Ⓑ Ⓒ Ⓓ	10 Ⓐ Ⓑ Ⓒ Ⓓ	17 Ⓐ Ⓑ Ⓒ Ⓓ	24 Ⓐ Ⓑ Ⓒ Ⓓ	31 Ⓐ Ⓑ Ⓒ Ⓓ
4 Ⓐ Ⓑ Ⓒ Ⓓ	11 Ⓐ Ⓑ Ⓒ Ⓓ	18 Ⓐ Ⓑ Ⓒ Ⓓ	25 Ⓐ Ⓑ Ⓒ Ⓓ	32 Ⓐ Ⓑ Ⓒ Ⓓ
5 Ⓐ Ⓑ Ⓒ Ⓓ	12 Ⓐ Ⓑ Ⓒ Ⓓ	19 Ⓐ Ⓑ Ⓒ Ⓓ	26 Ⓐ Ⓑ Ⓒ Ⓓ	33 Ⓐ Ⓑ Ⓒ Ⓓ
6 Ⓐ Ⓑ Ⓒ Ⓓ	13 Ⓐ Ⓑ Ⓒ Ⓓ	20 Ⓐ Ⓑ Ⓒ Ⓓ	27 Ⓐ Ⓑ Ⓒ Ⓓ	34 Ⓐ Ⓑ Ⓒ Ⓓ
7 Ⓐ Ⓑ Ⓒ Ⓓ	14 Ⓐ Ⓑ Ⓒ Ⓓ	21 Ⓐ Ⓑ Ⓒ Ⓓ	28 Ⓐ Ⓑ Ⓒ Ⓓ	35 Ⓐ Ⓑ Ⓒ Ⓓ

Subtest 4: Paragraph Comprehension

1 Ⓐ Ⓑ Ⓒ Ⓓ	4 Ⓐ Ⓑ Ⓒ Ⓓ	7 Ⓐ Ⓑ Ⓒ Ⓓ	10 Ⓐ Ⓑ Ⓒ Ⓓ	13 Ⓐ Ⓑ Ⓒ Ⓓ
2 Ⓐ Ⓑ Ⓒ Ⓓ	5 Ⓐ Ⓑ Ⓒ Ⓓ	8 Ⓐ Ⓑ Ⓒ Ⓓ	11 Ⓐ Ⓑ Ⓒ Ⓓ	14 Ⓐ Ⓑ Ⓒ Ⓓ
3 Ⓐ Ⓑ Ⓒ Ⓓ	6 Ⓐ Ⓑ Ⓒ Ⓓ	9 Ⓐ Ⓑ Ⓒ Ⓓ	12 Ⓐ Ⓑ Ⓒ Ⓓ	15 Ⓐ Ⓑ Ⓒ Ⓓ

Subtest 5: Mathematics Knowledge

1 Ⓐ Ⓑ Ⓒ Ⓓ	6 Ⓐ Ⓑ Ⓒ Ⓓ	11 Ⓐ Ⓑ Ⓒ Ⓓ	16 Ⓐ Ⓑ Ⓒ Ⓓ	21 Ⓐ Ⓑ Ⓒ Ⓓ
2 Ⓐ Ⓑ Ⓒ Ⓓ	7 Ⓐ Ⓑ Ⓒ Ⓓ	12 Ⓐ Ⓑ Ⓒ Ⓓ	17 Ⓐ Ⓑ Ⓒ Ⓓ	22 Ⓐ Ⓑ Ⓒ Ⓓ
3 Ⓐ Ⓑ Ⓒ Ⓓ	8 Ⓐ Ⓑ Ⓒ Ⓓ	13 Ⓐ Ⓑ Ⓒ Ⓓ	18 Ⓐ Ⓑ Ⓒ Ⓓ	23 Ⓐ Ⓑ Ⓒ Ⓓ
4 Ⓐ Ⓑ Ⓒ Ⓓ	9 Ⓐ Ⓑ Ⓒ Ⓓ	14 Ⓐ Ⓑ Ⓒ Ⓓ	19 Ⓐ Ⓑ Ⓒ Ⓓ	24 Ⓐ Ⓑ Ⓒ Ⓓ
5 Ⓐ Ⓑ Ⓒ Ⓓ	10 Ⓐ Ⓑ Ⓒ Ⓓ	15 Ⓐ Ⓑ Ⓒ Ⓓ	20 Ⓐ Ⓑ Ⓒ Ⓓ	25 Ⓐ Ⓑ Ⓒ Ⓓ

Subtest 6: Electronics Information

1 Ⓐ Ⓑ Ⓒ Ⓓ	5 Ⓐ Ⓑ Ⓒ Ⓓ	9 Ⓐ Ⓑ Ⓒ Ⓓ	13 Ⓐ Ⓑ Ⓒ Ⓓ	17 Ⓐ Ⓑ Ⓒ Ⓓ
2 Ⓐ Ⓑ Ⓒ Ⓓ	6 Ⓐ Ⓑ Ⓒ Ⓓ	10 Ⓐ Ⓑ Ⓒ Ⓓ	14 Ⓐ Ⓑ Ⓒ Ⓓ	18 Ⓐ Ⓑ Ⓒ Ⓓ
3 Ⓐ Ⓑ Ⓒ Ⓓ	7 Ⓐ Ⓑ Ⓒ Ⓓ	11 Ⓐ Ⓑ Ⓒ Ⓓ	15 Ⓐ Ⓑ Ⓒ Ⓓ	19 Ⓐ Ⓑ Ⓒ Ⓓ
4 Ⓐ Ⓑ Ⓒ Ⓓ	8 Ⓐ Ⓑ Ⓒ Ⓓ	12 Ⓐ Ⓑ Ⓒ Ⓓ	16 Ⓐ Ⓑ Ⓒ Ⓓ	20 Ⓐ Ⓑ Ⓒ Ⓓ

Subtest 7: Auto & Shop Information

1 Ⓐ Ⓑ Ⓒ Ⓓ	6 Ⓐ Ⓑ Ⓒ Ⓓ	11 Ⓐ Ⓑ Ⓒ Ⓓ	16 Ⓐ Ⓑ Ⓒ Ⓓ	21 Ⓐ Ⓑ Ⓒ Ⓓ
2 Ⓐ Ⓑ Ⓒ Ⓓ	7 Ⓐ Ⓑ Ⓒ Ⓓ	12 Ⓐ Ⓑ Ⓒ Ⓓ	17 Ⓐ Ⓑ Ⓒ Ⓓ	22 Ⓐ Ⓑ Ⓒ Ⓓ
3 Ⓐ Ⓑ Ⓒ Ⓓ	8 Ⓐ Ⓑ Ⓒ Ⓓ	13 Ⓐ Ⓑ Ⓒ Ⓓ	18 Ⓐ Ⓑ Ⓒ Ⓓ	23 Ⓐ Ⓑ Ⓒ Ⓓ
4 Ⓐ Ⓑ Ⓒ Ⓓ	9 Ⓐ Ⓑ Ⓒ Ⓓ	14 Ⓐ Ⓑ Ⓒ Ⓓ	19 Ⓐ Ⓑ Ⓒ Ⓓ	24 Ⓐ Ⓑ Ⓒ Ⓓ
5 Ⓐ Ⓑ Ⓒ Ⓓ	10 Ⓐ Ⓑ Ⓒ Ⓓ	15 Ⓐ Ⓑ Ⓒ Ⓓ	20 Ⓐ Ⓑ Ⓒ Ⓓ	25 Ⓐ Ⓑ Ⓒ Ⓓ

Subtest 8: Mechanical Comprehension

1 Ⓐ Ⓑ Ⓒ Ⓓ	6 Ⓐ Ⓑ Ⓒ Ⓓ	11 Ⓐ Ⓑ Ⓒ Ⓓ	16 Ⓐ Ⓑ Ⓒ Ⓓ	21 Ⓐ Ⓑ Ⓒ Ⓓ
2 Ⓐ Ⓑ Ⓒ Ⓓ	7 Ⓐ Ⓑ Ⓒ Ⓓ	12 Ⓐ Ⓑ Ⓒ Ⓓ	17 Ⓐ Ⓑ Ⓒ Ⓓ	22 Ⓐ Ⓑ Ⓒ Ⓓ
3 Ⓐ Ⓑ Ⓒ Ⓓ	8 Ⓐ Ⓑ Ⓒ Ⓓ	13 Ⓐ Ⓑ Ⓒ Ⓓ	18 Ⓐ Ⓑ Ⓒ Ⓓ	23 Ⓐ Ⓑ Ⓒ Ⓓ
4 Ⓐ Ⓑ Ⓒ Ⓓ	9 Ⓐ Ⓑ Ⓒ Ⓓ	14 Ⓐ Ⓑ Ⓒ Ⓓ	19 Ⓐ Ⓑ Ⓒ Ⓓ	24 Ⓐ Ⓑ Ⓒ Ⓓ
5 Ⓐ Ⓑ Ⓒ Ⓓ	10 Ⓐ Ⓑ Ⓒ Ⓓ	15 Ⓐ Ⓑ Ⓒ Ⓓ	20 Ⓐ Ⓑ Ⓒ Ⓓ	25 Ⓐ Ⓑ Ⓒ Ⓓ

Subtest 9: Assembling Objects

1 Ⓐ Ⓑ Ⓒ Ⓓ	6 Ⓐ Ⓑ Ⓒ Ⓓ	11 Ⓐ Ⓑ Ⓒ Ⓓ	16 Ⓐ Ⓑ Ⓒ Ⓓ	21 Ⓐ Ⓑ Ⓒ Ⓓ
2 Ⓐ Ⓑ Ⓒ Ⓓ	7 Ⓐ Ⓑ Ⓒ Ⓓ	12 Ⓐ Ⓑ Ⓒ Ⓓ	17 Ⓐ Ⓑ Ⓒ Ⓓ	22 Ⓐ Ⓑ Ⓒ Ⓓ
3 Ⓐ Ⓑ Ⓒ Ⓓ	8 Ⓐ Ⓑ Ⓒ Ⓓ	13 Ⓐ Ⓑ Ⓒ Ⓓ	18 Ⓐ Ⓑ Ⓒ Ⓓ	23 Ⓐ Ⓑ Ⓒ Ⓓ
4 Ⓐ Ⓑ Ⓒ Ⓓ	9 Ⓐ Ⓑ Ⓒ Ⓓ	14 Ⓐ Ⓑ Ⓒ Ⓓ	19 Ⓐ Ⓑ Ⓒ Ⓓ	24 Ⓐ Ⓑ Ⓒ Ⓓ
5 Ⓐ Ⓑ Ⓒ Ⓓ	10 Ⓐ Ⓑ Ⓒ Ⓓ	15 Ⓐ Ⓑ Ⓒ Ⓓ	20 Ⓐ Ⓑ Ⓒ Ⓓ	25 Ⓐ Ⓑ Ⓒ Ⓓ

Subtest 1: General Science

Time: 11 minutes for 25 questions

Directions: This subtest tests your knowledge of general science principles usually covered in high school classes. Pick the best answer for each question and then mark the space on your answer sheet that corresponds to the letter indicating your choice.

1. Which planet is named after the Greek god who personified the sky?

    (A) Earth

    (B) Mars

    (C) Pluto

    (D) Uranus

2. An animal that eats only meat is called a(n)

    (A) omnivore.

    (B) herbivore.

    (C) carnivore.

    (D) voracious.

3. The chemical process in which electrons are removed from a molecule is called

    (A) respiration.

    (B) recreation.

    (C) oxidation.

    (D) metabolism.

4. What is a single unit of quanta called?

    (A) quantum

    (B) quantumonium

    (C) quantus

    (D) quanfactorial

5. Light waves travel at a rate of about

    (A) 186,000 miles per hour.

    (B) 186,000 miles per minute.

    (C) 18,600 miles per hour.

    (D) 186,000 miles per second.

6. The largest planet in the solar system is

    (A) Earth.

    (B) Mars.

    (C) Saturn.

    (D) Jupiter.

7. The intestines are part of the

    (A) circulatory system.

    (B) nervous system.

    (C) respiratory system.

    (D) digestive system.

8. Joints that hold bones firmly together are called

    (A) hinge joints.

    (B) ball and socket joints.

    (C) fixed joints.

    (D) pivot joints.

9. Of the levels listed, the top or broadest level of the classification system for living organisms is called the

    (A) class.

    (B) phylum.

    (C) kingdom.

    (D) genus.

10. Which planet is the brightest object in the sky, aside from the sun and moon?

    (A) Saturn

    (B) Pluto

    (C) Venus

    (D) Mercury

11. The human heart includes

    (A) 2 chambers.

    (B) 3 chambers.

    (C) 4 chambers.

    (D) 5 chambers.

Go on to next page

12. White blood cells

    (A) produce antibodies.

    (B) fight infections.

    (C) carry oxygen and carbon dioxide.

    (D) both A and B

13. A measureable amount of protein can be found in all of the following foods EXCEPT

    (A) eggs.

    (B) meat.

    (C) peas.

    (D) apples.

14. What is the most abundant element, by mass, in the Earth's crust?

    (A) carbon

    (B) oxygen

    (C) gold

    (D) salt

15. Osmosis is

    (A) diffusion of water.

    (B) transfer of oxygen.

    (C) low blood sugar.

    (D) protein.

16. A meter consists of

    (A) 10 centimeters.

    (B) 100 millimeters.

    (C) 100 centimeters.

    (D) 10 millimeters.

17. One light-year is

    (A) the distance traveled by light in one year.

    (B) the brightness of light at 30,000 miles.

    (C) 17 standard Earth years.

    (D) Spock's birthday.

18. Electrons are particles that are

    (A) positively charged.

    (B) neutral.

    (C) able to move freely.

    (D) negatively charged.

19. The asteroid belt is located

    (A) around Mercury.

    (B) between Mars and Jupiter.

    (C) inside the orbit of Venus.

    (D) There is no such thing as an asteroid belt.

20. The atomic number of an atom is determined by

    (A) the size of its nucleus.

    (B) the number of protons.

    (C) the number of electrons.

    (D) its location in the periodic table.

21. The "control center" of a cell is called the

    (A) nucleus.

    (B) compound.

    (C) mitochondria.

    (D) atom.

22. How many planets in the solar system have rings?

    (A) one

    (B) two

    (C) three

    (D) four

23. The temperature at which a substance's solid and liquid states exist in equilibrium is its

    (A) melting point.

    (B) boiling point.

    (C) anti-freezing point.

    (D) concentration point.

Go on to next page

24. The atmosphere of Mars is composed mostly of

    (A) oxygen.

    (B) carbon dioxide.

    (C) helium.

    (D) Mars has no atmosphere.

25. Not counting the sun, the closest star to the Earth is

    (A) Rigel.

    (B) Proxima Centauri.

    (C) Antares.

    (D) Betelgeuse.

STOP DO NOT TURN THE PAGE UNTIL TOLD TO DO SO.
DO NOT RETURN TO A PREVIOUS TEST.

Subtest 2: Arithmetic Reasoning

Time: 36 minutes for 30 questions

Directions: This test contains questions about arithmetic. Each question is followed by four possible answers. Decide which answer is correct and then mark the space on your answer sheet that has the same number and letter as your choice. Use scratch paper for any figuring you want to do. A calculator is not allowed.

1. If a car is towed 12 miles to the repair shop and the tow charge is $3.50 per mile, how much does the tow cost?

   (A) $12.00

   (B) $3.50

   (C) $42.00

   (D) $100.00

2. The sum of two numbers is 70. One number is 8 more than the other. What's the smaller number?

   (A) 31

   (B) 33

   (C) 35

   (D) 36

3. A sales manager buys antacid in bottles by the gross. If he goes through 3 bottles of antacid every day, how long will the gross last?

   (A) 144 days

   (B) 3 days

   (C) 20 days

   (D) 48 days

4. Jenny's test grades are 93, 89, 96, and 98. If she wishes to raise her average to 95, what does she need to score on her next test?

   (A) 100

   (B) 99

   (C) 97

   (D) 95

5. A waitress earns an average tip of 12% of the cost of the food she serves. If she serves $375 worth of food in one evening, how much money in tips will she earn on average?

   (A) $37

   (B) $45

   (C) $42

   (D) $420

6. How many square feet of carpeting are needed to carpet a 12-foot x 12-foot room?

   (A) 24

   (B) 120

   (C) 48

   (D) 144

7. Carpet stain protector costs $0.65 per square yard to apply. How much will it cost to apply the protector to a 16-foot x 18-foot carpet?

   (A) $187.20

   (B) $62.40

   (C) $20.80

   (D) $96.00

8. A printing plant that produces baseball cards has a monthly overhead of $6,000. It costs 18 cents to print each card, and the cards sell for 30 cents each. How many cards must the printing plant sell each month in order to make a profit?

   (A) 30,000

   (B) 40,000

   (C) 50,000

   (D) 60,000

Go on to next page

9. Joe received an hourly wage of $8.15. His boss gave him a 7% raise. How much does Joe make per hour now?

    (A) $0.57

    (B) $8.90

    (C) $8.72

    (D) $13.85

10. Alice leaves her house, driving east at 45 miles per hour (mph). Thirty minutes later, her husband Dave notices she forgot her cell phone and sets off after her. How fast must Dave travel in order to catch up with Alice 3 hours after he leaves?

    (A) 49 mph

    (B) 50.5 mph

    (C) 52.5 mph

    (D) 54 mph

11. A baker made 20 pies. A Boy Scout troop buys one-fourth of his pies, a preschool teacher buys one-third of his pies, and a caterer buys one-sixth of his pies. How many pies does the baker have left?

    (A) $\frac{3}{4}$

    (B) 15

    (C) 12

    (D) 5

12. Miriam bought five cases of motor oil on sale. A case of motor oil normally costs $24.00, but she was able to purchase the oil for $22.50 a case. How much money did Miriam save on her entire purchase?

    (A) $7.50

    (B) $1.50

    (C) $8.00

    (D) $22.50

13. A security guard walks the equivalent of six city blocks when he makes a circuit around the building. If he walks at a pace of eight city blocks every 30 minutes, how long will it take him to complete a circuit around the building, assuming he doesn't run into any thieves?

    (A) 20.00 minutes

    (B) 3.75 minutes

    (C) 22.50 minutes

    (D) 7.5 minutes

14. The population of Grand Island, Nebraska, grew by 600,000 people between 1995 and 2005, one-fifth more than the town council predicted. The town council originally predicted the city's population would grow by

    (A) 400,000

    (B) 500,000

    (C) 300,000

    (D) 100,000

15. Joan is taking an admissions examination. If she has to get at least 40 of the 60 questions right to pass, what percent of the questions does she need to answer correctly?

    (A) 30%

    (B) 40%

    (C) $66\frac{1}{3}$%

    (D) $66\frac{2}{3}$%

16. A teacher deposits $3,000 in a retirement fund. If she doesn't add any more money to the fund, which earns an annual interest rate of 6%, how much money will she have in 1 year?

    (A) $180

    (B) $3,006

    (C) $3,180

    (D) $6,000

17. The high school track measures one-quarter of a mile around. How many laps would you have to run in order to run three and a half miles?

    (A) 12

    (B) 14

    (C) 16

    (D) 18

18. Karl is driving in Austria, where the speed limit is posted in kilometers per hour. The car's speedometer shows that he's traveling at a rate of 75 kilometers per hour. Karl knows that a kilometer is about $\frac{5}{8}$ of a mile. Approximately how many miles per hour is Karl traveling?

    (A) 47

    (B) 120

    (C) 50

    (D) 53

Go on to next page

19. A carpenter earns $12.30 an hour for a 40-hour week. His overtime pay is $1\frac{1}{2}$ times his base pay. If he puts in a 46-hour week, how much is his weekly pay?

(A) $602.70

(B) $492.00

(C) $565.80

(D) $110.70

20. An office building has 30 employees and provides 42 square feet of work space per employee. If five more employees are hired, how much less work space will each employee have?

(A) 6 square feet

(B) 7 square feet

(C) 7.5 square feet

(D) 36 square feet

21. Stan bought a monster truck for $2,000 down and payments of $450 a month for five years. What's the total cost of the monster truck?

(A) $4,250

(B) $29,000

(C) $27,000

(D) $34,400

22. Darla spent $120.37 on groceries in January, $108.45 in February, and $114.86 in March. What was the average monthly cost of Darla's groceries?

(A) $343.68

(B) $110.45

(C) $114.86

(D) $114.56

23. Keith is driving from Reno to Kansas City to meet his girlfriend. The distance between the two cities is 1,650 miles. If Keith can average 50 miles per hour, how many hours will it take him to complete his trip?

(A) 8 hours

(B) 30 hours

(C) 33 hours

(D) 82 hours

24. Michael needs 55 gallons of paint to paint an apartment building. He would like to purchase the paint for the least amount of money possible. Which of the following should he buy?

(A) two 25-gallon buckets at $550 each

(B) eleven 5-gallon buckets at $108 each

(C) six 10-gallon buckets at $215 each

(D) fifty-five 1-gallon buckets at $23 each

25. As a member of FEMA, you're required to set up a contingency plan to supply meals to residents of a town devastated by a tornado. A breakfast ration weighs 12 ounces and the lunch and dinner rations weigh 18 ounces each. Assuming a food truck can carry 3 tons and that each resident will receive 3 meals per day, how many residents can you feed from one truck during a 10-day period?

(A) 150 residents

(B) 200 residents

(C) 250 residents

(D) 300 residents

26. A train headed south for Wichita left the station at the same time a train headed north for Des Moines left the same station. The train headed for Wichita traveled at 55 miles per hour. The train headed for Des Moines traveled at 70 miles per hour. How many miles apart are the trains at the end of 3 hours?

(A) 210 miles

(B) 165 miles

(C) 125 miles

(D) 375 miles

27. A carpenter needs to cut four sections, each 3 feet, 8 inches long, from a piece of molding. If the board is only sold by the foot, what's the shortest length of board she can buy?

(A) 15 feet

(B) 14 feet

(C) 16 feet

(D) 12 feet

Go on to next page

28. Kiya had only one coupon for 10% off one frozen turkey breast. The turkey breasts cost $8.50 each, and Kiya wanted to buy two. How much did she pay?

    (A) $16.15

    (B) $17.00

    (C) $15.30

    (D) $7.65

29. A recruiter travels 1,100 miles during a 40-hour workweek. If she spends $\frac{2}{5}$ of her time traveling, how many hours does she spend traveling?

    (A) 22

    (B) $5\frac{1}{2}$

    (C) 16

    (D) 8

30. Your car uses gasoline at the rate of 21 miles per gallon. If gasoline costs $2.82 per gallon and you drive for 7 hours at a speed of 48 miles per hour, how much will you pay for gasoline for the trip?

    (A) $38.18

    (B) $45.12

    (C) $47.73

    (D) $59.27

STOP DO NOT TURN THE PAGE UNTIL TOLD TO DO SO.
DO NOT RETURN TO A PREVIOUS TEST.

Subtest 3: Word Knowledge

Time: 11 minutes for 35 questions

Directions: This test is about the meanings of words. Each question has a word underlined. You may be asked to decide which one of the four words in the choices *most nearly means* the same thing as the underlined word or which one of the four words means the opposite. If the underlined word is used in a sentence, decide which of the four choices most nearly means the same thing as the underlined word, as used in the context of the sentence. Mark the corresponding space on your answer sheet.

1. Tim promised to meet us at the apex.
    (A) top
    (B) bottom
    (C) canyon
    (D) river

2. Assimilate most nearly means
    (A) absorb.
    (B) react.
    (C) pretend.
    (D) lie.

3. Brittle most nearly means
    (A) soft.
    (B) fragile.
    (C) study.
    (D) hard.

4. Datum most nearly means
    (A) fiscal year date.
    (B) congruence.
    (C) fact.
    (D) positive result.

5. The exchange student was proficient in French, German, and English.
    (A) poor
    (B) knowledgeable
    (C) adept
    (D) exacting

6. The judge imposed a severe penalty due to Tom's actions.
    (A) scheduled
    (B) made an example of
    (C) levied
    (D) questioned

7. Mary went to the store and bought peanuts galore.
    (A) abundant
    (B) salty
    (C) on sale
    (D) roasted

8. He ran headlong into the fight.
    (A) headfirst
    (B) reluctantly
    (C) happily
    (D) recklessly

9. Frugal most nearly means
    (A) quiet.
    (B) amazing.
    (C) delayed.
    (D) economical.

10. The word most opposite in meaning to stimulate is
    (A) support.
    (B) arrest.
    (C) travel.
    (D) dislike.

Go on to next page

11. <u>Licit</u> most nearly means
    (A) historical.
    (B) lawful.
    (C) storied.
    (D) willfully.

12. <u>Vacate</u> most nearly means
    (A) crawl.
    (B) impel.
    (C) exhume.
    (D) leave.

13. The sergeant gave his <u>reasoned</u> opinion.
    (A) irate
    (B) logical
    (C) impressive
    (D) uninformed

14. <u>Tacit</u> most nearly means
    (A) loud.
    (B) understood.
    (C) commendable.
    (D) transparent.

15. The brass was not <u>burnished</u>.
    (A) yellow
    (B) dull
    (C) expensive
    (D) polished

16. The <u>commodity</u> was sold.
    (A) product
    (B) stock
    (C) idea
    (D) table

17. Her motives were <u>contrived</u>.
    (A) premeditated
    (B) emotional
    (C) obscure
    (D) amusing

18. <u>Supplicate</u> most nearly means
    (A) to make superior.
    (B) to be unnecessary.
    (C) to beg.
    (D) to be expansive.

19. The word most opposite in meaning to <u>hypocrisy</u> is
    (A) honesty.
    (B) happy.
    (C) angry.
    (D) threatening.

20. Bob found the peaches to be extremely <u>succulent</u>.
    (A) large
    (B) tasteless
    (C) old
    (D) juicy

21. The Army soldiers were ordered to immediate <u>garrison</u> duty.
    (A) field
    (B) combat
    (C) latrine
    (D) fort

22. <u>Furtherance</u> most nearly means
    (A) advancement.
    (B) finance.
    (C) practicality.
    (D) destruction.

23. <u>Domicile</u> most nearly means
    (A) office.
    (B) shopping.
    (C) home.
    (D) vacation.

24. <u>Abrogate</u> most nearly means
    (A) recover.
    (B) aid.
    (C) foreclose.
    (D) abolish.

Go on to next page

25. <u>Compensation</u> most nearly means
    (A) religion.
    (B) commission.
    (C) boathouse.
    (D) shower.

26. He gave a <u>brusque</u> account of the events.
    (A) passionate
    (B) lengthy
    (C) uncensored
    (D) abrupt

27. The vote resulted in the <u>demise</u> of the proposed new law.
    (A) passage
    (B) death
    (C) postponement
    (D) abatement

28. We <u>commemorated</u> our veterans during the ceremony.
    (A) denied
    (B) remembered
    (C) thanked
    (D) took pictures of

29. <u>Bore</u> most nearly means
    (A) deepen.
    (B) hide.
    (C) burrow.
    (D) jump.

30. That custom still <u>prevails</u>.
    (A) angers
    (B) persists
    (C) surprises
    (D) excites

31. <u>Defray</u> most nearly means
    (A) invade.
    (B) obstruct.
    (C) pay.
    (D) reverse.

32. <u>Chasm</u> most nearly means
    (A) abyss.
    (B) sky.
    (C) mountain.
    (D) valley.

33. <u>Fundamental</u> most nearly means
    (A) radical.
    (B) religious.
    (C) basic.
    (D) excessive.

34. <u>Susceptible</u> most nearly means
    (A) travel.
    (B) resistant.
    (C) limited.
    (D) vulnerable

35. <u>Emblem</u> most nearly means
    (A) symbol.
    (B) picture.
    (C) statue.
    (D) religion.

STOP DO NOT TURN THE PAGE UNTIL TOLD TO DO SO.
DO NOT RETURN TO A PREVIOUS TEST.

Subtest 4: Paragraph Comprehension

Time: 13 minutes for 15 questions

Directions: This test contains items that measure your ability to understand what you read. This section includes one or more paragraphs of reading material followed by incomplete statements or questions. Read the paragraph and select the choice that best completes the statement or answers the question. Mark your choice on your answer sheet, using the correct letter with each question number.

An important stage of personal time management is to take control of appointments. Determined by external obligation, appointments constitute interaction with other people and an agreed-on interface between your activities and those of others. Start with a simple appointment diary. List all appointments, including regular and recurring ones. Now, be ruthless and eliminate the unnecessary. There may be committees where you can't productively contribute or where a subordinate may be able to participate. Eliminate the waste of your time.

1. Effectively managing your appointments allows you to

   (A) spend more time with your subordinates.

   (B) delegate responsibility to subordinates.

   (C) make more efficient use of your time.

   (D) attend only the most important meetings.

The U.S. Congress consists of 100 senators and 435 representatives. Two senators are elected from each state. The number of representatives from each state is based on population, although each state has at least one representative. Senators serve six-year terms, and representatives serve two-year terms.

2. According to this passage,

   (A) there are equal numbers of senators and representatives.

   (B) the number of representatives from each state is decided by a lottery.

   (C) it's possible for a state to have no representatives.

   (D) senators and representatives have different term lengths.

Indo-European languages consist of those languages spoken by most of Europe and in those parts of the world that Europeans have colonized since the 16th century (such as the United States). Indo-European languages are also spoken in India, Iran, parts of western Afghanistan, and in some areas of Asia.

3. The author of this passage would agree that

   (A) Indo-European languages are spoken in areas all over the world.

   (B) Indo-European languages include all the languages spoken in the world.

   (C) only Europeans speak Indo-European languages.

   (D) Indo-European language speakers can easily understand one another.

In privatization, the government relies on the private sector to provide a service. However, the government divests itself of the entire process, including all assets. With privatized functions, the government may specify quality, quantity, and timeliness requirements, but it has no control over the operations of the activity. Also, the government may not be the only customer. Whoever the government chooses to provide the services would likely provide the same services to others.

4. This paragraph best supports the statement that

   (A) the government must closely supervise privatized functions.

   (B) privatized functions consist of a mixture of government employees, military personnel, and private contractors.

   (C) privatized functions are those institutions that provide services only to a government agency.

   (D) privatized functions provide essential services to the government.

Go on to next page →

The success or failure of a conference lies largely with its leader. A leader's zest and enthusiasm must be real, apparent, and contagious. The leader is responsible for getting the ball rolling and making the attendees feel as if the meeting is theirs and its success depends on their participation. A good, thorough introduction helps establish the right climate.

5. A good title to this paragraph would be

    (A) "Lead by Example."

    (B) "The Importance of Proper Introductions."

    (C) "Leading a Successful Conference."

    (D) "Conference Participation Basics."

Cloud seeding is accomplished by dropping particles of dry ice (solid carbon dioxide) from a plane onto super-cooled clouds. This process encourages condensation of water droplets in the clouds, which usually, but not always, results in rain or snow.

6. From this passage, it's reasonable to assume that

    (A) cloud seeding could be used to end a drought.

    (B) cloud seeding is prohibitively expensive.

    (C) cloud seeding is rarely used.

    (D) cloud seeding can be accomplished by using regular ice.

To write or not to write — that is the question. If assigned a writing task, there's no option. However, if someone is looking for a specific answer, find out if they need a short answer or a detailed one. Can the requirement be met with a telephone call, e-mail, or short note, or is something more necessary? A former CEO of a major corporation once commented that he had looked at 13,000 pieces of paper in a 5-day period. Think how much easier and more economical it would be if people would use the telephone, send an e-mail, or write a short note.

7. The main point of this passage is that

    (A) written records are important because they provide detailed documentation.

    (B) more businesspeople should invest time and energy improving their writing skills.

    (C) writing may not be the best way to communicate information.

    (D) it's pointless for businesspeople to spend time improving their writing skills.

The transistor, a small, solid-state device that can amplify sound, was invented in 1947. At first, it was too expensive and too difficult to produce to be used in cheap, mass-market products. By 1954, though, these cost and production problems had been overcome, and the first transistor radio was put on the market.

8. According to this passage,

    (A) there was no market for transistors before 1954.

    (B) when transistors could be produced cheaply and easily, the transistor radio was put on the market.

    (C) transistors were invented in 1947 by order of the Department of Defense.

    (D) transistors are still expensive to produce.

I returned from the City about three o'clock on that May afternoon pretty well disgusted with life. I had been three months in the Old Country and was fed up with it. If people had told me a year ago that I would've been feeling like that I should've laughed at them; but there was the fact. The weather made me liverish, the talk of the ordinary Englishman made me sick, I couldn't get enough exercise, and the amusements of London seemed as flat as soda water that had been standing in the sun.

9. The author is speaking of his travels in

    (A) Spain.

    (B) Great Britain.

    (C) Germany.

    (D) Scotland.

Surveys show that the average child under the age of 18 watches four hours of television per day. Although some of the programming may be educational, most isn't. Spending this much time watching television interferes with a child's ability to pursue other interests, such as reading, participating in sports, and playing with friends.

10. The author of this passage would agree that

    (A) television viewing should be restricted.

    (B) parents who let their children watch this much television are neglectful.

    (C) reading, participating in sports, playing with friends, and watching television should all be given equal time.

    (D) adults over 18 can watch as much television as they want.

Go on to next page

High school and college graduates attempting to find jobs should participate in mock job interviews. These mock interviews help students prepare for the types of questions they'll be asked, make them more comfortable with common interview formats, and help them critique their performance before facing a real interviewer. Because they're such a valuable aid, schools should organize mock job interviews for all of their graduating students.

11. The above passage states that mock job interviews

    (A) frighten students.

    (B) should be offered to the best students.

    (C) help prepare students for real job interviews.

    (D) should be organized by students.

12. From the above passage, it is reasonable to assume that

    (A) mock interviews can increase a student's confidence when he or she goes into a real job interview.

    (B) mock interviews are expensive to organize.

    (C) few students are interested in mock interviews.

    (D) students don't need job interview preparation.

Due process, the guarantee of fairness in the administration of justice, is part of the 5th Amendment to the U.S. Constitution. The 14th Amendment further requires states to abide by due process. After this amendment was enacted, the U.S. Supreme Court struck down many state laws that infringed on the civil rights guaranteed to citizens in the Bill of Rights.

13. According to the above passage, due process

    (A) is an outdated concept.

    (B) guarantees fairness in the justice system.

    (C) never became part of the U.S. Constitution.

    (D) is the process by which winning lottery tickets are selected.

14. According to the above passage, it's reasonable to assume that the 5th Amendment

    (A) is about taxes.

    (B) guarantees due process in all criminal and civil cases.

    (C) guarantees due process in federal law.

    (D) should never have become part of the Bill of Rights.

15. The author of the above passage would agree that

    (A) without the passage of the 14th Amendment, many laws restricting civil rights would still exist in various states.

    (B) the Supreme Court overstepped its jurisdiction when it struck down laws infringing on citizens' civil rights.

    (C) the Supreme Court had every right to strike down state laws before the passage of the 14th Amendment.

    (D) the 14th Amendment was opposed by all states.

STOP DO NOT TURN THE PAGE UNTIL TOLD TO DO SO.
DO NOT RETURN TO A PREVIOUS TEST.

Subtest 5: Mathematics Knowledge

Time: 24 minutes for 25 questions

Directions: This section tests your ability to solve general mathematical problems. Select the correct answer from the choices given, and then mark the corresponding space on your answer sheet. Use scratch paper to do any figuring.

1. If $x = 8$, what's the value of y in the equation $y = (x^2 \div 4) - 2$?
   - (A) 14
   - (B) 16
   - (C) 18
   - (D) 20

2. The cube of 5 is
   - (A) 125
   - (B) 25
   - (C) 15
   - (D) 50

3. $2.5 \times 3^3 =$
   - (A) 22.5
   - (B) 75.0
   - (C) 67.5
   - (D) 675.0

4. The fourth root of 16 is
   - (A) 4
   - (B) 1
   - (C) 3
   - (D) 2

5. What's the equation of a line that passes through points $(0, -1)$ and $(2, 3)$?
   - (A) $y = 2x - 1$
   - (B) $y = 2x + 1$
   - (C) $x = 2y - 1$
   - (D) $x = 2y + 1$

6. (12 yards + 14 feet) $\div 5 =$
   - (A) 12 feet
   - (B) $5\frac{1}{5}$ feet
   - (C) 10 feet
   - (D) $2\frac{1}{2}$ yards

7. $x^3 \cdot x^4 =$
   - (A) x^{12}
   - (B) $2x^7$
   - (C) $2x^{12}$
   - (D) x^7

8. $(x + 4)(x + 2) =$
   - (A) $x^2 + 6x + 6$
   - (B) $x^2 + 8x + 8$
   - (C) $x^2 + 8x + 6$
   - (D) $x^2 + 6x + 8$

9. $1.5 \times 10^3 =$
   - (A) 45
   - (B) 150
   - (C) 1,500
   - (D) 15

10. Which of the following is a prime number?
    - (A) 27
    - (B) 11
    - (C) 8
    - (D) 4

11. What's the mode of the following series of numbers? 4 4 8 8 8 10 10 12 12
    - (A) 9
    - (B) 8
    - (C) 11
    - (D) 10

12. If $a = 4$, then $a^3 \div a =$
    - (A) 4
    - (B) 12
    - (C) 64
    - (D) 16

Go on to next page ⇒

13. Solve: 5!
    (A) 25
    (B) 125
    (C) 120
    (D) 15

14. $(900 \times 2) \div 6 =$
    (A) 30
    (B) 300
    (C) 150
    (D) 3,000

15. If $x = 2$, then $x^x(x) =$
    (A) 8
    (B) $2x^x$
    (C) 4
    (D) 6

16. If $(5 + 1)(6 \div 3)(8 - 5) = (3 + 3)x$, then $x =$
    (A) 12
    (B) 3
    (C) 4
    (D) 6

17. $\sqrt{49} \times \sqrt{64} =$
    (A) 56
    (B) 15
    (C) 42
    (D) 3,136

18. Which of the following fractions is the largest?
    (A) $\frac{2}{5}$
    (B) $\frac{3}{8}$
    (C) $\frac{7}{10}$
    (D) $\frac{13}{16}$

19. If $2 + x \geq 4$, then $x \geq$
    (A) 6
    (B) 2
    (C) 4
    (D) $\frac{1}{2}$

20. If a circle has a radius of 12 feet, what's its circumference most nearly?
    (A) 24 feet
    (B) 72 feet
    (C) 75 feet
    (D) 36 feet

21. An aquarium measures 16 inches long x 8 inches deep x 18 inches high. What's its volume?
    (A) 2,304 cubic inches
    (B) 128 cubic inches
    (C) 42 cubic inches
    (D) 288 cubic inches

22. Triangle ABC is a(n)

    (A) right triangle.
    (B) obtuse triangle.
    (C) equilateral triangle.
    (D) isosceles triangle.

23. The sum of the measures of the angles of a trapezoid is
    (A) 360 degrees.
    (B) 540 degrees.
    (C) 180 degrees.
    (D) 720 degrees.

Go on to next page

24. Angles 1 and 2 are

   (A) supplementary.
   (B) complementary.
   (C) both obtuse.
   (D) both right angles.

25. Convert 24% to a fraction.

   (A) $\frac{6}{25}$

   (B) $\frac{1}{25}$

   (C) $\frac{6}{24}$

   (D) $\frac{1}{24}$

STOP DO NOT TURN THE PAGE UNTIL TOLD TO DO SO.
DO NOT RETURN TO A PREVIOUS TEST.

Subtest 6: Electronics Information

Time: 9 minutes for 20 questions

Directions: This test contains questions to challenge your knowledge of electrical, radio, and electronics information. Select the correct response from the choices given and then mark the corresponding space on your answer sheet.

1. Ohm's law states
   - (A) Voltage = Current × Resistance
   - (B) Amperes = Current × Resistance
   - (C) Voltage = Resistance ÷ Amperes
   - (D) Ohms = Current ÷ Voltage

2. A resistor's first three color bands are brown, black, and red. What is its value?
   - (A) 1,000 ohms
   - (B) 500 ohms
   - (C) 500 volts
   - (D) 50 volts

3. In the U.S., all metal equipment, electrical or not, connected to a swimming pool must be
   - (A) freestanding.
   - (B) bonded together.
   - (C) certified.
   - (D) none of the above

4. Voltage can also be expressed as
   - (A) watts.
   - (B) amps.
   - (C) current.
   - (D) electrical potential difference.

5. Newer cell phones contain a removable memory card, which is often called a
   - (A) SIM card.
   - (B) DIM chip.
   - (C) PIN card.
   - (D) PIN chip.

6. Made from a variety of materials, such as carbon, this inhibits the flow of current.
   - (A) resistor
   - (B) diode
   - (C) transformer
   - (D) generator

7. This is a type of semiconductor that only allows current to flow in one direction. It is usually used to rectify AC signals (conversion to DC).
   - (A) capacitor
   - (B) inductor
   - (C) diode
   - (D) transformer

8. Radar can operate at frequencies as high as
   - (A) 100,000 Hz.
   - (B) 100,000 kHz.
   - (C) 100,000 MHz.
   - (D) 500,000 MHz.

9. What do AC and DC stand for in the electrical field?
   - (A) amplified capacity and differential capacity
   - (B) alternating current and direct current
   - (C) accelerated climate and deduced climate
   - (D) none of the above

10. Changing AC to DC is called what?
    - (A) capacitance.
    - (B) impedance.
    - (C) rectification.
    - (D) induction.

Go on to next page

11. A 5,000 BTU air conditioner can efficiently cool up to 150 square feet, or a 10-foot x 15-foot room. What does BTU stand for?

    (A) basic thermal unit

    (B) basic temperature unit

    (C) British thermal unit

    (D) none of the above

12. Which is the most correct definition of current?

    (A) the measure of electrical pressure

    (B) the amount of electricity used in a heater

    (C) the electricity used in heating a kilo of water

    (D) the presence of electron flow

13. A device that transforms energy from one form to another is called

    (A) a capacitor.

    (B) a transducer.

    (C) a transformer.

    (D) magic.

14. Which one of the following is an active element?

    (A) 15 kΩ resistor

    (B) 10 mH inductor

    (C) 25 pF capacitor

    (D) 10 V power supply

15. A light bulb is 60 watts. Operated at 120 volts, how much current does it draw?

    (A) 0.5 amperes

    (B) 5.0 amperes

    (C) 50.0 amperes

    (D) 7,200 amperes

16. A number-12 wire, compared to a number-6 wire,

    (A) is longer.

    (B) is shorter.

    (C) is smaller in diameter.

    (D) is larger in diameter.

17. A fuse with a higher-than-required rating used in an electrical circuit

    (A) improves safety.

    (B) increases maintenance.

    (C) may not work properly.

    (D) is less expensive.

18. Neutral wire is always

    (A) whitish or natural.

    (B) black.

    (C) green with stripes.

    (D) blue.

19. To measure electrical power, you would use a(n)

    (A) ammeter.

    (B) ohmmeter.

    (C) voltmeter.

    (D) wattmeter.

20. What will happen if you operate an incandescent light bulb at less than its rated voltage?

    (A) The bulb will burn brighter and last longer.

    (B) The bulb will burn dimmer and last longer.

    (C) The bulb will burn brighter but won't last as long.

    (D) The bulb will burn dimmer but won't last as long.

STOP DO NOT TURN THE PAGE UNTIL TOLD TO DO SO.
DO NOT RETURN TO A PREVIOUS TEST.

Subtest 7: Auto & Shop Information

Time: 11 minutes for 25 questions

Directions: This test is about automobiles, shop practices, and the use of tools. Pick the best answer for each question and then mark the corresponding space on your answer sheet.

1. Overheating the engine can cause all of the following problems EXCEPT

   (A) burned engine bearings.

   (B) enlarged pistons.

   (C) melted engine parts.

   (D) improved fuel efficiency.

2. The device that converts an automobile's mechanical energy to electrical energy is called the

   (A) converter.

   (B) alternator.

   (C) battery.

   (D) brakes.

3. A primary advantage of the electronic ignition system over conventional ignition systems is that

   (A) the electronic ignition system is less expensive to repair.

   (B) the electronic ignition system requires a lower voltage to provide a higher voltage for spark.

   (C) the electronic ignition system allows for use of a lower octane fuel.

   (D) all of the above

4. The primary purpose of piston rings is to

   (A) seal the combustion chamber and allow the pistons to move freely.

   (B) connect the piston to the crankshaft.

   (C) allow fuel to enter the piston cylinder.

   (D) provide lubrication to the piston cylinder.

5. The crankshaft typically connects to a

   (A) flywheel.

   (B) fuel pump.

   (C) muffler.

   (D) battery.

6. What component allows the left and right wheels to turn at different speeds when cornering?

   (A) differential

   (B) camshaft

   (C) valve rotator

   (D) battery

7. If a car's ignition system, lights, and radio don't work, the part that's probably malfunctioned is the

   (A) cylinder block.

   (B) water pump.

   (C) carburetor.

   (D) battery.

8. A good tool to cut intricate shapes in wood would be a

   (A) ripsaw.

   (B) hacksaw.

   (C) coping saw.

   (D) pocket knife.

9. A two-stroke engine will normally be found on

   (A) small cars.

   (B) large diesel trucks.

   (C) trucks, vans, and some cars.

   (D) snowmobiles, chainsaws, and some motorcycles.

10. A belt sander would best be used to

    (A) cut wood.

    (B) finish wood.

    (C) shape wood.

    (D) keep your pants up.

Go on to next page

11. A car equipped with limited-slip differential

    (A) can be readily put into all-wheel (four-wheel) drive.

    (B) won't lock up when the brakes are applied steadily.

    (C) transfers the most driving force to the wheel with the greatest amount of traction.

    (D) is rated for off-road driving.

12. Big block engines generally have

    (A) more than 5.9 L of displacement.

    (B) better gas mileage than small block engines.

    (C) less than 6 L of displacement.

    (D) air conditioning.

13. A good tool for spreading and/or shaping mortar would be a

    (A) cement shaper.

    (B) hammer.

    (C) trowel.

    (D) broom.

14. Plumb-bobs are used to

    (A) clean pipes.

    (B) check vertical reference.

    (C) fix the toilet.

    (D) carve stones.

15. Rebar is used to

    (A) measure the depth of concrete.

    (B) reinforce concrete.

    (C) stir concrete.

    (D) smooth concrete.

16. Annular ring, clout, and spring head are types of

    (A) hammers.

    (B) saws.

    (C) nails.

    (D) screwdrivers.

17. A ripsaw cuts

    (A) against the grain of the wood.

    (B) with the grain of the wood.

    (C) most materials, including metal.

    (D) only plastic.

18. A cam belt is also known as a

    (A) piston.

    (B) timing belt.

    (C) transmission belt.

    (D) lug nut.

19. To check for horizontal trueness, the best tool to use is a

    (A) steel tape rule.

    (B) plumb bob.

    (C) level.

    (D) sliding T-bevel.

20. A bucking bar is used to

    (A) pull nails.

    (B) pry wood apart.

    (C) form rivet bucktails.

    (D) drive screws.

21. Washers that have teeth all around the circumference to prevent them from slipping are called

    (A) shake-proof washers.

    (B) jaw washers.

    (C) flat washers.

    (D) split-lock washers.

Go on to next page

22. The tool below measures

(A) an inside curve.
(B) an outside curve.
(C) the depth of a hole.
(D) the thickness of wire.

23. The object below is a type of

(A) nut.
(B) washer.
(C) screw.
(D) bolt.

24. The tool below is used to

(A) finish concrete.
(B) spread joint compound.
(C) smooth wallpaper.
(D) dress wood.

25. The chisel used to cut metal is

(A)

(B)

(C)

(D)

STOP DO NOT TURN THE PAGE UNTIL TOLD TO DO SO.
DO NOT RETURN TO A PREVIOUS TEST.

Subtest 8: Mechanical Comprehension

> **Time:** 19 minutes for 25 questions
>
> **Directions:** This test is about mechanical principles. Many of the questions use drawings to illustrate specific principles. Choose the correct answer and mark the corresponding space on the answer sheet.

1. An induction clutch works by

   (A) magnetism.

   (B) pneumatics.

   (C) hydraulics.

   (D) friction.

2. If a first-class lever with a resistance arm measuring 2 feet and an effort arm measuring 8 feet are being used, what's the mechanical advantage?

   (A) 2

   (B) 4

   (C) 6

   (D) 1

3. The bottoms of four boxes are shown below. The boxes all have the same volume. If postal regulations state that the sides of a box must meet a minimum height, which box is most likely to be too short to go through the mail?

   (A) No. 4

   (B) No. 2

   (C) No. 1

   (D) No. 3

4. Looking at the figure below, when Anvil B lands on the seesaw, Anvil A will

   (A) remain stationary.

   (B) hit the ground hard.

   (C) rise in the air quickly.

   (D) enter the stratosphere.

5. Air pressure at sea level is about 15 psi. What's the amount of force exerted on the top of your head, given a surface area of 24 square inches?

   (A) 360 pounds

   (B) 625 pounds

   (C) $\frac{5}{8}$ pound

   (D) 180 pounds

6. The force produced when a boxer's hand hits a heavy bag and "bounces" off it is called

   (A) response time.

   (B) bounce.

   (C) recoil.

   (D) gravity.

Go on to next page

7. In the figure below, if Gear 1 has 25 teeth and Gear 2 has 15 teeth, how many revolutions does Gear 2 make for every 10 revolutions Gear 1 makes?

1

(A) about $16\frac{2}{3}$

(B) 12

(C) about $\frac{1}{3}$ more

(D) about 20

8. A cubic foot of water weighs about 62.5 pounds. If an aquarium is 18 feet long, 10 feet deep, and 12 feet wide, what's the approximate pressure in pounds per square inch (psi) on the bottom of the tank?

(A) 2 psi

(B) 4 psi

(C) 5 psi

(D) 7 psi

9. Springs used in machines are usually made of

(A) plastic.

(B) bronze.

(C) nylon fiber.

(D) steel.

10. A clutch is a type of

(A) universal joint.

(B) coupling.

(C) gear differential.

(D) cam follower.

11. When Cam A completes one revolution, the lever will touch the contact point

(A) once.

(B) never.

(C) four times.

(D) twice.

12. A single block-and-fall is called a

(A) fixed pulley.

(B) gun tackle.

(C) runner.

(D) sheave.

13. In the figure below, if the fulcrum supporting the lever is moved closer to the anvil, the anvil will be

(A) easier to lift and will move higher.

(B) harder to lift but will move higher.

(C) easier to lift but will not move as high.

(D) harder to lift and will not move as high.

Go on to next page

14. The mechanical advantage of the block-and-tackle arrangement shown below is

(A) 2

(B) 4

(C) 6

(D) 1

15. In the figure below, if the cogs move up the track at the same rate of speed, Cog A will

(A) reach the top at the same time as Cog B.

(B) reach the top after Cog B.

(C) reach the top before Cog B.

(D) have greater difficulty staying on track.

16. If a house key, a wooden spoon, a plastic hanger, and a wool jacket are all the same temperature. On a cool day, which one feels the coldest?

(A) key

(B) spoon

(C) hanger

(D) jacket

17. In the figure below, assume the valves are all closed. To fill the tank but prevent it from filling entirely, which valves should be open?

(A) 1 and 2 only

(B) 1, 2, and 3 only

(C) 1, 2, and 4 only

(D) 1, 2, 3, and 5 only

18. If Gear A is turned to the left,

(A) Gear B turns to the right and Gear C turns to the left.

(B) Gear B turns to the left and Gear C turns to the left.

(C) Gear B turns to the right and Gear C turns to the right.

(D) Gear B turns to the left and Gear C turns to the right.

Go on to next page

19. If Gear 1 moves in a clockwise direction, which other gears also turn clockwise?

(A) 3 and 5

(B) 3, 4, and 5

(C) 2 and 5

(D) 3 and 4

20. The pressure gauge in the figure below shows a reading of

(A) 15.0

(B) 19.5

(C) 21.0

(D) 23.0

21. A way to determine the amount of power being used is to

(A) multiply the amount of work done by the time it takes.

(B) multiply the distance covered by the time it takes to move a load.

(C) divide the amount of work done by 550 pounds per second.

(D) divide the amount of work done by the amount of time it takes.

22. A wood tool, a silver tool, and a steel tool are placed in boiling water for cleaning. Which tool will get hot the fastest?

(A) steel

(B) wood

(C) silver

(D) All three are equally hot.

23. A runner is being used in the figure shown. How much effort is the boy who's lifting the 50-pound anvil using? Disregard friction, wind resistance, and the weight of the pulley and the rope.

50 pounds

(A) 50-pound effort

(B) 100-pound effort

(C) 25-pound effort

(D) 10-pound effort

Go on to next page

24. In the figure below, at what point was the ball traveling most slowly?

(A) A
(B) B
(C) C
(D) D

25. In the figure below, which angle is braced most solidly?

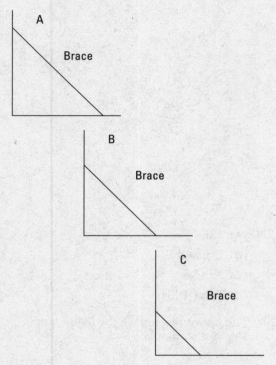

(A) A
(B) B
(C) C
(D) All are braced equally solidly.

STOP DO NOT TURN THE PAGE UNTIL TOLD TO DO SO.
DO NOT RETURN TO A PREVIOUS TEST.

Subtest 9: Assembling Objects

Time: 15 minutes for 25 questions

Directions: The Assembling Objects subtest consists of questions that measure your ability to mentally picture items in two dimensions. Each question is comprised of five separate drawings. The problem is presented in the first drawing, and the remaining four drawings are possible solutions. Determine which of the choices best solves the problem shown in the first picture and then mark the corresponding choice on your answer sheet.

Go on to next page

Chapter 17

Practice Exam 1:
Answers and Explanations

• •

With the first practice test out of the way, you're probably anxious to see how well you did. Use the answer keys in this chapter to score yourself on each of the nine subtests. Remember, your scores on this practice exam don't equate to scores on the actual ASVAB. That's because on the enlistment ASVAB, you get more points for answering harder questions correctly than you do for easier questions. The test is scored by comparing your raw score to the scores of other people, which produces a scaled score, so missing 20 out of 225 questions doesn't mean that your score is 205. The practice exam, however, is a valuable tool for determining which subject areas you need to brush up on. (Turn to Chapter 1 to find out how the ASVAB is scored.)

Subtest 1: General Science Answers

The General Science subtest tests your knowledge of science facts. If you missed a few questions, reread the questions and try to figure out where you went wrong. If you missed more than a few questions, review Chapter 10.

General Science is a broad field, but some of the following books may help you: *Chemistry For Dummies* by John T. Moore, *Biology For Dummies* by Donna Rae Siegfried, *Astronomy For Dummies,* 2nd Edition, by Stephen P. Maran, *Weather For Dummies* by John D. Cox, and *Physics I For Dummies* by Steven Holzner. You can find additional practice questions in Chapter 15.

1. **D**	4. **A**	7. **D**	10. **C**	13. **D**	16. **C**	19. **B**	22. **D**	25. **B**
2. **C**	5. **D**	8. **C**	11. **C**	14. **B**	17. **A**	20. **B**	23. **A**	
3. **C**	6. **D**	9. **C**	12. **D**	15. **A**	18. **D**	21. **A**	24. **B**	

Subtest 2: Arithmetic Reasoning Answers

Arithmetic Reasoning is one of the four ASVAB subtests that make up your Armed Force Qualification Test (AFQT) score, which determines whether you qualify to join the service branch of your choice (check Appendix A to see whether the jobs you're interested in require a score in this subtest). If you missed more than five or six questions, dig out that old high school math textbook and wrap your brain around some math problems. Chapters 7 and 8 may also help you out.

Some books that may help you score better on the Arithmetic Reasoning subtest include *Basic Math & Pre-Algebra For Dummies* by Mark Zegarelli, *Algebra I For Dummies* and *Algebra II For Dummies* by Mary Jane Sterling, and *Geometry For Dummies* by Mark Ryan, as well as the related workbooks. You can also check out Mark Zegarelli's *SAT Math For Dummies* and *ACT Math For Dummies* for some math test practice. Also see Chapter 9 for additional practice questions.

1. **C.** Multiply 12 miles by $3.50 per mile: $12 \times \$3.50 = \$42.00$.

2. **A.** Let x equal the smaller number and $x + 8$ equal the larger number. Because the sum of the two numbers is 70, you can express this mathematically as $x + x + 8 = 70$. Now all you have to do is solve for x. Combine the like terms: $2x + 8 = 70$. Then subtract 8 from both sides of the equation: $2x + 8 - 8 = 70 - 8$, or $2x = 62$. Divide both sides of the equation by 2, and you find that x is equal to 31.

3. **D.** 144 bottles are in a gross, and $144 \div 3$ (bottles per day) = 48 days.

4. **B.** To determine Jenny's average, add the test scores and divide the sum by the number of tests she took. You want to know what she needs on the next test to achieve an average of 95, so let x equal the unknown score. Set up the equation as $(93 + 89 + 96 + 98 + x) \div 5 = 95$. Combine the like terms: $(376 + x) \div 5 = 95$. Multiplying both sides by 5 results in $376 + x = 475$, so $x = 99$.

   Choice (A) is very close to the correct answer, but it isn't the best answer. If Jenny's next test score is 100, her average would be raised to 95.2.

5. **B.** Multiply the total amount spent on food, $375, by 12% (or 0.12) to determine the amount of tips: $\$375 \times 0.12 = \$45$.

6. **D.** You determine square footage by multiplying length by width: $12 \times 12 = 144$.

7. **C.** First determine the number of square feet of carpet you want to protect: $16 \text{ ft.} \times 18 \text{ ft.} = 288 \text{ ft.}^2$ The carpet stain protector is priced by the square yard, so divide 288 by 9 to convert square feet to square yards (because $1 \text{ yd.}^2 = 3 \text{ ft.} \times 3 \text{ ft.} = 9 \text{ ft.}^2$): $288 \text{ ft.}^2 \div 9 \text{ ft.}^2/\text{yd.} = 32 \text{ yd.}^2$

   Multiply the number of square yards by the cost of protection per square yard, $0.65, to get the correct answer: $32 \text{ yd.}^2 \times \$0.65/\text{yd.}^2 = \$20.80$

8. **C.** Let x equal the number of cards printed and sold each month. Each card costs $0.18 to print and sells for $0.30. Therefore, the cost is equal to $6,000 + 0.18x$, and revenue is equal to $0.30x$. You're looking for the point where revenue is greater than the cost (revenue > cost). The inequality is $0.30x > 6,000 + 0.18x$.

   Now solve for x. Subtract $0.18x$ from both sides of the inequality and then divide both sides by 0.12:

   $0.12x > 6,000$

   $x > 50,000$

   The printing plant would have to print and sell at least 50,000 cards per month to make a profit.

9. **C.** Joe gets a 7% raise. To calculate the new wage, start off by multiplying $\$8.15 \times 0.07 = \$0.57$. Then add that number (the amount of Joe's raise) to his original hourly wage. Joe's new hourly wage is $\$8.15 + \$0.57 = \$8.72$.

10. **C.** To find distance, you multiply speed by time. First find how far Alice travels before Dave catches up with her. By the time Dave leaves, Alice has already been traveling for half an hour. Three hours later, she would've been traveling for $3\frac{1}{2}$ hours at 45 mph, or 157.5 miles: $3.5 \text{ hr.} \times 45 \text{ mph} = 157.5 \text{ mi.}$ Dave has three hours to cover this distance. Now find his speed. To travel 157.5 miles in 3 hours, Dave would have to travel at 52.5 mph: $157.5 \text{ mi.} \div 3 \text{ hr.} = 52.5 \text{ mph}$.

11. **D.** To find the amount of pie purchased (which, by the way, does not give you the final answer), you have to add the fractions. But first the fractions need to have a common denominator. The denominators (4, 3, and 6) all divide evenly into 12, so use 12 as the common denominator.

To convert the fractions to the least common denominator of 12, do the following:

$$\frac{1}{4} \times \frac{3}{3} = \frac{3}{12}$$

$$\frac{1}{3} \times \frac{4}{4} = \frac{4}{12}$$

$$\frac{1}{6} \times \frac{2}{2} = \frac{2}{12}$$

Now you can add the fractions together:

$$\frac{3}{12} + \frac{4}{12} + \frac{2}{12} = \frac{3+4+2}{12} = \frac{9}{12}$$

Nine-twelfths of 20 pies is the same thing as $\frac{3}{4}$, or 75%, of the 20 pies. That equals 15 pies. But that's *not* what the question asks. One more step: Subtract the pies sold (15) from the original 20, leaving 5 pies, which makes Choice (D) correct.

12. **A.** Subtract the sale price from the regular price to find how much she saves on each case: $24.00 − $22.50 = $1.50. Multiply the answer by the total number of cases to get your final answer: $1.50 × 5 = $7.50.

13. **C.** Divide 30 by 8 to determine how long the security guard takes to walk one city block: 30 ÷ 8 = 3.75 minutes. Then multiply 3.75 by 6, the number of blocks it takes to complete the circuit. The answer is 22.50 minutes.

14. **B.** Let x equal the original number of how much Grand Island would grow. An additional $\frac{1}{5}$ would make the population growth $\frac{6}{5}$, or 120%, of x. You can express the equation as $1.2x = 600{,}000$. To solve for x, divide both sides of the equation by 1.2, which gives you $x = 500{,}000$.

15. **D.** Divide the number of questions she has to get right (40) by the total number of questions (60) to reach $66\frac{2}{3}$%.

16. **C.** The interest formula says that interest equals principal times rate times time, or $I = Prt$. To determine the amount of interest earned, multiply the principal ($3,000) by the interest rate (6%) and the number of years interest accrues (1 year): $3,000 × 0.06 × 1 = $180. Add the interest earned to the principal to show how much total money the teacher would have: $180 + $3,000 = $3,180.

17. **B.** Recognize that if the track is a quarter mile long, then 1 mile equals four laps. Therefore, multiply 4 times 3.5 miles; the answer is 14 laps.

18. **A.** One kilometer is approximately $\frac{5}{8}$ of 1 mile, so you can multiply $75 \times \frac{5}{8}$: $75 \times 5 = 375$, and $375 ÷ 8 =$ about 46.8. Therefore, Karl was traveling at 47 miles per hour.

19. **A.** You need to add the carpenter's base pay and overtime pay to find his total pay for the week. First find his base pay per week: $12.30/hr. × 40 hr. = $492. Then find his overtime rate per hour, which is $1\frac{1}{2}$ times his base pay: $12.30/hr. × 1.5 = $18.45. Multiply this rate by the number of hours of overtime to find his overtime pay: $18.45/hr. × 6 hr. = $110.70. Finally, add his base pay and overtime pay to find his total pay for the week: $492.00 + $110.70 = $602.70.

20. **A.** The office has 1,260 square feet of space (multiply 42 square feet by 30 employees). With 35 employees, each employee will have 36 square feet of work space (1,260 ÷ 35), which is 6 square feet less than originally.

21. **B.** The total cost is the down payment plus 5 years' worth of monthly payments. Five years contain 60 months, so multiply $450 (monthly payment) × 60 = $27,000 (total payments). Then add $27,000 (total payments) + $2,000 (down payment) = $29,000 (total cost).

22. **D.** Add the three monthly amounts to determine the total amount Darla spent on groceries: $120.37 + $108.45 + $114.86 = $343.68. Divide the total by 3 to determine the average monthly cost: $114.56.

23. **C.** Distance equals speed times time, so divide the total distance by Keith's average speed to find how long the trip took: 1,650 mi. ÷ 50 mph = 33 hr.

24. **B.** Choice (A) doesn't provide enough paint (2 × 25 gal. = 50 gal.), so it's wrong. Now determine the cost of each of the other options:

    Choice (B): 11 × $108 = $1,188

    Choice (C): 6 × $215 = $1,290

    Choice (D): 55 × $23 = $1,265

    The lowest price is $1,188, Choice (B).

25. **B.** First find how many ounces of rations each truck can hold. One ton is 2,000 pounds, so one truck can carry three times that, or 6,000 pounds. There are 16 ounces in a pound, so one truck can carry 96,000 ounces: 6,000 lbs. × 16 oz. = 96,000 oz.

    Then figure out how many daily rations are in a truckload. The total daily ration for each resident is 12 ounces + 18 ounces + 18 ounces, or 48 ounces. You can express the number of daily rations supplied as 96,000 oz. ÷ 48 oz./daily ration = 2,000 daily rations. These rations need to last 10 days. Dividing 2,000 by 10 days results in 200 residents who can be fed by one truck during this 10-day period.

26. **D.** The train headed for Wichita traveled 55 miles/hour × 3 hours = 165 total miles. The train headed for Des Moines traveled 70 miles/hour × 3 hours = 210 total miles. Adding the distances together gives you the number of miles apart the two trains are after three hours: 210 + 165 = 375. ***Another option:*** You can add the two rates of speed (55 + 70) and multiply the sum by 3 hours (125 × 3 hours = 375).

27. **A.** Convert the mixed number to inches: 3 feet, 8 inches equals 44 inches (12 in./ft. × 3 ft. = 36 in., and 36 in. + 8 in. = 44 in.). Forty-four inches (length each section needs to be) × 4 (number of sections needed) = 176 inches (total molding needed). To find the amount of molding needed in feet, convert 176 inches into feet by dividing 176 inches by 12 inches. You get $14\frac{2}{3}$ feet, so the shortest board length necessary is 15 feet.

28. **A.** One turkey breast costs $8.50 minus 10% of $8.50 (which is $0.85), or $8.50 − $0.85 = $7.65. The other turkey breast is full price, so add the two costs: $7.65 + $8.50 = $16.15.

29. **C.** Don't let the number of miles traveled confuse you. You don't use them to solve the problem. Finding $\frac{2}{5}$ of a 40-hour workweek is the same thing as multiplying 40 times 2, which is 80, and then dividing 80 by 5, which equals 16 hours the recruiter travels weekly.

30. **B.** Your first step is to determine the number of miles traveled. Multiply the rate of travel by the time: 48 × 7 = 336 mi. The amount of gas used is the total miles driven divided by the number of miles per gallon: 336 ÷ 21 = 16 gal. used. At the price of $2.82 per gallon, you spent $45.12 for gas: $2.82 × 16 = $45.12.

Subtest 3: Word Knowledge Answers

The Word Knowledge subtest is nothing more than a vocabulary test. However, it's very important because it's another one of the four subtests used to make up your AFQT score. If you find you need to improve your vocabulary, see Chapter 4.

A couple of other great study references are *Vocabulary For Dummies* by Laurie E. Rozakis (Wiley) and *SAT Vocabulary For Dummies* by Suzee Vlk (Wiley). Additionally, see Chapter 6 for more practice questions.

1. **A**	6. **C**	11. **B**	16. **A**	21. **D**	26. **D**	31. **C**
2. **A**	7. **A**	12. **D**	17. **A**	22. **A**	27. **B**	32. **A**
3. **B**	8. **D**	13. **B**	18. **C**	23. **C**	28. **B**	33. **C**
4. **C**	9. **D**	14. **B**	19. **A**	24. **D**	29. **C**	34. **D**
5. **C**	10. **B**	15. **D**	20. **D**	25. **B**	30. **B**	35. **A**

Subtest 4: Paragraph Comprehension Answers

Like Word Knowledge, your Paragraph Comprehension score goes toward your AFQT score, so pay special attention if you've missed more than a couple of these answers — you need some study time (see Chapter 5). Remember that rereading the paragraph several times to make sure you have the right answer is perfectly fine. You can find additional practice questions in Chapter 6.

1. **C.** Effective appointment management eliminates the waste of your time, as the last sentence of the passage explains.

2. **D.** The passage gives the numbers of senators and representatives, so Choice (A) is incorrect. The passage states that each state's population determines the number of representatives a state has, so Choice (B) is incorrect. As the passage states, each state has at least one representative, so Choice (C) is incorrect.

3. **A.** Many languages are excluded from the Indo-European language group, so Choice (B) is incorrect. Indians, Iranians, Asians, and Afghans aren't Europeans, so Choice (C) is incorrect. The passage gives no evidence to support Choice (D), which isn't true.

4. **D.** Privatized functions operate independently of the government, making Choices (A) and (B) incorrect. The passage states that privatized functions may sell goods and services to other customers as well as the government, so Choice (C) is also incorrect. Choice (D) is the correct answer, because privatized functions do perform essential services to government agencies.

5. **C.** Choice (A) — "Lead by Example" — is a good philosophy but isn't pertinent to the main point of the passage. Choices (B) and (D) are subpoints, which support the main point of the passage, which is how to lead a successful conference (C).

6. **A.** You can assume that causing rain or snow would end a drought, Choice (A). Nothing in the passage has to do with expense, so Choice (B) is incorrect. The passage says nothing about how frequently the process is used, so Choice (C) is incorrect. The passage specifies that dry ice (solid carbon dioxide) is used; regular ice (solid water) is a different substance, so Choice (D) is wrong.

7. **C.** Choices (A) and (B) may be true in certain situations, but they're not the point of this particular paragraph. The passage doesn't say anything about working to improve writing skills being a waste of time, so Choice (D) is incorrect. The main point of the paragraph is that writing may not be the most efficient way of communicating, depending on the situation.

8. **B.** Products with transistors weren't widely sold before 1954 because of the expense and difficulty of production, not because markets didn't exist, so Choice (A) is incorrect. Choice (C) has the right date, but the passage doesn't say who invented the transistor,

so it's wrong as well. Choice (D) is wrong because the passage states that the problem of transistors' being expensive to produce was solved by 1954. The last sentence notes that the first transistor radio went on the market after cost and production problems were overcome, so (B) is the right answer.

9. **B.** The words *London* and *Englishman* make it clear that the author is speaking of his travels in England, which is part of Great Britain.

10. **A.** The author makes no reference to parents in the passage, so Choice (B) is incorrect. The author doesn't imply anything about all these interests requiring equal time, so Choice (C) is incorrect. The passage is about children under 18; you can't draw a conclusion about what the author thinks people over 18 should do, so Choice (D) is incorrect.

11. **C.** The passage doesn't say anything about mock job interviews being frightening, so Choice (A) is wrong. The passage says that mock job interviews should be available to all students, so Choice (B) is wrong. The passage says that schools, not students, should organize mock interviews, so Choice (D) is incorrect.

12. **A.** Choices (B), (C), and (D) are the opposite of what the paragraph states and implies.

13. **B.** Nothing in the paragraph supports Choice (A), which is incorrect. When an amendment is passed, it becomes part of the Constitution, so Choice (C) is incorrect. The passage doesn't support Choice (D), because the passage doesn't mention anything related to lottery tickets. The passage defines *due process* as " the guarantee of fairness in the administration of justice," so (B) is correct.

14. **C.** Because the 14th Amendment guarantees due process in states' laws, the 5th Amendment must guarantee due process only in federal law, which makes Choice (C) right. Nothing in the passage implies that the 5th Amendment is about taxes, so Choice (A) is wrong. Because the passage states that the 14th Amendment had to be enacted to require states to abide by due process, Choice (B) is incorrect. Choice (D) is neither stated nor implied in the passage.

15. **A.** Because the Supreme Court struck down many state laws after the 14th Amendment was enacted, it's probably true that these laws would still exist if there'd been no 14th Amendment. The passage doesn't support Choices (B), (C), or (D).

Subtest 5: Mathematics Knowledge Answers

This subtest is also used to calculate your AFQT score, so it's important. If you miss more than four or five, consider brushing up on your basic math skills. Chapters 7 and 8 can help with this.

The following books may also be of some help: *Algebra I For Dummies* and *Algebra II For Dummies* by Mary Jane Sterling, *Geometry For Dummies* and *Calculus For Dummies* by Mark Ryan, and *SAT Math For Dummies* by Mark Zegarelli (all books published by Wiley). Chapter 9 also has some additional practice questions.

1. **A.** Substitute 8 for x in the equation and then solve for y:

$$y = (x^2 \div 4) - 2$$
$$= (8^2 \div 4) - 2$$
$$= (64 \div 4) - 2$$
$$= 16 - 2$$
$$= 14$$

2. **A.** The cube of 5 is 5^3, which is $5 \times 5 \times 5 = 125$.

3. **C.** Because of the order of operations, you need to find 3^3 first and then multiply by 2.5:

$$2.5 \times 3^3$$

$$= 2.5(3 \times 3 \times 3)$$

$$= 2.5 \times 27$$

$$= 67.5$$

4. **D.** Because $2^4 = 16$, the fourth root of 16 is 2.

5. **A.** To get the equation of the line, you need to know the line's slope and y-intercept. The slope of the line is equal to the change in y values divided by the change in x values. The change in y values is $3 - (-1) = 4$. The change in x values is $2 - 0 = 2$. Thus, the slope is $\frac{4}{2} = 2$. The line passes through the point $(0, 1)$, so to find the intercept, substitute 0 for x and -1 for y in the equation $y = 2x + b$:

$$-1 = 2(0) + b$$

$$b = -1$$

Therefore, $b = -1$, so the full equation is $y = 2x - 1$.

6. **C.** Do what's in parentheses first. You need consistent units of measurement, so convert 12 yards to feet; then add 14 feet:

$$(12 \text{ yd.} \times 3 \text{ ft./yd.}) + 14 \text{ ft.}$$

$$= 36 \text{ feet} + 14 \text{ feet}$$

$$= 50 \text{ feet}$$

The original problem asks for $(12 \text{ yards} + 14 \text{ feet}) \div 5$, so divide by 5 as instructed: $50 \text{ feet} \div 5 = 10 \text{ feet}$.

7. **D.** If two powers have the same base, you multiply them by keeping the base the same and adding the powers together: $x^3 \cdot x^4 = x^{3+4} = x^7$.

8. **D.** To find $(x + 4)(x + 2)$, you need to multiply every term in the first set of parentheses by every term in the second set and then add the results. The acronym FOIL (First, Outside, Inside, Last) can help you keep track of which terms you're multiplying:

- ✔ **First:** Multiply the first variable in the first set of parentheses by the first variable in the second set of parentheses: $x(x) = x^2$.

- ✔ **Outside:** Next, multiply the first variable in the first set of parentheses by the second number in the second set of parentheses: $x(2) = 2x$. So far, the results are $x^2 + 2x$.

- ✔ **Inside:** Now multiply the second number in the first set of parentheses by the first variable in the second set of parentheses: $4(x) = 4x$.

- ✔ **Last:** Next, multiply the second number in the first set of parentheses by the second number in the second set of parentheses: $4(2) = 8$.

The solution is $x^2 + 2x + 4x + 8$. Combining the like terms results in $x^2 + 6x + 8$.

9. **C.** You need to do powers (exponents) first, so find 10^3 and then multiply by 1.5:

$$1.5 \times 10^3$$

$$= 1.5 \times (10 \times 10 \times 10)$$

$$= 1.5 \times 1,000$$

$$= 1,500$$

10. **B.** A *prime number* is a number that can be divided evenly by itself or by 1 but not by any other number. Choices (A), (C), and (D) can all be divided evenly by other numbers.

11. **B.** The *mode* of a series of numbers is the number that appears in the series the most frequently. In this case, it's 8.

12. **D.** Substitute 4 for all a's in the problem and then solve, doing the powers first:

$$4^3 \div 4$$

$$= (4 \times 4 \times 4) \div 4$$

$$= 64 \div 4$$

$$= 16$$

13. **C.** The factorial (!) of a number is the number multiplied by the next-smallest whole number, then by the next smallest whole number, and so on down to 1:

$$5! = 5 \times 4 \times 3 \times 2 \times 1 = 120$$

14. **B.** Do what's in parentheses first:

$$(900 \times 2) \div 6 = 1{,}800 \div 6 = 300$$

15. **A.** Substitute 2 for all x's in the problem and then solve, starting with the powers:

$$2^2(2) = 4(2) = 8$$

16. **D.** The problem asks you to solve $(5 + 1)(6 \div 3)(8 - 5) = (3 + 3)x$ for x. Solve the first half of the equation, finding the values in parentheses first:

$$(6)(2)(3) = 36$$

Therefore, the whole equation becomes $36 = (3 + 3)x$, which turns into $36 = 6x$. Isolate x:

$$36 \div 6 = 6x \div 6$$

$$6 = x$$

To check your answer, substitute 6 for x.

17. **A.** The square root of 49 is 7; the square root of 64 is 8. And $7 \times 8 = 56$.

18. **D.** Find a common denominator for the fractions. In this case, 80 works for all the fractions. Convert all the fractions using the following method:

$$\frac{2}{5} \times \frac{16}{16} = \frac{32}{80}$$

$$\frac{3}{8} \times \frac{10}{10} = \frac{30}{80}$$

$$\frac{7}{10} \times \frac{8}{8} = \frac{56}{80}$$

$$\frac{13}{16} \times \frac{5}{5} = \frac{65}{80}$$

Comparing the fractions, you can see that $\frac{65}{80}$ $\left(\text{or } \frac{13}{16}\right)$ is the largest fraction.

19. **B.** Solve as you would solve for any unknown:

$$2 + x \geq 4$$

$$2 + x - 2 \geq 4 - 2$$

Therefore, $x \geq 2$. To check your answer, substitute 2 for x: $2 + 2 \geq 4$. That's true, so the answer is correct.

20. **C.** Circumference equals $\pi \times$ diameter, and diameter is equal to two times the radius (or mathematically, $C = \pi d$ and $d = 2r$). For this problem, $C = \pi \times 24$. If you round π to 3.14, the answer is about 75.36, or about 75 feet.

21. **A.** Volume equals length $\times$ width $\times$ height ($V = lwh$), so plug in the numbers and solve: $16 \times 8 \times 18 = 2{,}304$ in.^{3}

22. **C.** In an equilateral triangle, all sides are equal and all angles are equal.

23. **A.** All quadrilaterals (four-sided figures) have angles that total 360 degrees.

24. **B.** If the sum of two angles equals 90 degrees, they're called *complementary angles*.

25. **A.** $24\% = \frac{24}{100}$. You further reduce this fraction to $\frac{6}{25}$ by dividing the numerator and denominator by 4.

Subtest 6: Electronics Information Answers

The Electronics Information subtest is particularly important if you want to obtain a job that requires a solid score in this area. You can check Appendix A to see whether the job(s) you're interested in requires a high score in Electronics Information. If so, you shouldn't miss more than five questions in this practice exam. If you do, you may want to review Chapter 13.

If you need even more study, check out *Electronics For Dummies* by Cathleen Shamieh and Gordon McComb (Wiley) or consider enrolling in a quick course at a community college. You can also find additional practice questions in Chapter 15.

1. **A.** Ohm's law states that Voltage *(E)* = Current *(I)* × Resistance *(R)*. All other answers are incorrect expressions of this law.

2. **A.** You read a resistor's color bands from left to right. The first band denotes the first digit, the second band denotes the second digit, and the third band denotes the subsequent number of zeros. In this example, brown is one, black is zero, and red means there are two additional zeros.

3. **B.** Heaters, pumps, stairs, diving boards, railings, and rebar, among other things, must be bonded together by a minimum #8 wire for safety purposes.

4. **D.** *Voltage* is commonly used as a short name for electrical potential difference, and it is measured in volts.

5. **A.** SIM stands for *Subscriber Identity Module.* The card contains information such as your phone number, your billing information, and your address book. The card makes it easier to switch from one cell phone to another.

6. **A.** A resistor is so named because it resists (or inhibits) the flow of current.

7. **C.** A diode has two terminals, the anode and the cathode, which is why it's called a *diode*. It restricts current flow to only one direction.

8. **C.** Radar can operate as high as 100,000 MHz (megahertz).

9. **B.** *Current* is the flow of charged particles. The difference between *alternating current* (AC) and *direct current* (DC) is that the electrons in an AC circuit regularly reverse their direction. In a DC circuit, electrons always flow in the same direction.

10. **C.** Changing AC to DC is a process called *rectification.*

11. **C.** A British thermal unit (BTU) is a measure of heat energy.

12. **D.** *Current* is the presence of electron flow.

13. **B.** *Transducers,* which transform energy, can be switches, strain gauges, temperature sensors, or inductive switches.

14. **D.** *Active elements* are electronic devices that can create energy (such as voltage supplies and current supplies). *Passive elements* are electronic devices that cannot create energy.

15. **A.** Power = Current × Voltage or, written another way, Current = Power ÷ Voltage. Plug in the numbers and do the math: 60 watts ÷ 120 volts = 0.5 amperes.

16. **C.** The larger the number, the smaller the diameter of the wire.

17. **C.** Because fuses are designed to prevent current overload at a specific level, a fuse with a high rating may allow a higher current to flow through a circuit not designed to work at that higher current, possibly causing damage to the circuit.

18. **A.** Neutral wire is always whitish or natural colored.

19. **D.** Electrical power is measured in watts, so you use a wattmeter. An ammeter measures amps (current). An ohmmeter measures ohms (resistance). A voltmeter measures volts (voltage).

20. **B.** The bulb will burn dimmer because its full potential isn't used; it'll last longer for the same reason.

Subtest 7: Auto & Shop Information Answers

The Auto & Shop Information subtest is fairly straightforward. You either know the information or you don't. Not knowing the info may not matter to you as long as the career you want doesn't require a subtest score in this area (check the Appendix to see whether the jobs you're interested in require a score in this subtest). But if you do need to do well on this subtest and you've missed more than five answers, review the material in Chapter 11.

Reviewing *Auto Repair For Dummies* by Deanna Sclar (Wiley) may also help you score better on this subtest. *Home Improvement All-in-One For Dummies* by Roy Barnhart, James Carey, Morris Carey, Gene Hamilton, Katie Hamilton, Donald R. Prestly, and Jeff Strong (Wiley) can help you get a better handle on basic tools and their uses. You may even want to take a class at a nearby community college or at least hang out at the garage and help some mechanics for a couple of weeks. See Chapter 15 for some more practice questions.

1. D	4. A	7. D	10. B	13. C	16. C	19. C	22. B	25. A
2. B	5. A	8. C	11. C	14. B	17. B	20. C	23. A	
3. B	6. A	9. D	12. A	15. B	18. B	21. A	24. D	

Subtest 8: Mechanical Comprehension Answers

The Mechanical Comprehension subtest is important only if you want to pursue a military career that requires a good score on this subtest (check Appendix A to see whether the jobs you're interested in require a score in this subtest). Otherwise, spend your time studying more important areas of the ASVAB. If you're considering a military job that requires a high mechanical aptitude and you missed more than four or five questions on this subtest, give Chapter 12 another once over.

1. **A.** An induction clutch is a magnetic clutch. When a conductor (wire) is wrapped around a core and electricity is passed through the wire, it sets up a magnetic field. The same wire also acts as an inductor, which produces inductance, during AC current flow. It's similar to resistance in a resistor in that it "resists" current flow, but the value of inductance is based on the value of the inductor (written as L) and the frequency of the AC current. Therefore, an induction clutch uses magnetism to operate.

2. **B.** You can calculate mechanical advantage as Length of Effort Arm ÷ Length of Resistance Arm. Simply plug in the numbers: $MA = 8 \div 2 = 4$.

3. **D.** The box with the largest area on the bottom will have the shortest sides. If Length × Width × Height = Volume and all the boxes have equal volume, then the sides must be shortest on the box with the largest area on the bottom. Calculate the area of each box bottom:

   No. 1 = 20 square inches

   No. 2 = 35 square inches

   No. 3 = 48 square inches

   No. 4 = 27 square inches

   No. 3, which has the largest area, will have the shortest sides.

4. **C.** Anvil B's landing on the seesaw will propel Anvil A into the air.

5. **A.** Pressure equals force divided by area in square inches ($P = F \div A$). You can also state this formula as $F = A \times P$. Substitute the known quantities: $F = 15 \times 24 = 360$ pounds.

6. **C.** *Recoil* occurs when an object producing a force is kicked back.

7. **A.** To determine the answer, multiply the number of teeth Gear 1 has *(D)* and the number of revolutions it makes *(R)*. Divide that number by the number of teeth Gear 2 has *(d)* to determine the number of revolutions Gear 2 makes *(r)*. Because the gears are proportional, this formula shows you the ratio of teeth to revolutions.

$$r = \frac{DR}{d}$$
$$r = \frac{25 \times 10}{15}$$
$$r = \frac{250}{15} = \frac{50}{3} = 16\frac{2}{3}$$

8. **B.** You can determine the pressure of all that water by multiplying the volume of the aquarium by the weight of the water. Volume = *lwh*. The bottom of the tank is 18 feet long by 12 feet wide by 10 feet high for a total volume of 2,160 cubic feet: $18 \times 12 \times 10 = 2{,}160$ ft.³ A cubic foot of water weighs approximately 62.5 pounds, so multiply the volume of water by 62.5: $2{,}160 \times 62.5 = 135{,}000$.

   That gives an approximate pressure on the bottom of the tank of about 135,000 pounds over the entire surface area. The surface area of the bottom of the tank is length × width. Convert feet to inches and then find the area: $A = (18 \text{ ft.} \times 12 \text{ in./ft.}) \times (12 \text{ ft.} \times 12 \text{ in./ft.}) = 216 \text{ in.} \times 144 \text{ in.} = 31{,}104 \text{ in.}^2$.

   Dividing the pressure of 135,000 by the number of square inches of surface area gives an approximate psi of 4.

9. **D.** Machine springs are usually made of steel, although sometimes they're made of brass or other metal alloys.

10. **B.** Clutches connect and disconnect parts, so they're a type of coupling.

11. **D.** When the high point of the cam connects with the lever arm, the lever arm will touch the contact point. Two high points on the cam mean the lever arm will touch the contact point twice with each revolution of the cam.

12. **C.** A *single block-and-fall* is a way to get mechanical advantage by threading a rope through a pulley or stationary point, the load being attached to the end of the rope, and you pulling on the other end of the rope, hoisting the load. The device is also called a *runner*.

13. **C.** If the fulcrum is moved closer to the anvil, the length of the effort arm of the lever will be increased, making the anvil easier to raise, but the height to which the anvil can be raised will be reduced.

14. **A.** Because this block-and-tackle arrangement merely changes the direction of the pull, it has a mechanical advantage of only 2.

15. **C.** The larger cog (Cog A) covers a greater linear distance in a given period of time, so Cog A reaches the top first.

16. **A.** The key will feel coldest because metal is a better conductor than the other materials.

17. **D.** All but Valve 4 should be open. Opening Valves 1 and 2 allows water to enter the tank. Opening Valves 3 and 5 prevents water from filling the tank entirely. Opening Valve 4 allows water to leave the tank.

18. **A.** Gears with their teeth together in mesh turn in opposite directions. Gear A turns Gear B in the opposite direction (right), and Gear B turns Gear C in the opposite direction (left).

19. **A.** Gears with their teeth together in mesh turn in opposite directions. Gear 1 turns clockwise. Gear 2, in mesh with Gear 1, turns counterclockwise. Gear 3, in mesh with Gear 2, turns clockwise. Gear 4, in mesh with Gear 3, turns counterclockwise. Gear 5, in mesh with Gear 2, turns clockwise.

20. **C.** The gauge shows a reading of 21.

21. **D.** The formula for determining power is Power = Work ÷ Time.

22. **C.** Silver is the best conductor, so it will become hotter faster than the other objects because heat transfers faster into materials with greater conductivity than with those with lower conductivity.

23. **A.** Stationary pulleys give no mechanical advantage, so effort equals the weight of the crate, or 50 pounds.

24. **C.** At the height of the arc, the ball has no upward momentum, so it goes the slowest at that point.

25. **A.** The brace on Angle A covers more area of the angle, so it's more solidly braced.

Subtest 9: Assembling Objects Answers

If you plan on enlisting in the Navy, check Appendix A to see whether the jobs you're interested in require a score in this subtest. For more information about the Assembling Objects subtest, see Chapter 14. For additional practice questions, see Chapter 15.

1. C	4. D	7. C	10. B	13. D	16. A	19. C	22. D	25. C
2. A	5. A	8. D	11. A	14. C	17. B	20. A	23. B	
3. D	6. A	9. B	12. D	15. B	18. B	21. B	24. C	

Chapter 18

Practice Exam 2

I've designed the second practice test so you can see how much you've improved. This exam is exactly like the first one from Chapter 16, except (of course) the questions are different. I hope you used the results from the first practice exam to determine your weak areas and spent some time hitting the ol' books and recharging your thinking cap.

To get the most out of this practice exam, take it like you'd take the real ASVAB under the same conditions:

- Allow yourself about three hours to take the entire exam, and take the whole thing at one time.

- Find a quiet place where you won't be interrupted.

- Bring a timer that you can set for various lengths of time, some scratch paper, and a pencil.

- At the start of each subtest, set your timer for the specified period of time. Don't go on to the next section until the timer has gone off, and don't go back to a previous section. If you finish early, check your work for that section only.

- Use the answer sheet that's provided.

- You don't get any breaks in between subtests during the real thing, so try to keep moving along as best as you can.

After you complete the entire sample test, check your answers against the answer explanations and key in Chapter 19.

Answer Sheet for Practice Exam 2

Subtest 1: General Science

1 Ⓐ Ⓑ Ⓒ Ⓓ	6 Ⓐ Ⓑ Ⓒ Ⓓ	11 Ⓐ Ⓑ Ⓒ Ⓓ	16 Ⓐ Ⓑ Ⓒ Ⓓ	21 Ⓐ Ⓑ Ⓒ Ⓓ
2 Ⓐ Ⓑ Ⓒ Ⓓ	7 Ⓐ Ⓑ Ⓒ Ⓓ	12 Ⓐ Ⓑ Ⓒ Ⓓ	17 Ⓐ Ⓑ Ⓒ Ⓓ	22 Ⓐ Ⓑ Ⓒ Ⓓ
3 Ⓐ Ⓑ Ⓒ Ⓓ	8 Ⓐ Ⓑ Ⓒ Ⓓ	13 Ⓐ Ⓑ Ⓒ Ⓓ	18 Ⓐ Ⓑ Ⓒ Ⓓ	23 Ⓐ Ⓑ Ⓒ Ⓓ
4 Ⓐ Ⓑ Ⓒ Ⓓ	9 Ⓐ Ⓑ Ⓒ Ⓓ	14 Ⓐ Ⓑ Ⓒ Ⓓ	19 Ⓐ Ⓑ Ⓒ Ⓓ	24 Ⓐ Ⓑ Ⓒ Ⓓ
5 Ⓐ Ⓑ Ⓒ Ⓓ	10 Ⓐ Ⓑ Ⓒ Ⓓ	15 Ⓐ Ⓑ Ⓒ Ⓓ	20 Ⓐ Ⓑ Ⓒ Ⓓ	25 Ⓐ Ⓑ Ⓒ Ⓓ

Subtest 2: Arithmetic Reasoning

1 Ⓐ Ⓑ Ⓒ Ⓓ	7 Ⓐ Ⓑ Ⓒ Ⓓ	13 Ⓐ Ⓑ Ⓒ Ⓓ	19 Ⓐ Ⓑ Ⓒ Ⓓ	25 Ⓐ Ⓑ Ⓒ Ⓓ
2 Ⓐ Ⓑ Ⓒ Ⓓ	8 Ⓐ Ⓑ Ⓒ Ⓓ	14 Ⓐ Ⓑ Ⓒ Ⓓ	20 Ⓐ Ⓑ Ⓒ Ⓓ	26 Ⓐ Ⓑ Ⓒ Ⓓ
3 Ⓐ Ⓑ Ⓒ Ⓓ	9 Ⓐ Ⓑ Ⓒ Ⓓ	15 Ⓐ Ⓑ Ⓒ Ⓓ	21 Ⓐ Ⓑ Ⓒ Ⓓ	27 Ⓐ Ⓑ Ⓒ Ⓓ
4 Ⓐ Ⓑ Ⓒ Ⓓ	10 Ⓐ Ⓑ Ⓒ Ⓓ	16 Ⓐ Ⓑ Ⓒ Ⓓ	22 Ⓐ Ⓑ Ⓒ Ⓓ	28 Ⓐ Ⓑ Ⓒ Ⓓ
5 Ⓐ Ⓑ Ⓒ Ⓓ	11 Ⓐ Ⓑ Ⓒ Ⓓ	17 Ⓐ Ⓑ Ⓒ Ⓓ	23 Ⓐ Ⓑ Ⓒ Ⓓ	29 Ⓐ Ⓑ Ⓒ Ⓓ
6 Ⓐ Ⓑ Ⓒ Ⓓ	12 Ⓐ Ⓑ Ⓒ Ⓓ	18 Ⓐ Ⓑ Ⓒ Ⓓ	24 Ⓐ Ⓑ Ⓒ Ⓓ	30 Ⓐ Ⓑ Ⓒ Ⓓ

Subtest 3: Word Knowledge

1 Ⓐ Ⓑ Ⓒ Ⓓ	8 Ⓐ Ⓑ Ⓒ Ⓓ	15 Ⓐ Ⓑ Ⓒ Ⓓ	22 Ⓐ Ⓑ Ⓒ Ⓓ	29 Ⓐ Ⓑ Ⓒ Ⓓ
2 Ⓐ Ⓑ Ⓒ Ⓓ	9 Ⓐ Ⓑ Ⓒ Ⓓ	16 Ⓐ Ⓑ Ⓒ Ⓓ	23 Ⓐ Ⓑ Ⓒ Ⓓ	30 Ⓐ Ⓑ Ⓒ Ⓓ
3 Ⓐ Ⓑ Ⓒ Ⓓ	10 Ⓐ Ⓑ Ⓒ Ⓓ	17 Ⓐ Ⓑ Ⓒ Ⓓ	24 Ⓐ Ⓑ Ⓒ Ⓓ	31 Ⓐ Ⓑ Ⓒ Ⓓ
4 Ⓐ Ⓑ Ⓒ Ⓓ	11 Ⓐ Ⓑ Ⓒ Ⓓ	18 Ⓐ Ⓑ Ⓒ Ⓓ	25 Ⓐ Ⓑ Ⓒ Ⓓ	32 Ⓐ Ⓑ Ⓒ Ⓓ
5 Ⓐ Ⓑ Ⓒ Ⓓ	12 Ⓐ Ⓑ Ⓒ Ⓓ	19 Ⓐ Ⓑ Ⓒ Ⓓ	26 Ⓐ Ⓑ Ⓒ Ⓓ	33 Ⓐ Ⓑ Ⓒ Ⓓ
6 Ⓐ Ⓑ Ⓒ Ⓓ	13 Ⓐ Ⓑ Ⓒ Ⓓ	20 Ⓐ Ⓑ Ⓒ Ⓓ	27 Ⓐ Ⓑ Ⓒ Ⓓ	34 Ⓐ Ⓑ Ⓒ Ⓓ
7 Ⓐ Ⓑ Ⓒ Ⓓ	14 Ⓐ Ⓑ Ⓒ Ⓓ	21 Ⓐ Ⓑ Ⓒ Ⓓ	28 Ⓐ Ⓑ Ⓒ Ⓓ	35 Ⓐ Ⓑ Ⓒ Ⓓ

Subtest 4: Paragraph Comprehension

1 Ⓐ Ⓑ Ⓒ Ⓓ	4 Ⓐ Ⓑ Ⓒ Ⓓ	7 Ⓐ Ⓑ Ⓒ Ⓓ	10 Ⓐ Ⓑ Ⓒ Ⓓ	13 Ⓐ Ⓑ Ⓒ Ⓓ
2 Ⓐ Ⓑ Ⓒ Ⓓ	5 Ⓐ Ⓑ Ⓒ Ⓓ	8 Ⓐ Ⓑ Ⓒ Ⓓ	11 Ⓐ Ⓑ Ⓒ Ⓓ	14 Ⓐ Ⓑ Ⓒ Ⓓ
3 Ⓐ Ⓑ Ⓒ Ⓓ	6 Ⓐ Ⓑ Ⓒ Ⓓ	9 Ⓐ Ⓑ Ⓒ Ⓓ	12 Ⓐ Ⓑ Ⓒ Ⓓ	15 Ⓐ Ⓑ Ⓒ Ⓓ

Subtest 5: Mathematics Knowledge

1 Ⓐ Ⓑ Ⓒ Ⓓ	6 Ⓐ Ⓑ Ⓒ Ⓓ	11 Ⓐ Ⓑ Ⓒ Ⓓ	16 Ⓐ Ⓑ Ⓒ Ⓓ	21 Ⓐ Ⓑ Ⓒ Ⓓ
2 Ⓐ Ⓑ Ⓒ Ⓓ	7 Ⓐ Ⓑ Ⓒ Ⓓ	12 Ⓐ Ⓑ Ⓒ Ⓓ	17 Ⓐ Ⓑ Ⓒ Ⓓ	22 Ⓐ Ⓑ Ⓒ Ⓓ
3 Ⓐ Ⓑ Ⓒ Ⓓ	8 Ⓐ Ⓑ Ⓒ Ⓓ	13 Ⓐ Ⓑ Ⓒ Ⓓ	18 Ⓐ Ⓑ Ⓒ Ⓓ	23 Ⓐ Ⓑ Ⓒ Ⓓ
4 Ⓐ Ⓑ Ⓒ Ⓓ	9 Ⓐ Ⓑ Ⓒ Ⓓ	14 Ⓐ Ⓑ Ⓒ Ⓓ	19 Ⓐ Ⓑ Ⓒ Ⓓ	24 Ⓐ Ⓑ Ⓒ Ⓓ
5 Ⓐ Ⓑ Ⓒ Ⓓ	10 Ⓐ Ⓑ Ⓒ Ⓓ	15 Ⓐ Ⓑ Ⓒ Ⓓ	20 Ⓐ Ⓑ Ⓒ Ⓓ	25 Ⓐ Ⓑ Ⓒ Ⓓ

Subtest 6: Electronics Information

1 Ⓐ Ⓑ Ⓒ Ⓓ	5 Ⓐ Ⓑ Ⓒ Ⓓ	9 Ⓐ Ⓑ Ⓒ Ⓓ	13 Ⓐ Ⓑ Ⓒ Ⓓ	17 Ⓐ Ⓑ Ⓒ Ⓓ
2 Ⓐ Ⓑ Ⓒ Ⓓ	6 Ⓐ Ⓑ Ⓒ Ⓓ	10 Ⓐ Ⓑ Ⓒ Ⓓ	14 Ⓐ Ⓑ Ⓒ Ⓓ	18 Ⓐ Ⓑ Ⓒ Ⓓ
3 Ⓐ Ⓑ Ⓒ Ⓓ	7 Ⓐ Ⓑ Ⓒ Ⓓ	11 Ⓐ Ⓑ Ⓒ Ⓓ	15 Ⓐ Ⓑ Ⓒ Ⓓ	19 Ⓐ Ⓑ Ⓒ Ⓓ
4 Ⓐ Ⓑ Ⓒ Ⓓ	8 Ⓐ Ⓑ Ⓒ Ⓓ	12 Ⓐ Ⓑ Ⓒ Ⓓ	16 Ⓐ Ⓑ Ⓒ Ⓓ	20 Ⓐ Ⓑ Ⓒ Ⓓ

Subtest 7: Auto & Shop Information

1 Ⓐ Ⓑ Ⓒ Ⓓ	6 Ⓐ Ⓑ Ⓒ Ⓓ	11 Ⓐ Ⓑ Ⓒ Ⓓ	16 Ⓐ Ⓑ Ⓒ Ⓓ	21 Ⓐ Ⓑ Ⓒ Ⓓ
2 Ⓐ Ⓑ Ⓒ Ⓓ	7 Ⓐ Ⓑ Ⓒ Ⓓ	12 Ⓐ Ⓑ Ⓒ Ⓓ	17 Ⓐ Ⓑ Ⓒ Ⓓ	22 Ⓐ Ⓑ Ⓒ Ⓓ
3 Ⓐ Ⓑ Ⓒ Ⓓ	8 Ⓐ Ⓑ Ⓒ Ⓓ	13 Ⓐ Ⓑ Ⓒ Ⓓ	18 Ⓐ Ⓑ Ⓒ Ⓓ	23 Ⓐ Ⓑ Ⓒ Ⓓ
4 Ⓐ Ⓑ Ⓒ Ⓓ	9 Ⓐ Ⓑ Ⓒ Ⓓ	14 Ⓐ Ⓑ Ⓒ Ⓓ	19 Ⓐ Ⓑ Ⓒ Ⓓ	24 Ⓐ Ⓑ Ⓒ Ⓓ
5 Ⓐ Ⓑ Ⓒ Ⓓ	10 Ⓐ Ⓑ Ⓒ Ⓓ	15 Ⓐ Ⓑ Ⓒ Ⓓ	20 Ⓐ Ⓑ Ⓒ Ⓓ	25 Ⓐ Ⓑ Ⓒ Ⓓ

Subtest 8: Mechanical Comprehension

1 Ⓐ Ⓑ Ⓒ Ⓓ	6 Ⓐ Ⓑ Ⓒ Ⓓ	11 Ⓐ Ⓑ Ⓒ Ⓓ	16 Ⓐ Ⓑ Ⓒ Ⓓ	21 Ⓐ Ⓑ Ⓒ Ⓓ
2 Ⓐ Ⓑ Ⓒ Ⓓ	7 Ⓐ Ⓑ Ⓒ Ⓓ	12 Ⓐ Ⓑ Ⓒ Ⓓ	17 Ⓐ Ⓑ Ⓒ Ⓓ	22 Ⓐ Ⓑ Ⓒ Ⓓ
3 Ⓐ Ⓑ Ⓒ Ⓓ	8 Ⓐ Ⓑ Ⓒ Ⓓ	13 Ⓐ Ⓑ Ⓒ Ⓓ	18 Ⓐ Ⓑ Ⓒ Ⓓ	23 Ⓐ Ⓑ Ⓒ Ⓓ
4 Ⓐ Ⓑ Ⓒ Ⓓ	9 Ⓐ Ⓑ Ⓒ Ⓓ	14 Ⓐ Ⓑ Ⓒ Ⓓ	19 Ⓐ Ⓑ Ⓒ Ⓓ	24 Ⓐ Ⓑ Ⓒ Ⓓ
5 Ⓐ Ⓑ Ⓒ Ⓓ	10 Ⓐ Ⓑ Ⓒ Ⓓ	15 Ⓐ Ⓑ Ⓒ Ⓓ	20 Ⓐ Ⓑ Ⓒ Ⓓ	25 Ⓐ Ⓑ Ⓒ Ⓓ

Subtest 9: Assembling Objects

1 Ⓐ Ⓑ Ⓒ Ⓓ	6 Ⓐ Ⓑ Ⓒ Ⓓ	11 Ⓐ Ⓑ Ⓒ Ⓓ	16 Ⓐ Ⓑ Ⓒ Ⓓ	21 Ⓐ Ⓑ Ⓒ Ⓓ
2 Ⓐ Ⓑ Ⓒ Ⓓ	7 Ⓐ Ⓑ Ⓒ Ⓓ	12 Ⓐ Ⓑ Ⓒ Ⓓ	17 Ⓐ Ⓑ Ⓒ Ⓓ	22 Ⓐ Ⓑ Ⓒ Ⓓ
3 Ⓐ Ⓑ Ⓒ Ⓓ	8 Ⓐ Ⓑ Ⓒ Ⓓ	13 Ⓐ Ⓑ Ⓒ Ⓓ	18 Ⓐ Ⓑ Ⓒ Ⓓ	23 Ⓐ Ⓑ Ⓒ Ⓓ
4 Ⓐ Ⓑ Ⓒ Ⓓ	9 Ⓐ Ⓑ Ⓒ Ⓓ	14 Ⓐ Ⓑ Ⓒ Ⓓ	19 Ⓐ Ⓑ Ⓒ Ⓓ	24 Ⓐ Ⓑ Ⓒ Ⓓ
5 Ⓐ Ⓑ Ⓒ Ⓓ	10 Ⓐ Ⓑ Ⓒ Ⓓ	15 Ⓐ Ⓑ Ⓒ Ⓓ	20 Ⓐ Ⓑ Ⓒ Ⓓ	25 Ⓐ Ⓑ Ⓒ Ⓓ

Subtest 1: General Science

Time: 11 minutes for 25 questions

Directions: This exam tests your knowledge of general science principles usually covered in high school classes. Pick the best answer for each question and then mark the space on your answer sheet that corresponds to the question number and the letter indicating your choice.

1. What is the change in body form that an insect undergoes from birth to maturity?

    (A) transformation

    (B) metamorphosis

    (C) trinity

    (D) transmutation

2. An earthquake that measures 4 on the Richter scale would be how many times stronger than an earthquake that measured 2?

    (A) 2 times stronger

    (B) 4 times stronger

    (C) 10 times stronger

    (D) 100 times stronger

3. Muscles attach to bone with

    (A) nonconnective tissue.

    (B) ligaments.

    (C) tendons.

    (D) rubber bands.

4. The male part of a flower is called

    (A) the stamen.

    (B) the pistil.

    (C) the throttle.

    (D) stubborn.

5. Blood leaving the lungs is

    (A) hydrogenated.

    (B) coagulated.

    (C) watery.

    (D) oxygenated.

6. Which river is the longest?

    (A) Mississippi

    (B) Nile

    (C) Colorado

    (D) Congo

7. The branch of science that studies matter and energy is called

    (A) chemistry.

    (B) physics.

    (C) oceanography.

    (D) trigonometry.

8. Which type of cloud's name comes from the Latin word meaning "rain"?

    (A) nimbus

    (B) cirrus

    (C) strato

    (D) alto

9. Deoxyribonucleic acid is better known as

    (A) antacid.

    (B) carbohydrates.

    (C) triglyceride.

    (D) DNA.

10. The instrument used to measure wind speed is

    (A) barometer.

    (B) anemometer.

    (C) altimeter.

    (D) fanometer.

Go on to next page

11. Electric charges can be
    (A) positive or negative.
    (B) positive or neutral.
    (C) negative or neutral.
    (D) neutral only.

12. Which planet in the solar system has the most moons?
    (A) Neptune
    (B) Saturn
    (C) Jupiter
    (D) Uranus

13. The law of gravitation was discovered by
    (A) Albert Einstein.
    (B) Isaac Newton.
    (C) Alexander Graham Bell.
    (D) Rod Powers.

14. Which U.S. space program is responsible for putting 12 men on the moon?
    (A) Gemini
    (B) Titan
    (C) Voyager
    (D) Apollo

15. Animals that eat both plants and animals are called
    (A) herbivores.
    (B) carnivores.
    (C) omnivores.
    (D) ambidextrous.

16. Unlike most other fish, sharks have no
    (A) gills.
    (B) bones.
    (C) liver.
    (D) heart.

17. What human organ is responsible for detoxification of red blood cells?
    (A) liver
    (B) kidneys
    (C) intestines
    (D) stomach

18. Kinetic energy is the energy that
    (A) is produced by sound waves.
    (B) an object potentially has.
    (C) is possessed by a moving object.
    (D) results from the attraction of two magnets.

19. The terrestrial planets consist of
    (A) Jupiter, Saturn, Uranus, and Neptune.
    (B) Pluto and Neptune.
    (C) Mercury, Venus, Earth, and Mars.
    (D) any planet.

20. A step-up transformer
    (A) increases the voltage in a power line.
    (B) decreases the voltage in a power line.
    (C) doesn't affect the voltage in a power line.
    (D) measures the voltage in a power line.

21. Which animal has the heaviest brain?
    (A) human
    (B) elephant
    (C) rhinoceros
    (D) sperm whale

22. The sun is what type of star?
    (A) O type
    (B) G type
    (C) F type
    (D) M type

Go on to next page

23. Molecules are created when

    (A) matter is created.

    (B) matter is destroyed.

    (C) atoms combine together.

    (D) atoms are separated.

24. An example of an embryonic plant would be a

    (A) tree.

    (B) rose.

    (C) seed.

    (D) cabbage.

25. The vernal equinox is

    (A) the first day of winter.

    (B) near the equator.

    (C) the first day of spring.

    (D) a lunar eclipse.

STOP DO NOT TURN THE PAGE UNTIL TOLD TO DO SO. DO NOT RETURN TO A PREVIOUS TEST.

Subtest 2: Arithmetic Reasoning

Time: 36 minutes for 30 questions

Directions: The questions in the arithmetic test are each followed by four possible answers. Decide which answer is correct and then mark the space on your answer sheet that has the same number and letter as your choice. Use scratch paper for any figuring you need to do. Calculators are not allowed.

1. If you roll two six-sided dice, what's the probability of NOT rolling a five on either die?

    (A) $\frac{1}{36}$

    (B) $\frac{1}{6}$

    (C) $\frac{4}{36}$

    (D) $\frac{25}{36}$

2. Jack loaned Bob $1,500 at an annual interest rate of 7%. After one year, how much will Bob owe Jack?

    (A) $105

    (B) $1,500

    (C) $1,605

    (D) $1,507

3. A 2-ton truck is taxed at a rate of $0.12 per pound. How much is the total tax bill?

    (A) $480

    (B) $240

    (C) $120

    (D) $600

4. If $ab = 10$ and $a^2 + b^2 = 30$, solve for y in the equation $y = (a + b)^2$.

    (A) 40

    (B) 45

    (C) 50

    (D) 55

5. A half-pint of cream is what part of a gallon?

    (A) $\frac{1}{8}$

    (B) $\frac{1}{4}$

    (C) $\frac{1}{16}$

    (D) $\frac{1}{6}$

6. The cost of a protein bar increased from $2.50 to $2.80. The percent increase to the $2.80 rate was how much?

    (A) 16%

    (B) 10%

    (C) 15%

    (D) 12%

7. An aircraft flies over Boondock Air Force Base at 10:20 a.m. At 10:32 a.m., the aircraft passes over Sea Side Naval Air Station, 120 miles away. How fast is the aircraft traveling?

    (A) 400 mph

    (B) 500 mph

    (C) 600 mph

    (D) 700 mph

8. Last year, Margot grew 50 bushels of corn in her backyard. This year, the yield has increased 8%. How many bushels of corn did Margot grow this year?

    (A) 56

    (B) 52

    (C) 60

    (D) 54

Go on to next page

9. Junior has saved money in his piggy bank over the winter. He wants to buy a $30 computer game. If he has 14 one-dollar bills, 16 half dollars, 12 quarters, 8 dimes, 25 nickels, and 10 pennies, how much more does he need to borrow from Dad to buy the game?

    (A) $27.15

    (B) $2.85

    (C) $2.95

    (D) $1.85

10. Debbie receives a weekly salary of $80, plus a 5% commission on any sales. During the week, she has $800 in total sales. What's the ratio of her commission to her salary?

    (A) 2:1

    (B) 1:2

    (C) 3:1

    (D) 1:3

11. How many quart cans can be filled from 25 gallons of paint?

    (A) 50

    (B) 75

    (C) 100

    (D) 80

12. If a crew of four people can paint the barn in three days, how long will it take a crew of two people?

    (A) 4 days

    (B) $1\frac{1}{2}$ days

    (C) 8 days

    (D) 6 days

13. Brian works for five hours and is paid $24. Christina works for three hours and is paid $10.95. How much more per hour does Brian make than Christina?

    (A) $1.15

    (B) $1.25

    (C) $1.35

    (D) $1.37

14. Margaret is getting married and must be ready by 11:15 a.m. If it's now 8:30 a.m., how much time does she have to get ready?

    (A) $1\frac{1}{2}$ hours

    (B) $2\frac{1}{2}$ hours

    (C) $2\frac{3}{4}$ hours

    (D) $2\frac{1}{3}$ hours

15. An accounting-firm employee is asked to shred 900 documents. If he can shred documents at a rate of 7 per minute, the number of documents remaining after $1\frac{1}{2}$ hours of shredding is

    (A) 630

    (B) 90

    (C) 270

    (D) 810

16. A home stereo depreciates by 20% each year. What's the value of a stereo, purchased new for $1,200, after two years?

    (A) $768

    (B) $693

    (C) $827

    (D) $654

17. Janet's old pickup truck can only reach a speed of 45 miles per hour. If she drives at top speed, how long will it take her to reach a city 135 miles away?

    (A) 3 hours

    (B) 2 hours

    (C) 4 hours

    (D) $2\frac{1}{2}$ hours

18. A blouse normally costs $18.50. How much money is saved if the blouse is purchased at a 20% discount?

    (A) $1.85

    (B) $14.80

    (C) $4.50

    (D) $3.70

Go on to next page

19. A clerk's weekly salary of $320 is increased to $360. The percent increase is

    (A) $10\frac{1}{2}\%$

    (B) 11%

    (C) $12\frac{1}{2}\%$

    (D) 12%

20. Two go-carts are racing on a circular track with a circumference of 360 feet. Camera One is following Go-Cart One, and Camera Two is following Go-Cart Two. If the angle between the two cameras is 40 degrees, how far apart are the two go-carts?

    (A) 30 feet

    (B) 40 feet

    (C) 50 feet

    (D) 60 feet

21. Dinner at a nice restaurant costs $35.98. If Joan gave the cashier $40.00, how much change should she get back?

    (A) $5.02

    (B) $4.02

    (C) $3.92

    (D) $1.02

22. A balloonist circumnavigated the globe in 13 days, 12 hours, 16 minutes, and 13 seconds. A plane circumnavigates the globe in 4 days, 10 hours, 15 minutes, and 7 seconds. How much longer did it take for the balloon to go around the world?

    (A) 12 days, 7 hours, 11 minutes, and 35 seconds

    (B) 9 days, 2 hours, 1 minute, and 6 seconds

    (C) 8 days, 14 hours, 16 minutes, and 6 seconds

    (D) 9 days, 7 hours, 3 minutes, and 20 seconds

23. Darlene bought 12 boxes of cookies for $48.00. What was the cost of each box of cookies?

    (A) $4.00

    (B) $0.48

    (C) $0.40

    (D) $4.80

24. A tune-up increases a car's fuel efficiency by 5%. If a car averaged 20 miles per gallon before the tune-up, how many miles per gallon will it average after the tune-up?

    (A) 25

    (B) 22

    (C) $20\frac{1}{2}$

    (D) 21

25. A lumberjack wishes to drive a spike through the center of a tree with a circumference of 43.96 feet. What's the minimum length of the spike needed to go completely through the tree, passing through the center?

    (A) 14 feet

    (B) 15 feet

    (C) 16 feet

    (D) 17 feet

26. A bin of hard candy holds $10\frac{1}{2}$ pounds. How many $\frac{3}{4}$-pound boxes of candy can be filled from the bin?

    (A) 30 boxes

    (B) $15\frac{1}{4}$ boxes

    (C) $7\frac{7}{8}$ boxes

    (D) 14 boxes

27. A patio measures 12 feet by 14 feet. How many 8-inch-square paving stones are needed to pave the patio?

    (A) 21

    (B) 252

    (C) 378

    (D) 168

28. A computer programmer is making $25,000 per year, and 28% of her salary is withheld for federal and state deductions. How much is the computer programmer's net pay?

    (A) $20,000

    (B) $7,000

    (C) $18,750

    (D) $18,000

Go on to next page

29. Pam cuts a pie in half in a straight line. She then cuts a line from the center to the edge, creating a 55-degree angle. What's the supplement of that angle?

    (A) 55 degrees

    (B) 125 degrees

    (C) 70 degrees

    (D) 130 degrees

30. A stack of lumber is 6 feet high. If each piece of lumber is 4 inches thick, how many pieces of lumber are in the stack?

    (A) 72

    (B) 12

    (C) 18

    (D) 10

STOP DO NOT TURN THE PAGE UNTIL TOLD TO DO SO.
DO NOT RETURN TO A PREVIOUS TEST.

Subtest 3: Word Knowledge

Time: 11 minutes for 35 questions

Directions: This test's questions cover the meanings of words. Each question has an underlined word. You may be asked to decide which one of the four words in the choices *most nearly means* the same thing as the underlined word or which one of the four words means the opposite. If the underlined word is used in a sentence, decide which of the four choices most nearly means the same thing as the underlined word as used in the context of the sentence. Mark the corresponding space on your answer sheet.

1. <u>Abeyance</u> most nearly means
   - (A) trustworthiness.
   - (B) passion.
   - (C) suspension.
   - (D) business.

2. It was a <u>sturdy</u> table.
   - (A) well-built
   - (B) ugly
   - (C) thick
   - (D) small

3. <u>Bullock</u> most nearly means
   - (A) ox.
   - (B) inattentive.
   - (C) lazy.
   - (D) panther.

4. <u>Brevity</u> is the soul of wit.
   - (A) beauty
   - (B) intelligence
   - (C) terseness
   - (D) humor

5. <u>Paradigm</u> most nearly means
   - (A) twenty cents.
   - (B) model.
   - (C) heaven.
   - (D) basis.

6. He <u>facilitated</u> her promotion.
   - (A) hindered
   - (B) helped
   - (C) disliked
   - (D) ignored

7. <u>Quiescence</u> most nearly means
   - (A) kill.
   - (B) preserve.
   - (C) small.
   - (D) quiet.

8. The <u>spectator</u> enjoyed the game.
   - (A) competitor
   - (B) observer
   - (C) referee
   - (D) organizer

9. Joy <u>reclined</u> against the far wall.
   - (A) sat
   - (B) leaned
   - (C) jumped
   - (D) paraded

10. The teacher <u>cited</u> some examples.
    - (A) memorized
    - (B) finished
    - (C) specified
    - (D) examined

Go on to next page

11. <u>Surround</u> most nearly means
    (A) line.
    (B) benefit.
    (C) encircle.
    (D) speaker.

12. <u>Illustrious</u> most nearly means
    (A) illustrated.
    (B) famous.
    (C) foolish.
    (D) intelligent.

13. <u>Habitant</u> most nearly means
    (A) invalid.
    (B) nun.
    (C) seeker.
    (D) dweller.

14. Tim had a penchant for engaging in <u>subterfuge</u>.
    (A) religion
    (B) evasion
    (C) gambling
    (D) danger

15. Megan found the new shoes to be <u>ghastly</u>.
    (A) hideous
    (B) cute
    (C) large
    (D) comfortable

16. <u>Rigid</u> most nearly means
    (A) strong.
    (B) weak.
    (C) pliable.
    (D) inflexible.

17. Billy yearned to join the <u>fraternal</u> organization.
    (A) brotherly
    (B) large
    (C) fun
    (D) special

18. <u>Deplore</u> most nearly means
    (A) accept.
    (B) insult.
    (C) regret.
    (D) salute.

19. <u>Meager</u> most nearly means
    (A) space.
    (B) sparse.
    (C) brief.
    (D) thirsty.

20. <u>Weal</u> most nearly means
    (A) happiness.
    (B) blow.
    (C) scream.
    (D) tire.

21. To be <u>guileless</u>, I think your hair looks ugly.
    (A) helpful
    (B) kind
    (C) frank
    (D) serious

22. The customs agent <u>confiscated</u> the goods.
    (A) bought
    (B) noticed
    (C) seized
    (D) stole

23. <u>Dubious</u> most nearly means
    (A) long.
    (B) beautiful.
    (C) articulate.
    (D) doubtful.

24. <u>Illusion</u> most nearly means
    (A) mirage.
    (B) distant.
    (C) sight.
    (D) perspective.

Go on to next page

25. Becky developed a sudden <u>craving</u> for ice cream.
    - (A) disgust
    - (B) passion
    - (C) hatred
    - (D) desire

26. <u>Enmity</u> most nearly means
    - (A) enemy.
    - (B) hatred.
    - (C) anger.
    - (D) childish.

27. <u>Arbor</u> most nearly means
    - (A) native.
    - (B) tree.
    - (C) travel.
    - (D) delirious.

28. They <u>terminated</u> his contract.
    - (A) bought
    - (B) extended
    - (C) sold
    - (D) ended

29. Tim always considered Chuck to be a big <u>buffoon</u>.
    - (A) clown
    - (B) help
    - (C) liar
    - (D) pain

30. <u>Null</u> most nearly means
    - (A) zero.
    - (B) dull.
    - (C) unskilled.
    - (D) rapid.

31. Tom had to provide proof to the judge that he was not <u>indigent</u>.
    - (A) guilty
    - (B) rich
    - (C) poor
    - (D) ugly

32. <u>Impertinent</u> most nearly means
    - (A) fun.
    - (B) boring.
    - (C) rude.
    - (D) impatient.

33. <u>Lustrous</u> most nearly means
    - (A) expensive.
    - (B) lazy.
    - (C) cold.
    - (D) bright.

34. <u>Pardon</u> most nearly means
    - (A) courtesy.
    - (B) excuse.
    - (C) believe.
    - (D) respect.

35. <u>Veracious</u> most nearly means
    - (A) fast.
    - (B) slow.
    - (C) equal.
    - (D) truthful.

STOP DO NOT TURN THE PAGE UNTIL TOLD TO DO SO. DO NOT RETURN TO A PREVIOUS TEST.

Subtest 4: Paragraph Comprehension

Time: 13 minutes for 15 questions

Directions: This test measures your ability to understand what you read. This section includes one or more paragraphs of reading material followed by incomplete statements or questions. Read the paragraph and select the choice that best completes the statement or answers the question.

Questions 1 and 2 are based on the following passage.

There is not a single town of any size within a distance of forty miles, yet already the rural population of this county is quite large. The whole country, within a wide circuit north, south, east and west, partakes of the same general character; mountain ridges, half tilled, half wood, screening cultivated valleys, sprinkled with farms and hamlets, among which some pretty stream generally winds its way. The waters in our immediate neighborhood all flow to the southward, though only a few miles to the north of our village, the brooks are found running in an opposite course, this valley lying just within the borders of the dividing ridge. The river itself, though farther south it becomes one of the great streams of the country, cannot boast of much breadth so near its source, and running quietly among the meadows, half screened by the groves and thickets, scarcely shows in the general view.

1. According to this passage,
   (A) the author lives in a large city.
   (B) the author lives in the country.
   (C) the author lives on the seashore.
   (D) the author lives on Mars.

2. According to this passage, the brooks are running in which direction within the author's neighborhood?
   (A) north
   (B) south
   (C) east
   (D) west

The Panama Canal is a ship canal that cuts through the Isthmus of Panama, connecting the Atlantic and Pacific oceans. Although several foreign companies tried to build the canal throughout the 19th century, none were successful. After the U.S. helped Panama revolt against Columbia, the U.S. was given rights to the land the canal occupied. The U.S. government finished the canal in 1914.

3. According to this passage,
   (A) Panama and Columbia fought a war over the Panama Canal.
   (B) the U.S. was given rights to the canal land.
   (C) foreign companies built the canal before the U.S. stepped in.
   (D) Panama built the canal in 1914.

Extreme care must be exercised to ensure proper handling and cleaning of soiled U.S. flags. A torn flag may be professionally mended, but a badly torn or tattered flag should be destroyed. When the flag is in such a condition that it's no longer a fitting emblem for display, destroy it in a dignified manner, preferably by burning.

4. According to this passage, torn flags should be
   (A) mended.
   (B) burned.
   (C) destroyed.
   (D) all of the above

Go on to next page

Medieval guilds were similar to modern-day labor unions. These groups of merchants or craftspeople set rules regarding economic activity in order to protect themselves. Some guilds held considerable economic power, but even small guilds protected members. Guilds also served a social purpose.

5. According to this passage, guilds

    (A) had only one purpose.

    (B) had little in common with modern labor unions.

    (C) exploited workers.

    (D) held considerable economic power.

After a series of well-publicized failures by various inventors, Orville and Wilbur Wright succeeded in flying and controlling a heavier-than-air craft on December 17, 1903. The War Department, stung by its investment in a failed effort by Samuel Langley and compounded by the Wright's own secretiveness, initially rejected the brothers' overtures toward the government to buy the aircraft. Prevailing sentiments held that the immediate future still belonged to the balloon. In August 1908, the two brothers delivered the first Army aircraft to the U.S. Government. That the U.S. government managed to purchase an airplane was a minor miracle. For more than four years after the Wright brothers' successful flight at Kitty Hawk, North Carolina, the government refused to accept the fact that man had flown in a heavier-than-air machine.

6. Which of the following statements is NOT supported by the above passage?

    (A) The U.S. Government felt that balloons were more practical than airplanes.

    (B) The Wright brothers' own secretiveness contributed to their problems in getting the government interested in their aircraft.

    (C) The historic flight took place on the East Coast.

    (D) It took more than six years for the Wright brothers to interest the U.S. Government in their airplane.

If anyone should be inclined to overrate the state of our present knowledge of mental life, all that would be needed to force him to assume a modest attitude would be to remind him of the function of memory. No psychologic theory has yet been able to account for the connection between the fundamental phenomena of remembering and forgetting; indeed, even the complete analysis of that which one can actually observe has as yet scarcely been grasped. Today forgetting has perhaps grown more puzzling than remembering, especially since we have learned from the study of dreams and pathologic states that even what for a long time we believed forgotten may suddenly return to consciousness.

7. The primary subject of this paragraph is

    (A) bowling.

    (B) puzzles.

    (C) memory.

    (D) government service.

Troy weight is based on a pound of 12 ounces and an ounce of 480 grains. Common, or avoirdupois, weight is based on a pound having 16 ounces and an ounce having 437.5 grains. A common pound has 7,000 grains while a troy pound has 5,760.

8. According to this passage,

    (A) in common weight, an ounce is less than 438 grains.

    (B) a troy pound and a common pound are the same weight.

    (C) common weight and avoirdupois weight are different measures.

    (D) a troy ounce equals 437.5 grains.

Go on to next page

Good leaders get involved in their subordinates' careers. People merely obey arbitrary commands and orders, but they respond quickly and usually give extra effort for leaders who genuinely care for them. An often neglected leadership principle in today's environment of technology and specialization is knowing the workers and showing sincere interest in their problems, career development, and welfare. Leadership is reflected in the degree of efficiency, productivity, morale, and motivation demonstrated by subordinates. Leadership involvement is the key ingredient to maximizing worker performance.

9. A key leadership principle that's often ignored is

   (A) leading by example.

   (B) showing sincere interest in the problems of the workers.

   (C) ensuring workers have access to the most modern technology.

   (D) maximizing worker performance.

Leukemia is a blood disease in which white blood cells in the blood or bone marrow reproduce rapidly, interfering with the body's ability to produce red blood cells. Red blood cells are needed to perform vital bodily functions.

10. According to this passage,

    (A) white blood cells perform no vital function in the body.

    (B) no treatment for leukemia exists.

    (C) leukemia makes it hard for the body to produce red blood cells.

    (D) white blood cells are found only in the blood.

Questions 11 and 12 are based on the following passage.

Any discussion of distinctive military capabilities would be incomplete without looking at their relationship to the Joint Service vision of the future. JV 2020 guides all the Services into the next century with its vision of future war fighting. JV 2020 sets forth four overarching operational concepts: dominant maneuver, precision engagement, focused logistics, and full-dimensional protection. Each of these operational concepts reinforces the others. The aggregate of these four concepts, along with their interaction with information superiority and innovation, allows joint forces to dominate the full range of military operations from humanitarian assistance through peace operations to the highest intensity conflict.

11. According to the passage above, which of the following is NOT an operational concept?

    (A) dominant maneuver

    (B) focused logistics

    (C) high intensity conflict

    (D) precision engagement

12. The document discussed in the above passage is primarily about

    (A) military operations of the past.

    (B) present military operations.

    (C) military operations in the future.

    (D) training for future military operations.

Go on to next page

Questions 13 through 15 are based on the following passage.

Genetics is a branch of science dealing with heredity. The field is concerned with how genes operate and the way genes are transmitted to offspring. Subdivisions in the field include cytogenetics, which is the study of the cellular basis of inheritance; microbial genetics, the study of inheritance in microbes; molecular genetics, the study of the biochemical foundation of inheritance; and human genetics, the study of how people inherit traits that are medically and socially important. Genetic counselors are primarily concerned with human genetics. They advise couples and families on the chances of their offspring having specific genetic defects.

13. In the passage above, cytogenetics is defined as

(A) the study of the psychological impact of genetics.

(B) the study of the cellular foundation of inheritance.

(C) the study of molecular genetics.

(D) the study of human genetics.

14. According to the passage, genetics

(A) concerns how genes operate and how they're passed along.

(B) is a field of study populated by quacks, fakes, and frauds.

(C) is a field of study only concerned with human genetics.

(D) is a new field of study.

15. According to the passage, it's reasonable to assume that genetic counseling

(A) is restricted to the very rich.

(B) is used to diagnose diseases.

(C) can be used by parents to learn if their offspring are likely to inherit a disease one of the parents has.

(D) can be used by parents to prevent their offspring from inheriting a specific genetic defect.

STOP DO NOT TURN THE PAGE UNTIL TOLD TO DO SO.
DO NOT RETURN TO A PREVIOUS TEST.

Subtest 5: Mathematics Knowledge

Time: 24 minutes for 25 questions

Directions: This test is a test of your ability to solve general mathematical problems. Select the correct answer from the choices given and then mark the corresponding space on your answer sheet. Use scratch paper to do any figuring.

1. $x^2(x^4) =$
    (A) x^6
    (B) x^8
    (C) $2x^6$
    (D) $2x^8$

2. If a rectangle has a perimeter of 36 feet and is 4 feet wide, what's its area?
    (A) 56 square feet
    (B) 128 square feet
    (C) 112 square feet
    (D) 16 square feet

3. The cube root of 64 is
    (A) 3
    (B) 9
    (C) 2
    (D) 4

4. Convert 314,000 to scientific notation.
    (A) 3.14×10^5
    (B) 3.14×10^{-5}
    (C) 314×10
    (D) 31.4×100

5. The reciprocal of $\frac{1}{6}$ is
    (A) 1
    (B) 3
    (C) 6
    (D) $\frac{1}{3}$

6. If $0.05 \div x = 1$, then $x =$
    (A) 0.05
    (B) 0.5
    (C) 50.0
    (D) 5.0

7. Factor $x^2 - 6x + 9$.
    (A) $(x + 6)(x + 6)$
    (B) $(x - 6)(x + 6)$
    (C) $(x - 3)^2$
    (D) $(x + 3)^2$

8. $(3 \times 2)(7 - 2)(6 + 2) = (6 \times 4)x$. What's the value of x?
    (A) –5
    (B) 5
    (C) 10
    (D) 1

9. Solve for x: $2x - 6 = x + 5$.
    (A) 3
    (B) 11
    (C) 7
    (D) 5

10. If $I = Prt$, and $P = \$1,000$, $r = 7\%$, and $t = 1$, what does I equal?
    (A) \$35
    (B) \$1,000
    (C) \$700
    (D) \$70

Go on to next page ⟹

11. Solve for x in the equation $(x - 7)^2 - 4 = (x + 1)^2$.

    (A) $2\frac{1}{2}$

    (B) $2\frac{3}{4}$

    (C) $4\frac{1}{2}$

    (D) $4\frac{3}{4}$

12. A circle has a radius of 5 inches. What's its approximate area?

    (A) 78.5 inches

    (B) 70.0 inches

    (C) 314.0 inches

    (D) 25.0 inches

13. Solve the following inequality:
    $\frac{2}{3}(6x - 9) + 4 > 5x + 1$.

    (A) $x > 6$

    (B) $x < 6$

    (C) $x > -3$

    (D) $x < -3$

14. A tube has a radius of 3 inches and a height of 5 inches. What's its approximate volume?

    (A) 34 cubic inches

    (B) 141 cubic inches

    (C) 565 cubic inches

    (D) 45 cubic inches

15. Triangle *ABC* (shown below) is a(n)

    (A) right triangle.

    (B) equilateral triangle.

    (C) scalene triangle.

    (D) isosceles triangle.

16. The following figure is what type of quadrilateral?

    (A) square

    (B) rhombus

    (C) trapezoid

    (D) parallelogram

17. The angle shown below is a(n)

    (A) complementary angle.

    (B) supplementary angle.

    (C) acute angle.

    (D) obtuse angle.

18. Solve for x: $-x^2 - x + 30 = 0$.

    (A) 4, –8

    (B) –6, 5

    (C) –4, 5

    (D) 6, –3

19. A square box has a volume of 64 cubic inches. What's the perimeter of one of its faces?

    (A) 8 inches

    (B) 16 inches

    (C) 64 inches

    (D) 32 inches

20. A cube has a volume of 64 cubic inches. What's its surface area?

    (A) 16 square inches

    (B) 64 square inches

    (C) 96 square inches

    (D) 32 square inches

Go on to next page

21. $(x^3)^3 =$

    (A) $3x^3$

    (B) x^6

    (C) x^9

    (D) $2x^6$

22. $4! =$

    (A) 16

    (B) 40

    (C) 0

    (D) 24

23. If $a^3 + b^3 = a^3 + x^3$, then $b =$

    (A) $b^3 - a^3$

    (B) x

    (C) $a^3 - b^3$

    (D) a

24. What's the sum of the integers from 1 to 300?

    (A) 38,243

    (B) 45,150

    (C) 49,923

    (D) 52,024

25. $(y^2)^3 + y^2 =$

    (A) y^7

    (B) $y^6 + y^2$

    (C) $y^8 + y^2$

    (D) $3y^2$

STOP DO NOT TURN THE PAGE UNTIL TOLD TO DO SO. DO NOT RETURN TO A PREVIOUS TEST.

Subtest 6: Electronics Information

Time: 9 minutes for 20 questions

Directions: This part tests your knowledge of electrical, radio, and electronics information. Select the correct response from the choices given and then mark the corresponding space on your answer sheet.

1. What is used to measure current that is going through a circuit?

    (A) multimeter

    (B) amp gauge

    (C) currentometer

    (D) tri-gauge

2. Which of the following isn't a component of a DC motor?

    (A) rotor bars

    (B) armature

    (C) field poles

    (D) yoke

3. The television broadcast standards in the United States is

    (A) NTSC.

    (B) RGB.

    (C) SECAM.

    (D) RTSC.

4. In a closed electrical circuit,

    (A) one terminal is always positive, and one terminal is always negative.

    (B) both terminals can be positive.

    (C) both terminals can be negative.

    (D) terminals are neither positive nor negative.

5. Electrical current is counted in what measurement?

    (A) hertz

    (B) voltage

    (C) amps

    (D) ohms

6. The following symbol is a/an

    (A) resistor.

    (B) fuse.

    (C) capacitor.

    (D) inductor.

7. In the United States, what is the specification for an electrical outlet in a bathroom near a sink?

    (A) If within 6 feet of a sink, an outlet must have a childproof cover.

    (B) If within 2 feet of a sink, an outlet must not be GFCI protected.

    (C) If within 6 feet of a sink, an outlet must be GFCI protected.

    (D) If within 2 feet of a sink, an outlet must also be within reach of the bathtub.

8. The following symbol is a/an

    (A) lamp.

    (B) fuse.

    (C) inductor.

    (D) bell.

Go on to next page

9. When a circuit breaker trips, in what position will you find the operating handle?

   (A) on position

   (B) off position

   (C) halfway between on and off

   (D) three-fourths of the way between the on position and the off position

10. Which wire is smallest?

    (A) 00 AWG

    (B) 4 AWG

    (C) 10 AWG

    (D) 12 AWG

11. Which of the following is the best conductor of electricity?

    (A) plastic

    (B) wood

    (C) aluminum

    (D) copper

12. How many paths of electrical flow can be found in a series circuit?

    (A) one

    (B) two

    (C) two or more

    (D) It can't be determined from the information given.

13. A microwave is rated at 1,200 watts. At 120 volts, how much current does it draw?

    (A) 1 amp

    (B) 10 amps

    (C) 100 amps

    (D) 1,440 amps

14. Electricians use the term *low potential* to refer to

    (A) electrical circuits with a low potential for overload.

    (B) building codes that reduce the risk of fire.

    (C) the likelihood of getting a raise this year.

    (D) 600 watts or less.

15. Which of the following isn't a conductor of electricity?

    (A) water

    (B) graphite

    (C) gold

    (D) glass

16. The ground wire is always

    (A) green.

    (B) black.

    (C) whitish.

    (D) blue.

17. What does AM mean?

    (A) amp metrics

    (B) alien mothers

    (C) amplitude modulation

    (D) annoid matrix

18. Silver is a better conductor than copper. But copper is more often used because of

    (A) the cost of silver.

    (B) the brittleness of copper.

    (C) the low melting point of silver.

    (D) the tendency of silver to tarnish.

19. Electronic circuits that produce high frequencies are called

    (A) amplifiers.

    (B) regulators.

    (C) transformers.

    (D) oscillators.

20. If you plug an appliance designed for AC into a DC power source, the appliance

    (A) will operate normally.

    (B) will produce excessive heat.

    (C) won't operate.

    (D) will explode into tiny pieces.

Subtest 7: Auto & Shop Information

Time: 11 minutes for 25 questions

Directions: This test is about automobiles, shop practices, and the use of tools. Pick the best answer for each question and then mark the corresponding space on your answer sheet.

1. If a car uses too much oil, which of the following parts may be worn?

    (A) camshaft

    (B) connecting rods

    (C) fuel pump

    (D) piston rings

2. Clean air filters are important because

    (A) dirty filters can cause a decrease in fuel mileage.

    (B) they remove pollutants, which can decrease engine performance.

    (C) they keep the oil from becoming contaminated.

    (D) both A and B

3. The alternator

    (A) starts the engine.

    (B) supplies regulated power to the battery.

    (C) connects the ignition system to the engine.

    (D) can be used as an alternative to motor oil.

4. In which automotive system would you find a "wishbone"?

    (A) transmission

    (B) engine

    (C) exhaust

    (D) oil pan

5. If the electrolyte solution in a battery is too low, you should add

    (A) sulfuric acid.

    (B) antifreeze.

    (C) distilled water.

    (D) gasoline.

6. What area of your car should be flushed periodically to maintain optimum performance?

    (A) exhaust system

    (B) brake system

    (C) cooling system

    (D) ignition system

7. The primary purpose of a carburetor is to

    (A) maintain engine timing.

    (B) regulate oil pressure.

    (C) mix fuel and air.

    (D) monitor tire pressure.

8. Car restorers often seek NOS parts. What does NOS stand for?

    (A) Near Original Specifications

    (B) NASCAR Operating Standards

    (C) New Old Stock

    (D) none of the above

9. To make spark plugs work effectively, the coil and breaker

    (A) provide a gap between the electrodes.

    (B) ignite the spark.

    (C) transfer the electricity to the correct spark plug.

    (D) create a very high electrical voltage.

10. Schrader valves can be found in your car's

    (A) tires.

    (B) engine.

    (C) transmission.

    (D) electronic ignition.

Go on to next page

11. A bent frame causes

    (A) improper tracking.

    (B) auto accidents.

    (C) poor visibility

    (D) excessive rust.

12. In the tire designation 205/55 R 15 92 H, what does the "H" signify?

    (A) tread type

    (B) tire height

    (C) maximum sustained speed

    (D) turning radius

13. When the tightness of screws and/or bolts is important, it's best to use

    (A) a screwdriver.

    (B) a torque wrench.

    (C) tin snips.

    (D) a coping saw.

14. Hammer faces are commonly made of each of the following materials EXCEPT

    (A) steel.

    (B) brass.

    (C) plastic.

    (D) lead.

15. Hammers, mallets, and sledges are all striking tools, but mallets and sledges don't have

    (A) claws.

    (B) metal parts.

    (C) as much durability.

    (D) heads.

16. Round objects can be measured most exactly using a

    (A) rigid steel rule.

    (B) folding rule.

    (C) set of calipers.

    (D) depth gauge.

17. The best chisel to use when making a circular cut in metal is a

    (A) cold chisel.

    (B) socket chisel.

    (C) butt chisel.

    (D) round chisel.

18. A pipe wrench is also known as a

    (A) strap wrench.

    (B) hammer.

    (C) plumb-bob.

    (D) Stillson wrench.

19. Painting on a surface with too much moisture

    (A) causes no problems.

    (B) causes bubbling.

    (C) requires an extra coat of paint.

    (D) takes longer.

20. A tool used to control the location and/or motion of another tool is called a

    (A) control tool.

    (B) jig.

    (C) nail.

    (D) static rectifier.

21. An 8-point saw

    (A) has 7 teeth per inch.

    (B) weighs 8 ounces.

    (C) can saw 8 kinds of material.

    (D) is 8 inches long.

22. Concrete is made by mixing

    (A) cement and sand.

    (B) cement, sand, and water.

    (C) cement and water.

    (D) cement, sand, gravel, and water.

Go on to next page

23. Which of the following tools isn't used to cut metal?

(A)

(C)

(B)

(D)

24. The following tool is used to

(A) cut tile.
(B) cut wire.
(C) turn screws.
(D) cut bolts.

25. The following tool is a(n)

(A) Phillips screwdriver.
(B) Allen wrench.
(C) socket wrench.
(D) offset screwdriver.

STOP DO NOT TURN THE PAGE UNTIL TOLD TO DO SO.
DO NOT RETURN TO A PREVIOUS TEST.

Subtest 8: Mechanical Comprehension

Time: 19 minutes for 25 questions

Directions: This test is about mechanical principles. Many of the questions use drawings to illustrate specific principles. Choose the correct answer and mark the corresponding space on the answer sheet.

1. A simple pulley gives a mechanical advantage of

    (A) 2

    (B) 3

    (C) 1

    (D) unknown

2. The baskets are balanced on the arm in the figure below. If cherries are removed from Basket B, then to rebalance the arm,

    Basket A   Basket B

    fulcrum

    (A) the fulcrum will have to be moved to the right.

    (B) Basket B will have to be moved to the right.

    (C) Basket A will have to be moved to the left.

    (D) Basket A will have to be moved to the right.

3. If both Wheel A and Wheel B revolve at the same rate in the figure below, Wheel A will cover a linear distance of 12 feet

    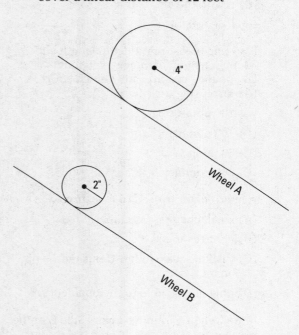

    (A) faster than Wheel B.

    (B) slower than Wheel B.

    (C) in about the same time as Wheel B.

    (D) half as quickly as Wheel B.

4. If a force of 200 pounds is exerted over an area of 10 square inches, what's the psi?

    (A) 10

    (B) 15

    (C) 20

    (D) 200

Go on to next page

5. In the following figure, if you move Anvil A toward the middle of the seesaw, Anvil B will

Anvil A   Anvil B

(A) remain stationary.

(B) move toward the ground.

(C) rise in the air.

(D) lose weight.

6. If a ramp measures 6 feet in length and 3 feet in height, an object weighing 200 pounds requires how much effort to move using the ramp?

(A) 200 pounds

(B) 100 pounds

(C) 50 pounds

(D) 300 pounds

7. A micrometer is used to measure

(A) small changes in temperature.

(B) changes in psi.

(C) thicknesses to a few thousandths of an inch.

(D) objects invisible to the unaided eye.

8. If the weight is removed from Side B of the seesaw, what happens to the weight on Side A?

Side A   Side B

(A) The weight will never move from Side B.

(B) The weight on Side A will move up in the air.

(C) The weight on Side A will move toward the ground.

(D) Nothing will happen.

9. The force produced when two objects rub against each other is called

(A) gravity.

(B) recoil.

(C) magnetism.

(D) friction.

10. Normally, atmospheric pressure is approximately

(A) 14.7 psi

(B) 23.2 psi

(C) 7.0 psi

(D) 10.1 psi

11. For Gear A and Gear B to mesh properly in the following figure,

(A) they must be the same size.

(B) they must turn at different rates.

(C) they must both turn in the same direction.

(D) their teeth must be of equal size.

12. Torsion springs

(A) produce a direct pull.

(B) exert no pull.

(C) produce a twisting action.

(D) coil but do not uncoil.

Go on to next page

13. To move a 400-pound crate from the floor of a warehouse to the bed of a truck 4 feet off the ground, the most efficient device to use is a

    (A) lever.

    (B) inclined plane.

    (C) fixed pulley.

    (D) jackscrew.

14. Water in an engine can cause damage in winter weather because

    (A) it can vaporize.

    (B) water expands when it freezes.

    (C) ice is heavier than water.

    (D) cold water creates more steam than warm water.

15. The weight of the load is being carried on the backs of the two anvils shown in the figure. Which anvil is carrying the most weight?

    Anvil A   Anvil B

    (A) Anvil A

    (B) Anvil B

    (C) Both are carrying an equal amount of weight.

    (D) It can't be determined without more information.

16. When the block-and-tackle arrangement shown in the figure is used to lift a load, all the following parts remain stationary EXCEPT

    Upper Block

    Lower Block

    LOAD

    (A) the upper hook.

    (B) the upper block.

    (C) the lower block.

    (D) all the parts move.

17. In the following figure, what effort (E) must be applied to lift the anvil?

    3'   9'

    E

    21–pound anvil

    (A) 7.0 pounds

    (B) 9.0 pounds

    (C) 21.0 pounds

    (D) 10.5 pounds

Go on to next page

18. In the figure below, for each complete revolution the cam makes, how many times will the valve open?

(A) 1

(B) 6

(C) 3

(D) 2

19. In the following figure, assume the valves are all open. Which valves need to be closed for the tank to fill up completely?

(A) 3 and 4 only

(B) 3, 4, and 5

(C) 2, 3, and 4

(D) 4 only

20. If Gear A turns left in the figure below, Gear B

(A) won't turn.

(B) turns left.

(C) turns right.

(D) It can't be determined.

21. If Gear 1 makes 10 complete clockwise revolutions per minute in the figure below, then

(A) Gear 2 makes 10 complete clockwise revolutions per minute.

(B) Gear 2 makes 20 complete counter-clockwise revolutions per minute.

(C) Gear 2 makes 5 complete counter-clockwise revolutions per minute.

(D) Gear 3 keeps Gear 2 from making any revolutions.

Go on to next page

22. For the fuel to travel from Reservoir A to Reservoir B, passing through Filters C and D on the way, which valves must be open?

Filter C

Reservoir A   Filter D   Reservoir B

(A) 1, 2, 4, and 8

(B) 1, 2, and 3

(C) 6, 7, and 8

(D) 4, 6, and 7

23. A yellow flame on a gas furnace indicates that

(A) everything is fine.

(B) the fuel-air mixture is too rich.

(C) the fuel-air mixture is too lean.

(D) the gas pressure is too low.

24. If a water tank on a toilet keeps overflowing, the problem is probably a

(A) defective float.

(B) clogged pipe.

(C) crimped chain.

(D) improper seal.

25. In the figure below, the board holds the anvil. The board is placed on two identical scales. Each scale reads

(A) 24

(B) 10

(C) 12

(D) 40

STOP DO NOT TURN THE PAGE UNTIL TOLD TO DO SO.
DO NOT RETURN TO A PREVIOUS TEST.

Subtest 9: Assembling Objects

Time: 15 minutes for 25 questions

Directions: The Assembling Objects subtest consists of questions that measure your ability to mentally picture items in two dimensions. Each question is comprised of five separate drawings. The problem is presented in the first drawing and the remaining four drawings are possible solutions. Determine which of the choices best solves the problem shown in the first picture; then mark the corresponding choice on your answer sheet.

Go on to next page

17. A B C D

18. A B C D

19. A B C D

20. A B C D

21. A B C D

22. A B C D

23. A B C D

Go on to next page →

24.

A   B   C   D

25.

A   B   C   D

Chapter 19

Practice Exam 2: Answers and Explanations

∙∙

Here are the answers and explanations for the practice exam in Chapter 18. Read over each question from Chapter 18 as you check your answers. Doing so reminds you what the question is about and serves as a helpful review. If you look at each question and the possible answers, you can also identify some of the traps that you may run across on the ASVAB.

You don't have to be an algebra ace to determine whether you're making progress through your review efforts. Simply compare the number of wrong answers you got on Practice Exam 1 (Chapter 16) against the number of wrong answers you got on this test. If you put the work in, you'll probably find that you made fewer errors on Practice Exam 2.

By the time you've scored Practice Exam 2, you should have a good idea of your strengths and weaknesses. If some subjects or subtests still give you problems, keep studying — just follow the cross-references for some tips and additional practice questions. If you find you need in-depth study, check out Chapter 17, where I name some books on various subjects covered in the subtests.

The ASVAB is technically scored by comparing your raw score to the scores of other people, which produces a scaled score. Turn to Chapter 2 to find out how the ASVAB is scored.

Subtest 1: General Science Answers

The answers to the questions on the General Science subtest are fairly straightforward — you either know the answer or you don't. This can be a hard subject to study for because General Science includes the entire scope of scientific disciplines. The good news is you may not even have to score well on this subtest — it depends on the job you're interested in. See Appendix A for military jobs that require a good General Science score. You can find additional science practice questions in Chapter 15.

1. **B**	6. **B**	11. **A**	16. **B**	21. **D**
2. **D**	7. **B**	12. **C**	17. **A**	22. **B**
3. **C**	8. **A**	13. **B**	18. **C**	23. **C**
4. **A**	9. **D**	14. **D**	19. **C**	24. **C**
5. **D**	10. **B**	15. **C**	20. **A**	25. **C**

Subtest 2: Arithmetic Reasoning Answers

This subtest is one of the most important because it makes up a portion of your AFQT score, the score that determines your overall mental qualifications to enlist in the military.

If you think you need more in-depth study, review Chapters 7 and 8 or see whether you can find some high school–level math textbooks at your local library. Chapter 9 has some additional practice questions.

1. **D.** For each die, the probability of rolling a 5 is 1 out of 6 $\left(\text{that is}, \frac{1}{6}\right)$, so the probability of not rolling a 5 is $1 - \frac{1}{6}$, or $\frac{5}{6}$. With two dice, the probability of not rolling a 5 is $\frac{5}{6} \times \frac{5}{6}$, or $\frac{25}{36}$.

2. **C.** Multiply $1,500 by 7%, or 0.07, and get $105. Then add $105 to $1,500 to find the answer, $1,605.

   Sometimes you can actually save time by *not* working the problem. In this problem, simply recognizing that the answer has to be more than $1,500 makes it obvious that Choices (A) and (B) are wrong. It also should be obvious that 7% of $1,500 has to be more than $7, so Choice (D) is also wrong. That only leaves the correct answer, Choice (C).

3. **A.** Two tons = 4,000 pounds; $4,000 \times \$0.12 = \$480$.

4. **C.** $y = (a + b)^2$. Expanding the equation results in $y = a^2 + b^2 + 2ab$. You know that $a^2 + b^2 = 30$ and $ab = 10$. When you substitute these known values into the equation, you get $y = 30 + 2(10)$. Solving for y results in $y = 50$.

5. **C.** There are 2 pints in a quart, and 4 quarts make up a gallon; therefore, a gallon contains $2 \times 4 = 8$ pints, or 16 half-pints. One half-pint equals $\frac{1}{16}$ of a gallon.

6. **D.** First subtract the old cost from the new cost: $2.80 - \$2.50 = \$0.30$. Then divide the difference by the old cost to find the percent difference: $0.30 \div \$2.50 = 0.12 = 12\%$.

7. **C.** The aircraft travels 120 miles in 12 minutes, which is $\frac{1}{5}$ of an hour. Therefore, in $\frac{5}{5}$ (or 1 hour), it would travel 5×120, or 600 miles. The aircraft is traveling 600 miles per hour.

8. **D.** Multiply 50 bushels by 8% to find the yield increase in bushels: $50 \times 0.08 = 4$. Add 4 bushels (the amount of the increase) to 50 bushels (the original yield) to determine that an 8% increase equals 54 bushels.

9. **B.** Convert the change to dollars or fractions of dollars and add:

14 dollars	= $14.00
16 half dollars	= $8.00
12 quarters	= $3.00
8 dimes	= $0.80
25 nickels	= $1.25
10 pennies	= $0.10
	= $27.15

   Subtract the total from $30.00 to determine how much money Junior has to borrow: $30.00 - \$27.15 = \$2.85$.

10. **B.** Her commission for the week was $40 (because $0.05 \times 800 = 40$). The ratio of her commission to her salary is 40:80, which can be reduced to 1:2.

11. **C.** A gallon consists of 4 quarts, and $4 \times 25 = 100$.

12. **D.** Four members is twice as many as two members. Multiply the number of days it would take four people to paint by 2 (that is, $3 \times 2 = 6$) to determine how long it would take two people to do the same task.

13. **A.** Brian's hourly wage is $24 \div 5 = \$4.80$. Christina's hourly wage is $10.95 \div 3 = \$3.65$. $\$4.80 - \$3.65 = \$1.15$.

14. **C.** The amount of time from 8:30 a.m. to 11:15 a.m. is 2 hours, 45 minutes. From 8:30 a.m. until 10:30 a.m. is 2 hours. From 10:30 until 11:15 is 45 minutes, or $\frac{3}{4}$ of an hour, for a total of $2\frac{3}{4}$ hours.

15. **C.** At a rate of 7 documents per minute, the employee can shred 630 documents in 90 minutes. How do you come up with that number? Multiply 7 by 90 (the number of minutes in $1\frac{1}{2}$ hours). Subtract 630 from 900 total documents to determine that after $1\frac{1}{2}$ hours of shredding, 270 documents remain.

16. **A.** If the stereo depreciates 20%, the value of the stereo then becomes 80% of its original value. After depreciation, the value of the stereo the first year is $960 ($0.8 \times 1,200$). The value of the stereo after the second year is $768 ($0.8 \times 960$). $768 is Choice (A).

17. **A.** Divide the distance (135 miles) by the speed (45 miles per hour) to determine that Janet will take 3 hours to reach the city.

18. **D.** Multiply the price of the blouse by the amount of the discount: $18.50 \times 0.20 = \$3.70$.

19. **C.** Subtract the original salary from the new salary to get the difference in salary: $360 - $320 = $40. Then divide the difference in salary ($40) by the original salary ($320) to determine the percent increase: $40 \div 320 = 0.125 = 12.5\%$.

20. **B.** A circle is 360 degrees, so 40 degrees is $\frac{1}{9}$ of a circle ($360° \div 40° = 9$). To get the answer, multiply the circumference of the track by $\frac{1}{9}$: $\left(360 \text{ ft.} \times \frac{1}{9} = 40 \text{ ft.}\right)$.

21. **B.** Subtract $35.98 from $40.00 to get $4.02.

22. **B.** Subtract the time of the plane from the time of the balloon to determine how much longer it took the balloonist:

13 days	12 hours	16 minutes	13 seconds
− 4 days	10 hours	15 minutes	7 seconds
9 days	2 hours	1 minute	6 seconds

23. **A.** Divide the total cost by the number of boxes purchased to determine the cost per box: $48 \div 12 = $4.

24. **D.** Multiply 20×0.05 to determine how many more miles per gallon the car will get. The answer is 1. Then add the number of additional miles per gallon the car will get to the original number of miles per gallon the car gets to reach the new average: $1 + 20 = 21$.

25. **A.** The minimum length of spike is equal to the diameter of the tree. To find the diameter of the tree, use the formula, $C = \pi d$, where $C = 43.96$ and $\pi \approx 3.14$: $43.96 = 3.14 \times d$; $d = 43.96 \div 3.14$; $d = 14$.

26. **D.** Divide $10\frac{1}{2}$ by $\frac{3}{4}$. You can perform this operation by multiplying $10\frac{1}{2}$ by the reciprocal of $\frac{3}{4}$: $10\frac{1}{2} \times \frac{4}{3} = \frac{21}{2} \times \frac{4}{3} = \frac{84}{6}$. Divide 84 by 6, and the answer is 14.

27. **C.** First figure out how many stones will be needed along the 12-foot side of the patio and then how many stones will be needed along the 14-foot side of the patio. Then multiply those two numbers together to get the total number of stones required. Here's the math: Convert 12 feet to inches: 12 ft. × 12 in./ft. = 144 inches. The paving stones are 8 inches square, so divide 144 inches by 8 inches (144 ÷ 8), which gives you 18 stones.

Do the same math for the 14-foot length: 14 ft. × 12 in./ft. = 168 in., and 168 ÷ 8 = 21. Therefore, 21 stones are needed on the 14-foot side.

Now multiply the stones: 18 stones × 21 stones = 378 stones, which is Choice (C).

28. **D.** Calculate the amount of the deduction by multiplying her salary by the percent deducted: $25,000 × 28% = $25,000 × 0.28 = $7,000. Subtract that product from the salary to determine the net pay: $25,000 − $7,000 = $18,000.

29. **B.** When the sum of two angles is 180 degrees, the angles are said to be supplementary to each other. To find the supplement, subtract 55 from 180: 180 − 55 = 125.

30. **C.** Multiply the height of the stack in feet by 12 to determine the height of the stack in inches: 6 × 12 = 72 inches. Divide that number by 4 inches, the thickness of each board, to determine the number of pieces of lumber in the stack: 72 ÷ 4 = 18.

Subtest 3: Word Knowledge Answers

Keep in mind that your score on the Word Knowledge subtest counts toward your AFQT score (see Chapter 1), so make sure you're getting comfortable with this portion of the test.

If your score on the Word Knowledge subtest has improved since you took the first test, congratulations! If not, don't be too surprised. Improving your score on this subtest in a short period of time is difficult, but it can be done. Review the information from Chapter 4 and set aside time each day (maybe several times a day, depending on how soon you plan on taking the ASVAB) to memorize words, roots, prefixes, and suffixes. Chapter 6 has some additional practice questions for you to sink your dictionaries into.

1. **C**	8. **B**	15. **A**	22. **C**	29. **A**
2. **A**	9. **B**	16. **D**	23. **D**	30. **A**
3. **A**	10. **C**	17. **A**	24. **A**	31. **C**
4. **C**	11. **C**	18. **C**	25. **D**	32. **C**
5. **B**	12. **B**	19. **B**	26. **B**	33. **D**
6. **B**	13. **D**	20. **A**	27. **B**	34. **B**
7. **D**	14. **B**	21. **C**	28. **D**	35. **D**

Subtest 4: Paragraph Comprehension Answers

Like Word Knowledge, the Paragraph Comprehension subtest also counts toward your AFQT score. If you're missing more answers than you should, review the info in Chapter 5 and concentrate on improving your analytical reading skills. For example, when you're reading the evening newspaper, ask yourself what the main point of an article is. Or when you finish a news story, set the paper down and try to remember what the President said about the budget deficit. Think of this technique as a workout for your mind. You can find more practice questions in Chapter 6.

1. **B.** The author is describing a quaint country setting.

2. **B.** The passage states that the brooks in the village run south, so the answer is Choice (B). A few miles north, the brooks run in an opposite direction (north).

3. **B.** The passage states that Panama revolted against Columbia, not that they fought over the canal, so Choice (A) is incorrect. The passage states that the foreign companies were unsuccessful in building the canal, so Choice (C) is incorrect. The United States, not Panama, built the canal, so Choice (D) is wrong. In the next to last sentence, the passage states that the U.S. was given rights to the land the canal occupied, making Choice (B) the correct answer.

4. **D.** According to the passage, a torn U.S. flag can be professionally mended, but a severely torn flag should be destroyed. The preferred method of destruction is by burning.

5. **D.** The passage states that guilds had economic and social purposes, so Choice (A) is incorrect. The passage states that guilds were similar to labor unions, so Choice (B) is incorrect. The passage states that guilds protected merchants and craftspeople; it says nothing about exploiting workers, so Choice (C) is incorrect. The third sentence states that some guilds held considerable economic power, but even small guilds protected members, making Choice (D) the correct answer.

6. **D.** According to the passage, it took more than four years for the government to believe that anyone had flown a heavier-than-air craft. The historic flight was in December 1903, and the Wright brothers delivered the first aircraft to the government in August 1908, 4.5 years later. The passage supports all the other statements.

7. **C.** Freud comments on the characteristics of memory throughout the entire passage.

8. **A.** The passage describes how troy and common weights are different, so Choice (B) is incorrect. Common and avoirdupois are the same system, so Choice (C) is incorrect. A troy ounce is 480 grains, so Choice (D) is incorrect. Choice (A) is the correct answer because the second sentence states that a common ounce is 437.5 grains, which is just shy of 438 grains.

9. **B.** The passage doesn't address leading by example or use of technology by workers, so Choices (A) and (C) are incorrect. Maximizing worker performance is a result of leadership involvement, not a principle of leadership, making Choice (D) incorrect. The correct answer, showing interest in workers' problems, is in the third sentence of the passage.

10. **C.** The passage doesn't support Choices (A) or (B). The passage states that white blood cells are found in blood and bone marrow, so Choice (D) is wrong. The correct answer, Choice (C), can be found in the first sentence. The passage states that leukemia interferes with "the body's ability to produce red blood cells."

11. **C.** High intensity conflict is listed as a type of military operation (in the last sentence), not one of the four operational concepts.

12. **C.** The JV 2020 guides all the military services with its vision of future war fighting. Although Choice (D) is close, the passage doesn't specifically reference military training.

13. **B.** Cytogenetics is the study of the cellular basis of inheritance; the text doesn't support Choices (A), (C), or (D).

14. **A.** Nothing in the passage supports Choices (B) or (D). Although human genetics is an important subfield of genetics, nothing in the passage suggests that it's the only concern of geneticists. Microbial genetics, as the passage mentions, is a subfield in genetics that has nothing to do with humans, so Choice (C) is incorrect. Choice (A) is the correct answer — the second sentence mentions genes and their transmission to offspring.

15. **C.** Nothing in the passage supports Choices (A), (B), or (D). Choice (C) is the correct answer because the last sentence in the passage states, "[Genetic counselors] advise couples and families on the chances of their offspring having specific genetic defects." Note it does not state that genetic counselors use genetics to *prevent* offspring from inheriting defects, which is what Choice (D) states, making Choice (D) an incorrect answer.

Subtest 5: Mathematics Knowledge Answers

Although the military doesn't expect you to be the next Einstein, a solid grasp of mathematics is important because math skills make up half of your AFQT score. If you're still struggling on this subtest, it's time to hit the books. (Actually, as much as you may feel like it, I don't recommend that you actually hit the books — just study them.) See Chapter 9 for some more fun practice questions.

1. **A.** If two exponents have the same base, you can multiply them by keeping the base and adding the exponents together: $x^2(x^4) = x^{2+4} = x^6$.

2. **A.** To find area, multiply length times width *(A = lw)*. You have the width, so you need to find the length. For a rectangle, $P = 2l + 2w$, so plug in the values you know and solve for *l*. To determine the length, subtract two times the width from the perimeter: $36 - 2(4) = 36 - 8 = 28$. Divide the answer by 2 to determine the length of one side: $28 \div 2 = 14$. Then multiply length times width to determine the area: $A = 14 \times 4 = 56$.

3. **D.** The cube of 4 is $4 \times 4 \times 4 = 64$, so 4 is the cube root of 64.

4. **A.** To convert this number to scientific notation, move the decimal point to the left until it's to the immediate right of the first number, while counting the number of moves. In this case, you move it five places. The result is then multiplied by 10 raised to the power of the number of places the decimal point was moved. The exponent is positive here because the original number, 314,000, is larger than 3.14. Choice (B), 3.14×10^{-5}, is equal to 0.0000314, so it's incorrect.

5. **C.** A reciprocal is the number by which a number can be multiplied to produce 1. The reciprocal $\frac{1}{6}$ is 6, because $\frac{1}{6} \times 6 = 1$.

6. **A.** You start with $0.05 \div x = 1$. Multiply both sides of the equation by *x*: $0.05 = 1x$ or $x = 0.05$. Check by substituting 0.05 for *x* in the original equation.

7. **C.** $x^2 - 6x + 9 = (x - 3)(x - 3) = (x - 3)^2$

8. **C.** You start with $(3 \times 2)(7 - 2)(6 + 2) = (6 \times 4)x$. Solve the left side of the equation first. $(6)(5)(8) = (30)(8) = 240$. Therefore, $240 = (6 \times 4)x$, which equals $240 = 24x$. Now isolate *x* by dividing both sides of the equation by 24: $240 \div 24 = 24x \div 24$, or $10 = x$. Check your answer by substituting 10 for *x* in the original equation.

9. **B.** Isolate *x* on one side of the equation. Subtract *x* from both sides of the equation and then add 6 to both sides:

$$2x - 6 = x + 5$$
$$x - 6 = 5$$
$$x = 11$$

Check by substituting 11 for *x* in the original equation.

10. **D.** Solve for *I*. $I = (1,000)(7\%)(1)$, or $I = (1,000)(0.07)(1) = 70$.

11. **B.** Multiply out what's in parentheses. Then simplify and solve for *x*:

$$(x-7)^2 - 4 = (x+1)^2$$
$$(x-7)(x-7) - 4 = (x+1)(x+1)$$
$$x^2 - 7x - 7x + 49 - 4 = x^2 + x + x + 1$$
$$x^2 - 14x + 45 = x^2 + 2x + 1$$
$$-14x + 45 = 2x + 1$$
$$-16x = -44$$
$$x = \frac{11}{4} = 2\frac{3}{4}$$

12. **A.** The area of a circle is $A = \pi r^2$. $A = \pi 5^2$. The number π is approximately 3.14, so 3.14×25 means A is approximately 78.5 square inches.

13. **D.** Distribute the $\frac{2}{3}$, simplify, and solve for x. Note that when you divide by a negative number, you have to switch the direction of the inequality sign.

$$\frac{2}{3}(6x - 9) + 4 > 5x + 1$$
$$4x - 6 + 4 > 5x + 1$$
$$4x - 2 > 5x + 1$$
$$4x > 5x + 3$$
$$-x > 3$$
$$x < -3$$

14. **B.** For cylinders, Volume $= \pi r^2 h$. In this problem, $V = \pi(3^2)(5)$. Assume π is approximately 3.14. V is approximately equal to $(3.14)(9)(5)$, or 141 cubic inches.

15. **A.** A right triangle has one right angle (one 90° angle).

16. **D.** Parallelograms have opposite sides of equal length.

17. **D.** Angles measuring more than 90 degrees are obtuse angles.

18. **B.** This is a quadratic equation, which you solve by factoring. First factor out the -1; then factor the quadratic expression and solve for x:

$$-x^2 - x + 30 = 0$$
$$-1(x^2 + x - 30) = 0$$
$$x^2 + x - 30 = 0$$
$$(x + 6)(x - 5) = 0$$
$$x + 6 = 0 \quad x - 5 = 0$$
$$x = -6 \quad\quad x = 5$$

19. **B.** Volume equals length times width times height ($V = lwh$). In this case, $V = 64$, so one edge of the box is 4 inches long (because 4 is the cube root of 64: $64 = 4 \times 4 \times 4$). Find the perimeter by adding the four sides together: $4 + 4 + 4 + 4 = 16$.

20. **C.** You calculate volume by multiplying length times width times height ($V = lwh$). Because the edges are equal on a cube, each edge is 4 inches (because $4 \times 4 \times 4 = 64$). The area of one face of the cube is $4 \times 4 = 16$ square inches, and because a cube has 6 sides, you multiply 16×6 to find the surface area of the cube, 96 square inches.

21. **C.** $(x^3)^3$ is the same as $(x^3)(x^3)(x^3)$. Multiply exponents with the same base by keeping the base and adding the exponents: $(x^3)(x^3)(x^3) = x^{3+3+3} = x^9$.

22. **D.** 4! (4 factorial) $= 4 \times 3 \times 2 \times 1 = 24$.

23. **B.** You start with $a^3 + b^3 = a^3 + x^3$. To solve, subtract a^3 from both sides of the equation and then take the cube root:

$$a^3 + b^3 - a^3 = a^3 + x^3 - a^3$$
$$b^3 = x^3$$
$$b = x$$

24. **B.** The formula to find the sum of a finite arithmetic sequence is $S = \frac{n}{2}(a+b)$, where n is the number of terms, a is the first term in the sequence, and b is the last term in the sequence. In this case there are 300 terms (n), and the first term is 1 and the final term is 300.

$$S = \frac{n}{2}(a+b)$$
$$S = \frac{300}{2}(1+300)$$
$$S = 150(301)$$
$$S = 45,150$$

25. **B.** $(y^2)^3$ is the same as $(y^2)(y^2)(y^2)$. Multiply exponents with the same base by keeping the base and adding the exponents: $(y^2)(y^2)(y^2) = y^{2+2+2} = y^6$. The second y^2 in the equation cannot be added into the first term because now they are not like terms, so the answer is Choice (B), $y^6 + y^2$. Tricky, eh?

Subtest 6: Electronics Information Answers

If you're having difficulty defining the difference between AC and DC, you may want to spend some additional time studying basic electronic information. Reviewing Chapter 13 can help. You can also wrap your wires around the practice questions in Chapter 15.

On the other hand, you may not be interested in a military job that requires a decent score on this subtest (see Appendix A), in which case, try not to worry too much. Your main goal is to score well in all areas of the ASVAB. The better you do on each subtest, the more desirable you become as a candidate for all the available jobs.

1. **A.** A multimeter includes several pieces of test equipment, including an ammeter, which measures inline current.

2. **A.** Rotor bars are only on AC induction motors, not DC motors.

3. **A.** NTSC stands for National Television Analog Committee and, although gradually being replaced by ATSC (Advanced Television Systems Committee), NTSC is currently the broadcast standard in the U.S. Choice (B) is incorrect because RGB stands for red, green, and blue — the colors of light used to create an image. Although most televisions use this standard, it is not a broadcast standard. Choice (C) is incorrect because SECAM (*Séquentiel couleur avec mémoire,* or sequential color with memory) is a standard used in other countries. Choice (D) is RTSC, which stands for Raytheon Technical Services Company and is obviously not the correct answer.

4. **A.** In a closed circuit, one terminal is always positive, and the other is always negative.

5. **C.** Amperes (or amps) are the unit of measure of electric current. Hertz is the unit of measurement of frequency, not current. Current equals voltage divided by resistance. Resistance is measured in ohms. Therefore, neither voltage nor ohms can be the unit of measure for current.

6. **B.** The symbol is a fuse. Fuses are designed to *blow* (melt) if the current flowing through it exceeds a specified value.

7. **C.** This is code prescribed by the NEC (National Electric Code). Outlets within 6 feet of a sink need to be GFCI protected for safety reasons.

8. **A.** The symbol is a lamp. A *lamp* is a transducer that converts electrical energy to light.

9. **C.** Conventional circuit breaker handles have four positions: on, off, trip, and reset. When tripped, the handle moves to the middle position.

10. **D.** The smaller the wire, the larger the number.

11. **D.** Plastic does not conduct, and wood is a poor conductor. Aluminum is a good conductor but not better than copper.

12. **A.** A series circuit has only one path, so if you break the circuit's path at any point, electricity stops flowing. An example of a series circuit is a string of Christmas lights that no longer works if a single bulb burns out.

13. **B.** *I* (current) = Power (watts) ÷ Effort (volts). In this case, *I* = 1,200 ÷ 120 = 10 amperes.

14. **D.** *Potential* equals voltage; *low potential* is anything less than 600 watts.

15. **D.** Glass is an insulator. Other insulators include plastics, paper, and rubber.

16. **A.** Ground wires are always green.

17. **C.** Amplitude modulation (AM) was the first type of audio modulation to be used in radio. It works well with high frequency (HF) and Morse code.

18. **A.** Silver is a better conductor, but it's more brittle than copper and more expensive.

19. **D.** Oscillators produce high frequencies. An *amplifier* changes the amplitude of a signal. A *regulator* is a circuit that maintains a constant voltage. A *transformer* is a device that changes (transforms) the voltage at its input side to a different voltage on its output side.

20. **B.** When DC is applied to an AC appliance, the amount of resistance is less, so more current flows through the wire and heat builds up.

Subtest 7: Auto & Shop Information Answers

You need to do well on this subtest to qualify for certain military jobs (see Appendix A). If you care about those jobs and you're missing more than a few questions on this subtest, it's time for more extreme measures — like taking your mother's car apart and putting it back together (or going back over Chapter 11).

Drive back to Chapter 15 for more practice questions.

1. **D**	6. **C**	11. **A**	16. **C**	21. **A**
2. **D**	7. **C**	12. **C**	17. **D**	22. **D**
3. **B**	8. **C**	13. **B**	18. **D**	23. **B**
4. **A**	9. **D**	14. **C**	19. **B**	24. **D**
5. **C**	10. **A**	15. **A**	20. **B**	25. **B**

Subtest 8: Mechanical Comprehension Answers

If you need to do well on the Mechanical Comprehension subtest (as in you're hoping for a military career that requires a score for this subtest) but you're still missing more answers than you should be, ask yourself whether your math skills need work. Go back to Chapters 7 and 8 if they do. Many of the formulas you need to know for this subtest require an understanding of arithmetic and basic algebra.

Usually, improving your arithmetic and basic-algebra skills will improve your score on the Mechanical Comprehension subtest. Improving your knowledge of physics is also beneficial. Take a gander at Chapter 12 and the practice questions in Chapter 15.

1. **C.** A simple pulley gives no mechanical advantage, although it does make work easier by spreading out the work needed over several tries. The mechanical advantage is 1.

2. **D.** Moving Basket A to the right counterbalances the loss of cherries from Basket B.

3. **A.** Wheel B has to make more revolutions to cover the same ground as Wheel A, so it covers the distance more slowly.

4. **C.** You can calculate psi as Pressure = Force ÷ Area. So in this problem, $P = 200 \div 10 = 20$.

5. **B.** If you move Anvil A toward the center, Anvil B will move toward the ground.

6. **B.** The formula to determine mechanical advantage of an inclined plane is Length of Ramp ÷ Height of Ramp = Weight of Object ÷ Effort. Plugging in the numbers gives you

$$\frac{6}{3} = \frac{200}{E}$$
$$6E = 600$$
$$E = 100$$

7. **C.** Micrometers measure very small but not microscopic objects.

8. **C.** Reducing the weight on Side B will cause Side A to move toward the ground.

9. **D.** Objects rubbing together produce friction.

10. **A.** Normal atmospheric pressure (the average atmospheric pressure at sea level) is 14.7 psi.

11. **D.** Gears of unequal size can mesh properly as long as their teeth are of equal size.

12. **C.** Torsion springs coil or uncoil and produce a twisting action, not a direct pull; in other words, torsion springs apply torque.

13. **B.** To move a heavy object a few feet in height, the inclined plane is the most efficient device (of those listed) to use. ***Note:*** The mechanical advantage of an inclined plane is equal to the slope of the plane divided by the height. The longer the slope is (compared to the height), the greater the mechanical advantage will be.

14. **B.** Water expands when it freezes, possibly damaging engine components.

15. **A.** The load is closer to Anvil A, so it's carrying the greater portion of the weight.

16. **C.** All the listed parts remain stationary except the lower block.

17. **A.** Apply the leverage formula: Length of Effort Arm ÷ Length of Resistance Arm = Resistance Force ÷ Effort Force:

$$\frac{9}{3} = \frac{21}{E}$$
$$3 = \frac{21}{E}$$
$$3E = 21$$
$$E = 7$$

18. **C.** The valve will open each time a high point of the cam hits it. The cam has three high points, so the valve will open three times per revolution.

19. **A.** Closing only Valves 3 and 4 keeps the water from leaving the tank.

20. **C.** Gears in mesh always turn in opposite directions.

21. **B.** If Gear 1 turns at 10 rpm, then Gear 2, which is half the size, turns twice as fast, at a rate of 20 rpm.

22. **A.** Opening Valves 1, 2, 4, and 8 allows the fuel to travel through the filters. Opening Valves 1, 2, and 3 doesn't allow the fuel to travel through Filter D. Opening Valves 6, 7, and 8 doesn't allow the fuel to travel through the filters. Opening Valves 4, 6, and 7 doesn't allow fuel to travel to Reservoir B.

23. **B.** A yellow flame indicates too much fuel or not enough air. More air should be allowed to enter and mix with the gas. Thus, the fuel-air mixture is too rich.

24. **A.** The float measures the water level in the tank. If the tank overflows, the float is probably defective.

25. **C.** The 20-pound anvil and the 4-pound board weigh 24 pounds total or, divided by 2, 12 pounds per scale.

Subtest 9: Assembling Objects Answers

So far, only the Navy has elected to use scores from the Assembling Objects subtest and only for a few jobs. If you're planning on joining the Navy and you're interested in a Navy career that requires a score on this subtest (see Appendix A), review Chapter 14 for help on improving your score. For additional practice questions, see Chapter 15.

1. B	6. A	11. C	16. D	21. A
2. A	7. B	12. B	17. C	22. D
3. C	8. C	13. A	18. B	23. C
4. D	9. D	14. B	19. C	24. B
5. C	10. D	15. D	20. C	25. D

Chapter 20

Practice Exam 3

●●

I suggest you take the third practice exam a week or so before you're scheduled to take the real ASVAB. Use it to refresh your memory of the material or to cram for any of the subtests that you have to do better on than you've been doing.

Don't forget to use the test-taking strategies and the guessing tips in each of the subtest chapters earlier in this book. Chapter 3 provides additional information on how to improve your score just by using smart test-taking strategies.

This sample test features nine subtests and follows the same format as the actual ASVAB. To get the most out of this sample test, take it under the same conditions as the real ASVAB:

- ✔ Allow yourself about three hours to take the entire exam, and take the whole thing at one time.

- ✔ Find a quiet place where you won't be interrupted.

- ✔ Bring a timer that you can set for various lengths of time, some scratch paper, and a pencil.

- ✔ At the start of each subtest, set your timer for the specified period of time. Don't go on to the next section until the timer has gone off, and don't go back to a previous section. If you finish early, check your work for that section only.

- ✔ Use the answer sheet that's provided.

- ✔ Don't take a break during any subtest. You can take a short one- or two-minute break between subtests if you need it.

After you complete the entire test, check your answers against the answer keys and explanations in Chapter 21. Then compare the results to your results on Practice Exams 1 and 2. You should see some improvement.

Answer Sheet for Practice Exam 3

Subtest 1: General Science

1 Ⓐ Ⓑ Ⓒ Ⓓ	6 Ⓐ Ⓑ Ⓒ Ⓓ	11 Ⓐ Ⓑ Ⓒ Ⓓ	16 Ⓐ Ⓑ Ⓒ Ⓓ	21 Ⓐ Ⓑ Ⓒ Ⓓ
2 Ⓐ Ⓑ Ⓒ Ⓓ	7 Ⓐ Ⓑ Ⓒ Ⓓ	12 Ⓐ Ⓑ Ⓒ Ⓓ	17 Ⓐ Ⓑ Ⓒ Ⓓ	22 Ⓐ Ⓑ Ⓒ Ⓓ
3 Ⓐ Ⓑ Ⓒ Ⓓ	8 Ⓐ Ⓑ Ⓒ Ⓓ	13 Ⓐ Ⓑ Ⓒ Ⓓ	18 Ⓐ Ⓑ Ⓒ Ⓓ	23 Ⓐ Ⓑ Ⓒ Ⓓ
4 Ⓐ Ⓑ Ⓒ Ⓓ	9 Ⓐ Ⓑ Ⓒ Ⓓ	14 Ⓐ Ⓑ Ⓒ Ⓓ	19 Ⓐ Ⓑ Ⓒ Ⓓ	24 Ⓐ Ⓑ Ⓒ Ⓓ
5 Ⓐ Ⓑ Ⓒ Ⓓ	10 Ⓐ Ⓑ Ⓒ Ⓓ	15 Ⓐ Ⓑ Ⓒ Ⓓ	20 Ⓐ Ⓑ Ⓒ Ⓓ	25 Ⓐ Ⓑ Ⓒ Ⓓ

Subtest 2: Arithmetic Reasoning

1 Ⓐ Ⓑ Ⓒ Ⓓ	7 Ⓐ Ⓑ Ⓒ Ⓓ	13 Ⓐ Ⓑ Ⓒ Ⓓ	19 Ⓐ Ⓑ Ⓒ Ⓓ	25 Ⓐ Ⓑ Ⓒ Ⓓ
2 Ⓐ Ⓑ Ⓒ Ⓓ	8 Ⓐ Ⓑ Ⓒ Ⓓ	14 Ⓐ Ⓑ Ⓒ Ⓓ	20 Ⓐ Ⓑ Ⓒ Ⓓ	26 Ⓐ Ⓑ Ⓒ Ⓓ
3 Ⓐ Ⓑ Ⓒ Ⓓ	9 Ⓐ Ⓑ Ⓒ Ⓓ	15 Ⓐ Ⓑ Ⓒ Ⓓ	21 Ⓐ Ⓑ Ⓒ Ⓓ	27 Ⓐ Ⓑ Ⓒ Ⓓ
4 Ⓐ Ⓑ Ⓒ Ⓓ	10 Ⓐ Ⓑ Ⓒ Ⓓ	16 Ⓐ Ⓑ Ⓒ Ⓓ	22 Ⓐ Ⓑ Ⓒ Ⓓ	28 Ⓐ Ⓑ Ⓒ Ⓓ
5 Ⓐ Ⓑ Ⓒ Ⓓ	11 Ⓐ Ⓑ Ⓒ Ⓓ	17 Ⓐ Ⓑ Ⓒ Ⓓ	23 Ⓐ Ⓑ Ⓒ Ⓓ	29 Ⓐ Ⓑ Ⓒ Ⓓ
6 Ⓐ Ⓑ Ⓒ Ⓓ	12 Ⓐ Ⓑ Ⓒ Ⓓ	18 Ⓐ Ⓑ Ⓒ Ⓓ	24 Ⓐ Ⓑ Ⓒ Ⓓ	30 Ⓐ Ⓑ Ⓒ Ⓓ

Subtest 3: Word Knowledge

1 Ⓐ Ⓑ Ⓒ Ⓓ	8 Ⓐ Ⓑ Ⓒ Ⓓ	15 Ⓐ Ⓑ Ⓒ Ⓓ	22 Ⓐ Ⓑ Ⓒ Ⓓ	29 Ⓐ Ⓑ Ⓒ Ⓓ
2 Ⓐ Ⓑ Ⓒ Ⓓ	9 Ⓐ Ⓑ Ⓒ Ⓓ	16 Ⓐ Ⓑ Ⓒ Ⓓ	23 Ⓐ Ⓑ Ⓒ Ⓓ	30 Ⓐ Ⓑ Ⓒ Ⓓ
3 Ⓐ Ⓑ Ⓒ Ⓓ	10 Ⓐ Ⓑ Ⓒ Ⓓ	17 Ⓐ Ⓑ Ⓒ Ⓓ	24 Ⓐ Ⓑ Ⓒ Ⓓ	31 Ⓐ Ⓑ Ⓒ Ⓓ
4 Ⓐ Ⓑ Ⓒ Ⓓ	11 Ⓐ Ⓑ Ⓒ Ⓓ	18 Ⓐ Ⓑ Ⓒ Ⓓ	25 Ⓐ Ⓑ Ⓒ Ⓓ	32 Ⓐ Ⓑ Ⓒ Ⓓ
5 Ⓐ Ⓑ Ⓒ Ⓓ	12 Ⓐ Ⓑ Ⓒ Ⓓ	19 Ⓐ Ⓑ Ⓒ Ⓓ	26 Ⓐ Ⓑ Ⓒ Ⓓ	33 Ⓐ Ⓑ Ⓒ Ⓓ
6 Ⓐ Ⓑ Ⓒ Ⓓ	13 Ⓐ Ⓑ Ⓒ Ⓓ	20 Ⓐ Ⓑ Ⓒ Ⓓ	27 Ⓐ Ⓑ Ⓒ Ⓓ	34 Ⓐ Ⓑ Ⓒ Ⓓ
7 Ⓐ Ⓑ Ⓒ Ⓓ	14 Ⓐ Ⓑ Ⓒ Ⓓ	21 Ⓐ Ⓑ Ⓒ Ⓓ	28 Ⓐ Ⓑ Ⓒ Ⓓ	35 Ⓐ Ⓑ Ⓒ Ⓓ

Subtest 4: Paragraph Comprehension

1 Ⓐ Ⓑ Ⓒ Ⓓ	4 Ⓐ Ⓑ Ⓒ Ⓓ	7 Ⓐ Ⓑ Ⓒ Ⓓ	10 Ⓐ Ⓑ Ⓒ Ⓓ	13 Ⓐ Ⓑ Ⓒ Ⓓ
2 Ⓐ Ⓑ Ⓒ Ⓓ	5 Ⓐ Ⓑ Ⓒ Ⓓ	8 Ⓐ Ⓑ Ⓒ Ⓓ	11 Ⓐ Ⓑ Ⓒ Ⓓ	14 Ⓐ Ⓑ Ⓒ Ⓓ
3 Ⓐ Ⓑ Ⓒ Ⓓ	6 Ⓐ Ⓑ Ⓒ Ⓓ	9 Ⓐ Ⓑ Ⓒ Ⓓ	12 Ⓐ Ⓑ Ⓒ Ⓓ	15 Ⓐ Ⓑ Ⓒ Ⓓ

Subtest 5: Mathematics Knowledge

1 Ⓐ Ⓑ Ⓒ Ⓓ	6 Ⓐ Ⓑ Ⓒ Ⓓ	11 Ⓐ Ⓑ Ⓒ Ⓓ	16 Ⓐ Ⓑ Ⓒ Ⓓ	21 Ⓐ Ⓑ Ⓒ Ⓓ
2 Ⓐ Ⓑ Ⓒ Ⓓ	7 Ⓐ Ⓑ Ⓒ Ⓓ	12 Ⓐ Ⓑ Ⓒ Ⓓ	17 Ⓐ Ⓑ Ⓒ Ⓓ	22 Ⓐ Ⓑ Ⓒ Ⓓ
3 Ⓐ Ⓑ Ⓒ Ⓓ	8 Ⓐ Ⓑ Ⓒ Ⓓ	13 Ⓐ Ⓑ Ⓒ Ⓓ	18 Ⓐ Ⓑ Ⓒ Ⓓ	23 Ⓐ Ⓑ Ⓒ Ⓓ
4 Ⓐ Ⓑ Ⓒ Ⓓ	9 Ⓐ Ⓑ Ⓒ Ⓓ	14 Ⓐ Ⓑ Ⓒ Ⓓ	19 Ⓐ Ⓑ Ⓒ Ⓓ	24 Ⓐ Ⓑ Ⓒ Ⓓ
5 Ⓐ Ⓑ Ⓒ Ⓓ	10 Ⓐ Ⓑ Ⓒ Ⓓ	15 Ⓐ Ⓑ Ⓒ Ⓓ	20 Ⓐ Ⓑ Ⓒ Ⓓ	25 Ⓐ Ⓑ Ⓒ Ⓓ

Subtest 6: Electronics Information

1 Ⓐ Ⓑ Ⓒ Ⓓ	5 Ⓐ Ⓑ Ⓒ Ⓓ	9 Ⓐ Ⓑ Ⓒ Ⓓ	13 Ⓐ Ⓑ Ⓒ Ⓓ	17 Ⓐ Ⓑ Ⓒ Ⓓ
2 Ⓐ Ⓑ Ⓒ Ⓓ	6 Ⓐ Ⓑ Ⓒ Ⓓ	10 Ⓐ Ⓑ Ⓒ Ⓓ	14 Ⓐ Ⓑ Ⓒ Ⓓ	18 Ⓐ Ⓑ Ⓒ Ⓓ
3 Ⓐ Ⓑ Ⓒ Ⓓ	7 Ⓐ Ⓑ Ⓒ Ⓓ	11 Ⓐ Ⓑ Ⓒ Ⓓ	15 Ⓐ Ⓑ Ⓒ Ⓓ	19 Ⓐ Ⓑ Ⓒ Ⓓ
4 Ⓐ Ⓑ Ⓒ Ⓓ	8 Ⓐ Ⓑ Ⓒ Ⓓ	12 Ⓐ Ⓑ Ⓒ Ⓓ	16 Ⓐ Ⓑ Ⓒ Ⓓ	20 Ⓐ Ⓑ Ⓒ Ⓓ

Subtest 7: Auto & Shop Information

1 Ⓐ Ⓑ Ⓒ Ⓓ	6 Ⓐ Ⓑ Ⓒ Ⓓ	11 Ⓐ Ⓑ Ⓒ Ⓓ	16 Ⓐ Ⓑ Ⓒ Ⓓ	21 Ⓐ Ⓑ Ⓒ Ⓓ
2 Ⓐ Ⓑ Ⓒ Ⓓ	7 Ⓐ Ⓑ Ⓒ Ⓓ	12 Ⓐ Ⓑ Ⓒ Ⓓ	17 Ⓐ Ⓑ Ⓒ Ⓓ	22 Ⓐ Ⓑ Ⓒ Ⓓ
3 Ⓐ Ⓑ Ⓒ Ⓓ	8 Ⓐ Ⓑ Ⓒ Ⓓ	13 Ⓐ Ⓑ Ⓒ Ⓓ	18 Ⓐ Ⓑ Ⓒ Ⓓ	23 Ⓐ Ⓑ Ⓒ Ⓓ
4 Ⓐ Ⓑ Ⓒ Ⓓ	9 Ⓐ Ⓑ Ⓒ Ⓓ	14 Ⓐ Ⓑ Ⓒ Ⓓ	19 Ⓐ Ⓑ Ⓒ Ⓓ	24 Ⓐ Ⓑ Ⓒ Ⓓ
5 Ⓐ Ⓑ Ⓒ Ⓓ	10 Ⓐ Ⓑ Ⓒ Ⓓ	15 Ⓐ Ⓑ Ⓒ Ⓓ	20 Ⓐ Ⓑ Ⓒ Ⓓ	25 Ⓐ Ⓑ Ⓒ Ⓓ

Subtest 8: Mechanical Comprehension

1 Ⓐ Ⓑ Ⓒ Ⓓ	6 Ⓐ Ⓑ Ⓒ Ⓓ	11 Ⓐ Ⓑ Ⓒ Ⓓ	16 Ⓐ Ⓑ Ⓒ Ⓓ	21 Ⓐ Ⓑ Ⓒ Ⓓ
2 Ⓐ Ⓑ Ⓒ Ⓓ	7 Ⓐ Ⓑ Ⓒ Ⓓ	12 Ⓐ Ⓑ Ⓒ Ⓓ	17 Ⓐ Ⓑ Ⓒ Ⓓ	22 Ⓐ Ⓑ Ⓒ Ⓓ
3 Ⓐ Ⓑ Ⓒ Ⓓ	8 Ⓐ Ⓑ Ⓒ Ⓓ	13 Ⓐ Ⓑ Ⓒ Ⓓ	18 Ⓐ Ⓑ Ⓒ Ⓓ	23 Ⓐ Ⓑ Ⓒ Ⓓ
4 Ⓐ Ⓑ Ⓒ Ⓓ	9 Ⓐ Ⓑ Ⓒ Ⓓ	14 Ⓐ Ⓑ Ⓒ Ⓓ	19 Ⓐ Ⓑ Ⓒ Ⓓ	24 Ⓐ Ⓑ Ⓒ Ⓓ
5 Ⓐ Ⓑ Ⓒ Ⓓ	10 Ⓐ Ⓑ Ⓒ Ⓓ	15 Ⓐ Ⓑ Ⓒ Ⓓ	20 Ⓐ Ⓑ Ⓒ Ⓓ	25 Ⓐ Ⓑ Ⓒ Ⓓ

Subtest 9: Assembling Objects

1 Ⓐ Ⓑ Ⓒ Ⓓ	6 Ⓐ Ⓑ Ⓒ Ⓓ	11 Ⓐ Ⓑ Ⓒ Ⓓ	16 Ⓐ Ⓑ Ⓒ Ⓓ	21 Ⓐ Ⓑ Ⓒ Ⓓ
2 Ⓐ Ⓑ Ⓒ Ⓓ	7 Ⓐ Ⓑ Ⓒ Ⓓ	12 Ⓐ Ⓑ Ⓒ Ⓓ	17 Ⓐ Ⓑ Ⓒ Ⓓ	22 Ⓐ Ⓑ Ⓒ Ⓓ
3 Ⓐ Ⓑ Ⓒ Ⓓ	8 Ⓐ Ⓑ Ⓒ Ⓓ	13 Ⓐ Ⓑ Ⓒ Ⓓ	18 Ⓐ Ⓑ Ⓒ Ⓓ	23 Ⓐ Ⓑ Ⓒ Ⓓ
4 Ⓐ Ⓑ Ⓒ Ⓓ	9 Ⓐ Ⓑ Ⓒ Ⓓ	14 Ⓐ Ⓑ Ⓒ Ⓓ	19 Ⓐ Ⓑ Ⓒ Ⓓ	24 Ⓐ Ⓑ Ⓒ Ⓓ
5 Ⓐ Ⓑ Ⓒ Ⓓ	10 Ⓐ Ⓑ Ⓒ Ⓓ	15 Ⓐ Ⓑ Ⓒ Ⓓ	20 Ⓐ Ⓑ Ⓒ Ⓓ	25 Ⓐ Ⓑ Ⓒ Ⓓ

Subtest 1: General Science

Time: 11 minutes for 25 questions

Directions: This test challenges your knowledge of general science principles usually covered in high school classes. Pick the best answer for each question and then mark the space on your answer sheet that corresponds to the question number and the letter indicating your choice.

1. The moon completes a revolution around the Earth approximately every
    - (A) 28 days.
    - (B) 365 days.
    - (C) 24 hours.
    - (D) 7 days.

2. Carcinogens are chemicals that cause
    - (A) high blood pressure.
    - (B) genome mutations.
    - (C) blood clots.
    - (D) diabetes.

3. A paramecium is
    - (A) a one-celled organism.
    - (B) algae.
    - (C) bacteria.
    - (D) a many-celled organism.

4. What substance is essential for the function of the thyroid gland?
    - (A) potassium chloride (salt)
    - (B) hemoglobin
    - (C) calcium
    - (D) iodine

5. The brainstem controls
    - (A) vision.
    - (B) voluntary muscle movements.
    - (C) your sense of balance.
    - (D) some involuntary activities.

6. Which element is the most abundant one in the atmosphere?
    - (A) oxygen
    - (B) nitrogen
    - (C) helium
    - (D) hydrogen

7. Minerals are necessary for
    - (A) respiration.
    - (B) eliminating waste.
    - (C) preventing night blindness.
    - (D) metabolic function.

8. What's the only metallic element found as a liquid at room temperature?
    - (A) bromine
    - (B) tellurium
    - (C) mercury
    - (D) silver

9. Which of the following isn't a type of telescope?
    - (A) reflecting
    - (B) convexing
    - (C) refracting
    - (D) catadioptric

10. A dekagram
    - (A) is larger than a kilogram.
    - (B) is smaller than a kilogram.
    - (C) is the same as a kilogram.
    - (D) doesn't exist.

Go on to next page

11. The aurora borealis can be seen only in the

    (A) winter.

    (B) summer.

    (C) Southern Hemisphere.

    (D) Northern Hemisphere.

12. The three important properties of sound waves are

    (A) wavelength, speed, and crest.

    (B) speed, frequency, and reflection.

    (C) wavelength, frequency, and vibration.

    (D) wavelength, frequency, and speed.

13. Between which two planets can most of the asteroids in the solar system be found?

    (A) Mars and Jupiter

    (B) Saturn and Jupiter

    (C) Earth and Mars

    (D) Mercury and Venus

14. At room temperature, an element is a

    (A) gas.

    (B) liquid or gas.

    (C) gas or solid.

    (D) liquid, gas, or solid.

15. The elements hydrogen and helium comprise what percentage of almost all matter in the universe?

    (A) 75%

    (B) 82%

    (C) 90%

    (D) 98%

16. Compounds are created when

    (A) atoms of two or more like elements are combined.

    (B) atoms of two or more different elements are combined.

    (C) two or more molecules are combined.

    (D) a molecule decomposes.

17. What theory suggests the universe will come to an end when its ever-increasing rate of expansion causes all matter to fly apart?

    (A) The Big Rip

    (B) The Big Bang

    (C) The Big Crunch

    (D) The Big Easy

18. A watt-hour measures

    (A) how much electricity is converted.

    (B) the number of electrons moving past a specific point.

    (C) resistance.

    (D) voltage.

19. Which of the following planets, known as *gas giants,* have no rings?

    (A) Neptune

    (B) Jupiter

    (C) Uranus

    (D) They all have rings.

20. Gas particles move

    (A) more slowly than liquid particles.

    (B) more slowly than solid particles.

    (C) more quickly than liquid particles.

    (D) at the same rate as all other particles.

21. Absolute zero is

    (A) 0 degrees Fahrenheit.

    (B) 0 degrees Celsius.

    (C) –273 degrees Celsius.

    (D) –32 degrees Fahrenheit.

22. Radiology is employed when doing which of the following?

    (A) using a Magnetic Resonance Imaging machine

    (B) using a blood pressure cuff

    (C) blood typing

    (D) breathing

Go on to next page

23. Which of the following statements is NOT true?

    (A) The human female chin is usually more rounded or pointed than the human male chin.

    (B) The human female pelvis is usually narrower than the human male pelvis.

    (C) The human male skull is usually larger than the human female skull.

    (D) The human male skull has a larger brow ridge than the human female skull.

24. A lunar eclipse occurs when

    (A) the Earth moves into the moon's shadow.

    (B) the sun blocks the moon from view.

    (C) the Earth moves into the sun's shadow.

    (D) the moon moves into the Earth's shadow.

25. What chemical can be used to detect blood, even if it's been wiped from a surface?

    (A) luminol

    (B) cyanide

    (C) ninhydrin

    (D) alcohol

STOP DO NOT TURN THE PAGE UNTIL TOLD TO DO SO. DO NOT RETURN TO A PREVIOUS TEST.

Subtest 2: Arithmetic Reasoning

Time: 36 minutes for 30 questions

Directions: This test is about arithmetic. Each question is followed by four possible answers. Decide which answer is correct and then mark the space on your answer sheet that has the same number and letter as your choice. Calculators are not permitted. Use scratch paper for any figuring you need to do.

1. A baker sells a dozen donuts for $3.99. The cost to make three donuts is $0.45. How much is the total profit on 5 dozen donuts?

   (A) $17.70

   (B) $13.20

   (C) $2.19

   (D) $10.95

2. Your piggy bank contains $19.75 in dimes and quarters. There are 100 coins in all. How many dimes are there?

   (A) 25

   (B) 30

   (C) 35

   (D) 40

3. A bricklayer charges $8 per square foot to lay a patio. How much would it cost for the bricklayer to lay a 12-foot by 16-foot patio?

   (A) $960

   (B) $192

   (C) $224

   (D) $1,536

4. Terry earns three times more per hour than Tim. Tim earns $2 more per hour than Angie. As a group, they earn $43 per hour. What's Angie's hourly wage?

   (A) $7.00

   (B) $8.00

   (C) $9.00

   (D) $10.00

5. If four people can run eight machines, how many machines can two people run?

   (A) 2

   (B) 4

   (C) 1

   (D) 3

6. The price of daily admission at an amusement park is $36. The park sells an unlimited season pass for $240. How many trips would you need to make with the season pass in order for it to cost less than paying the daily admission rate?

   (A) 6

   (B) 7

   (C) 8

   (D) 9

7. A plumber needs four lengths of pipe, each 3 feet, 6 inches long. Pipes are sold by the foot. How many feet does he need to buy?

   (A) 15

   (B) 16

   (C) 14

   (D) 12

8. The product of two consecutive odd numbers is 399. What are the numbers?

   (A) 17 and 19

   (B) 19 and 21

   (C) 21 and 23

   (D) 25 and 27

Go on to next page

9. A personal trainer earns a 65% commission on her training sales. If she sells $530 worth of training, how much commission does she make?

    (A) $874.50

    (B) $34.45

    (C) $344.50

    (D) $185.50

10. A rectangle is 1 inch longer than it is wide. Its diagonal is 5 inches. What's the width of the rectangle?

    (A) 2 inches

    (B) 3 inches

    (C) 4 inches

    (D) 5 inches

11. A treasure map is drawn to a scale of 2 inches equals 3 miles. On the map, the distance between Point A and X-marks-the-spot is $9\frac{1}{2}$ inches. How many actual miles does this represent?

    (A) $20\frac{1}{2}$ miles

    (B) $14\frac{1}{4}$ miles

    (C) $6\frac{1}{3}$ miles

    (D) 19 miles

12. A painter has painted a picture on a piece of canvas that measures 10 by 14 inches. To accommodate a frame, he has left an unpainted margin of 1 inch all the way around. What part of the canvas has been painted?

    (A) 96%

    (B) 91%

    (C) 65%

    (D) 69%

13. A dog trainer is building a rectangular dog run that measures 9 by 16 feet. If she wants to fence the perimeter of the run, how many feet of chain link fence will she need?

    (A) 144 feet

    (B) 25 feet

    (C) 32 feet

    (D) 50 feet

14. A rectangle is $1\frac{1}{2}$ times as long as it is wide. The perimeter of the rectangle is 100 inches. What's the length of the rectangle?

    (A) 20 inches

    (B) 30 inches

    (C) 40 inches

    (D) 45 inches

15. Miguel passed seven of his history quizzes and failed three. The fraction of quizzes he passed is correctly expressed as

    (A) $\frac{7}{3}$

    (B) $\frac{3}{7}$

    (C) $\frac{7}{10}$

    (D) $\frac{3}{5}$

16. A 3-yard-long ribbon was used to trim four dresses. Each dress used the same amount of ribbon. How much ribbon was used for each dress?

    (A) 1 yard

    (B) $\frac{2}{3}$ yard

    (C) $\frac{1}{2}$ yard

    (D) $\frac{3}{4}$ yard

17. Kelly bought a painting at an antiques sale for $500 and the following day she was able to sell it for an additional $30. What percentage of the sale price was her profit?

    (A) 5%

    (B) 6%

    (C) 7%

    (D) 4%

18. A bin of bolts at the hardware store contains 7 dozen bolts when full. The stock clerk is supposed to reorder bolts when the bin is $\frac{1}{6}$ full. How many bolts are in the bin when it's time to reorder?

    (A) 14 bolts

    (B) 1 bolt

    (C) 84 bolts

    (D) 12 bolts

Go on to next page

19. Two bicyclists head toward each other from the opposite ends of Main Street, which is 6 miles long. The first biker started at 2:05 going 12 mph. The second biker began peddling 4 minutes later at a rate of 14 mph. What time will they meet?

    (A) 2:13

    (B) 2:24

    (C) 2:21

    (D) 2:34

20. A recipe calls for 8 ounces of black beans or red beans. The cheapest option to buy and use would be

    (A) two 4-ounce cans of black beans at $0.79 each.

    (B) one 8-ounce can of red beans at $1.49.

    (C) two 3-ounce cans of black beans at $0.59 each.

    (D) three 3-ounce cans of red beans at $0.65 each.

21. A street vendor sells $25.70 worth of pretzels on Friday, $32.30 on Saturday, and $31.80 on Sunday. He spends a fourth of the money over the weekend. How much money does he have left?

    (A) $89.80

    (B) $22.45

    (C) $44.90

    (D) $67.35

22. A recruit has $30.00. He saw some camouflage socks for $3.95 a pair. How many pairs of socks can he buy?

    (A) 9

    (B) 7

    (C) 6

    (D) 4

23. A crate containing a puppy weighs 60 pounds, 5 ounces. The puppy weighs 43 pounds, 7 ounces. How much does the crate alone weigh?

    (A) 16 pounds, 8 ounces

    (B) 16 pounds, 2 ounces

    (C) 17 pounds

    (D) 16 pounds, 14 ounces

24. In a manufacturing plant that produces new computers, a 0.15 probability exists that a computer will be defective. If five computers are manufactured, what's the probability that all of them will be defective?

    (A) 7.6

    (B) 0.60

    (C) 0.00042

    (D) 0.000076

25. A house contains one 12-foot x 14-foot bedroom, one 12-foot x 10-foot bedroom, and one 8-foot x 12-foot bedroom. What's the total amount of carpeting needed to carpet all three bedrooms?

    (A) 383 square yards

    (B) 128 square yards

    (C) 88 square yards

    (D) 43 square yards

26. Rafael can type 9 pages an hour. How long will it take him to type 126 pages?

    (A) 14 hours

    (B) 9 hours

    (C) 7 hours

    (D) 16 hours

27. In a 60-minute gym class, 48 girls want to play volleyball, but only 12 can play at a time. For each player to get the same amount of playing time, how many minutes should each person play?

    (A) $1\frac{1}{2}$ minutes

    (B) 6 minutes

    (C) 30 minutes

    (D) 15 minutes

28. The movie-rental store charges $2.00 for the first day a rented DVD is overdue and $1.25 for each day after that. If a person paid $8.25 in late fees, how many days was the DVD overdue?

    (A) 7 days

    (B) 6 days

    (C) 4 days

    (D) 5 days

Go on to next page

29. Janet is trying to watch her weight. A half-cup of pudding has 150 calories. The same amount of broccoli has 60 calories. How much broccoli can Janet eat to equal the same number of calories in the $\frac{1}{2}$ cup of pudding?

    (A) 2 cups

    (B) $2\frac{1}{2}$ cups

    (C) $1\frac{1}{2}$ cups

    (D) $1\frac{1}{4}$ cups

30. The neighbor's dog barks at a raccoon every 15 minutes at night. If he first barks at 10 p.m., when you're trying to fall asleep, how many times will he have barked by 2 a.m., when you give up trying to sleep and decide to read a book instead?

    (A) 16 times

    (B) 132 times

    (C) 17 times

    (D) 15 times

STOP DO NOT TURN THE PAGE UNTIL TOLD TO DO SO.
DO NOT RETURN TO A PREVIOUS TEST.

Subtest 3: Word Knowledge

Time: 11 minutes for 35 questions

Directions: This test is about the meanings of words. Each question has an underlined word. You may be asked to decide which one of the four words in the choices *most nearly means* the same thing as the underlined word or which one of the four words means the opposite. If the underlined word is used in a sentence, decide which of the four choices most nearly means the same thing as the underlined word as used in the context of the sentence. Mark the corresponding space on your answer sheet.

1. <u>Lackadaisical</u> most nearly means
   (A) flowerless.
   (B) listless.
   (C) promiscuous.
   (D) suitable.

2. The fruit was <u>edible</u>.
   (A) waxy
   (B) expensive
   (C) foreign
   (D) digestible

3. Universities and colleges should be designed to cater to the <u>philomaths</u>.
   (A) athletes
   (B) scholars
   (C) teachers
   (D) faculty

4. <u>Pretense</u> most nearly means
   (A) politeness.
   (B) dishonesty.
   (C) stress.
   (D) appearance.

5. At an early age Jane showed a <u>proclivity</u> for music and dancing.
   (A) predisposition
   (B) interest
   (C) dislike
   (D) fever

6. Her conversation was <u>incoherent</u>.
   (A) eloquent
   (B) succinct
   (C) unintelligible
   (D) amusing

7. The week following Joe DiMaggio's death was filled with often <u>mawkish</u> eulogies.
   (A) long
   (B) sentimental
   (C) boring
   (D) detailed

8. She <u>established</u> proof.
   (A) offered
   (B) invented
   (C) demanded
   (D) demonstrated

9. <u>Ephemeral</u> most nearly means
   (A) short-lived.
   (B) mythical.
   (C) dead.
   (D) exceptional.

10. <u>Avocation</u> most nearly means
    (A) hobby.
    (B) occupation.
    (C) vacation.
    (D) education.

Go on to next page

11. <u>Kvetch</u> most nearly means

    (A) assert.

    (B) yell.

    (C) complain.

    (D) argue.

12. Her eyesight was <u>acute</u>.

    (A) sharp

    (B) poor

    (C) unusual

    (D) tested

13. <u>Inamorata</u> most nearly means

    (A) boyfriend.

    (B) mistress.

    (C) best friend.

    (D) acquaintance.

14. Her thoughts on the matter were <u>inconsequential</u>.

    (A) profound

    (B) disturbing

    (C) irrelevant

    (D) confused

15. <u>Debouch</u> most nearly means

    (A) emerge.

    (B) fight.

    (C) relax.

    (D) capture.

16. He was an <u>amateur</u> astronomer.

    (A) veteran

    (B) novice

    (C) interested

    (D) pleased

17. She had no idea how to react to her <u>ludic</u> boyfriend.

    (A) playful

    (B) cheating

    (C) crazy

    (D) lazy

18. The rose was <u>crimson</u>.

    (A) blooming

    (B) colorful

    (C) fragrant

    (D) red

19. The word *most opposite* in meaning to <u>benison</u> is

    (A) theft.

    (B) replaceable.

    (C) curse.

    (D) heavy.

20. She was <u>exempt</u> from gym class.

    (A) banned

    (B) excused

    (C) tired

    (D) refreshed

21. The <u>eldritch</u> light of the desert can play tricks on your eyes.

    (A) bright

    (B) wavering

    (C) strange

    (D) yellow

22. <u>Defective</u> most nearly means

    (A) flawed.

    (B) noticeable.

    (C) rare.

    (D) durable.

23. <u>Allot</u> most nearly means

    (A) plow.

    (B) assign.

    (C) property.

    (D) test.

24. The doctor gave the patient a <u>cursory</u> examination.

    (A) in-depth

    (B) painful

    (C) unnecessary

    (D) superficial

Go on to next page

25. <u>Arcanum</u> most nearly means
    - (A) rare.
    - (B) secret.
    - (C) tangible.
    - (D) false.

26. Her answer was <u>terse</u>.
    - (A) defensive
    - (B) angry
    - (C) lengthy
    - (D) brief

27. The <u>dulcet</u> songs of the band got the attention of the audience.
    - (A) harmonious
    - (B) love
    - (C) jazzy
    - (D) loud

28. He was arrested on a <u>misdemeanor</u> charge.
    - (A) theft
    - (B) serious
    - (C) petty crime
    - (D) bogus

29. <u>Embonpoint</u> most nearly means
    - (A) plumpness.
    - (B) height.
    - (C) quickness.
    - (D) cold.

30. He <u>concocted</u> a story about me.
    - (A) told
    - (B) rehearsed
    - (C) invented
    - (D) remembered

31. He spent his days searching fruitlessly for that <u>chimera</u>, his true self.
    - (A) personality
    - (B) enigma
    - (C) talent
    - (D) monster

32. Her <u>former</u> home was in Colorado.
    - (A) previous
    - (B) current
    - (C) second
    - (D) abandoned

33. <u>Mulct</u> most nearly means
    - (A) complain.
    - (B) play.
    - (C) work.
    - (D) defraud.

34. My voice is <u>strident</u>.
    - (A) soft
    - (B) melodious
    - (C) harsh
    - (D) baritone

35. <u>Raffish</u> most nearly means
    - (A) clean.
    - (B) serene.
    - (C) tawdry.
    - (D) expensive.

STOP DO NOT TURN THE PAGE UNTIL TOLD TO DO SO.
DO NOT RETURN TO A PREVIOUS TEST.

Subtest 4: Paragraph Comprehension

Time: 13 minutes for 15 questions

Directions: This test measures your ability to understand what you read. This section includes paragraphs of reading material followed by incomplete statements or questions. Read each paragraph and select the choice that best completes the statement or answers the question. Mark your choice on your answer sheet by using the correct letter with each question number.

Because leadership is charged with bringing new ideas, methods, or solutions into use, innovation is inextricably connected with the process of being an effective leader. Innovation means change, and change requires leadership. Leaders must be the chief transformation officers in their organizations and learn everything there is to know about the change before it even takes place. Furthermore, they must learn how to deal with the emotions that result from the chaos and fear associated with change.

1. According to the passage,

   (A) leaders should resist making changes that subordinates are likely to resist.

   (B) innovation and change are distinctly different processes.

   (C) it's not necessary for the leader to know everything about a change before it's implemented.

   (D) change is often associated with panic and disorder.

Cougars are the most wide-ranging big cats in North America, inhabiting a wide variety of environments. A cougar, also called a puma or a mountain lion, lives about 18 years in the wild, can jump 20 feet (in distance) at a time, and can range 50 miles when on the prowl for food.

2. According to this passage,

   (A) a cougar isn't the same thing as a mountain lion.

   (B) cougars are an endangered species.

   (C) cougars live in many areas of North America.

   (D) cougars live only a few years in the wild.

A helping relationship refers to interactions in which the counselor makes a determined effort to contribute in a positive way to the counselee's improvement. In counseling, the counselor establishes a helping relationship by drawing on practices that help the counselee live more in harmony with himself or herself and others and with a greater self-understanding. The relationship develops because the counselee needs assistance, instruction, or understanding.

3. Which of the following statements is NOT supported by the passage?

   (A) Successful counseling requires developing a relationship.

   (B) Most counselees initially reject advice given by the counselor.

   (C) Counseling helps a counselee develop a greater understanding of him/herself.

   (D) Counseling relationships are developed by relying on helpful practices.

Many small cities and towns rely on volunteer fire departments to put out fires. A professional fire department, however, has more training, more expertise, and more experience in fighting fires and investigating their causes. In many cases, it's worthwhile for even very small towns to hire professional firefighters.

4. According to this passage, it's reasonable to assume that

   (A) volunteer firefighters have less training, expertise, and experience than professional firefighters.

   (B) volunteer firefighters have the skills and resources to investigate the causes of fires.

   (C) professional firefighters don't know what causes fires.

   (D) a professional fire department is cost-prohibitive for small towns.

Go on to next page →

The idea being an alarming one, he scrambled out of bed and groped his way to the window. He was obliged to rub the frost off with the sleeve of his dressing-gown before he could see anything and could see very little then. All he could make out was that it was still very foggy and extremely cold and that there was no noise of people running to and fro and making a great stir, as there unquestionably would've been if night had beaten off bright day, and taken possession of the world.

5. This story takes place

(A) in Ireland.

(B) on a calm summer evening.

(C) on a winter night.

(D) both A and C.

Epidemiology is the study of what causes diseases, injuries, and other physiological damage to humans and why such problems occur. Epidemiologists examine where and when disease outbreaks occur. By using statistics and other scientific methods, epidemiologists determine what factors affect the frequency and severity of disease patterns. The primary goal of epidemiology is to control or prevent outbreaks of disease — other goals are subordinate.

6. What would be the best title for this passage?

(A) "Epidemiology: The Study of Disease Patterns"

(B) "Goals for the Future of Epidemiology"

(C) "Using Statistical Methods in Epidemiology"

(D) "Employment Outlook for Epidemiologists"

Buddhism is a religion that must be viewed from many angles. Its original form, as preached by Gautama in India and developed in the early years succeeding and as embodied in the sacred literature of early Buddhism, isn't representative of the actual Buddhism of any land today.

7. According to this passage,

(A) most Buddhists live in India.

(B) Buddhist teachings have changed over the years.

(C) Buddhism draws its teachings from early Christianity.

(D) Buddhist temples can be found in any land of the world.

Questions 8 and 9 are based on the following passage.

Many criminal-law statutes permit more severe punishment of a person convicted of a crime if he or she intended to harm another person. For example, voluntary manslaughter carries a heavier penalty than involuntary manslaughter in most states. Planned crimes are also punished more severely than spur-of-the-moment crimes.

The problem is that juries find it difficult to know what the intent of a person was at the time he or she committed a crime. Many defendants will deny that they intended to harm the other person and claim that any harm that occurred was "accidental." The law asks too much of juries when it expects them to determine what a person was thinking. Juries should only be asked to weigh objective evidence.

8. The author of this passage would agree that

(A) laws should not punish people based on intention.

(B) juries aren't intelligent enough to weigh evidence.

(C) more laws should distinguish between crimes committed with intent and crimes committed on the spur of the moment.

(D) lawyers will lie about anything.

9. According to this passage,

(A) most states don't distinguish between voluntary and involuntary manslaughter.

(B) punishing people more severely for voluntary manslaughter is unconstitutional.

(C) it's difficult for juries to determine a defendant's intentions at the time a crime was committed.

(D) prosecutors can, through careful questioning, show a defendant's intention at the time a crime was committed.

Questions 10 through 12 are based on the following passage.

Ergonomics is the science of designing and arranging workspaces so that people and objects interact efficiently and safely. Lack of attention to ergonomics causes thousands of workers to

Go on to next page

suffer repetitive stress injury, eye fatigue, muscle soreness, and many other medical problems each year.

Adequate lighting, well-designed chairs, and clutter-free work areas contribute to effective ergonomic design. The opportunity to take short breaks every hour or two, especially for desk-bound workers, is also helpful. It's also important for workers to avoid performing the same movements over and over for hours at a time. Variety in the type of work being done can decrease the chance of injury.

10. According to this passage,

   (A) ergonomics can cause injuries.

   (B) ergonomics is about designing and arranging workspaces efficiently and safely.

   (C) ergonomics is expensive and time-consuming.

   (D) few people experience problems due to poor ergonomics.

11. According to this passage,

   (A) adequate lighting and well-designed chairs, although important, have nothing to do with ergonomics.

   (B) repetition in the type of work people do helps them accomplish their tasks safely and efficiently.

   (C) short breaks aren't important for desk-bound employees because they do little heavy labor.

   (D) ergonomic design also includes keeping work areas well-lit and clutter-free.

12. According to this passage, it's reasonable to assume that

   (A) employers should invest in ergonomic design to protect workers.

   (B) lack of ergonomic design isn't dangerous.

   (C) labor unions have opposed ergonomic design.

   (D) poor design is responsible for most employee accidents.

Questions 13 through 15 are based on the following passage.

Electricity is the most inefficient and costly way to heat a home. One kilowatt-hour of electricity creates about 3,400 British thermal units (BTUs). (BTUs are a standard heat measurement.) The price of electricity per kilowatt-hour is between $0.10 and $0.25 or between $29.35 and $73.13 per million BTUs.

In contrast, fuel oil, which produces 140,000 BTUs per gallon, costs about $8.33 to $13.89 per million BTUs. Natural gas, which produces 100,000 BTUs per therm, can be purchased for $5.00 to $22.50 per million BTUs. Oak firewood, which produces 26,000,000 BTUs per cord, costs $5.77 to $13.46 per million BTUs.

Choosing the right heating method for your home, based on the cost of fuel, may be more expensive at installation but will be cheaper in the long run.

13. According to the passage, a BTU

   (A) is an unusual method of measuring heat.

   (B) stands for "British thermal unit."

   (C) is the abbreviation for a "big thermal unit."

   (D) can heat a 9 x 12 room.

14. According to the passage,

   (A) heating with fuel oil is always cheaper than other methods.

   (B) oak firewood produces fewer BTUs per dollar than the other types of fuel.

   (C) natural gas costs more than all other fuels except oak firewood.

   (D) electricity is always the most expensive way to heat a house.

15. The title of this passage should be

   (A) "Choosing the Right Heating Method"

   (B) "Heating Methods for Houses"

   (C) "Know Your BTUs"

   (D) "Price List for Fuel"

STOP DO NOT TURN THE PAGE UNTIL TOLD TO DO SO. DO NOT RETURN TO A PREVIOUS TEST.

Subtest 5: Mathematics Knowledge

> **Time:** 24 minutes for 25 questions
>
> **Directions:** This section tests your ability to solve general mathematical problems. Select the correct answer from the choices given and then mark the corresponding space on your answer sheet. Use scratch paper to do any figuring.

1. If $y = 6$, then $2y \cdot y =$
   - (A) 12
   - (B) 72
   - (C) 18
   - (D) 242

2. If $0.05x = 1$, then x equals
   - (A) $\frac{1}{20}$
   - (B) 20
   - (C) 10
   - (D) 5

3. $\sqrt{25x^2} =$
   - (A) x
   - (B) x^2
   - (C) $5x$
   - (D) $-5x^2$

4. Factor: $9x^3 + 18x^2 - x - 2$
   - (A) $(9x^2 - 1)(x + 2)$
   - (B) $(9x^2 + 1)(x - 2)$
   - (C) $(9x^2 + 2)(x - 1)$
   - (D) $(9x^2 - 2)(x + 1)$

5. Solve for x: $5x + 7 = 6(x - 2) - 4(2x - 3)$
   - (A) 1
   - (B) -1
   - (C) 2
   - (D) -2

6. $x(x^2) =$
   - (A) x^2
   - (B) $2x$
   - (C) $2x^2$
   - (D) x^3

7. $\sqrt{(5 + x)^2} =$
   - (A) $5 - x$
   - (B) $5 + x$
   - (C) $\sqrt{5} - \sqrt{x}$
   - (D) $\sqrt{5} + \sqrt{x}$

8. $(3 \times 3)(5 - 3)(6 + 2) = x^2$. What's the value of x?
   - (A) 6
   - (B) 12
   - (C) 144
   - (D) 64

9. If $-5x = 25$, x equals
   - (A) -5
   - (B) 5
   - (C) 10
   - (D) 0

10. A circle measures 12 feet in diameter. What's its area to the nearest foot?
    - (A) 452
    - (B) 24
    - (C) 113
    - (D) 48

Go on to next page

11. A square box has 6-inch sides. What's its volume?

    (A) 18 cubic inches

    (B) 216 cubic inches

    (C) 12 cubic inches

    (D) 36 cubic inches

12. A circle has a diameter of 10 inches. What's its approximate area?

    (A) $\pi(10^2)$

    (B) $\pi(25)$

    (C) $\pi(5)$

    (D) $\pi(10^2)(10)$

13. A cylinder has a diameter of 12 inches and a height of 10 inches. What's its approximate volume?

    (A) 4,521 cubic inches

    (B) 120 cubic inches

    (C) 1,130 cubic inches

    (D) 1,440 cubic inches

14. Triangle *ABC* is a(n)

    (A) equilateral triangle.

    (B) right triangle.

    (C) scalene triangle.

    (D) isosceles triangle.

15. The angles of the following quadrilateral

    (A) are all right angles.

    (B) each equal 45 degrees.

    (C) are all unequal.

    (D) total 180 degrees.

16. In the following figure, the sum of Angles 1 and 2 equals

    (A) 180 degrees.

    (B) 90 degrees.

    (C) 45 degrees.

    (D) 360 degrees.

17. Solve for *x*: $3(2x - 5) - 2(4x + 1) = -5(x + 3) - 2.$

    (A) 0

    (B) 1

    (C) 2

    (D) 3

18. A cube has a volume of 64 cubic inches. What's the length of one side of the cube?

    (A) 4 inches

    (B) 16 inches

    (C) 8 inches

    (D) 32 inches

19. $(x^3)^2 =$

    (A) x^5

    (B) x^6

    (C) x^9

    (D) $2x^3$

20. If *i* inches of rain fall in one minute, how many inches fall in *h* hours?

    (A) $ih \div 60$

    (B) $60i - h$

    (C) ih

    (D) $60ih$

21. If $x = y$, then $6 + 4(x - y) =$

    (A) $6xy + 4$

    (B) $6 + 4xy$

    (C) $10x - 10y$

    (D) 6

Go on to next page

22. $\sqrt{820}$ is a number between
    (A) 20 and 30.
    (B) 10 and 20.
    (C) 80 and 90.
    (D) 40 and 50.

23. $(x + 2)(x + 2) =$
    (A) $x^2 + 2x + 4$
    (B) $x^2 + 4x + 4$
    (C) $x^2 + 4x + 2$
    (D) $x^2 + 2x + 0$

24. Evaluate the expression $6a - 3x - 2y$ if $a = -3$, $x = -7$, and $y = 4$.
    (A) -5
    (B) -40
    (C) 31
    (D) 40

25. $(x + 4)(3x + 5) =$
    (A) $3x^2 + 9x + 20$
    (B) $3x^2 + 17x + 15$
    (C) $3x^2 + 17x + 20$
    (D) $3x^2 + 9x + 15$

STOP DO NOT TURN THE PAGE UNTIL TOLD TO DO SO.
DO NOT RETURN TO A PREVIOUS TEST.

Subtest 6: Electronics Information

> **Time:** 9 minutes for 20 questions
>
> **Directions:** This section tests your knowledge of electrical, radio, and electronics information. Select the correct response from the choices given and then mark the corresponding space on your answer sheet.

1. What effect does a speaker wire's gauge have on speaker sound quality?

    (A) higher gauge wires are thicker with better sound quality

    (B) lower gauge wires are thicker with better sound quality

    (C) lower gauge wires are thicker with lesser sound quality

    (D) higher gauge wires are thicker with lesser sound quality

2. What's the primary advantage of a quad-band cell phone over a dual-band cell phone?

    (A) transmission strength

    (B) coverage area

    (C) reception strength

    (D) smaller phone size

3. When working with electricity, you should assume that all electrical equipment is alive unless you know for certain otherwise. This prevents

    (A) damage to circuits.

    (B) personal injury.

    (C) unnecessary labor.

    (D) overheating the equipment.

4. The heat effect of current occurs

    (A) when the pressure of the current in the wire breaks up impurities in the wire, creating heat.

    (B) when the current in the wire decays electrons, causing them to move more quickly, creating heat.

    (C) when the current overcomes resistance in the wire, creating heat.

    (D) The heat effect of current is only theoretical; it has never been proven to exist.

5. What special type of diode is commonly used to regulate voltage?

    (A) capacitor

    (B) transistor

    (C) Zener

    (D) LED

6. This symbol means

    (A) ohm.

    (B) ampere.

    (C) high voltage.

    (D) wattage.

7. Electromotive force is another way of saying

    (A) frequency.

    (B) watts.

    (C) cycles per second.

    (D) voltage.

8. A primary advantage of using a Li-Ion battery instead of a NiMH battery in your cell phone is

    (A) Li-Ion batteries are lighter.

    (B) Li-Ion batteries last longer.

    (C) Li-Ion batteries don't interfere with signal quality.

    (D) none of the above.

Go on to next page

9. Transistors contain at least three terminals called the

   (A) base, emitter, and collector.

   (B) base, positive terminal, and negative terminal.

   (C) emitter, amplifier, and collector.

   (D) base and two gates.

10. To control a light fixture from two different wall switches, you should use

    (A) a single-pole switch and a four-way switch.

    (B) two three-way switches.

    (C) two four-way switches.

    (D) two single-pole switches.

11. A transistor is also called a(n)

    (A) rectifier.

    (B) cathode.

    (C) amplifier.

    (D) semiconductor.

12. This symbol means

    (A) ground.

    (B) resistor.

    (C) diode.

    (D) battery.

13. To decrease capacitance, capacitors

    (A) should have less voltage applied to them.

    (B) should be connected in parallel.

    (C) should be connected in series.

    (D) should be eliminated.

14. A resistor marked 2.5K ohms has the value of

    (A) 2.5 ohms.

    (B) 250 watts.

    (C) 2,500 ohms.

    (D) 25,000 ohms.

15. A 9-volt transistor contains

    (A) 1 cell.

    (B) 6 cells.

    (C) 9 cells.

    (D) 3 cells.

16. The hot wire is always

    (A) purple.

    (B) green.

    (C) whitish.

    (D) black.

17. How wide is the full AT motherboard?

    (A) 11 inches

    (B) 11.5 inches

    (C) 12 inches

    (D) 12.5 inches

18. The following symbol represents a(n)

    (A) relay.

    (B) on-off switch.

    (C) push switch.

    (D) connected wire.

19. If a 120-volt current is protected by a 25-amp circuit breaker, what's the largest number of watts an appliance can safely use?

    (A) 1,200 watts

    (B) 1,800 watts

    (C) 3,000 watts

    (D) 3,600 watts

20. The following symbol represents a

    (A) rheostat.

    (B) capacitor.

    (C) relay.

    (D) potentiometer.

STOP DO NOT TURN THE PAGE UNTIL TOLD TO DO SO.
DO NOT RETURN TO A PREVIOUS TEST.

Subtest 7: Auto & Shop Information

Time: 11 minutes for 25 questions

Directions: This test contains questions about automobiles, shop practices, and the use of tools. Pick the best answer for each question and then mark the corresponding space on your answer sheet.

1. A symptom of worn piston rings is
   - (A) a knocking and pinging sound when driving.
   - (B) soft and spongy acceleration.
   - (C) the smell of exhaust in the car.
   - (D) an engine using excessive amounts of oil.

2. What term refers to the rebuilding of an engine to precise factory specifications?
   - (A) blueprinting
   - (B) speccing
   - (C) gold rebuild
   - (D) silver rebuild

3. The number of cranks a crankshaft has on a V-8 engine is
   - (A) 6.
   - (B) 4.
   - (C) 3.
   - (D) 8.

4. When an engine runs on after the ignition key is turned off, it's called
   - (A) dieseling.
   - (B) sputtering.
   - (C) ignition recharge.
   - (D) ignition malfunction.

5. If a radiator fails, the engine
   - (A) will idle roughly.
   - (B) may burn fuel less efficiently.
   - (C) works hard to maintain speed.
   - (D) can quickly overheat.

6. On modern automobile engines, what's the purpose of the intake manifold?
   - (A) It regulates airflow to the cooling system.
   - (B) It provides airflow to the air-conditioner and heater.
   - (C) It connects the air/fuel management device to the head.
   - (D) It regulates fuel pump pressure.

7. Brake systems work by
   - (A) applying friction to the wheels to stop their rotation.
   - (B) reversing power to the wheels.
   - (C) applying pressure to the axle.
   - (D) interrupting power to the transmission.

8. Which of the following isn't a component of the cooling system?
   - (A) heater core
   - (B) radiator
   - (C) thermostat
   - (D) hydrator

9. A catalytic converter
   - (A) combines the fuel-air mixture.
   - (B) reduces dangerous exhaust emissions.
   - (C) converts the up-and-down motion of the pistons to rotary motion.
   - (D) charges the battery when the engine is in operation.

10. If the steering wheel vibrates at high speeds, the most likely problem is
    - (A) front end alignment.
    - (B) front tire balance.
    - (C) cracked steering column.
    - (D) overinflated tires.

Go on to next page →

11. During the compression stroke on a four-cycle engine,

   (A) the intake valve opens to fill the cylinder with fuel.

   (B) the burning fuel mixture forces the piston to the bottom of the cylinder.

   (C) the intake valve closes, and the piston moves to the top of the cylinder.

   (D) the exhaust valve releases the burned gas.

12. On older cars, the air filter can be found

   (A) on top of the engine.

   (B) under the engine.

   (C) behind the engine.

   (D) on the left or right side of the engine.

13. Glazing is the process of

   (A) cutting glass to size.

   (B) using putty to hold glass to a window frame.

   (C) polishing glass before using.

   (D) removing glass from a window.

14. A wrench with fixed, open jaws is called a(n)

   (A) adjustable wrench.

   (B) Allen wrench.

   (C) socket wrench.

   (D) open-end wrench.

15. All hammers have a

   (A) head, face, and handle.

   (B) head, toe, and handle.

   (C) head and foot.

   (D) head and claw.

16. To determine the number of threads per inch on a fastener, use a

   (A) depth gauge.

   (B) thread gauge.

   (C) thickness gauge.

   (D) wire gauge.

17. To chip or cut wood in close, the best tool is a

   (A) screwdriver.

   (B) butt chisel.

   (C) framing chisel.

   (D) mortising chisel.

18. Machine screws

   (A) are made by machines.

   (B) can be used interchangeably with wood screws.

   (C) fasten metal parts.

   (D) are machined to fine tolerances.

19. Double-headed nails are used

   (A) to reinforce a joint.

   (B) on temporary construction.

   (C) to make frames for furniture.

   (D) when a larger striking surface is needed.

20. To thin oil-based paint, use

   (A) turpentine.

   (B) baby oil.

   (C) benzene.

   (D) varnish.

21. When finishing a piece of wood, it's best to sand

   (A) diagonal to the grain.

   (B) against the grain.

   (C) with the grain.

   (D) in small circles.

22. To transfer an angle, the best tool to use is a

   (A) square.

   (B) caliper.

   (C) level.

   (D) sliding T-bevel.

Go on to next page

23. The following tool is a(n)

(A) pipe wrench.

(B) socket wrench.

(C) adjustable crescent wrench.

(D) box-end wrench.

24. Which of the following screw heads requires a Phillips screwdriver?

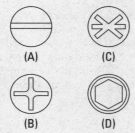

25. The following tool is used to

(A) punch holes.

(B) drive nails.

(C) measure thickness.

(D) set nails.

STOP DO NOT TURN THE PAGE UNTIL TOLD TO DO SO.
DO NOT RETURN TO A PREVIOUS TEST.

Subtest 8: Mechanical Comprehension

Time: 19 minutes for 25 questions

Directions: This test is about mechanical principles. Many of the questions use drawings to illustrate specific principles. Choose the correct answer and mark the corresponding space on the answer sheet.

1. Helical gears have

    (A) straight teeth.

    (B) slanted teeth.

    (C) teeth of unequal size.

    (D) no advantage over spur gears.

2. In the following figure, which pillar supports the greater load of the anvil?

    (A) Pillar A

    (B) Pillar B

    (C) Both pillars support the anvil equally.

    (D) It's impossible to determine from the information given.

3. Wheel A has a diameter of 10 feet. Wheel B has a diameter of 8 feet. If both wheels revolve at the same rate, Wheel B will cover a linear distance of 16 feet

    (A) at the same time as Wheel A.

    (B) more slowly than Wheel A.

    (C) in twice the time as Wheel A.

    (D) faster than Wheel A.

4. What effort must be used to lift a 30-pound anvil (see the following figure) using a first-class lever? (Don't include the weight of the lever in your calculations.)

    (A) 10 pounds

    (B) 15 pounds

    (C) 50 pounds

    (D) 5 pounds

Go on to next page ⇒

5. What mechanical advantage does the block-and-tackle arrangement in the following figure give?

(A) 1

(B) 3

(C) 2

(D) 4

6. If a ramp is 8 feet long and 4 feet high, how much effort is required to move a 400-pound object up the ramp?

(A) 35 pounds

(B) 150 pounds

(C) 800 pounds

(D) 200 pounds

7. 33,000 foot-pounds of work done in one minute is called

(A) a job for an enlisted soldier.

(B) 1 horsepower.

(C) 330 psi.

(D) meaningful force.

8. A 130-pound woman is wearing shoes with high heels that measure 1-inch square. If the woman is standing on one heel, what psi does the heel exert as it rests on the ground? (Disregard atmospheric pressure from your calculations.)

(A) 130

(B) 65

(C) 260

(D) 11

9. Clothes from the dryer stick together because of

(A) gravity.

(B) magnetism.

(C) friction.

(D) static electricity.

10. An aneroid barometer measures

(A) atmospheric pressure.

(B) water pressure.

(C) hydraulic-fluid pressure.

(D) the ambient temperature.

11. If Gear A is revolving in a clockwise manner, as in the following figure, Gear B

(A) remains stationary.

(B) revolves in a clockwise manner.

(C) revolves in a counterclockwise manner.

(D) turns more slowly than Gear A.

12. Springs are used for all of the following purposes EXCEPT

(A) to store energy for part of a mechanical cycle.

(B) to force a mechanical component to maintain contact with another component.

(C) to reduce shock or impact.

(D) to increase the weight of a mechanism.

Go on to next page →

13. The floats in Tubes A and B measure specific gravity. Which tube contains the liquid with the higher specific gravity?

A   B

(A) Tube A

(B) Tube B

(C) It can't be determined.

(D) Both Tube A and Tube B have the same specific gravity.

14. Universal joints are used to

(A) connect ball bearings.

(B) fix two shafts so they don't pivot or rotate.

(C) connect shafts in a U-shape.

(D) couple two shafts set at different angles.

15. The try-cock in the following schematic measures

(A) temperature of water.

(B) pressure of water.

(C) pressure of steam buildup.

(D) level of water.

16. The steel plate below is held in place by different machine screws, each indicated by different symbols. How many different types of machine screws have been used?

(A) 6

(B) 15

(C) 5

(D) 9

17. The amount of force (F) needed to balance the lever in the following figure is most nearly

(A) 15 pounds.

(B) 13 pounds.

(C) 7.5 pounds.

(D) 20 pounds.

18. With one complete revolution of the cable winch shown below, the load will move

Drum circumference 24 inches

LOAD

(A) 12 inches.

(B) 6 inches.

(C) 24 inches.

(D) 36 inches.

19. In the following figure, assume the valves are all closed. Which valves need to be open to fill the tank entirely?

(A) 1 and 2 only

(B) 1 only

(C) 1, 2, and 3

(D) 2 only

20. If Gear 1 in the following figure makes 10 complete clockwise revolutions per minute, then

(A) Gear 2 makes 2 clockwise revolutions per minute.

(B) Gear 3 makes 8 clockwise revolutions per minute.

(C) Gear 3 makes 30 clockwise revolutions per minute.

(D) Gear 3 makes 9 counterclockwise revolutions per minute.

21. A gear and pinion have a ratio of 1 to 4. If the gear makes 200 revolutions per minute, the speed of the pinion is

(A) 50 rpm.

(B) 800 rpm.

(C) 400 rpm.

(D) 200 rpm.

22. The gas gauge in an automobile relies on what mechanical device to measure the amount of gas in the tank?

(A) ball and cock

(B) automatic valve

(C) float

(D) mechanical switch

23. Using a runner gives you a mechanical advantage of

(A) 4.

(B) 2.

(C) 3.

(D) 1.

Go on to next page

24. For the valve shown in the figure below to open once each second, the cam must revolve at a rate of

(A) 6 rpm.

(B) 10 rpm.

(C) 15 rpm.

(D) 3 rpm.

25. The following figure represents a water tank. Which of the following statements is NOT true?

(A) If Valves 1 and 2 are open and Valves 3, 4, and 5 are closed, the tank will eventually overflow.

(B) If all valves are open, the water will remain at a constant level as long as the rate of intake is equal to the rate of discharge.

(C) Water in the tank will rise if Valves 1 and 2 are open and Valves 3 and 4 are closed.

(D) The tank will empty entirely if Valves 1 and 2 are closed and Valves 4 and 5 are open.

STOP DO NOT TURN THE PAGE UNTIL TOLD TO DO SO. DO NOT RETURN TO A PREVIOUS TEST.

Subtest 9: Assembling Objects

Time: 15 minutes for 25 questions

Directions: The Assembling Objects subtest consists of questions that measure your ability to mentally picture items in two dimensions. Each question is comprised of five separate drawings. The problem is presented in the first drawing and the remaining four drawings are possible solutions. Determine which of the choices best solves the problem shown in the first picture, and then mark the corresponding choice on your answer sheet.

Go on to next page

24.

25.

Chapter 21

Practice Exam 3: Answers and Explanations

• •

*R*ead over each question from Chapter 20 as you check the answer key. I hope you did well on this practice exam. If you find you need to study more for any subtest, follow the cross-references. (And for in-depth study, check out some of the book recommendations in Chapter 17.)

Subtest 1: General Science Answers

If you're still having problems figuring out the difference between an isotope and an ion, remember you may not have to do well on this subtest. It depends on the military career you're interested in. (See Appendix A for a list of military jobs that require a competent General Science score.) If this subtest is important to your military career aspirations, consider putting in some extra study. You can find additional information in Chapter 10, and Chapter 15 has a few more practice questions.

1. **A**	6. **B**	11. **D**	16. **B**	21. **C**
2. **B**	7. **D**	12. **D**	17. **A**	22. **A**
3. **A**	8. **C**	13. **A**	18. **A**	23. **B**
4. **D**	9. **B**	14. **D**	19. **D**	24. **D**
5. **D**	10. **B**	15. **D**	20. **C**	25. **A**

Subtest 2: Arithmetic Reasoning Answers

You have to do well on this subtest to qualify for military enlistment — your score from the Arithmetic Reasoning subtest counts toward your AFQT score. If you're still doing poorly on this test, you may want to postpone taking the ASVAB until you have more study time under your belt (and perhaps take a math class or two). You may also want to review Chapters 7 and 8 and the practice questions in Chapter 9.

1. **D.** Multiply \$0.45 (the cost of making three donuts) by 4 to find the cost of making a dozen donuts: $\$0.45 \times 4 = \$1.80$. Then subtract the cost of making one dozen donuts from the selling price of one dozen donuts to get the profit on one dozen donuts: $\$3.99 - \$1.80 = \$2.19$.

Because the baker sold five dozen donuts, multiply the profit on one dozen donuts times 5 to determine the profit on five dozen donuts: $\$2.19 \times 5 = \$10.95$.

2. **C.** Let x equal the number of dimes. Then $100 - x$ represents the number of quarters. You have $0.10x$ in dimes and $0.25(100 - x)$ in quarters, so set up your equation and solve for x:

$$0.10x + 0.25(100 - x) = 19.75$$
$$0.10x + 25 - 0.25x = 19.75$$
$$-0.15x = -5.25$$
$$x = 35$$

3. **D.** First determine the square footage of the patio: 12 feet $\times$ 16 feet = 192 square feet. Then multiply this number by the cost per square foot to determine what the bricklayer charges: $192 \times \$8 = \$1,536$.

4. **A.** Let x equal Angie's hourly wage; $x + 2$ would then represent Tim's hourly wage, and $3(x + 2)$ would represent Terry's hourly wage. Set up your equation and solve for x:

$$x + (x + 2) + 3(x + 2) = 43$$
$$x + x + 2 + 3x + 6 = 43$$
$$5x + 8 = 43$$
$$5x = 35$$
$$x = 7$$

5. **B.** Two people is half as many as four people. Multiply the number of machines four people can run by $\frac{1}{2}$ to determine how many machines two people can run: $8 \times \frac{1}{2} = 4$.

6. **B.** Let x equal the number of daily tickets you would purchase; $36x$ equals the daily ticket cost:

$$240 < 36x$$
$$\frac{240}{36} < x$$
$$6\frac{2}{3} < x$$

You would need to use the ticket more than $6\frac{2}{3}$ times (or 7 times) for it to be cheaper to use the season ticket.

7. **C.** You can convert the lengths of the pipes from feet and inches to inches and then divide the total inches needed by 12 to get the total number of feet of pipe needed. However, the easiest and fastest way to do this problem is to realize that 3 feet, 6 inches is 3.5 feet. Multiply the number of pipes needed by 3.5 feet to get the number of feet of pipe needed.

$$4 \times 3.5 = 14$$

8. **B.** The fastest way to solve this is to simply multiply the possible choices together ($19 \times 21 = 399$). However, you can also solve this with algebra. Let x equal the first number and $x + 2$ equal the second number:

$$x(x + 2) = 399$$
$$x^2 + 2x = 399$$

This is a quadratic equation that you can solve by setting it equal to zero and factoring.

$$x^2 + 2x - 399 = 0$$
$$(x - 19)(x + 21) = 0$$
$$x - 19 = 0 \qquad \text{or} \qquad x + 21 = 0$$
$$x = 19 \qquad\qquad x = -21$$
$$x + 2 = 21 \qquad\qquad x + 2 = -19$$

Two solutions are possible: 19 and 21, and −21 and −19. Because the latter pair isn't one of the answer choices, the first pair is the correct answer.

9. **C.** Multiply her total sales by her percent commission to find her commission: $530 × 0.65 = $344.50.

10. **B.** The formula for the length of the diagonal of a rectangle is $d^2 = l^2 + w^2$ (this is the Pythagorean theorem, where l and w are the sides of a right triangle and d is the hypotenuse). In this case, $d = 5$ and $l = w + 1$. Substituting the known values into the formula results in $5^2 = (w + 1)^2 + w^2$.

$$5^2 = (w + 1)(w + 1) + w^2$$
$$25 = w^2 + 2w + 1 + w^2$$
$$25 = 2w^2 + 2w + 1$$

This equation is a quadratic equation, which you can solve by setting it equal to zero and factoring.

$$0 = 2w^2 + 2w - 24$$
$$\frac{1}{2}(0) = \frac{1}{2}(2w^2 + 2w - 24)$$
$$0 = w^2 + w - 12$$
$$0 = (w - 3)(w + 4)$$
$$w - 3 = 0 \quad \text{or} \quad w + 4 = 0$$
$$w = 3 \qquad\qquad w = -4 \text{ (not a possible solution)}$$

11. **B.** If 2 inches = 3 miles, then 1 inch equals 1.5 miles: $3 ÷ 2 = 1.5$. Multiply 1.5 miles × 9.5 inches to determine the actual distance: $1.5 × 9.5 = 14.25$, or $14\frac{1}{4}$ miles.

12. **D.** The area of the entire piece of canvas = 10 inches × 14 inches = 140 square inches. The portion painted on equals 8 inches × 12 inches = 96 square inches. (This is determined by subtracting 2 inches — 1 inch on each side — from the length of each side to account for the margins.) Divide 96 by 140 to determine that about 68.5% of the canvas is covered with paint. You can round up to 69%.

13. **D.** Calculate perimeter by adding the lengths of all four sides of a quadrilateral: 9 + 9 + 16 + 16 = 50 feet.

14. **B.** The formula for the perimeter of a rectangle is $P = 2l + 2w$. In this case, $P = 100$ and $l = 1.5w$. Set up your equation and solve for w:

$$100 = 2(1.5w) + 2w$$
$$100 = 3w + 2w$$
$$100 = 5w$$
$$w = 20$$

The width of the rectangle is 20 inches. Because the length is $1\frac{1}{2}$ times the width, $1.5 × 20 = 30$.

15. **C.** The total number of quizzes is 10. If he passed seven of them, the fraction would be expressed as $\frac{7}{10}$.

16. **D.** Divide the amount of ribbon (in yards) used by the number of dresses to determine how much ribbon (in yards) was used in each dress: $3 ÷ 4 = \frac{3}{4}$. Three-quarters of a yard of ribbon was used to make each dress.

17. **B.** Divide $30 by $530 ($500 + $30) to determine the percentage of the sale price that the profit comprised: $30 ÷ 530 = 0.056 = 6\%$.

18. **A.** First find how many bolts a full bin contains: 7 × 12 = 84 bolts. Then multiply the total number of bolts in a full bin by $\frac{1}{6}$ to find how many bolts are in the bin when it's $\frac{1}{6}$ full: $84 × \frac{1}{6} = \frac{84}{6} = 14$ bolts.

Tip: A shortcut is to find $\frac{1}{6}$ of a dozen first and then multiply by 7, the number of dozens. That is, $12 \times \frac{1}{6} = 2$ bolts, and $2 \times 7 = 14$ bolts. You can do this because multiplication is *commutative* — you can multiply the numbers in any order.

19. **C.** The first bike got a $\frac{4}{5}$-mile head start ($12 \text{ mph} \times \frac{4}{60} \text{ hr.} = \frac{48}{60} = \frac{4}{5} \text{ mi.}$). Therefore, by the time the second bike leaves, there are $5\frac{1}{5}$ miles between them ($6 - \frac{4}{5}$). Their combined rate of travel is $12 + 14 = 26$ mph. Let t = the number of hours the second bike travels.

$$26t = 5\frac{1}{5}$$
$$26t = \frac{26}{5}$$
$$t = \frac{26}{5} \div \frac{26}{1}$$
$$t = \frac{26}{5} \times \frac{1}{26}$$
$$t = \frac{1}{5}$$

One-fifth of an hour = $60 \div 5 = 12$ minutes. The second bike left at 2:09, so both bikes will meet at 2:21.

20. **B.** Choice (B) is the cheapest option that gives you enough beans. Calculate each answer option and compare:

    ✓ **Choice (A):** $2 \times \$0.79 = \$1.58$

    ✓ **Choice (B):** $\$1.49$

    ✓ **Choice (C):** Two 3-ounce cans give you less than 8 ounces, so this answer can't be correct.

    ✓ **Choice (D):** $3 \times \$0.65 = \$1.95$

21. **D.** Add the sales amounts together: $\$25.70 + \$32.30 + \$31.80 = \$89.80$. Then multiply the total sales by $\frac{3}{4}$ to determine how much money he has left: $\$89.80 \times 0.75 = \$67.35$.

22. **B.** Divide $\$30.00$ by $\$3.95$. The whole number is the number of pairs of socks the recruit could buy: $\$30.00 \div \$3.95 = 7.59$, or 7 pairs of socks.

23. **D.** Subtract 43 pounds, 7 ounces (the weight of the puppy) from 60 pounds, 5 ounces (the weight of the crate). Converting an additional pound of the crate to ounces makes the subtraction possible. Sixteen ounces make a pound, so 60 pounds, 5 ounces is the same as 59 pounds, 21 ounces. Do the subtraction:

59 pounds	21 ounces
− 43 pounds	7 ounces
16 pounds	14 ounces

24. **D.** The probability that all five computers will be defective is $0.15 \times 0.15 \times 0.15 \times 0.15 \times 0.15 = 0.0000759$ (round up to 0.000076).

25. **D.** Find the area of each bedroom and add them together: $12 \times 14 = 168$; $12 \times 10 = 120$; $8 \times 12 = 96$; and $168 + 120 + 96 = 384$ square feet. Then, because 9 square feet make up a square yard, divide the total area in square feet by 9 to determine the number of square yards needed: $384 \div 9 = 42.6$ square yards. You can round up to 43 square yards.

26. **A.** Divide the total number of pages to be typed by the number of pages Rafael can type per hour to find the number of hours it will take him to type the pages: 126 pages $\div$ 9 pages per hour = 14 hours.

27. **D.** Divide the group of 48 girls by the number of girls who can play at the same time: $48 \div 12 = 4$. This means four groups of girls have to share the 60 minutes: 60 minutes $\div$ 4 = 15 minutes. Thus, each girl plays for 15 minutes.

28. **B.** Subtract the first day's late charge from the total: $8.25 - $2.00 = $6.25. Then divide that amount by $1.25 to determine the number of additional days the movie was overdue: $6.25 $\div$ $1.25 = 5. Add those 5 days to the first day the movie was late to find that the movie was 6 days overdue.

29. **D.** Divide the number of calories in the pudding by the number of calories in the broccoli: $150 \div 60 = 2.5$. Janet can eat 2.5 times the amount of broccoli as she can eat pudding for the same number of calories. Multiply 2.5 by 0.5 cup (the amount of pudding that contains 150 calories) to find how many cups of broccoli she can eat for 150 calories: $2.5 \times 0.5 = 1.25 = 1\frac{1}{4}$ cups.

30. **C.** The dog is barking every 15 minutes, or 4 times per hour. The time between 10 p.m. and 2 a.m. is 4 hours. Multiply the total number of hours in the time period by 4 barks per hour. Then add 1 because the dog barked at the beginning of the period also: $(4 \times 4) + 1 = 16 + 1 = 17$.

Subtest 3: Word Knowledge Answers

The Word Knowledge subtest is another one of the "big four" that counts toward your AFQT score. If you're not seeing the improvement in your scores that you need to see, work with a partner who can quiz you on vocabulary. Review your vocabulary words intensely, even several times a day, to ensure your success on this subtest. See Chapter 4 for more help on improving your word knowledge. Additional practice questions are available in Chapter 6, and you also have a chance to practice this subtest in the practice AFQT in Chapter 22.

1. **B**	8. **D**	15. **A**	22. **A**	29. **A**
2. **D**	9. **A**	16. **B**	23. **B**	30. **C**
3. **B**	10. **A**	17. **A**	24. **D**	31. **D**
4. **B**	11. **C**	18. **D**	25. **B**	32. **A**
5. **A**	12. **A**	19. **C**	26. **D**	33. **D**
6. **C**	13. **B**	20. **B**	27. **A**	34. **C**
7. **B**	14. **C**	21. **C**	28. **C**	35. **C**

Subtest 4: Paragraph Comprehension Answers

Because the military bigwigs use the Paragraph Comprehension subtest to determine whether you even qualify for enlistment (it counts toward your AFQT score), you need to do well here. If you're still struggling, remember to take your time when you read the passages. And after you read each question, you can quickly reread the passage just to make sure you're on the money. The information is in the paragraph; you just have to concentrate to pull it out. Turn to Chapter 5 and the practice questions in Chapter 6 if you still need additional help to pull off a good score on this subtest. An additional opportunity to practice taking this subtest is in the next chapter.

1. **D.** The last sentence in the passage states that chaos and fear are associated with change, making Choice (D) the correct choice. The passage states that leaders must learn to deal with negative emotions connected with change, making Choice (A) incorrect. The second sentence makes it clear that innovation means change, so Choice (B) is incorrect. The third sentence clearly states that leaders must learn everything there is to know about the change, making Choice (C) the wrong choice.

2. **C.** The first sentence says cougars are wide-ranging big cats in North America, making Choice (C) correct. The passage states that pumas, mountain lions, and cougars are the same thing, so Choice (A) is incorrect. Nothing in the passage supports Choice (B), which says cougars are endangered. The passage states that cougars live about 18 years in the wild, so Choice (D) is incorrect.

3. **B.** The counseling process works because the counselee feels the need for assistance, instruction, or understanding. Therefore, Choice (B) — counselees initially reject the advice of their counselors — isn't supported by the passage. The other three choices are all supported by the content of the paragraph.

4. **A.** The second sentence says that professional fire departments have more training, expertise, and experience. Therefore, the reader can infer that volunteer departments have less training, expertise, and experience than professionals. The passage says that professionals, not volunteers, have the skills needed to investigate fires, so Choice (B) is incorrect. The passage states that professional firefighters have more experience investigating the causes of fires, so Choice (C) is incorrect. The passage states that hiring professional firefighters is worthwhile, so Choice (D) is incorrect.

5. **C.** The passage doesn't state the locale of the story, so Choices (A) and (D) are incorrect. The references to extreme cold and lack of light makes Choice (B) an incorrect answer. In sentence three, the author says it was still very foggy and extremely cold, so Choice (C) is the answer.

6. **A.** The main point of the passage is to define epidemiology, as evidenced by the opening sentence. Epidemiology is the study of what causes diseases. Choices (B), (C), and (D) aren't the main points of the passage.

7. **B.** The only statement that's supported by the passage is Choice (B), which says Buddhist teachings have changed. In fact, this sentence is the primary theme of the passage. The other choices aren't supported by information contained in the paragraph.

8. **A.** Choice (B), which questions jurors' intelligence, isn't supported by the passage. Choice (C), which asks for more laws that take intent into consideration, is the opposite of what the author argues. The text doesn't support Choice (D), which calls lawyers liars. The first line of the passage states that statutes permit more severe punishment of a person convicted of a crime if he or she intended to harm another person. The last sentence says juries should only be asked to weigh objective evidence, so the author would no doubt agree that laws should not punish people based on intention, Choice (A).

9. **C.** The passage says that most states punish voluntary manslaughter more severely than involuntary manslaughter, so Choice (A) is incorrect. The argument that punishing people more severely for voluntary manslaughter is unconstitutional isn't made in the passage, so Choice (B) is incorrect. The passage doesn't support Choice (D), which says prosecutors can establish intent. The first sentence of the second paragraph states that juries find it difficult to know what the intent of a person was at the time he or she committed a crime, so Choice (C) is correct.

10. **B.** Lack of attention to ergonomics, not ergonomics itself, can cause injury, so Choice (A) is incorrect. The passage doesn't support Choice (C), which discusses cost and time. The passage states that many people suffer injuries when sufficient attention isn't paid to ergonomics, so Choice (D) is incorrect. The first says, "Ergonomics is the science of designing and arranging workspaces so that people and objects interact efficiently and safely," so Choice (B) is correct.

11. **D.** The passage states that adequate lighting and well-designed chairs are part of ergonomic design, so Choice (A) is incorrect. The passage states that repetitious work can cause injury, so Choice (B) is incorrect. The passage states that desk-bound workers should take breaks, so Choice (C) is incorrect. The first sentence in the second paragraph states that adequate lighting, well-designed chairs, and clutter-free work areas contribute to effective ergonomic design, so Choice (D) is correct.

12. **A.** The passage makes it clear that lack of ergonomic design is dangerous, so Choice (B) is incorrect. Nothing in the passage supports Choice (C), which brings up labor unions. Although the passage claims that lack of ergonomic design causes injury, nothing in the passage supports Choice (D). The passage's second sentence says that lack of attention to ergonomics causes thousands of workers to suffer repetitive stress injury, eye fatigue, muscle soreness, and many other medical problems, so it's reasonable to assume that employers should invest in ergonomic design to protect workers, which makes Choice (A) correct.

13. **B.** The passage says that BTUs are the standard measure of heat, so Choice (A) is incorrect. BTU stands for British thermal unit, so Choice (C) is incorrect. Nothing in the passage supports Choice (D), which names room dimensions.

14. **D.** The passage shows that fuel oil can be more expensive than other heating methods, so Choice (A) is incorrect. Oak firewood is sometimes less expensive than other types of fuel, so Choice (B) is incorrect. Natural gas can sometimes cost less than firewood, so Choice (C) is incorrect. The first sentence states that electricity is always the most inefficient and costly way to heat a home, which makes Choice (D) correct.

15. **A.** The main point of this passage deals with choosing the right fuel based on price; only Choice (A) summarizes this point. Choices (B), (C), and (D) are less important points. The final sentence makes Choice (A) correct.

Subtest 5: Mathematics Knowledge Answers

The Mathematics Knowledge subtest is used to determine whether you qualify for enlistment, so you need to do well. If you're still missing too many questions, you may need to take more drastic measures, such as enrolling in a basic-algebra class at a local community college. If your scores are improving, keep hitting the books and testing yourself up until the day of the ASVAB. Turn to Chapter 7 and the practice questions in Chapter 9 for more information. The practice AFQT in Chapter 22 also gives you a chance to gauge your progress.

1. **B.** Substitute 6 for y in the equation: $2(6) \times 6 = 12 \times 6 = 72$.

2. **B.** Divide both sides of the equation by 0.05 to isolate x: $0.05x \div 0.05 = 1 \div 0.05$, or $x = 20$. To check your answer, substitute 20 for x in the original equation.

3. **C.** $\sqrt{25x^2} = \sqrt{(5x)^2} = 5x$

4. **A.** $9x^3 + 18x^2 - x - 2 = 9x^2(x + 2) - 1(x + 2) = (9x^2 - 1)(x + 2)$.

   The fully factored answer is $(3x - 1)(3x + 1)(x + 2)$, but that's not what the question asks. Make sure you look for the answer to the question.

5. **B.** Solve for x:

$$5x + 7 = 6(x - 2) - 4(2x - 3)$$
$$5x + 7 = 6x - 12 - 8x + 12$$
$$5x + 7 = -2x$$
$$7x + 7 = 0$$
$$7x = -7$$
$$x = -1$$

6. **D.** If two powers have the same base, they can be multiplied by keeping the base and adding the exponents together. In this case, x is the same as x^1: $x + x^2 = x^{1+2} = x^3$.

7. **B.** This is so easy that it may tempt you to think that the correct answer is too obvious. The square root of $(5 + x)^2$ is simply $5 + x$.

8. **B.** You start with $(3 \times 3)(5 - 3)(6 + 2) = x^2$. First solve the left side of the equation: $(9)(2)(8) = 144$. So $x^2 = 144$. Find the square root of each side: $x = 12$.

9. **A.** You start with $-5x = 25$. Isolate x by dividing each side of the equation by -5: $x = -5$.

10. **C.** The area of a circle equals π times the radius squared. The radius is half the diameter, which is 12 in this problem. Plug in the known values: $A = \pi r^2$; $A = \pi 6^2 = 36\pi$. If π is approximately 3.14, the area of the circle is approximately 3.14×36, or 113 square feet.

11. **B.** Volume equals length $\times$ width $\times$ height ($V = lwh$): $6 \times 6 \times 6 = 36 \times 6 = 216$ cubic inches.

12. **B.** The area of a circle is $A = \pi r^2$. Radius is half the diameter, so the radius is 5. In this problem, $A = \pi 5^2 = 25\pi$.

13. **C.** For cylinders, Volume $= \pi r^2(h)$. Because the radius is half the diameter, you can calculate the problem this way: $V = \pi(6^2)10 = \pi(36)10$. If π is approximately 3.14, then $3.14 \times 36 \times 10 = 1{,}130$ cubic inches.

14. **D.** In an isosceles triangle, sides a and c are equal, and angles 1 and 2 are equal.

15. **A.** Rectangles have four equal angles, and all angles are right angles.

16. **A.** Supplementary angles always equal 180 degrees.

17. **A.** Solve for x:

$$3(2x - 5) - 2(4x + 1) = -5(x + 3) - 2$$
$$6x - 15 - 8x - 2 = -5x - 15 - 2$$
$$-2x - 17 = -5x - 17$$
$$3x - 17 = -17$$
$$3x = 0$$
$$x = 0$$

18. **A.** Volume equals length $\times$ width $\times$ height ($V = lwh$). Finding the cube root of 64 shows that each edge measures 4 inches ($4 \times 4 \times 4 = 64$).

19. **B.** $(x^3)^2$ is the same as $(x^3)(x^3)$. To multiply exponents with the same base, keep the base and add the exponents: $(x^3)(x^3) = x^{3+3} = x^6$.

20. **D.** To find out how much rain falls in an hour, multiply the amount that falls in one minute by 60, because 60 minutes make up an hour. In h hours, the amount of rain is $60ih$.

21. **D.** Because $x = y$, you can plug in x for each y in the problem. Therefore, $6 + 4(x - x) = 6 + 4(0) = 6 + 0 = 6$.

22. **A.** The problem asks for the square root of 810. You know that $20^2 = 400$ and $30^2 = 900$, so the range of 20 to 30 is correct.

23. **B.** The problem asks you to find $(x + 2)(x + 2)$. Using the FOIL method (First, Outside, Inside, Last), systematically multiply each term in the first set of parentheses by each term in the second set of parentheses:

✔ **Multiply the First terms:** $x(x) = x^2$.

✔ **Multiply the Outside term** 2) $= 2x$.

> ✔ **Multiply the Inside terms:** $2(x) = 2x$.
>
> ✔ **Multiply the Last terms:** $2 \times 2 = 4$.

Now add all the products together, and you get $x^2 + 2x + 2x + 4$. Add like terms to get the final answer of $x^2 + 4x + 4$.

24. **A.** Replace the unknowns with the numbers given: $6(-3) - 3(-7) - 2(4) = -18 + 21 - 8 = -5$.

25. **C.** The problem asks you to find $(x + 4)(3x + 5)$. Use the FOIL method:

> ✔ **Multiply the First terms:** $x(3x) = 3x^2$.
>
> ✔ **Multiply the Outside terms:** $x(5) = 5x$.
>
> ✔ **Multiply the Inside terms:** $4(3x) = 12x$.
>
> ✔ **Multiply the Last terms:** $4(5) = 20$.

Now add all the products together, and you get $3x^2 + 5x + 12x + 20$. Add like terms to get the final answer, $3x^2 + 17x + 20$.

Subtest 6: Electronics Information Answers

If you need to do well on the Electronics Information subtest to qualify for a certain military career (see Appendix A) and you're still missing questions, review Chapter 13 and spend some time memorizing key electronics concepts, including the mathematical formulas (like Power = Voltage × Current) that help you solve all kinds of electronics problems.

You can find additional practice questions in Chapter 15.

1. **B.** Unless a specific gauge is specified by the speaker manufacturer, you should always choose lower gauges for better sound quality.

2. **B.** There are four frequency bands used throughout the world. A quad-band cell phone would be able to access any of these frequency bands.

3. **B.** The greatest concern when dealing with electricity is personal injury.

4. **C.** *Heat effect* occurs when electrical current must overcome the resistance of the wire. Heat effect can be quite obvious or very subtle.

5. **C.** Like other diodes, Zener diodes allow current in only one direction, except if the voltage across it is greater than a threshold voltage (called *breakdown voltage*), at which point, current also flows through the Zener diode in the opposite direction. This action allows the Zener diode to regulate voltage.

6. **A.** The symbol stands for *ohm*.

7. **D.** *Electromotive force* is the difference of potential, so the term is another way of saying *voltage*.

8. **A.** Lithium-ion (Li-Ion) batteries are much lighter than nickel metal hydride (NiMH) batteries.

9. **A.** The three terminals a transistor must have are the base, emitter, and collector.

10. **B.** To control a light fixture from two different positions, use two three-way switches.

11. **C.** *Amplifier* is another name for *transistor*.

12. **A.** The symbol means *ground.*

13. **C.** Capacitance is the ability to hold an electrical charge. Connecting capacitors in series reduces the capacitance.

14. **C.** 2.5K ohms is 2,500 ohms. K = 1 kilo, or 1,000.

15. **B.** A cell is equal to about 1.5 volts, so 9 ÷ 1.5 = 6.

16. **D.** Primary live wires are black.

17. **C.** A motherboard is the physical arrangement in a computer that contains the computer's basic circuitry and components. Motherboards come in various sizes and component arrangements referred to as *form factors* to fit standard case sizes, components required, and so on. AT is a standard form factor that has a width of 12 inches and a length of 13.8 inches.

18. **B.** An on-off switch allows current to flow only when it's in the closed (on) position.

19. **C.** Determine the wattage that could cause the circuit breaker to trip with this formula: Watts = Volts × Amps, or 120 × 25 = 3,000 watts.

20. **A.** A rheostat is a type of variable resister that's usually used to control voltage.

Subtest 7: Auto & Shop Information Answers

If you have your heart set on fixing Jeeps and tanks or doing other related military jobs (see Appendix A) and you're still struggling on this test, review Chapter 11 and do the practice questions in Chapter 15.

1. D	6. C	11. C	16. B	21. C
2. A	7. A	12. A	17. B	22. D
3. D	8. D	13. B	18. C	23. C
4. A	9. B	14. D	19. B	24. B
5. D	10. B	15. A	20. A	25. A

Subtest 8: Mechanical Comprehension Answers

If you need to do well on the Mechanical Comprehension subtest, don't forget to apply your math skills to the concepts. (A little extra physics study wouldn't hurt, either.) But simply using your common sense can help you quite a bit, too. For example, you may not know exactly *why* a metal spoon feels colder than a wooden spoon when they're at the same temperature, but at least you know that it feels colder. And knowing that may help you answer a question correctly. See Chapter 12 and the additional practice questions in Chapter 15 for more information.

1. **B.** The teeth of helical gears are slanted.

2. **B.** The anvil is closer to Pillar B, so Pillar B bears more weight.

3. **B.** Wheel B is smaller. It has to make more revolutions than Wheel A to cover the same amount of distance, so it will take longer.

4. **A.** *E* stands for *effort needed*. Here's how to set up the equation: 30 (weight of the anvil) $\times$ 2 (length of resistance arm) = x(6) (length of effort arm). Do a little multiplication, and you get $60 = 6x$. To isolate x, divide each side by 6: $10 = x$.

5. **A.** A fixed, simple pulley gives no mechanical advantage, so its mechanical advantage number is 1.

6. **D.** The formula to determine the mechanical advantage of an inclined plane is Length of Ramp ÷ Height of Ramp = Weight of Object ÷ Effort:

$$\frac{8}{4} = \frac{400}{E}$$
$$8E = 400(4)$$
$$8E = 1,600$$
$$E = 200$$

7. **B.** One horsepower equals 33,000 foot-pounds per minute.

8. **A.** Pressure = Force ÷ Area. *Psi* stands for pounds per square inch, so you don't have to change the units of measurement. Just plug in your numbers: $P = 130$ lbs. ÷ 1 in.^{2} = 130 psi.

9. **D.** *Static electricity* is the buildup of electrical charge on surfaces, which causes materials to "stick" together this way.

10. **A.** An aneroid barometer measures atmospheric pressure.

11. **C.** Meshed gears always turn in opposite directions.

12. **D.** Springs are used for all the listed purposes except to add weight.

13. **B.** *Specific gravity* is a comparison between the density of a liquid and the density of water. The liquid with the higher specific gravity will have a float that rises higher.

14. **D.** Universal joints are used to connect shafts that aren't in the same plane.

15. **D.** Try-cocks are valves that measure water level. Water seeks a level throughout a system, so in the schematic, the try-cock correctly indicates the water level.

16. **A.** There are six different symbols, so six different types of machine screws were used.

17. **B.** To determine the amount of force the anvils exert, first multiply the length of the resistance arm (as it applies to the anvil) by the weight of each anvil and add the products together. The 10-pound anvil is supported by the entire weight of the resistance arm, so $5 \times 10 = 50$. The 5-pound anvil is being supported by 3 feet of the resistance arm, so $3 \times 5 = 15$. Add 'em up: $50 + 15 = 65$. This number is equal to the length of the resistance arm times effort (force), or $65 = 5F$. To isolate F, divide both sides by 5: $13 = F$.

18. **C.** One revolution of the winch will move the weight 24 inches, the circumference of the winch drum.

19. **A.** Valves 1 and 2 need to be open to fill the tank.

20. **B.** The number of revolutions a gear makes is inversely proportional to its difference in size from the gear that's turning it. Gear 1 makes 10 clockwise revolutions per minute. Gear 2 is half the size of Gear 1, so to determine the number of revolutions it makes, multiply the number of revolutions Gear 1 makes by the inverse (reciprocal) of $\frac{1}{2}$, which is $\frac{2}{1}$ (or just 2): $10 \times 2 = 20$. Therefore, Gear 2 makes 20 counterclockwise revolutions per minute. Gear 3 is 2.5 times (or $\frac{5}{2}$ times) the size of Gear 2. To determine the number of revolutions Gear 3 makes, multiply the inverse of $\frac{5}{2}$ by the number of revolutions Gear 2 makes: $\frac{2}{5} \times 20 = \frac{40}{5} = 8$ revolutions per minute.

21. **B.** The pinion turns four times as often as the gear: $4 \times 200 = 800$ rpm.

22. **C.** A float indicates the level of liquid in a container.

23. **B.** Using a *runner* (a single, moveable pulley) gives a mechanical advantage of 2.

24. **A.** Because 60 seconds comprise a minute, the valve must open 60 times per minute. The cam will open the valve 10 times per revolution, and $60 \div 10 = 6$. The cam must make 6 revolutions per minute to raise the valve 60 times per minute.

25. **D.** Because Valve 4 is above the bottom of the tank, some water will remain in the tank below the level of the valve, so the tank will never be completely empty.

Subtest 9: Assembling Objects Answers

At present, only the Navy uses the scores from this subtest. If you plan to sail the Seven Seas and you want one of the few Navy jobs that requires you to put parts A and B together, you may want to go over the practice subtests again. For additional practice questions, see Chapter 15.

1. **C**	6. **D**	11. **D**	16. **C**	21. **B**
2. **A**	7. **C**	12. **A**	17. **A**	22. **D**
3. **A**	8. **C**	13. **C**	18. **B**	23. **D**
4. **B**	9. **B**	14. **B**	19. **A**	24. **A**
5. **C**	10. **A**	15. **D**	20. **C**	25. **C**

Chapter 22

Practice AFQT Exam

· ·

If you're wondering what in the world this exam is doing in a book on the ASVAB, don't be confused. The *Armed Forces Qualification Test,* or AFQT, is part of the ASVAB — in a way, it's a test within a test. Your scaled AFQT score is derived from four subtests of the ASVAB, and it determines your overall mental qualification to join the service branch of your choice. Each of the five branches of military service has set its own minimum AFQT score in order to qualify for enlistment. The four subtests that can make or break your chances of joining the military are Arithmetic Reasoning (AR), Word Knowledge (WK), Paragraph Comprehension (PC), and Mathematics Knowledge (MK).

Because I like you (and because you were kind enough to buy this book), I've included an extra chance for you to evaluate your communication and math skills before you head over to the MEPS (Military Entrance Processing Station) or your school or the local National Guard Armory for the real deal.

After you complete the entire practice test, check your answers in Chapter 23.

Your goal here is to determine where you may still need to spend some more study time. If you miss only one question on the Word Knowledge subtest but you miss 15 on Arithmetic Reasoning, you may want to dedicate some extra study time to further develop your math skills before you take the actual ASVAB.

Answer Sheet for Practice AFQT Exam

Subtest 1: Arithmetic Reasoning

1 Ⓐ Ⓑ Ⓒ Ⓓ	7 Ⓐ Ⓑ Ⓒ Ⓓ	13 Ⓐ Ⓑ Ⓒ Ⓓ	19 Ⓐ Ⓑ Ⓒ Ⓓ	25 Ⓐ Ⓑ Ⓒ Ⓓ
2 Ⓐ Ⓑ Ⓒ Ⓓ	8 Ⓐ Ⓑ Ⓒ Ⓓ	14 Ⓐ Ⓑ Ⓒ Ⓓ	20 Ⓐ Ⓑ Ⓒ Ⓓ	26 Ⓐ Ⓑ Ⓒ Ⓓ
3 Ⓐ Ⓑ Ⓒ Ⓓ	9 Ⓐ Ⓑ Ⓒ Ⓓ	15 Ⓐ Ⓑ Ⓒ Ⓓ	21 Ⓐ Ⓑ Ⓒ Ⓓ	27 Ⓐ Ⓑ Ⓒ Ⓓ
4 Ⓐ Ⓑ Ⓒ Ⓓ	10 Ⓐ Ⓑ Ⓒ Ⓓ	16 Ⓐ Ⓑ Ⓒ Ⓓ	22 Ⓐ Ⓑ Ⓒ Ⓓ	28 Ⓐ Ⓑ Ⓒ Ⓓ
5 Ⓐ Ⓑ Ⓒ Ⓓ	11 Ⓐ Ⓑ Ⓒ Ⓓ	17 Ⓐ Ⓑ Ⓒ Ⓓ	23 Ⓐ Ⓑ Ⓒ Ⓓ	29 Ⓐ Ⓑ Ⓒ Ⓓ
6 Ⓐ Ⓑ Ⓒ Ⓓ	12 Ⓐ Ⓑ Ⓒ Ⓓ	18 Ⓐ Ⓑ Ⓒ Ⓓ	24 Ⓐ Ⓑ Ⓒ Ⓓ	30 Ⓐ Ⓑ Ⓒ Ⓓ

Subtest 2: Word Knowledge

1 Ⓐ Ⓑ Ⓒ Ⓓ	8 Ⓐ Ⓑ Ⓒ Ⓓ	15 Ⓐ Ⓑ Ⓒ Ⓓ	22 Ⓐ Ⓑ Ⓒ Ⓓ	29 Ⓐ Ⓑ Ⓒ Ⓓ
2 Ⓐ Ⓑ Ⓒ Ⓓ	9 Ⓐ Ⓑ Ⓒ Ⓓ	16 Ⓐ Ⓑ Ⓒ Ⓓ	23 Ⓐ Ⓑ Ⓒ Ⓓ	30 Ⓐ Ⓑ Ⓒ Ⓓ
3 Ⓐ Ⓑ Ⓒ Ⓓ	10 Ⓐ Ⓑ Ⓒ Ⓓ	17 Ⓐ Ⓑ Ⓒ Ⓓ	24 Ⓐ Ⓑ Ⓒ Ⓓ	31 Ⓐ Ⓑ Ⓒ Ⓓ
4 Ⓐ Ⓑ Ⓒ Ⓓ	11 Ⓐ Ⓑ Ⓒ Ⓓ	18 Ⓐ Ⓑ Ⓒ Ⓓ	25 Ⓐ Ⓑ Ⓒ Ⓓ	32 Ⓐ Ⓑ Ⓒ Ⓓ
5 Ⓐ Ⓑ Ⓒ Ⓓ	12 Ⓐ Ⓑ Ⓒ Ⓓ	19 Ⓐ Ⓑ Ⓒ Ⓓ	26 Ⓐ Ⓑ Ⓒ Ⓓ	33 Ⓐ Ⓑ Ⓒ Ⓓ
6 Ⓐ Ⓑ Ⓒ Ⓓ	13 Ⓐ Ⓑ Ⓒ Ⓓ	20 Ⓐ Ⓑ Ⓒ Ⓓ	27 Ⓐ Ⓑ Ⓒ Ⓓ	34 Ⓐ Ⓑ Ⓒ Ⓓ
7 Ⓐ Ⓑ Ⓒ Ⓓ	14 Ⓐ Ⓑ Ⓒ Ⓓ	21 Ⓐ Ⓑ Ⓒ Ⓓ	28 Ⓐ Ⓑ Ⓒ Ⓓ	35 Ⓐ Ⓑ Ⓒ Ⓓ

Subtest 3: Paragraph Comprehension

1 Ⓐ Ⓑ Ⓒ Ⓓ	4 Ⓐ Ⓑ Ⓒ Ⓓ	7 Ⓐ Ⓑ Ⓒ Ⓓ	10 Ⓐ Ⓑ Ⓒ Ⓓ	13 Ⓐ Ⓑ Ⓒ Ⓓ
2 Ⓐ Ⓑ Ⓒ Ⓓ	5 Ⓐ Ⓑ Ⓒ Ⓓ	8 Ⓐ Ⓑ Ⓒ Ⓓ	11 Ⓐ Ⓑ Ⓒ Ⓓ	14 Ⓐ Ⓑ Ⓒ Ⓓ
3 Ⓐ Ⓑ Ⓒ Ⓓ	6 Ⓐ Ⓑ Ⓒ Ⓓ	9 Ⓐ Ⓑ Ⓒ Ⓓ	12 Ⓐ Ⓑ Ⓒ Ⓓ	15 Ⓐ Ⓑ Ⓒ Ⓓ

Subtest 4: Mathematics Knowledge

1 Ⓐ Ⓑ Ⓒ Ⓓ	6 Ⓐ Ⓑ Ⓒ Ⓓ	11 Ⓐ Ⓑ Ⓒ Ⓓ	16 Ⓐ Ⓑ Ⓒ Ⓓ	21 Ⓐ Ⓑ Ⓒ Ⓓ
2 Ⓐ Ⓑ Ⓒ Ⓓ	7 Ⓐ Ⓑ Ⓒ Ⓓ	12 Ⓐ Ⓑ Ⓒ Ⓓ	17 Ⓐ Ⓑ Ⓒ Ⓓ	22 Ⓐ Ⓑ Ⓒ Ⓓ
3 Ⓐ Ⓑ Ⓒ Ⓓ	8 Ⓐ Ⓑ Ⓒ Ⓓ	13 Ⓐ Ⓑ Ⓒ Ⓓ	18 Ⓐ Ⓑ Ⓒ Ⓓ	23 Ⓐ Ⓑ Ⓒ Ⓓ
4 Ⓐ Ⓑ Ⓒ Ⓓ	9 Ⓐ Ⓑ Ⓒ Ⓓ	14 Ⓐ Ⓑ Ⓒ Ⓓ	19 Ⓐ Ⓑ Ⓒ Ⓓ	24 Ⓐ Ⓑ Ⓒ Ⓓ
5 Ⓐ Ⓑ Ⓒ Ⓓ	10 Ⓐ Ⓑ Ⓒ Ⓓ	15 Ⓐ Ⓑ Ⓒ Ⓓ	20 Ⓐ Ⓑ Ⓒ Ⓓ	25 Ⓐ Ⓑ Ⓒ Ⓓ

Subtest 1: Arithmetic Reasoning

Time: 36 minutes for 30 questions

Directions: This test contains questions about arithmetic. Each question is followed by four possible answers. Decide which answer is correct and then mark the space on your answer sheet that has the same number and letter as your choice. Use scratch paper for any figuring you need to do. Calculators are not allowed.

1. If a barber is capable of cutting the hair of 35 people per day and he works 7 days per week, how many haircuts could he give during the months of April, May, and June?

   (A) 3,185

   (B) 3,150

   (C) 2,545

   (D) 2,555

2. If you type 45 words per minute, how many words can you type in 12 minutes?

   (A) 490

   (B) 540

   (C) 605

   (D) 615

3. Tom is flying a kite at the end of a 500-foot string. His friend Kathy is standing directly under the kite 300 feet away from Tom. How high is the kite flying?

   (A) 300 feet

   (B) 350 feet

   (C) 400 feet

   (D) 450 feet

4. Amy wants to fence in a yard using 400 feet of fencing. If she wants the yard to be 30 feet wide, how long will it be?

   (A) 170 feet

   (B) 175 feet

   (C) 180 feet

   (D) 185 feet

5. A three-digit code must be used to access a computer file. The first digit must be an *A* or a *B*. The second digit must be a number between 0 and 9. The final digit is a single letter from the alphabet from *A* to *Z*. How many possible access codes can there be?

   (A) 38

   (B) 468

   (C) 520

   (D) 640

6. The sun is 93 million miles from Earth, and light travels at a rate of 186,000 miles per second. How long does it take for light from the sun to reach the Earth?

   (A) 5 minutes

   (B) $6\frac{1}{2}$ minutes

   (C) 7 minutes

   (D) $8\frac{1}{3}$ minutes

7. A tanning-bed pass for unlimited tanning costs $53 per month this year, but it was only $50 per month last year. What was the percentage of increase?

   (A) 5%

   (B) 5.5%

   (C) 6%

   (D) 6.5%

8. Eleven plus forty-one is divided by a number. If the result is thirteen, what's the number?

   (A) 2

   (B) 4

   (C) 6

   (D) 8

Go on to next page

9. Mark received an hourly wage of $9.25. His boss gave him a 4% raise. How much does Mark make per hour now?

   (A) $9.29

   (B) $9.62

   (C) $9.89

   (D) $9.99

10. How many pounds of nails costing $7 per pound must be mixed with 6 pounds of nails costing $3 per pound to yield a mixture costing $4 per pound?

    (A) 2 pounds

    (B) 2.5 pounds

    (C) 3 pounds

    (D) 3.5 pounds

11. Theodore has 24 baseball cards. He sells $\frac{1}{4}$ of his cards to Tom and $\frac{1}{3}$ of his cards to Larry, and his Mom accidently throws away $\frac{1}{6}$ of his cards. How many baseball cards does Theodore have left?

    (A) 2

    (B) 18

    (C) 12

    (D) 6

12. Theresa bought five karaoke CDs on sale. A karaoke CD normally costs $24, but she was able to purchase the CDs for $22.50 each. How much money did Theresa save on her entire purchase?

    (A) $7.50

    (B) $1.50

    (C) $8.00

    (D) $22.50

13. On a trip to the beach, you travel 200 miles in 300 minutes. How fast did you travel?

    (A) 30 mph

    (B) 40 mph

    (C) 50 mph

    (D) 60 mph

14. Twenty-one students, or 60% of the class, passed the final exam. How many students are in the class?

    (A) 45

    (B) 40

    (C) 35

    (D) 30

15. Joan invests $4,000 in an account that earns 3% simple interest. How much will Joan have in the account in 10 years?

    (A) $4,500

    (B) $4,800

    (C) $5,200

    (D) $5,400

16. A rectangle has a perimeter of 36 inches. Its length is 3 inches greater than twice the width. What's the rectangle's length?

    (A) 5 inches

    (B) 13 inches

    (C) 18 inches

    (D) 20 inches

17. A backyard is 50 feet by 100 feet. What's its area?

    (A) 150 square feet

    (B) 500 square feet

    (C) 2,500 square feet

    (D) 5,000 square feet

18. Eric is driving a car in which the speedometer is calibrated in kilometers per hour (kph). He notes that his car is traveling at a rate of 75 kph, when he passes a speed limit sign stating the limit is 40 miles per hour (mph). He knows that a kilometer is about $\frac{5}{8}$ of a mile. If a police officer stops him at this point, how many miles per hour over the limit will the ticket read?

    (A) 5

    (B) 7

    (C) 9

    (D) 11

Go on to next page ➡

19. Three apples and twice as many pears add up to one-half the number of grapes in a fruit basket. How many grapes are in the basket?

    (A) 8

    (B) 18

    (C) 28

    (D) 38

20. Apples are on sale for "Buy 2 pounds get 1 free." How many pounds must Janet purchase to get 2 pounds free?

    (A) 2 pounds

    (B) 4 pounds

    (C) 6 apples

    (D) 3 pounds

21. If four pipes of equal length measure 44 feet when they're connected together, how long is each pipe?

    (A) 11 feet

    (B) 4 feet

    (C) 22 feet

    (D) 9 feet

22. A German Shepherd and an Alaskan Malamute are both headed toward the same fire hydrant. The German Shepherd is 120 feet away from the hydrant, and the Alaskan Malamute is 75 feet away from the hydrant. How much closer to the hydrant is the Alaskan Malamute?

    (A) 45 feet

    (B) 25 feet

    (C) 75 feet

    (D) 195 feet

23. A recruit reporting to boot camp took a bus from her home to the military processing center in another city. The trip took 14 hours. If she left at 6 a.m., what time did she arrive at the processing center?

    (A) 7 p.m.

    (B) 12 a.m.

    (C) 8 p.m.

    (D) 9 p.m.

24. A farmer sold 3 pints of strawberries for $1.98 each, 5 pints of raspberries for $2.49 each, and a bushel of peaches for $5.50 at his roadside stand. How much money did the farmer make?

    (A) $9.97

    (B) $23.89

    (C) $18.39

    (D) $18.91

25. A librarian wants to shelve 532 books. If four books fit on a 1-foot length of shelving, how many feet of shelving does she need to shelve all the books?

    (A) 13

    (B) 45

    (C) 33

    (D) 133

26. A student buys a science textbook for $18.00, a math textbook for $14.50, and a dictionary for $9.95. What's the total cost of the books?

    (A) $27.95

    (B) $42.45

    (C) $41.95

    (D) $38.50

27. Debra works an 8-hour shift on Friday. How many minutes does she work on Friday?

    (A) 480 minutes

    (B) 800 minutes

    (C) 240 minutes

    (D) 400 minutes

28. Six people can run three machines in the factory. How many machines can 18 people run?

    (A) 7

    (B) 9

    (C) 6

    (D) 8

Go on to next page

29. On a map drawn to scale, $\frac{1}{2}$ inch equals 1 mile. What length on the map equals 5 miles?

    (A) 2.5 inches

    (B) 5.0 inches

    (C) 10.0 inches

    (D) 1.5 inches

30. A man bought a pair of jeans for $23.00, a shirt for $14.95, and two ties for $7.98 each. What was the total cost of his clothing?

    (A) $53.91

    (B) $45.93

    (C) $51.99

    (D) $54.50

STOP DO NOT TURN THE PAGE UNTIL TOLD TO DO SO.
DO NOT RETURN TO A PREVIOUS TEST.

Subtest 2: Word Knowledge

Time: 11 minutes for 35 questions

Directions: This test has questions about the meanings of words. Each question has an underlined word. You need to decide which one of the four words in the choices *most nearly means* the same thing as the underlined word and then mark the corresponding space on your answer sheet.

1. The <u>abhorrent</u> smell from the lake over-powered the picnickers gathered on the shore.

   (A) strong
   (B) pleasant
   (C) offensive
   (D) tantalizing

2. <u>Belie</u> most nearly means

   (A) pleasure.
   (B) rule.
   (C) pretend.
   (D) misrepresent.

3. The water was calm that day with <u>detritus</u> slowly moving in the small eddies.

   (A) fish
   (B) lily pads
   (C) plants
   (D) debris

4. The prime minister was always cautious about leaving his <u>redoubt</u> in Belgrade.

   (A) city
   (B) stronghold
   (C) house
   (D) country

5. Mike was afraid he might be <u>ostracized</u> for stepping out of line.

   (A) banished
   (B) scolded
   (C) assaulted
   (D) arrested

6. The hotel was specifically designed for the <u>wayworn</u> traveler.

   (A) lost
   (B) weary
   (C) demanding
   (D) happy

7. The park has no showers and no <u>potable</u> water.

   (A) usable
   (B) clear
   (C) drinkable
   (D) tasty

8. <u>Decamp</u> most nearly means

   (A) to backpack.
   (B) to leave.
   (C) to doubt.
   (D) to act with abandon.

9. <u>Glorious</u> most nearly means

   (A) splendid.
   (B) particular.
   (C) delayed.
   (D) contentious.

10. <u>Hypocrisy</u> most nearly means

    (A) hyperactivity.
    (B) god-like.
    (C) insincerity.
    (D) criticalness.

Go on to next page

11. <u>Mallet</u> most nearly means
   (A) sermon.
   (B) participate.
   (C) hammer.
   (D) fish.

12. <u>Hosiery</u> most nearly means
   (A) dangerous.
   (B) illegal.
   (C) stocking.
   (D) automatic.

13. <u>Hale</u> most nearly means
   (A) old.
   (B) healthy.
   (C) customary.
   (D) uninformed.

14. <u>Magnitude</u> most nearly means
   (A) importance.
   (B) peculiar.
   (C) alone.
   (D) tantamount.

15. His <u>vapid</u> presentation earned him a C in the class.
   (A) mediocre
   (B) plagiarized
   (C) dull
   (D) polished

16. Percival was unpopular at the meeting because he imparted so much <u>extraneous</u> data.
   (A) extensive
   (B) unwelcome
   (C) superfluous
   (D) radical

17. She was often <u>solicitous</u> of her father's feelings.
   (A) careful
   (B) ignorant
   (C) forgetful
   (D) abusive

18. I could never get over her liquid blue, <u>limpid</u> eyes.
   (A) bright
   (B) clear
   (C) attentive
   (D) dull

19. The goal of the treaty is to develop international <u>amity</u> and reciprocal trade.
   (A) agreement
   (B) friendship
   (C) standards
   (D) understanding

20. He often bragged about the bravery of his favorite <u>cohort</u>.
   (A) person
   (B) teacher
   (C) companion
   (D) employee

21. <u>Speechlessness</u> most nearly means
   (A) well spoken.
   (B) silence.
   (C) restlessness.
   (D) talkative.

22. <u>Indigenous</u> most nearly means
   (A) poor.
   (B) rich.
   (C) immigrant.
   (D) native.

23. <u>Illusive</u> most nearly means
   (A) insignificant.
   (B) deceptive.
   (C) useful.
   (D) hidden.

24. <u>Hesitate</u> most nearly means
   (A) slam.
   (B) slow to act.
   (C) foreclose.
   (D) end.

Go on to next page

25. <u>Gravity</u> most nearly means

(A) planet.

(B) relationship.

(C) earn.

(D) seriousness.

26. <u>Fondle</u> most nearly means

(A) stir.

(B) handle.

(C) ogle.

(D) radiate.

27. <u>Fete</u> most nearly means

(A) festival.

(B) criticize.

(C) approve.

(D) eat.

28. <u>Encore</u> most nearly means

(A) play.

(B) applause.

(C) repetition.

(D) excite.

29. <u>Diverse</u> most nearly means

(A) various.

(B) hidden.

(C) nestled.

(D) pastime.

30. <u>Detest</u> most nearly means

(A) anger.

(B) hate.

(C) surprise.

(D) excite.

31. Tim was known as a smart aleck, able to deliver <u>acerbic</u> one-liners with no effort.

(A) funny

(B) cheap

(C) sharp

(D) poetic

32. It took a great degree of <u>inexorable</u> force to break into the cavern.

(A) strong

(B) unyielding

(C) acute

(D) powerful

33. Attendents were stationed at intervals, with the obvious intent to <u>hector</u> those who moved too slowly.

(A) hurry

(B) harass

(C) encourage

(D) note

34. Reggy was as <u>gauche</u> in this group of polite company as he always had been.

(A) funny

(B) entertaining

(C) tactless

(D) embarrassed

35. <u>Confident</u> most nearly means

(A) assured.

(B) positive.

(C) intelligent.

(D) educated.

STOP DO NOT TURN THE PAGE UNTIL TOLD TO DO SO. DO NOT RETURN TO A PREVIOUS TEST.

Subtest 3: Paragraph Comprehension

Time: 13 minutes for 15 questions

Directions: This test contains items that measure your ability to understand what you read. This section includes one or more paragraphs of reading material followed by incomplete statements or questions. Read the paragraph and select the choice that best completes the statement or answers the question. Mark your choice on your answer sheet by using the correct letter with each question number.

On June 22, 1944, President Franklin Delano Roosevelt signed into law one of the most significant pieces of legislation ever produced by the United States government: The Servicemembers' Readjustment Act of 1944, commonly known as the GI Bill of Rights. By the time the original GI Bill ended in July 1956, 7.8 million World War II veterans had participated in an education or training program, and 2.4 million veterans had home loans backed by the Veterans Administration (VA).

1. The G.I. Bill provided

    (A) free housing, training, and education.

    (B) medical coverage, education, and assistance to veterans.

    (C) home loan guarantees, training, and education for many former military members.

    (D) a means to exempt veterans from Social Security taxes.

You can put up to $3,000 a year into an individual retirement account (IRA) on a tax-deductible basis if your spouse isn't covered by a retirement plan at work or as long as your combined income isn't too high. You also can put the same amount tax-deferred into an IRA for a nonworking spouse if you file your income tax return jointly.

2. The maximum amount that a married couple could possibly save in a tax-deferred IRA during a year is

    (A) $3,000.

    (B) $6,000.

    (C) $9,000.

    (D) The question can't be answered based on the information contained in the passage.

Presidential appointments are an ongoing effort. Some of a president's appointments require Senate confirmation. These appointments are for positions throughout the federal government, for the Cabinet and subcabinet, for members of regulatory commissions, for ambassadorships, for judgeships, and for members of numerous advisory boards.

3. Which of the following statements is NOT true?

    (A) All presidential appointments require Senate confirmation.

    (B) A position on a regulatory commission is an example of a presidential appointment.

    (C) Presidential appointments happen throughout the president's term in office.

    (D) All of the above statements are true.

Go on to next page

A link between advertising and alcohol consumption is intuitively compelling but hasn't been consistently supported by research. Because alcohol advertising is pervasive, econometric studies may not be sensitive to change or assess in a range where change actually makes a difference. In dealing with advertising, partial bans aren't likely to be effective, and total bans aren't practical. Advertising bans in one medium also are weakened by substitution of increased advertising in alternative media and/or other promotions.

4. The author of this passage believes that

    (A) advertisement of alcoholic beverages should be illegal.

    (B) partial bans on alcohol advertising could be effective in some cases.

    (C) bans on alcohol advertising aren't likely to work.

    (D) clear links have been established between alcohol consumption and advertising.

The etymology of the word or name *Alabama* has evoked much discussion among philological researchers. It was the name of a noted southern Indian tribe whose habitat when first known to Europeans was in what is now central Alabama. One of the major waterways in the state was named for this group and from this river, in turn, the name of the state was derived. According to some investigations, the tribal name Alabama must be sought in the Choctaw tongue, because it isn't uncommon for tribes to accept a name given them by a neighboring tribe.

5. The state of Alabama was named after

    (A) a Choctaw Indian tribe.

    (B) European settlers.

    (C) a river.

    (D) an Indian chief.

Each of the 94 federal judicial districts handles bankruptcy matters, and in almost all districts, bankruptcy cases are filed in the bankruptcy court. Bankruptcy cases can't be filed in state court. Bankruptcy laws help people who can no longer pay their creditors get a fresh start by liquidating their assets to pay their debts or by creating a repayment plan. Bankruptcy laws also protect troubled businesses and provide for orderly distributions to business creditors through reorganization or liquidation.

6. Which of the following statements is NOT supported by the passage?

    (A) Bankruptcy must be filed in a federal court.

    (B) Bankruptcy is designed to help individuals and protect businesses.

    (C) Businesses can be reorganized or liquidated through bankruptcy.

    (D) Bankruptcy must be filed in the bankruptcy court.

Questions 7 and 8 are based on the following passage.

The U.S. Department of Justice has prepared a report about hate crimes in the United States between 1997 and 1999. In 60% of hate crime incidents, the most serious offense was a violent crime, most commonly intimidation or simple assault. The majority of incidents motivated by race, ethnicity, sexual orientation, or disability involved a violent offense, while two-thirds of incidents motivated by religion involved a property offense, most commonly vandalism. Younger offenders were responsible for most hate crimes. Thirty-one percent of violent offenders and 46% of property offenders were under age 18.

7. Most property offense hate crimes were motivated by

    (A) religion.

    (B) race.

    (C) sexual orientation.

    (D) abortion.

8. The majority of hate crimes during this period can be classified as

    (A) property offenses.

    (B) violent crimes.

    (C) assault.

    (D) intimidation.

Go on to next page

Linewatch operations are conducted near international boundaries and coastlines in areas of Border Patrol jurisdiction to prevent the illegal entry and smuggling of aliens into the United States and to intercept those who do enter illegally before they can escape from border areas. Signcutting is the detection and the interpretation of any disturbances in natural terrain conditions that indicate the presence or passage of people, animals, or vehicles.

9. The activity that's designed to detect changes in the natural environment, which may indicate passage of illegal aliens, is called

(A) linewatching.

(B) signcutting.

(C) Border Patrol Operations.

(D) Terrain Observation.

Wales was in ancient times divided into three parts nearly equal, consideration having been paid, in this division, more to the value than to the just quantity or proportion of territory. They were Venedotia, now called North Wales; Demetia, or South Wales, which in British is called Deheubarth, that is, the southern part; and Powys, the middle or eastern district. Roderic the Great, or Rhodri Mawr, who was king over all Wales, was the cause of this division. He had three sons, Mervin, Anarawt, and Cadell, amongst whom he partitioned the whole principality.

10. Wales was divided into divisions because

(A) natural boundaries such as rivers and mountains made the division necessary.

(B) Wales was too large for the King to oversee personally.

(C) the King of Wales wanted his sons to rule.

(D) all of the above

Questions 11 and 12 are based on the following passage.

The fierce and warlike tribe, called the Huns, who'd driven the Goths to seek new homes, came from Asia into Southeastern Europe and took possession of a large territory lying north of the River Danube. During the first half of the fifth century, the Huns had a famous king named Attila. He was only 21 years old when he became their king. But although he was young, he was very brave and ambitious, and he wanted to be a great and powerful king. As soon as his army was ready, he marched with it into countries, which belonged to Rome. He defeated the Romans in several great battles and captured many of their cities. The Roman Emperor Theodosius had to ask for terms of peace. Attila agreed that there should be peace, but soon afterwards he found out that Theodosius had formed a plot to murder him. He was so enraged at this that he again began war. He plundered and burned cities wherever he went, and at last the emperor had to give him a large sum of money and a portion of the country south of the Danube.

11. A good title for the above paragraph would be

(A) "The Burning of Rome"

(B) "Emperor Theodosius"

(C) "Attila the Hun"

(D) "Rome For Dummies"

12. After terms of peace were offered, Attila resumed the war against Rome because

(A) he discovered the emperor wanted to assassinate him.

(B) he wanted to further expand his kingdom.

(C) the emperor of Rome offered too little money in the peace terms.

(D) Danube, his second-in-charge, advised him not to accept the peace terms.

Go on to next page

Questions 13 through 15 are based on the following passage.

In the military, as in all professions, the issue of competence is directly relevant to professional integrity. Because human life, national security, and expenditures from the national treasury are so frequently at issue when the military acts, the obligation to be competent isn't merely prudential. That obligation is a moral one, and culpable incompetence here is clearly a violation of professional integrity. Part of the social aspect of professional integrity involves the joint responsibility for conduct and competence shared by all members of the profession. Only fellow professionals are capable of evaluating competence in some instances; hence, fellow professionals must accept the responsibility of upholding the standards of the profession. Fellow military members can spot derelictions of duty, failures of leadership, failures of competence, and the venalities of conduct that interfere with the goals of the military mission. Often, the obligations of professional integrity may be pitted against personal loyalties or friendships; and, where the stakes for society are so high, professional integrity should win out.

13. One word that best describes the primary theme of this passage would be

(A) proficiency.

(B) equality.

(C) evaluations.

(D) relationships.

14. Professional competence is

(A) a moral obligation.

(B) directly relevant to professional integrity.

(C) essential because military operations impact human life, national security, and use of taxpayer funds.

(D) all of the above

15. The author of the passage would agree that

(A) friendship must often take a back seat to professional integrity.

(B) only fellow professionals should evaluate competence.

(C) professional competence is a direct result of effective training programs.

(D) all of the above

STOP DO NOT TURN THE PAGE UNTIL TOLD TO DO SO. DO NOT RETURN TO A PREVIOUS TEST.

Subtest 4: Mathematics Knowledge

> **Time:** 24 minutes for 25 questions
>
> **Directions:** This section is a test of your ability to solve general mathematical problems. Select the correct answer from the choices given and then mark the corresponding space on your answer sheet. Use scratch paper to do any figuring. Calculators are not allowed.

1. Solve for x: $5x - 2x = 7x + 2x - 24$
   - (A) 2
   - (B) −2
   - (C) 4
   - (D) −4

2. The cube of 6 is
   - (A) 125
   - (B) 225
   - (C) 216
   - (D) 238

3. In the equation $3x + 7y = 21$, at what point is the x-axis intersected?
   - (A) (7, 0)
   - (B) (0, 7)
   - (C) (0, 4)
   - (D) (4, 0)

4. $x + y = 6$ and $x - y = 4$. Solve for x.
   - (A) 3
   - (B) 5
   - (C) 7
   - (D) 8

5. Solve for y: $4(y + 3) + 7 = 3$
   - (A) 2
   - (B) −2
   - (C) 4
   - (D) −4

6. (12 yards + 14 feet) ÷ 2 =
   - (A) 25 feet
   - (B) 12 feet
   - (C) 32 feet
   - (D) 8 feet

7. $x^3(x^3) =$
   - (A) x^9
   - (B) $2x^9$
   - (C) $2x^6$
   - (D) x^6

8. $4\frac{1}{5} + 1\frac{2}{5} + 3\frac{3}{10} =$
   - (A) $6\frac{1}{5}$
   - (B) $8\frac{9}{10}$
   - (C) $5\frac{1}{2}$
   - (D) $7\frac{1}{5}$

9. $1.5 \times 10^2 =$
   - (A) 45
   - (B) 150
   - (C) 1,500
   - (D) 15

10. The average of 54, 61, 70, and 75 is
    - (A) 50
    - (B) 52
    - (C) 55
    - (D) 65

Go on to next page

11. 2 feet, 4 inches + 4 feet, 8 inches =

   (A) 6 feet, 8 inches

   (B) 7 feet

   (C) 7 feet, 2 inches

   (D) 8 feet

12. If $x = 4$, then $x^4 \div x =$

   (A) 12

   (B) 36

   (C) 64

   (D) 72

13. Solve for x: $5 - 3x \geq 14 + 6x$

   (A) $x \geq -1$

   (B) $x \leq -1$

   (C) $x > -1$

   (D) $x < -1$

14. $(900 \times 3) \div 6 =$

   (A) 45

   (B) 450

   (C) 55

   (D) 550

15. If $x = 2$, then $x^x(x^x) =$

   (A) 16

   (B) $2x^x$

   (C) 8

   (D) 24

16. Solve for x: $x^2 - 2x - 15 = 0$

   (A) 4, –2

   (B) 3, –3

   (C) 5, –3

   (D) –1, 1

17. $\sqrt{49} \div \sqrt{64} =$

   (A) $\frac{1}{4}$

   (B) $\frac{1}{2}$

   (C) $\frac{1}{3}$

   (D) $\frac{7}{8}$

18. If $5y^2 = 80$, then y is

   (A) a positive number.

   (B) a negative number.

   (C) either a positive or negative number.

   (D) an imaginary number.

19. If $2 + x \geq 15$, what's the value of x?

   (A) $x < 13$

   (B) $x > 13$

   (C) $x \geq 13$

   (D) $x \leq 13$

20. If a circle has a radius of 15 feet, what is its circumference most nearly?

   (A) 24 feet

   (B) 72 feet

   (C) 94 feet

   (D) 36 feet

21. What's the volume of a box measuring 12 inches long by 8 inches deep by 10 inches high?

   (A) 960 cubic inches

   (B) 128 cubic inches

   (C) 42 cubic inches

   (D) 288 cubic inches

22. The following figure is a(n)

   (A) parallelogram.

   (B) obtuse triangle.

   (C) trapezoid.

   (D) rectangle.

Go on to next page

23. The sum of the measures of the angles of a parallelogram is

    (A) 360 degrees.

    (B) 540 degrees.

    (C) 180 degrees.

    (D) 720 degrees.

24. What is the prime factorization of 100?

    (A) 2×50

    (B) $2^2 \times 5^2$

    (C) 4×25

    (D) 25^2

25. $\sqrt{-9}$ is an example of a(n)

    (A) real number.

    (B) imaginary number.

    (C) irrational number.

    (D) sloping number.

STOP DO NOT TURN THE PAGE UNTIL TOLD TO DO SO. DO NOT RETURN TO A PREVIOUS TEST.

Chapter 23

Practice AFQT Exam: Answers and Explanations

*U*se this answer key to score the Practice AFQT Exam in Chapter 22. Note that the actual AFQT is scored by comparing your raw score to the scores of other people, which produces a scaled score. Turn to Chapter 1 to find out how the AFQT score is derived from the Arithmetic Reasoning, Word Knowledge, Paragraph Comprehension, and Mathematics Knowledge subtests. Keep in mind that these four subtests determine whether you can even get into the military. If you find you're still struggling in any of these subtest areas, you may want to concentrate some additional study effort before knocking on the recruiter's door to say, "I'm ready!"

Subtest 1: Arithmetic Reasoning Answers

Mathematical word problems can be tough for some people. You have to develop a skill for determining which factors are relevant to the problem and then be able to convert those factors into a mathematical formula to arrive at a correct solution. Yikes! No wonder there are so many math books on the market! If you still need work on this subtest, I recommend a few good math books in Chapter 17. Reviewing Chapters 7 and 8 and the additional practice questions in Chapter 9 may also help.

1. **A.** There are 30 days in April, 31 days in May, and 30 days in June for a total of 91 days. Multiply the number of days by the number of haircuts per day: $91 \times 35 = 3,185$.

2. **B.** Multiply the number of words you can type per minute (45) by the number of minutes you'll be typing (12): $45 \times 12 = 540$.

3. **C.** Visualize a right triangle, where the kite string represents the hypotenuse and the line between Tom and Kathy represents one of the legs. The Pythagorean theorem states that if you know the length of two sides of a right triangle, you can determine the length of the third side using the formula $a^2 + b^2 = c^2$. In this case, $300^2 + b^2 = 500^2$. Solve for b:

$$90,000 + b^2 = 250,000$$
$$b^2 = 250,000 - 90,000$$
$$b^2 = 160,000$$
$$b = \sqrt{160,000}$$
$$b = 400$$

4. **A.** The formula used to determine the perimeter of a rectangle is $P = 2(l + w)$. The width is 30, and the perimeter is 400. Plug in the numbers and solve for l:

$$400 = 2(l + 30)$$
$$400 = 2l + 60$$
$$340 = 2l$$
$$l = 170$$

5. **C.** There are two possibilities for the first digit *(A or B),* 10 possibilities for the second digit (0 to 9), and 26 possibilities for the third digit. Using the multiplication principle, $2 \times 10 \times 26 = 520$ possible access codes.

6. **D.** The distance formula is distance equals rate times time, or *d = rt.* Substitute the known values: $93,000,000 = 186,000t$. Therefore, $t = 500$ seconds. Divide 500 by 60 to convert to minutes: 500 seconds ÷ 60 seconds/minute = $8\frac{1}{3}$ minutes.

7. **C.** The difference in the price is $3, so divide the difference by the original price: $3 ÷ $50 = 0.06, or 6%.

8. **B.** Let *x* = the unknown number. Set up the formula as $\frac{11+41}{x} = 13$. Then solve for *x:*

$$\frac{11+41}{x} = 13$$
$$\frac{52}{x} = 13$$
$$52 = 13x$$
$$x = 4$$

9. **B.** Mark received a 4% raise, so to calculate the new wage, start off by taking $9.25 × 0.04 = $0.37. Then add that number (the amount of Mark's raise) to his original hourly wage. Mark's new hourly wage is $9.25 + $0.37 = $9.62.

10. **A.** Let *x* = the number of nails costing $7 per pound. The total cost of the mixture *(M)* equals the sum of the cost for each type of nail, or *M = A + B,* where *A = 7x, B =* 3(6), and *M =* 4(6 + *x*). Substitute the known values into the equation and solve for *x:*

$$4(6 + x) = 7x + 18$$
$$24 + 4x = 7x + 18$$
$$24 - 18 = 7x - 4x$$
$$6 = 3x$$
$$x = 2$$

11. **D.** You need to add the fractions, so convert the different denominators to a common denominator — 4, 3, and 6 all divide evenly into 12, so use 12 as the common denominator. To convert $\frac{1}{4}$, divide 12 (the new common denominator) by 4 (the original common denominator) to get 3. Then multiply $\frac{1}{4}$ by $\frac{3}{3}$ (another way of saying 1). The product is $\frac{3}{12}$ (that is, $\frac{1}{4} = \frac{3}{12}$). Do the same calculation for the other fractions: $\frac{1}{3} = \frac{4}{12}$ and $\frac{1}{6} = \frac{2}{12}$.

To add the fractions, first add the new numerators together: $3 + 4 + 2 = 9$. Place the added numerator over the new denominator, 12, and you can see that $\frac{9}{12}$ of the cards have been sold or lost. You can reduce $\frac{9}{12}$ to $\frac{3}{4}$, which equals 75%. Now find 75% of 24: $24 \times 0.75 = 18$. Eighteen of 24 cards have been sold or lost, so subtract to find the remaining cards: $24 - 18 = 6$ cards remaining.

12. **A.** Subtract the sale price from the regular price: $24.00 – $22.50 = $1.50. Multiply the difference by the number of CDs to find out how much Theresa saved altogether: $1.50 × 5 = $7.50.

13. **B.** First convert the 300 minutes to hours by dividing by 60 (300 minutes ÷ 60 minutes/hour = 5 hours). Use the distance formula *(d = rt)* and substitute the known values: 200 = 5*r; r* = 40 mph.

14. **C.** Let *x* = the number of people in the class; 60% of *x* = 21, so $0.60x = 21$, and $x = 35$.

15. **C.** Use the interest formula *(I = Prt)* to determine the amount of interest earned, where the principal *(P)* is 4,000, the rate *(r)* is 0.03 (3%), and the time *(t)* is 10. *I =* 4,000(0.03)(10), or *I* = $1,200. Add the interest earned to the original amount invested: $4,000 + $1,200 = $5,200.

16. **B.** A rectangle's perimeter is determined by the formula $P = 2(l + w)$. The length of this rectangle is $3 + 2w$. Substituting the known values into the formula results in

$$36 = 2(w + 3 + 2w)$$

$$36 = 2(3w + 3)$$

$$18 = 3w + 3$$

$$15 = 3w$$

$$w = 5$$

The length is $3 + 2w$, so $l = 3 + 2(5) = 13$.

17. **D.** The area of a rectangle is the length × the width of the rectangle, or $A = lw$: $50 \times 100 = 5,000$ square feet.

18. **B.** A kilometer is $\frac{5}{8}$ of a mile, so multiply $75 \times \frac{5}{8} = \frac{375}{8}$. Divide 375 by 8 to determine that Eric was traveling at about 47 miles per hour, 7 mph over the 40 mph posted limit.

19. **B.** Let x = the number of grapes; 3 apples and 6 pears (twice the number of apples) equals $\frac{1}{2}$ of x, or

$$3 + 6 = \frac{1}{2}x$$

$$9 = \frac{1}{2}x$$

$$2(9) = x$$

$$x = 18$$

20. **B.** If Janet must purchase 2 pounds of apples to get 1 free pound, then to get 2 free pounds, she would need to purchase twice as many apples, or 4 pounds of apples.

21. **A.** All pipes are equal in length, so divide the total length, 44 feet, by the total number of pipes, 4. The answer, 11, is the length of each individual pipe. You can check this answer by multiplying: $4 \times 11 = 44$.

22. **A.** Subtract the Malamute's distance from the German Shepherd's distance ($120 - 75 = 45$) to determine how much closer the Malamute is to the hydrant.

23. **C.** Simply add 14 hours to 6 a.m. to reach 8 p.m. Twelve hours from 6 a.m. is 6 p.m., and two hours after that brings you to 8 p.m.

24. **B.** Multiply 3 pints of strawberries at $1.98 ($3 \times \$1.98 = \$5.94$), 5 pints of raspberries at $2.49 ($5 \times \$2.49 = \$12.45$), and 1 bushel of peaches at $5.50 ($1 \times \$5.50 = \$5.50$). Add the products together to determine the amount of cash the farmer earned: $\$5.94 + \$12.45 + \$5.50 = \$23.89$.

25. **D.** Divide 532 by 4 to determine how many feet of shelving will be needed: 532 books ÷ 4 books/foot = 133 feet.

26. **B.** Simply add the cost of all the books: $\$18.00 + \$14.50 + \$9.95 = \$42.45$.

27. **A.** 8 hours × 60 minutes/hour = 480 minutes.

28. **B.** Eighteen people can run three times the number of machines six people can run, because $18 = 3 \times 6$ (divide 18 by 6). Six people can run three machines, so multiply 3×3 machines = 9 machines. Therefore, 18 people can run nine machines.

29. **A.** Multiply the scale measurement for 1 mile ($\frac{1}{2}$ inch per mile) by 5 miles: $\frac{1}{2} \times 5 = \frac{1}{2} \times \frac{5}{1} = \frac{5}{2}$. Divide 5 by 2, and you get 2.5 inches.

30. **A.** Simply add the cost of all the items: $\$23.00 + \$14.95 + \$7.98 + \$7.98 = \$53.91$.

Subtest 2: Word Knowledge Answers

I hope you did well on this subtest. (I was crossing my fingers the whole time!) If not, you may want to take another gander at Chapter 4 and the practice questions in Chapter 6.

1. C	8. B	15. C	22. D	29. A
2. D	9. A	16. C	23. B	30. B
3. D	10. C	17. A	24. B	31. C
4. B	11. C	18. B	25. D	32. B
5. A	12. C	19. B	26. B	33. B
6. B	13. B	20. C	27. A	34. C
7. C	14. A	21. B	28. C	35. A

Subtest 3: Paragraph Comprehension Answers

If you still need to boost your score, engage in some more reading practice. Improving your vocabulary can also help improve your reading comprehension skills. See Chapter 5 for some tips. You may also want to try a few of the practice questions in Chapter 6.

1. **C.** According to the passage, millions of veterans received home loan guarantees, education, and training, making Choice (C) the correct answer. Be careful here, because Choice (A) is tempting, but nothing in the passage indicates that the housing, education, and training were totally free.

2. **B.** The paragraph states that the maximum amount one can place into a tax-deferred IRA is $3,000, plus an additional $3,000 if the spouse isn't employed. The question asks about a couple, so add $3,000 + $3,000 to get $6,000.

3. **A.** Although many presidential appointments require Senate confirmation, not all do. The passage mentions only *some* appointments, so Choice (A) is an incorrect statement.

4. **C.** The author specifically states that partial bans on alcohol advertising isn't likely to be effective and that total bans wouldn't be practical.

5. **C.** According to the passage, a river was named after the Alabama Indian Tribe, and the state derived its name from this river.

6. **D.** The first sentence states that bankruptcy is usually (not always) filed in bankruptcy court, making Choice (D) an incorrect statement.

7. **A.** The second sentence states that most violent crimes were motivated by such factors as race and sexual orientation, and most property crimes were motivated by religion. The question refers to property crimes, so Choice (A) is the right answer.

8. **B.** Sixty percent of all hate crimes during the period were violent crimes. Assault and intimidation are examples of violent crimes.

9. **B.** The last sentence in the passage describes the signcutting operation.

10. **C.** The rationale for the division is explained in the final sentence, which mentions the king's sons. The passage makes no reference to the size of Wales or the natural boundaries.

11. **C.** The primary subject of this paragraph is Attila, who was king of the Huns.

12. **A.** Attila agreed to peace but soon after discovered that the Roman emperor had launched a plot to kill him.

13. **A.** The primary theme of the passage is stated in the first sentence. *Proficiency* is closest in meaning to the word *competence,* which is the primary theme of the passage.

14. **D.** The passage directly supports all the statements.

15. **A.** The author specifically states that when pitted against friendship, professional integrity should win out. The author explains that only fellow professionals can evaluate other professionals in some (not all) cases, making Choice (B) incorrect. Choice (C) isn't supported by information in the passage.

Subtest 4: Mathematics Knowledge Answers

It's too bad the ASVAB folks don't allow calculators! That would make this subtest a breeze. Don't be discouraged. The problems are purposely designed so that they can be solved using only a scratch paper, the ol' No. 2 pencil, and a little brain sweat. If you're still having difficulty, give Chapter 7 another gander. There are additional practice questions in Chapter 9.

1. **C.** $5x - 2x = 7x + 2x - 24$; $3x = 9x - 24$; $-6x = -24$; $6x = 24$; $x = 4$

2. **C.** The cube of 6 is $6^3 = 6 \times 6 \times 6 = 216$.

3. **A.** The equation $3x + 7y = 21$ is the equation for a line, and a line intersects the x-axis at the point where the y-coordinate is 0 ($y = 0$). Substitute 0 for the y variable in the equation and solve for x: $3x + 7y = 21$; $3x + 7(0) = 21$; $3x = 21$; $x = 7$. The point's coordinates are (7, 0).

4. **B.** This problem gives you a system of equations — two equations with two variables. You can find x by solving one of the equations for y and plugging that value into the other equation. First, $x + y = 6$, so $y = 6 - x$. Substitute this known value for y in the second equation and solve for x:

$$x - y = 4$$
$$x - (6 - x) = 4$$
$$x - 6 + x = 4$$
$$2x - 6 = 4$$
$$2x = 10$$
$$x = 5$$

5. **D.**

$$4(y + 3) + 7 = 3$$
$$4y + 12 + 7 = 3$$
$$4y + 19 = 3$$
$$4y = -16$$
$$y = -4$$

6. **A.** Convert 12 yards, 14 feet to feet: (12 yards × 3 feet/yard) + 14 feet = 36 feet + 14 feet = 50 feet. Divide by 2 as instructed: 50 feet ÷ 2 = 25 feet.

7. **D.** If two powers have the same base, the numbers can be multiplied by keeping the base the same and adding the powers (exponents) together: $x^3(x^3) = x^{3+3} = x^6$.

8. **B.** Convert to the lowest common denominator (which is 10), and then add:
$4\frac{1}{5} + 1\frac{2}{5} + 3\frac{3}{10} = 4\frac{2}{10} + 1\frac{4}{10} + 3\frac{3}{10} = 8\frac{9}{10}$.

9. **B.** Following the order of operations, you have to find the power (10^2) before multiplying: $1.5 \times 10^2 = 1.5 \times (10 \times 10) = 1.5 \times 100 = 150$.

10. **D.** Add the numbers and then divide by the number of terms to find the mean. The sum is $54 + 61 + 70 + 75 = 260$. You have four numbers, and $260 \div 4 = 65$.

11. **B.** 2 feet + 4 feet = 6 feet, and 4 inches plus 8 inches = 12 inches (the equivalent to 1 foot). Therefore, you have a total of 7 feet.

12. **C.** Your first reaction may be to substitute 4 for each x and then do the math. But you can save yourself some work (and time) by first dividing x^4 by x, which is x^3. Then substitute 4 for each x, and you find that the equation is now $4 \times 4 \times 4$. Then multiply: 4×4 is 16, and 16×4 is 64, which is your final answer.

13. **B.** As you solve this inequality, remember that when you multiply or divide an inequality by a negative number, you need to reverse the direction of the inequality sign:

$$5 - 3x \geq 14 + 6x$$
$$5 - 3x - 6x \geq 14$$
$$-9x \geq 14 - 5$$
$$-9x \geq 9$$
$$x \leq -1$$

14. **B.** $(900 \times 3) \div 6 = 2{,}700 \div 6 = 450$.

15. **A.** Substitute 2 for all the x's: $x^x(x^x) = 2^2 \times 2^2 = 4 \times 4 = 16$.

16. **C.** This is a quadratic equation that you can solve by factoring and setting each factor equal to zero:

$$x^2 - 2x - 15 = 0$$
$$(x - 5)(x + 3) = 0$$
$$x - 5 = 0 \quad \text{or} \quad x + 3 = 0$$
$$x = 5 \qquad\qquad x = -3$$

17. **D.** Find the square roots before dividing. The square root of 49 is 7, and the square root of 64 is 8. Now divide: $7 \div 8 = \frac{7}{8}$.

18. **C.** The square root of a positive number can be either positive or negative. For instance, the square root of 16 is ± 4, because 4^2 and $(-4)^2$ both give you the positive number 16.

19. **C.** Solving this equation doesn't require multiplying or dividing by a negative number, so the inequality sign remains the same: $2 + x \geq 15$; $x \geq 13$.

20. **C.** Circumference equals π times diameter, and diameter is equal to two times the radius. In other words, $C = \pi d$, and $d = 2r$. Thus, $C = \pi(2)(15) = \pi 30$. If you round π to 3.14, the answer is 94.2, or about 94 feet.

21. **A.** Volume equals length times width times height ($V = lwh$). Plug in the numbers and solve: $V = 12 \times 8 \times 10 = 960$ cubic inches.

22. **C.** In a trapezoid, two of four sides are parallel to each other.

23. **A.** All quadrilaterals have angles that total 360 degrees.

24. **B.** Here's how you may have found the prime factors of 100: $100 = 4 \times 25 = 2 \times 2 \times 5 \times 5 = 2^2 \times 5^2$.

25. **B.** The square root of a negative number doesn't exist as far as real numbers are concerned. In mathematics, this is called an *imaginary number,* and it's represented by the letter i.

Part VI
The Part of Tens

The 5th Wave   By Rich Tennant

"Okay—now that the paramedic is here with the defibrillator and smelling salts, prepare to open your test booklets..."

In this part . . .

You can put your pencil down now — no more quizzes or sample tests like the ones in Part V. This part is the Part of Tens, which features my personal ASVAB top-ten lists. I couldn't write a *For Dummies* book and not include this part.

I give you important information for doing well on the ASVAB, offer some pointers for memorizing crucial concepts, and point you in the right direction for finding more information if you need it. This part presents material in quick tidbits so you can get into the chapters and then get out.

Good luck taking your ASVAB. I hope you get stationed in Hawaii!

Chapter 24

Ten Surefire Ways to Fail the ASVAB

In This Chapter

▶ Avoiding common ASVAB-preparation mistakes

▶ Steering clear of other people's mistakes

Technically, you can't fail the ASVAB — it's not a pass/fail test but instead a tool the military uses to measure your potential for learning military duties and military occupations. But realistically, each of the branches has established minimum Armed Forces Qualification Test (AFQT) scores to qualify for enlistment and minimum line scores to qualify for certain military jobs. If you don't qualify to join the service branch of your choice or don't qualify for the job you want, you haven't technically failed, but you may have to take the test again (after some study sessions) to get into the branch of service your heart desires.

But if you avoid the mistakes outlined in this chapter, you can improve your chances of qualifying for enlistment and getting the military job of your dreams.

Choosing Not to Study at All

Many people think that they don't need to study for the ASVAB. They assume that because they studied many of the subjects in high school, they'll do fine even if they just wing it.

This train of thought isn't true (and it's kind of crazy). Why wouldn't you study? At the very least, brushing up on vocabulary and math concepts definitely helps you score higher on the ASVAB. Using a calculator is a no-no on the ASVAB, so you may want to revisit some math tricks for doing calculations by hand. Auto, Shop, and Mechanical Comprehension aren't required high school courses, so these subjects may be completely new to you and require additional attention.

Using study guides like this one not only gives you an idea of what to expect but also allows you to sharpen some skills that may have gotten a little dull.

Failing to Realize How Scores Are Used

The military powers that be use the nine subtests on the ASVAB to determine which military jobs you qualify for. If you don't know how the scores are used, you can't decide which parts of the exam are most important for you to study.

Check out Chapters 1 and 2 for an explanation of how the military uses ASVAB subtest scores to determine your qualifications. Also head to Appendix A to see the scores that you need to get into the various branches of and careers in the military.

Studying for Unnecessary Subtests

If you don't want to be a mechanic in the military, what are you doing studying for the Auto & Shop Information subtest? You should be spending your time on the math and vocabulary review, because the math and vocabulary subtests of the ASVAB are used to compute the all-important AFQT score, which determines whether you can join the military branch of your choice.

It's easier to study subject areas that you find easy or have an interest in, but if you're already an electronics whiz, don't waste your time studying a subject area that you're already going to ace. Spend your time studying subject areas that you aren't quite so confident of.

Losing Focus

I'm not going to sugarcoat this: The ASVAB is tiring. You have to take nine subtests that cover some really diverse subjects. You have about three hours to complete the actual test, so if you lose focus while you're taking the test, time has a tendency of slipping away, and you may not get to all the questions. It's hard, but keep your mind focused on the task at hand throughout the whole test. It'll be over soon.

Here are some tips that can help you maintain focus:

- **Arrive at the test location with time to spare.** This gives you a few minutes to sit and relax before you have to dive into the test questions.

- **Leave your baggage at the door.** Don't worry about whether you'll get the military job you want or whether you'll pass the physical the next morning. You'll have plenty of time to worry about that after you've finished the test.

- **Concentrate on one subtest at a time.** Don't waste time rehashing the questions on the previous subtest or trying to anticipate the questions on the next subtest. Focus on the subtest you're taking at the time.

- **Take a few moments to relax and refocus between subtests.** If you finish a subtest with time to spare, close your eyes for a bit and take some deep breaths before you begin the next subtest.

When you answer the final question on one subtest on the CAT-ASVAB, you move immediately to the next subtest. If the timer on the computer screen says you have a few minutes of time left on the subtest, use that time to relax and refocus before submitting that final answer.

Panicking Over Time

Yes, you have only a limited time to do the test, but don't worry about it. The more you panic, the more likely you are to make mistakes. Just work at a steady pace, and you'll do fine.

Don't spend too much time on any single question. If you're drawing a blank, make a guess and move on. (See "Making Wild Guesses or Not Guessing at All," later in this chapter.)

If you're taking the CAT-ASVAB, there will be a timer on the computer screen, counting down the number of minutes you have to finish that subtest. If you're taking the pencil and paper version of the test, check the clock on the wall. The proctor will generally write the start and finish time for the current subtest on a chalkboard. Keep your eye on the time remaining, but don't panic over it.

Deciding Not to Check the Answers

You should always double-check your answers before you commit to them — you don't want to be tripped up by silly mistakes. Don't mark your answer and then check your work. Check your work first.

Do *not* second-guess yourself (see "Changing Answers," later in this chapter). Just check for accuracy (like in mathematical equations). Be sure to mark your answer sheet correctly, too, verifying that the number of the question matches the number on your answer sheet (you don't have to worry about this with the computerized version of the ASVAB). Getting just one question off can mess up the rest of the answer sheet.

Making Wild Guesses or Not Guessing at All

Take the time to eliminate answers you know are incorrect before choosing among the remaining answer options. And here's the number one rule: Don't leave any blank spaces. In most cases, guessing if you have to is the way to go — at least you have a higher chance at getting the right answer, as opposed to a 0 percent chance if you leave the answer blank. If you can eliminate answers you know are wrong before guessing, you increase your chances of answering correctly even more. For tips on smart guessing, see Chapter 3.

Changing Answers

After you double-check your math, decide that Choice (C) is correct, and mark it on the answer sheet, don't change your answer on the paper version of the ASVAB! You're almost certain to change a right answer to a wrong one when you play that game. Plus, you can drive yourself crazy by second-guessing (and third- and fourth-guessing) your decision. Mark the answer and move on.

Memorizing the Practice Test Questions

Don't waste your time trying to memorize the practice questions in this book. I can almost guarantee you won't see any of the practice questions in this book (or any other study guide) on the actual ASVAB. Military test materials are highly controlled items, and no author of an ASVAB preparation book has access to them. In fact, military members and military civilian employees who disclose actual ASVAB test questions or answers can go to jail — and I'm not planning on going to the big house any time soon!

Just use the practice questions in this book as a measurement tool of which subject areas you should spend your time concentrating on.

Misunderstanding the Problem

Make sure that you know what the question wants from you and then give the question what it wants. If the problem asks for the *sum* of two numbers, don't multiply the numbers. Don't mistake a division sign for an addition sign. By familiarizing yourself with the types of questions on the ASVAB, you'll be able to zero in on what you're supposed to do a lot more quickly than those poor folks who didn't have the brilliant idea to buy this book.

Chapter 25

Ten Tips for Doing Well on the AFQT

. . . .

In This Chapter

▶ Using your scratch paper wisely

▶ Reading carefully

▶ Performing math operations

▶ Making sure your answers make sense

. . . .

Commonly referred to as the *ASVAB score,* the Armed Forces Qualification Test (AFQT) score is actually computed only from the reading and math skills subtests of the ASVAB. The AFQT score determines whether you're even qualified to enlist in the service of your choice. (For the full scoop, see Chapter 1.) The ten concepts presented in this chapter help you score better on the four subtests of the ASVAB that are used to calculate your AFQT score.

As Soon as the Test Starts, Write Down What You're Likely to Forget

You can't bring your own scratch paper to the test, but the test proctors will give you as many sheets of scratch paper as you want. Not only is your scratch paper useful to take the place of the calculator you're not allowed to use, but you can also use it to write notes at the very beginning of the test, things that you're worried you may forget. For example, if you're worried that you'll forget the math order of operations, write it down first thing.

Read All the Answer Choices before Deciding

I think that those people who write the ASVAB questions must go through a special course about being tricky. Many of the answer choices given on the ASVAB are "close but no cigar." In other words, these tricksters often try to pull a fast one over on you with an incorrect answer that's *almost* correct but not quite.

The best defense against this type of trickery is to read each answer choice completely, even if you think the first or second choice looks plausible. You're looking for the answer that's *most correct.*

Don't Expect Perfect Word Matches

The Word Knowledge subtest of the ASVAB contains questions that ask you to find the word that is *closest in meaning* to a given word. Don't get confused and think that you have to find the word that means *exactly* the same thing as the given word. Just follow the directions. Because some of the answer options may have similar meanings, you need to choose the answer that's closest in meaning to the given word — the answer that's most right.

Read Passages before the Questions

Some of the Paragraph Comprehension questions can be tricky. The question asks you to come to a conclusion based on the information presented in the paragraph. The only way to do this effectively is to understand the entire paragraph and what the author wants to convey. If you instead read the question first, you may find yourself wasting time by looking for information that isn't directly stated.

Reread to Find Specific Information

The Paragraph Comprehension subtest often asks you to find specific information in a passage. Go back and reread the paragraph. You shouldn't have to guess what this information is — it's in the passage, or you can easily deduce it from the passage. For instance, if a paragraph includes the sentence, "Six out of ten smokers will contract some form of cancer," and a question asks, "How many smokers won't contract some form of cancer?" you can easily deduce that four is the correct number.

Base Conclusions Only on What You Read

You may have to draw inferences or conclusions from what you've read. You must use only the information presented in the paragraph to reach this conclusion instead of relying on your own ideas and opinions. In other words, ask yourself, "Would the author agree with this statement, based on what he or she has written in this paragraph?" Apply this test to each answer option to choose the best answer.

Change Percents to Decimals

To perform math operations, you often have to change a percent to a fraction or a decimal. To change a percent to a fraction, multiply the percent by $\frac{1}{100}$ and drop the percent sign:

$$5\% = 5 \times \frac{1}{100} = \frac{5}{100}$$

To change a percent to a decimal, move the decimal point over two places to the left and drop the percent sign:

$$5\% = 0.05$$

Understand Inverses

Inverse operations are opposite operations. The opposite of addition is subtraction, and vice versa. And the opposite of multiplication is division, and vice versa.

But when it comes to numbers, the term *inverse* is not the same as *opposite*. The *opposite* of 5 is –5, but the *inverse* of 5 is $\frac{1}{5}$. When you deal with numbers, think of writing the inverse of a number as standing the number on its head: The inverse (reciprocal) of 5, or $\frac{5}{1}$, is $\frac{1}{5}$.

Remember How Ratios, Rates, and Scales Compare

You need to understand the differences among ratios, rates, and scales:

- **Ratio:** A ratio represents any relationship between two objects. If Luis invests $10 in Lotto tickets and Joe invests $20 in Lotto tickets, then for every dollar Luis invests, Joe invests two. That's a ratio of 1:2.

- **Rate:** A rate is an expression of the relationship between two *unlike* elements. For example, if Anna's car can travel a distance of 450 miles per tank of gas and her gas tank holds 15 gallons, then her car consumes gas at a rate of 30 miles per gallon, or 30 mpg (*miles* and *gallons* being unlike elements). Mathematically, 450 (miles) ÷ 15 (gallons in the tank) = 30 miles to the gallon.

- **Scale:** A scale expresses a relationship between two *like* elements, although the units of measure may differ. A map drawn to scale may use 1 inch to represent 1 mile. Although an inch and a mile aren't the same unit of measure, they measure the same thing (distance).

Make Sure Your Answers Are Reasonable

On the Arithmetic Reasoning and Mathematics Knowledge subtests, you have a very short amount of time to answer each question, approximately a minute. But if you use your time wisely, you should have plenty of time to double-check and make sure you've chosen the correct answer.

Your answers should make sense, or they're probably wrong. For example, if you're required to compute the average speed that a car maintains during a 2,000 mile trip and your answer is 2,000 mph, your answer is probably not correct. If a question includes a formula (such as $2 + x = 10$), plug in your answer for the variable and see whether both sides are equal. So if you answered 8, plug in 8 for x and find that 10 = 10. That means your answer checks out.

Those crazy test-writers who designed the test questions often include wrong answers that you may chose if you make a common mistake when solving the problem. Double-checking your answers allows you to catch your errors.

Chapter 26

Ten Ways to Boost Your Math and English Skills

In This Chapter
▶ Getting used to doing math correctly by hand
▶ Knowing key rules and formulas
▶ Expanding your vocabulary
▶ Becoming a better reader

The ASVAB includes two math and two English subtests: Mathematics Knowledge, Arithmetic Reasoning, Word Knowledge, and Paragraph Comprehension. These four subtests are probably the most important subtests of the ASVAB, because they comprise your AFQT score, which is the score that determines whether or not you qualify to join the branch of your choice. (Check out Chapter 1 for more info on the AFQT and Chapter 22 for a sample AFQT. You can also peruse my book *AFQT For Dummies* [published by Wiley].)

Because these four subtests are so important, this chapter includes ten surefire ways to build your skills in these critical areas before you take the test.

Practice Doing Math Problems

The best way to get a firm grasp of certain types of math is by *doing* math problems and not simply reading them. Take advantage of the practice math questions in this book, and visit the public library to see what kind of high school math textbooks it has to lend. The more you *do* math, the better you'll get at it.

Put Away Your Calculator

You're not allowed to use a calculator when you take the ASVAB, so the time to get used to solving basic math problems without one is now, not during the test. You may have been taught to rely on a calculator for high school math, but you have to leave your calculator at home when you take the ASVAB. Practice working out problems by hand, and make sure you know your multiplication tables and other basic calculations. The ASVAB math questions are written by people who know how to compute 2 + 2 in their heads.

As you solve math problems by hand, you can get a feel for what works and what doesn't. For instance, some questions ask you to find the square root of a number, which you may find hard without a calculator. But a little logic can help. If you know the square root of 9 is 3 ($3 \times 3 = 9$) and you know the square root of 16 is 4 ($4 \times 4 = 16$), then you can conclude that the square root of 12 falls between 3 and 4.

Memorize the Order of Operations

Mathematical equations with multiple steps must be solved in a specific order. Otherwise, you won't get the correct answer. Memorize the order in which you do certain calculations when you're solving equations, and practice applying these rules well before test day.

When solving an equation involves multiple steps, the correct order of operations is

1. **Whatever's within parentheses (and other grouping symbols)**

   If you have multiple parentheses nested inside each other, do the innermost set first. On the ASVAB, the other grouping symbols you run across are the fraction bar and the square root sign. Do what's beneath the square root bar before taking the root. Do any operation above the fraction bar and any operation below the fraction bar before dividing.

2. **Exponents**

3. **Multiplication and division**

   Operate from left to right.

4. **Addition and subtraction**

   Again, work from left to right.

For example, $3 + 2 \times 3$ isn't equal to 5×3, or 15. The correct answer is 9. You first do the multiplication and then the addition. You can remember order of operations as "Please Excuse My Dear Aunt Sally," or *PEMDAS*. Check out Chapter 7 for more explanation.

Know Your Geometry Formulas

You encounter some math questions that require you to calculate area, perimeter, and volume on the ASVAB. Memorize the following area formulas:

- **Area of a rectangle:** For any rectangle, Area = Length × Width: $A = lw$.
- **Area of a triangle:** For triangles, Area = Base × Height (or altitude) divided by 2: $A = \frac{1}{2}bh$.
- **Area of a circle:** For circles, area is π (approximately 3.14) times the radius squared: $A\pi r^2$.

Know these perimeter and circumference formulas:

- **Perimeter of polygon (a shape with straight sides):** Calculate the perimeter of any quadrilateral (four-sided figure) or triangle by adding the lengths of all the sides together.
- **Circumference of a circle:** Find the circumference of a circle by multiplying π times the diameter: $C = \pi d$. ***Note:*** Diameter equals 2 times the radius.

And know these formulas for the volume of 3-D solids:

- ✔ **Volume of a box:** Find the volume of a rectangular solid by multiplying Length × Width × Height: $V = lwh$.

- ✔ **Volume of a cylinder:** Find the volume of a cylinder by multiplying the area of the circular base (π times the base's radius squared) by the cylinder's height: $V = \pi r^2 h$.

Keep a Word List

The English language has well over 200,000 words in it, so nobody expects you to know them all. However, the ASVAB writers do expect you to have a good grasp of many vocabulary words. One way to improve your vocabulary is to keep a word list.

How does a word list work? As you read, write down the words that you don't know. Quickly look them up in the dictionary. You can then apply your word list in your day-to-day life. Of course, you can't remember every single word, but you can focus on mastering one new word every day and using it in conversation. Check out Chapter 4 for more tips on building your vocabulary.

Don't waste your time and choose little-known words, such as *absquatulate* (which means to leave hurriedly or secretly). You're unlikely to see obscure words on the ASVAB, but you should make a practice of learning the meaning of as many common English words as possible.

Study Latin and Greek

You can skip the grammar and pronunciation, but you should get to know some of the roots, prefixes, and suffixes that English has borrowed from Latin and Greek. These word parts are the building blocks of much of the English language, and they can give you clues about what words mean.

If you see an unfamiliar word on the Word Knowledge section, try to figure out its root. For example, if you know the meaning of *mercy,* you can figure out the meaning of *merciful.* Remember that prefixes and suffixes can be added onto a root to change the word's meaning or function. Here are some examples:

- ✔ **Changing meaning:** The prefix *a-* usually means *opposite,* so the word *atypical* means the opposite of *typical,* not a typical thing.

- ✔ **Changing parts of speech:** *Establish* is a verb meaning *to make stable* or *to prove,* whereas *establishment* (with a suffix) is a noun meaning *a thing that has been established.*

For a list of common word parts you should know, check out Chapter 4.

Use Flashcards

Flashcards help you remember important facts through the process of spaced repetition. Learning psychologists agree that this is one of the most effective methods of memorizing new information. Plus, it's cheap — all you need is a set of blank index cards and a pen to create your very own studying machine.

You can use flashcards to improve both your mental math and vocabulary — write down vocab words, roots, prefixes, and suffixes, practice matching square roots and square numbers, or just make sure you know your math formulas.

Read More, Watch TV Less

The best way to improve your reading comprehension is simple: Read more. If you spend four hours a day watching TV or surfing the Web, you can instead use those four hours to read a novel or the newspaper or a book about car repair — whatever interests you the most. You'll be surprised at how fast your reading speed and comprehension improve with just a little daily practice.

Practice Finding Main and Supporting Points

All writing should have a point. The *main point* is the thing that the writer wants you to take away from his or her words. Some passages include more than one point. Usually, such passages have one main point and one or more subpoints that support the main idea. As you're reading passages on the ASVAB (and in real life), you want to be able to easily identify the main point. You should practice identifying the points during your own reading sessions. Read each paragraph and then ask yourself what information the author is trying to convey to you.

Use a Study Guide

In my humble opinion, there is no better commercial ASVAB study guide available than this one. Read the chapters carefully and then utilize the practice tests to see where you need more study.

Use the practice questions only to test your own knowledge of the subject. Don't expect to see the same questions on the actual ASVAB. Those test-makin' hooligans who write the actual ASVAB tests keep a close eye on commercial study guides, like this one, and try to avoid having the same questions.

Appendix A

Matching ASVAB Scores to Military Jobs

The military has hundreds of enlisted job opportunities, ranging from washing and sewing clothing items to translating foreign languages. Each of the military services has established its own individual *line score* requirements (a combination of various ASVAB subtest scores) for specific enlisted jobs. The tables in this appendix show the minimum line scores that the services have established for entry-level enlisted jobs.

Just because you achieve the minimum ASVAB line score for the job of your choice doesn't mean you'll absolutely get that job. Other factors are considered, including the current needs of the service, security clearance qualification, and medical exam results.

The charts in this appendix are as accurate as they can be at press time. However, military jobs and qualification standards are subject to change with little or no notice. For the most up-to-date information and for complete job descriptions and qualification factors, see your local military recruiter or visit the military enlisted-job pages on the About.com U.S. Military Information site (usmilitary.about.com).

Army Enlisted Jobs

The Army calls its enlisted jobs *Military Occupational Specialties* (MOSs), and more than 150 such specialties exist for entry-level recruits. Table A-1 shows entry-level Army MOSs and the ASVAB line scores required to qualify for the jobs. Scan the table and see whether you find a job that interests you.

Line scores are abbreviated as follows: Clerical (CL), Combat (CO), Electronics (EL), Field Artillery (FA), General Maintenance (GM), General Technical (GT), Mechanical Maintenance (MM), Operators and Food (OF), Surveillance and Communications (SC), and Skilled Technical (ST). See Chapter 2 for an explanation of which ASVAB subtest scores are used to calculate each of the line scores.

Table A-1		Army Enlisted Jobs and Required ASVAB Scores					
MOS	**Title**	**Score**	**MOS**	**Title**	**Score**	**MOS**	**Title**	**Score**
09L	Interpreter/ Translator	N/A	**11B**	Infantryman	CO-90	**11C**	Indirect Fire Infantryman	CO-90
12B	Combat Engineer	CO-98	**12C**	Bridge Crewmember	CO-87	**12D**	Diver	ST-106 or GM-98 and GT-107
12G	Quarrying Specialist	GM-93	**12K**	Plumber	GM-88	**12M**	Firefighter	GM-88
12N	Horizontal Construction Engineer	GM-90	**12Q**	Power Distribution Specialist	EL-93	**12R**	Interior Electrician	EL-93
12T	Technical Engineer	ST-101	**12V**	Concrete and Asphalt Equipment Operator	GM-88	**12W**	Carpentry and Masonry Specialist	GM-88
12Y	Geospatial Engineer	ST-95	**13B**	Cannon Crewmember	FA-95	**13C**	Tactical Automated Fire Control Systems Specialist	FA-95
13D	Field Artillery Automated Tactical Data Systems Specialist	FA-100	**13E**	Cannon Fire Direction Specialist	FA-95	**13F**	Fire Support Specialist	FA-100
13M	Multiple Launch Rocket System Crewmember	OF-105	**13P**	Multiple Launch Rocket System Operations/ Fire Direction Specialist	FA-100	**13R**	Field Artillery Firefinder Radar Operator	SC-98
13T	Field Artillery Surveyor/ Meteor-ological Crewmember	EL-95	**14E**	Patriot Fire Control Enhanced Operator/ Maintainer	MM-104	**14G**	Air Defense Battle Management System Operator	GT-98 and MM-99
14H	Air Defense Early Warning System Operator	GT-98 and MM-99	**14J**	Air Defense C41 Tactical Operations Center Enhanced Operator Maintainer	GT-98 and MM-99	**14S**	Air and Missile Defense (AMD) Crewmember	OF-85
14T	PATRIOT Launching Station Enhanced Operator/ Maintainer	OF-92	**15B**	Aircraft Power Plant Repairer	MM-104	**15D**	Aircraft Powertrain Repairer	MM-104
15E	Unmanned Aircraft Systems Repairer	EL-93 and MM-104	**15F**	Aircraft Electrician	MM-104	**15G**	Aircraft Structural Repairer	MM-104

MOS	Title	Score	MOS	Title	Score	MOS	Title	Score
15H	Aircraft Pneudraulics Repairer	MM-104	15J	OH-58D/ARH Armament/ Electrical/ Avionics Systems Repairer	EL-93 and MM-104	15M	Utility Helicopter Repairer (Reserves Only)	MM-104
15N	Avionic Mechanic	EL-93	15P	Aviation Operations Specialist	ST-91	15Q	Air Traffic Control Operator	ST-101
15R	AH-64 Attack Helicopter Repairer	MM-99	15S	OH-58D Helicopter Repairer	MM-100	15T	UH-60 Helicopter Repairer	MM-105
15U	CH-47 Helicopter Repairer	MM-104	15V	Observation/ Scout Helicopter Repairer	MM-102	15W	Unmanned Aerial Vehicle Operator	SC-102
15X	AH-64A Armament/ Electrical/ Avionic Systems Repairer	MM-102 and EL 98	15Y	AH-64D Armament/ Electrical/ Avionics Systems Repairer	EL-98 and MM-102	18B	Special Forces (Weapons)	GT-110 and CO-100
18C	Special Forces (Engineer)	GT-110 and CO-100	18D	Special Forces (Medical)	GT-100 and CO-87	18E	Special Forces (Communications)	GT-110 and SC-100
19D	Cavalry Scout	CO-90	19K	M1 Armor Crewman	CO-87	25B	Information Technology Specialist	ST-95
25C	Radio Operator/ Maintainer	SC-98 and EL-98	25F	Network Switching Systems Operator/ Maintainer	SC-105 and EL-102	25L	Cable Systems Installer/ Maintainer	SC-89 and EL-89
25M	Multimedia Illustrator	EL-93 and ST-91	25P	Microwave Systems Operator/ Maintainer	EL-107	25Q	Multichannel Transmission Systems Operator/ Maintainer	EL-98 and SC-98
25R	Visual Information Equipment Operator/ Maintainer	EL-107	25S	Satellite Communication Systems Operator/ Maintainer	EL-117	25U	Signal Support Systems Specialist	SC-92 and EL-93
25V	Combat Documentation/ Production Specialist	EL-93 and ST-91	35F	Intelligence Analyst	ST-101	35G	Geospatial Intelligence Imagery Analyst	ST-101
35M	Human Intelligence Collector	ST-101	35N	Signals Intelligence Analyst	ST-101	35P	Cryptologic Linguist	ST-91

(continued)

Table A-1 *(continued)*

MOS	Title	Score	MOS	Title	Score	MOS	Title	Score
35Q	Cryptologic Network Warfare Specialist	ST-105	35S	Signals Collector/ Analyst	ST-101	35T	Military Intelligence Systems Maintainer/ Integrator	ST-112
36B	Financial Management Technician	CL-101	37F	Psychological Operations Specialist	ST-101	38A	Civil Affairs Specialist	ST-100
38B	Intelligence and Combat Support	ST-96	42A	Human Resources Specialist	CL-90	42F	Information Systems Technician	CL-101
42L	Administrative Specialist	CL-95	42R	Band Member	N/A	46Q	Public Affairs Specialist	GT-107
46R	Public Affairs Broadcast Specialist Journalist	GT-107	56M	Chaplain Assistant	CL-90	68D	Operating Room Specialist	ST-91
68E	Dental Specialist	ST-91	68G	Patient Administration Specialist	CL-90	68H	Optical Laboratory Specialist	GM-98
68J	Medical Logistics Specialist	CL-90	68K	Medical Laboratory Specialist	ST-106	68M	Nutrition Care Specialist	OF-95
68P	Radiology Specialist	ST-106	68Q	Pharmacy Specialist	ST-95	68R	Veterinary Food Inspection Specialist	ST-95
68S	Preventive Medicine Specialist	ST-101	68T	Animal Care Specialist	ST-91	68V	Respiratory Specialist	ST-102
68W	Healthcare Specialist	ST-101 and GT-107	68X	Mental Health Specialist	ST-101	69A	Biomedical Equipment Specialist	EL-107
74D	Chemical Operations Specialist	ST-91	88H	Cargo Specialist	GM-88	88K	Watercraft Operator	MM-99
88L	Watercraft Engineer	MM-99	88M	Motor Transport Operator	OF-85	88N	Transportation Management Coordinator	CL-95
88P	Railway Equipment Repairer	MM-97	88T	Railway Section Repairer	MM-87	88U	Railway Operations Crewmember	MM-92
89A	Ammunition Stock Control and Accounting Specialist	ST-91	89B	Ammunition Specialist	ST-91	89D	Explosive Ordnance Disposal (EOD) Specialist	ST-110
91A	M1 Abrams Tank System Maintainer	MM-99 or MM-88 and GT-92	91B	Wheeled Vehicle Mechanic	MM-92 or MM-87 and GT-85	91C	Utilities Equipment Repairer	GM-98 or GM-88 and GT-83

MOS	Title	Score	MOS	Title	Score	MOS	Title	Score
91D	Power Generation Equipment	GM-98 or GM-88 and GT-88	91E	Allied Trade Specialist	GM-98 or GM-88 and GT-92	91F	Small Arms/ Artillery Repairer	GM-93 or GM-88 and GT-85
91G	Fire Control Repairer	EL-98 or EL-93 and GT-88	91H	Track Vehicle Repairer	MM-92 or MM-87 and GT-85	91J	Quarter-master and Chemical Equipment Repairer	MM-92 or MM-87 and GT-85
91L	Construction Equipment Repairer	MM-92 or MM-87 and GT-85	91M	Bradley Fighting Vehicle System Maintainer	MM-99 or MM-88 and GT-92	91P	Artillery Mechanic	MM-99 or MM-88 and GT-88
91S	Stryker Systems Maintainer	MM-92 or MM-87 and GT-85	92A	Automated Logistical Specialist	CL-90	92F	Petroleum Supply Specialist	CL-86 and OF-85
92G	Food Service Specialist	OF-85	92L	Petroleum Laboratory Specialist	ST-91	92M	Mortuary Affairs Specialist	GM-88
92R	Parachute Rigger	GM 88 and CO 87	92S	Shower/ Laundry and Clothing Repair Specialist	GM-84	92W	Water Treatment Specialist	GM-88
92Y	Unit Supply Specialist	CL-90	94A	Land Combat Electronic Missile System Repairer	EL-102	94D	Air Traffic Control Equipment Repairer	EL-102
94E	Radio and Communica-tions Security Repairer	EL-102	94F	Computer/ Detection Systems Repairer	EL-102	94H	Test Measure-ment and Diagnostic Equipment Support Specialist	EL-107
94L	Avionic Communica-tions Equipment Repairer	EL-98	94M	Radar Repairer	EL-107	94P	Multiple Launch Rocket System Repairer	EL-93
94R	Avionic and Survivability Equipment Repairer	EL-98	94S	Patriot System Repairer	EL-107	94T	Avenger System Repairer	EL-98
94Y	Integrated Family of Test Equipment Operator and Maintainer	N/A						

Air Force Enlisted Jobs

The United States Air Force has about 120 entry-level enlisted jobs for new recruits. The Air Force refers to enlisted jobs as *Air Force Specialty Codes* (AFSCs). Table A-2 shows the Air Force entry-level AFSCs and the line scores required to qualify for each job. The table is organized by AFSC number, so browse the table and see which AFSCs pique your interest.

Line scores are abbreviated as follows: General (G), Electronic (E), Mechanical (M), and Administrative (A). See Chapter 2 for information on which ASVAB subtest scores are used by the Air Force to calculate the various line scores.

Table A-2			Air Force Enlisted Jobs and Required ASVAB Scores					
AFSC	**Title**	**Score**	**AFSC**	**Title**	**Score**	**AFSC**	**Title**	**Score**
1A0X1	In-Flight Refueling	G-55	1A1X1	Flight Engineer	M-47 or E-38	1A2X1	Aircraft Loadmaster	G-57
1A3X1	Airborne Communications and Electronic Systems	E-70	1A4X1	Airborne Battle Management Systems	G-55	1A5X1	Airborne Missions Systems	E-70
1A7X1	Aerial Gunner	M-60 or E-45	1A8X1	Airborne Cryptologic Linguist	G-72	1C0X1	Airfield Management	A-41
1C1X1	Air Traffic Control	G-55 and M-55	1C2X1	Combat Control	G-44	1C3X1	Command Post	G-49
1C4X1	Tactical Air Command and Control	G-49	1C5X1	Aerospace Control and Warning Systems	G-55	1C6X1	Space Systems Operations	E-60
1C7X1	Airfield Management	G-50 and M-40	1N0X1	Operations Intelligence	G-57	1N1X1	Imagery Analysis	G-66
1N2X1	Communications Signals Intelligence Production	G-53	1N3XX	Cryptologic Linguist	G-72	1N4X1	Network Intelligence Analysis	G-62
1N5X1	Electronic Signal Intelligence Exploitation	G-72	1N6X1	Electronic Systems Security Assessment	G-62	1T0X1	Survival, Evasion, Resistance, and Escape Operations	G-55
1T1X1	Aircrew Life Support	G-34	1T2X1	Pararescue	G-44	1U0X1	Unmanned Aerospace Systems Sensor Operator	G-64 or E-54
1W0X1	Weather	G-66 and E-50	2A0X1	Avionics Test Stations and Components	E-70	2A3X1	A-10, F-15, and U-2 Avionics Systems	E-70

AFSC	Title	Score	AFSC	Title	Score	AFSC	Title	Score
2A3X2	F-16, F-117, RQ-1, and CV-22 Avionics Systems	E-70	2A3X1	Tactical Aircraft Maintenance	M-47	2A5X1	Aerospace Maintenance	M-47
2A5X2	Helicopter Maintenance	M-56	2A5X3	Integrated Avionics Systems	E-70	2A6X1	Aerospace Propulsion	M-56
2A6X2	Aerospace Ground Equipment	M-47 and E-28	2A6X3	Aircrew Egress Systems	M-56	2A6X4	Aircraft Fuel Systems	M-47
2A6X5	Aircraft Hydraulic Systems	M-56	2A7X1	Aircraft Metals Technology	M-47	2A7X2	Non-destructive Inspection	M-42
2A7X3	Aircraft Structural Maintenance	M-47	2A7X4	Survival Equipment	M-40	2E0X1	Ground Radar Systems	E-70
2E1X1	Satellite, Wideband, and Telemetry Systems	E-70	2E1X2	Meteorological and Navigations Systems	E-70	2E1X3	Ground Radio Communications	E-70
2E1X4	Visual Imagery and Intrusion Detection Systems	E-70	2E2X1	Computer, Network, Switching, and Cryptographic Systems	E-70	2E6X2	Communications Cable and Antenna Systems	M-47
2E6X3	Telephone Systems	E-45	2F0X1	Fuels	M-47 and G-38	2G0X1	Logistics Plans	A-56
2M0X1	Missile and Space Systems Electrical Maintenance	E-70	2M0X2	Missile and Space Systems Maintenance	M-47	2M0X3	Missile and Space Facilities	E-50
2P0X1	Precision Measurement Equipment Laboratory	E-70	2R0X1	Maintenance Data Systems Analysis	G-55	2R1X1	Maintenance Scheduling	G-44
2S0X1	Material Management	A-41 or G-44	2S0X2	Supply Systems Analysis	A-47	2T0X1	Traffic Management	A-35
2T1X1	Vehicle Operations	M-40	2T2X1	Air Transportation	M-47 and A-28	2T3X1	Special Purpose Vehicle and Equipment Maintenance	M-47
2T3X2	Special Vehicle Maintenance	M-40	2T3X5	Vehicle Body Maintenance	M-56	2T3X7	Vehicle Management and Analysis	A-41
2W0X1	Munitions Systems	M-55 or G-55	2W1X1	Aircraft Armament Systems	M-60 or E-45	2W2X1	Nuclear Weapons	M-60
3A0X1	Information Management	A-28	3C0X1	Computer Systems Operations	G-64	3C0X2	Computer Systems Programming	G-64

(continued)

Table A-2 *(continued)*

AFSC	Title	Score	AFSC	Title	Score	AFSC	Title	Score
3C1X1	Radio Communication Systems	A-41	3C1X2	Electromagnetic Spectrum Management	G-44	3C2X1	Computer Systems Control	E-70
3C3X1	Computer Systems Planning and Implementation	G-62	3M0X1	Services	G-24	3N0X1	Public Affairs	G-72
3N0X2	Radio and TV Broadcasting	G-72	3N1X1	Regional Band	A-21 or G-24	3P0X1	Security Forces	G-33
3E0X1	Electrical Systems	E-28	3E0X2	Electric Power Production	M-56 and E-40	3E1X1	Heating, Ventilation, Air Conditioning, and Refrigeration	M-47 or E-28
3E2X1	Pavement and Construction Equipment	M-40	3E3X1	Structural	M-47	3E4X1	Utilities Systems	M-47
3E4X2	Liquid Fuel Systems Maintenance	M-47	3E4X3	Pest Management	G-38	3E5X1	Engineering	G-49
3E6X1	Operations Management	G-44	3E7X1	Fire Protection	G-38	3E8X1	Explosive Ordnance Disposal	G-64 and M-60
3E9X1	Readiness	G-62	3S0X1	Personnel	A-41	3V0X1	Visual Information	G-44
3V0X2	Still Photograph	G-44	3V0X2	Visual Information Production-Documentation	G-62	4A0X1	Health Services Management	G-44
4A1X1	Medical Materiel	G-44	4A2X1	Biomedical Equipment	E-70 and M-60	4B0X1	Bio-environmental Engineering	G-49
4C0X1	Mental Health Services	G-55	4D0X1	Diet Therapy	G-44	4E0X1	Public Health	G-44
4H0X1	Cardiopulmonary Lab	G-44	4J0X2	Physical Medicine	G-49	4M0X1	Aerospace Physiology	G-44
4N0X1	Aerospace Medical Service	G-44	4N1X1	Surgical Services	G-44	4P0X1	Pharmacy	G-44
4R0X1	Diagnostic Imaging	G-44	4T0X1	Medical Laboratory	G-62	4T0X2	Histopathology	G-44
4T0X3	Cytotechnology	G-44	4V0X1	Optometry	G-55	4Y0X1	Dental Assistant	G-44
4Y0X2	Dental Lab	G-66	5R0X1	Chaplain Assistant	G-44 or A-35	6C0X1	Contracting	G-72
6F0X1	Financial Management and Comptroller	G-57	9S100	Technical Applications Specialist	M-88 and E-85			

Navy Enlisted Jobs

The Navy calls its enlisted jobs *ratings* and has about 75 types of jobs available for entry-level recruits. This branch doesn't use line scores for job-qualification purposes. Instead, the Navy combines scores from the various ASVAB subtests for each of its enlisted ratings.

Table A-3 (in ratings order) shows combinations of ASVAB subtest scores that are required to qualify for Navy enlisted jobs. Peruse the list and see which jobs may best suit you. The ASVAB subtests are abbreviated as follows: General Science (GS), Arithmetic Reasoning (AR), Word Knowledge (WK), Paragraph Comprehension (PC), Auto & Shop Information (AS), Mathematics Knowledge (MK), Mechanical Comprehension (MC), Electronics Information (EI), Assembling Objects (AO), and Verbal Expression (VE).

Table A-3			Navy Enlisted Jobs and Required ASVAB Scores					
Rating	**Title**	**Score**	**Rating**	**Title**	**Score**	**Rating**	**Title**	**Score**
ABE	Aviation Boatswain's Mate — Equipment	VE + MR + MK + AS = 184	**ABF**	Aviation Boatswain's Mate — Fuels	VE + AR + MK + AS = 184	**ABH**	Aviation Boatswain's Mate — Handling	VE + AR + MK + AS = 184
AC	Air Traffic Controller	VE + AR + MK + MC = 220 or VE + MK + MC + CS = 220	**AD**	Aviation Machinist's Mate	VE + AR + MK + AS = 210 or VE + AR + MK + MC = 210	**AE**	Aviation Electrician's Mate	AR + MK + EI + GS = 222 or VE + AR + MK + MC = 222
AECF	Advanced Electronics Computer Field	AR + MK + EI + GS = 222	**AG**	(Aviation) Aerographer's Mate	VE + MK + GS = 162	**AIR-CREW**	Aircrew Program	VE + AR + MK + MC = 210 or VE + AR + MK + AS = 210
AM	Aviation Structural Mechanic	VE + AR + MK + AS = 210 or VE + AR + MK + MC = 210	**AME**	Aviation Structural Mechanic — Equipment	VE + AR + MK + AS = 210 or VE + AR + MK + MC = 210	**AO**	Aviation Ordnanceman	VE + AR + MK + AS = 185 or MK + AS + AO = 140

(continued)

Table A-3 (continued)

Rating	Title	Score	Rating	Title	Score	Rating	Title	Score
AS	Aviation Support Equipment Technician	VE + AR + MK + AS = 210 or VE + AR + MK + MC = 210	AT	Aviation Electronics Technician	AR + MK + EI + GS = 222 or VE + AR + MK + MC = 222	AW	Aviation Warfare Systems Operator	VE + AR + MK + MC = 210.
AWF	Aircrewman Mechanical	VE + AR + MK + MC = 210	AWO	Aircrewman Operator	VE + AR + MK + MC = 210	AWR	Aircrewman Tactical Helicopter	VE + AR + MK + MC = 210
AWS	Aircrewman Helicopter	VE + AR + MK + MC = 210	AWV	Aircrewman Avionics	VE + AR + MK + MC = 210	AZ	Aviation Maintenance Administrationman	VE + AR = 102
BM	Boatswain's Mate	VE + AR + MK + AS = 175	BU	Builder	AR + MC + AS = 140	CE	Construction Electrician	AR + MK + EI + GS = 200
CM	Construction Mechanic	AR + MC + AS = 158	CS	Culinary Specialist	VE + AR = 89	CS(SS)	Culinary Specialist (Submarine)	AR + MK + EI + GS = 200 or VE + AR + MK + MC = 200
CTA	Cryptologic Technician — Administration	VE + MK = 105	CTI	Cryptologic Technician — Interpretive	VE + MK + GS = 165	CTM	Cryptologic Technician — Maintenance	MK + EI + GS + AR = 223
CTN	Cryptologic Technician — Networks	AR + 2MK + GS = 235 or VE + AR + MK + MC = 235	CTR	Cryptologic Technician — Collection	VE + AR = 110	CTT	Cryptologic Technician — Technical	VE + MK + GS = 162 or AR + MK + EI + GS = 223

Rating	Title	Score	Rating	Title	Score	Rating	Title	Score
DC	Damage Controlman	VE + MK + GS = 162 or AR + MK + EI + GS = 223	EA	Engineering Aide	AR + 2MK + GS = 210	EM	Electrician's Mate	VE + AR + MK + MC = 210
EN	Engineman	VE + AR + MK + AS = 195 or VE + AR + MK + AO = 200	EO	Equipment Operator	AR + MC + EI + GS = 204	EOD	Explosive Ordnance Disposal	AR + VE = 109 and MC = 51
ET	Electronics Technician	MK + EI + GS = 156 + AR = 223	ET(SS)	Electronics Technician (Submarine)	AR + MK + EI + GS = 222	FC	Fire Controlman	AR + MK + EI + GS = 218 and MK + EI + GS and MK = 57 and AR = 57
FT(SS)	Fire Control Technician (Submarine)	AR + MK + EI + GS = 222 or VE + AR + MK + MV = 222	GM	Gunner's Mate	AR + MK + EI + GS = 204	GSE	Gas Turbine Systems Technician — Electrical	VE + AR + MK + MC = 210
GSM	Gas Turbine Systems Technician — Mechanical	VE + AR + MK + AS = 195 or VE + AR + MK + AO = 200	HM	Hospital Corpsman	VE + MK + GS = 149	HT	Hull Technician	VE + MC + AS = 158

(continued)

Table A-3 *(continued)*

Rating	Title	Score	Rating	Title	Score	Rating	Title	Score
IC	Interior Communications Electrician	VE + AR + MK + MC = 210	IS	Intelligence Specialist	VE + AR = 108	IT	Information System Technician	AR + 2MK + GS = 222 or AR + MK + EI + GS = 222
LS	Logistics Specialist	VE + AR = 102	MA	Master at Arms	AR + WK = 95 and WK > 43	MC	Mass Communications Specialist	VE + AR = 115
MM	Machinist's Mate	VE + AR + MK + AS = 195 or VE + AR + MK + AO = 200	MM(SS)	Machinist's Mate (Submarine)	VE + AR + MK + MC = 210 or VE + AR + MK + AS = 210	MN	Mineman	VE + MC + AS = 158
MR	Machinery Repairman	VE + AR + MK + AS = 200 or MK + AS + AO = 150	MT	Missile Technician	AR + MK + EI + GS = 222 or VE + AR + MK + MC = 222	ND	Navy Diver	AR + VE = 103 and MC = 51
NUC	Nuclear Program	AR + MK + EI + GS = 252 or VE + AR + MK + MC = 252	OS	Operations Specialist	VE + MK + CS = 157 or AR + 2MK + GS = 210	PC	Postal Clerk	VE + AR = 108
PR	Aircrew Survival Equipment-man	VE + AR + MK + AS = 185 or MK + AS + AO = 140	PS	Personnel Specialist	VE + MK = 105	QM	Quartermaster	VE + AR = 96

Rating	Title	Score	Rating	Title	Score	Rating	Title	Score
RP	Religious Program Specialist	VE + MK = 105	SH	Ship Serviceman	VE + AR = 95	SK	Storekeeper	VE + AR = 103
SK(SS)	Storekeeper (Submarines)	AR + MK + EI + GS = 200 or VE + AR + MK + MC = 200	SN(SS)	Seaman (Submarine)	AR + MK + EI + GS = 200 or VE + AR + MK + MC = 200	STG	Sonar Technician (Surface)	AR + MK + EI + GS = 222
ST(SS)	Sonar Technician (Submarine)	AR + MK + EI + GS = 222 or VE + AR + MK + MC = 200	SO	Special Warfare Operator (SEAL)	GS + MC + EI = 165 or VE + MK + MC + CS = 220	SW	Steelworker	VE + MC + AS = 140
TM	Torpedoman's Mate	AR + 2MK + GS = 194	UT	Utilitiesman	AR + MK + EI + GS = 200	YN	Yeoman	VE + MK = 105
YN(SS)	Yeoman (Submarine)	AR + MK + EI + GS = 200 or VE + AR + MK + MC = 200						

Marine Corps Enlisted Jobs

The United States Marine Corps needs a few good men (and women) to fill about 120 enlisted entry-level job specialties. Like the Army, the Marine Corps calls its enlisted jobs *Military Occupational Specialties* (MOSs). The Marine Corps has only three line scores, and they're abbreviated in Table A-4 as follows: Mechanical Maintenance (MM), Electronics (EL), and General Technical (GT).

See Chapter 2 for information regarding which subtest scores of the ASVAB are used to comprise these line scores.

Table A-4		Marine Corps Enlisted Jobs and Required ASVAB Scores				
MOS	*Title*	*Score*	*MOS*	*Title*	*Score*	*MOS*	*Title*	*Score*

MOS	Title	Score	MOS	Title	Score	MOS	Title	Score
0121	Personnel Clerk	CL-100	0151	Administrative Clerk	CL-100	0161	Postal Clerk	CL-90
0231	Intelligence Specialist	GT-100	0241	Imagery Analysis Specialist	GT-100	0251	Interrogator/ Debriefer	GT-100
0261	Geographic Intelligence Specialist	EL-100	0311	Rifleman	GT-80	0313	LAV Crewman	GT-90
0321	Reconnais-sance Man	GT-105	0341	Mortarman	GT-80	0351	Assaultman	GT-80
0352	Antitank Assault Guided Missileman	GT-90	0411	Maintenance Management Specialist	GT-100	0431	Logistics/ Embarkation and Combat Service Support (CSS) Specialist	GT-100
0451	Air Delivery Specialist	GT-100	0481	Landing Support Specialist	GT-95 and MM-100	0511	MAGTF Planning Specialist	GT-110
0612	Field Wireman	EL-90	0613	Construction Wireman	EL-90	0614	Unit Level Circuit Switch (ULCS) Operator/ Maintainer	EL-100
0621	Field Radio Operator	EL-90	0622	Mobile Multichannel Equipment Operator	EL-100	0624	High Frequency Communica-tion Central Operator	EL-100
0626	Fleet SATCOM Terminal Operator	EL-100	0627	Ground Mobile Forces SATCOM Operator	EL-100	0811	Field Artillery Cannoneer	GT-90
0842	Field Artillery Radar Operator	GT-105	0844	Field Artillery Fire Control Man	GT-105	0847	Artillery Meteoro-logical Man	GT-105
1141	Electrician	EL-90	1142	Electrical Equipment Repair Specialist	EL-100	1161	Refrigeration Mechanic	MM-105
1171	Hygiene Equipment Operator	MM-85	1181	Fabric Repair Specialist	MM-85	1316	Metal Worker	MM-95
1341	Engineer Equipment Mechanic	MM-95	1345	Engineer Equipment Operator	MM-95	1361	Engineer Assistant	GT-100
1371	Combat Engineer	MM-105	1391	Bulk Fuel Specialist	MM-85	1812	M1A1 Tank Crewman	GT-90

MOS	Title	Score	MOS	Title	Score	MOS	Title	Score
1833	Assault Amphibious Vehicle (AAV) Crewman	GT-90	2111	Small Arms Repairer/ Technician	MM-95	2131	Towed Artillery Systems Technician	MM-95
2141	Assault Amphibious Vehicle (AAV) Repairer/ Technician	MM-105	2146	Main Battle Tank (MBT) Repairer/ Technician	MM-105	2147	Light Armored Vehicle (LAV) Repairer/ Technician	MM-105
2161	Machinist	MM-105	2171	Electro-Optical Ordnance Repairer	MM-105 and EL-105	2311	Ammunition Technician	GT-100
2336	Explosive Ordnance Disposal Technician	GT-110	2621	Communications Signal Collection/ Manual Morse Operator/ Analyst	GT-100	2631	Electronic Intelligence (ELINT) Intercept Operator/ Analyst	GT-100
2651	Special Intelligence System Administrator/ Communicator	GT-100	267X	Cryptologic Linguist	GT-105	2811	Telephone Technician	EL-115
2818	Personal Computer (PC)/Tactical Office Machine Repairer	EL-115	2821	Computer Technician	EL-115	2822	Electronic Switching Equipment Technician	EL-115
2831	Multichannel Equipment Repairer	EL-115	2832	Multichannel Equipment Technician	EL-115	2834	Satellite Communications (SATCOM) Technician	EL-115
2841	Ground Radio Repairer	EL-115	2844	Ground Communications Organizational Repairer	EL-115	2846	Ground Radio Intermediate Repairer	EL-115
2871	Test Measurement and Diagnostic Equipment Technician	EL-115	2881	Communication Security Equipment Technician	EL-115	2886	Artillery Electronic System Repairer	EL-115
2887	Counter Mortar Radar Repairer	EL-115	3043	Supply Administration and Operations Clerk	GT-110	3051	Warehouse Clerk	GT-90
3052	Packaging Specialist	GT-80	3112	Traffic Management Specialist	GT-90	3361	Subsistence Supply Clerk	GT-90

(continued)

Table A-4 *(continued)*

MOS	Title	Score	MOS	Title	Score	MOS	Title	Score
3381	Food Service Specialist	GT-90	3432	Finance Technician	GT-110	3441	NAF Audit Technician	GT-110
3451	Fiscal/Budget Technician	GT-110	3521	Organizational Automotive Mechanic	MM-95	3531	Motor Vehicle Operator	MM-85
4066	Small Computer Systems Specialist	GT-110	4067	Programmer	GT-110	4113	Morale, Welfare, Recreation (MWR) Specialist	GT-110
4341	Combat Cor-respondent	GT-105 and VE-40	4421	Legal Services Specialist	GT-100	46XX	Visual Information	GT-100
55XX	Band	GT-50	5711	Nuclear Biological and Chemical (NBC) Defense Specialist	GT-110	5811	Military Police	GT-100
5821	Criminal Investigator	GT-110	5831	Correctional Specialist	GT-100	5937	Aviation Radio Repairer	EL-105
5942	Aviation Radar Technician	EL-105	5952	Air Traffic Control Navigational Aids Technician	EL-105	5953	Air Traffic Control Radar Technician	EL-105
5954	Air Traffic Control Communications Technician	EL-105	5962	Tactical Data Systems Equipment (TDSE) Repairer	EL-105	5963	Tactical Air Operations Module Repairer	EL-105
6042	Individual Material Readiness List (IMRL) Asset Manager	GT-100	6046	Aircraft Maintenance Administration Specialist	GT-100	6048	Flight Equipment Technician	MM-105
6061	Aircraft Intermediate Level Hydraulic/Pneumatic Mechanic	MM-105	6071	Aircraft Maintenance Support Equipment (SE) Mechanic	MM-105	6091	Aircraft Intermediate Level Structures Mechanic	MM-105
611X	Helicopter Mechanic	MM-105	612X	Helicopter Power Plants Mechanic	MM-105	615X	Helicopter/Tiltrotor Airframe Mechanic	MM-105
617X	Helicopter Crew Chief	MM-105	621X	Fixed-Wing Aircraft Mechanic	MM-105	622X	Fixed-Wing Aircraft Power Plants Mechanic	MM-105

MOS	Title	Score	MOS	Title	Score	MOS	Title	Score
6232	Fixed-Wing Aircraft Flight Mechanic	MM-105	625X	Fixed-Wing Aircraft Airframe Mechanic	MM-105	628X	Fixed-Wing Aircraft Safety Equipment Mechanic	MM-105
63XX	Aircraft Communications/ Navigation/ Electrical/ Weapon Systems Technician	EL-105	64XX	Aircraft Communications/ Navigation Systems Technician	EL-105	6511	Aircraft Ordnance Technician	GT-105
6672	Aviation Supply Clerk	GT-100	6673	Automated Information Systems (AIS) Computer Operator	GT-100	6821	Weather Observer	GT-105
7011	Expeditionary Airfield Systems Technician	MM-105	7041	Aviation Operations Specialist	GT-100	7051	Aircraft Firefighting and Rescue Specialist	MM-95
7212	Low Altitude Air Defense (LAAD) Gunner	GT-90	7234	Air Control Electronics Operator	GT-105	7242	Air Support Operations Operator	GT-100
7251	Air Traffic Controller	GT-105	7314	Unmanned Aerial Vehicle (UAV) Air Vehicle Operator	GT-105	7371	Aerial Navigator	GT-110
7381	Airborne Radio Operator/ Inflight Refueling Observer/ Loadmaster	GT-110						

Coast Guard Enlisted Jobs

The smallest U.S. Military service, the Coast Guard, has only 19 types of entry-level jobs for enlisted members. Like the Navy, the Coast Guard calls its enlisted jobs *ratings*. Also like the Navy, the Coast Guard doesn't use line scores for job qualification purposes. Instead, it uses the sums of various ASVAB subtest scores.

Table A-5 shows combinations of ASVAB subtest scores that are required to qualify for Coast Guard enlisted jobs. The ASVAB subtests are abbreviated as follows: General Science (GS), Arithmetic Reasoning (AR), Word Knowledge (WK), Paragraph Comprehension (PC), Auto & Shop Information (AS), Mathematics Knowledge (MK), Mechanical Comprehension (MC), Electronics Information (EI), Assembling Objects (AO), and Verbal Expression (VE).

Table A-5   Coast Guard Enlisted Jobs and Required ASVAB Scores

Rating	Title	Score	Rating	Title	Score	Rating	Title	Score
AMT	Aviation Maintenance Technician	AR + MC + AS + EI = 213 (minimum AR = 52)	AST	Aviation Survival Technician	VE + MC + AS = 159 (minimum AR = 52)	AV	Avionics Technician	MK + EI + GS = 171 (minimum AR = 52)
BM	Boatswain's Mate	VE + AR = 101	DC	Damage Controlman	VE + MC + AS = 152	EM	Electrician's Mate	MK + EI + GS = 152 (minimum AR = 52)
ET	Electronics Technician	MK + EI + GS = 171 (minimum AR = 52) or AFQT = 66	FS	Food Service Specialist	VE + AR = 106	GM	Gunner's Mate	AR + MK + EI + GS = 208
HS	Health Services Technician	VE + MK + GS = 154	IT	Information Systems Technician	MK + EI + GS = 171 (minimum AR = 52)	MK	Machinery Technician	AR + MC + AS = 150 or VE + AR = 106
MST	Marine Science Technician	VE + AR = 115 (minimum MK = 58)	MU	Musician	N/A	OS	Operations Specialist	VE + AR = 106
PA	Public Affairs Specialist	VE + AR = 110 (minimum VE = 60)	PS	Port Security Specialist (CG Reserves Only)	VE + AR = 101	SK	Storekeeper	VE + AR = 106 (minimum VE = 52)
YN	Yeoman	VE + AR 106						

Appendix B

About the CD and Online Content

As technology prevails in our daily lives, not as many people rely on pencil and paper, and the military's no different. More than 90 percent of candidates who take the ASVAB for the purpose of joining the military take the CAT-ASVAB, the computerized version of the test. You can find the three ASVAB tests included in this book as well as three additional computerized ASVAB-style tests at *ASVAB For Dummies Online* to help you practice for the ASVAB; I include the AFQT from Chapter 22 on the companion CD and online. Use these tests to simulate taking the real CAT-ASVAB as closely as possible. The CD also includes bonus material, such as info on scoring and military jobs. If you need to bone up on your vocabulary before you take the ASVAB, check out the 300 flashcards at *ASVAB For Dummies Online*.

This appendix explains how to use the companion CD and website, what they contain, and what to do if you run into problems. *Note:* If you are using a digital version of this book, please go to `http://booksupport.wiley.com` for access to the CD content.

System Requirements

Make sure that your computer meets the minimum system requirements shown in the following list. If your computer doesn't match up to most of these requirements, you may have problems using the files on the CD and accessing the content on the website.

- A PC with a 2.33 GHz or faster x86-compatible; or a Mac OS computer with an Intel Core Duo 1.83 GHz or faster processor.

- Microsoft Windows XP or later; or a Macintosh running Apple OS X v10.6 or later.

- At least 512MB of total RAM installed on your computer; for best performance, 1GB RAM is recommended.

- A monitor capable of displaying at least 256 colors or grayscale and 128MB of graphics memory.

- A modem with a speed of at least 14,400 bps and browser if neither of these software programs is already installed on your PC:

- Adobe Reader for viewing the PDFs. If you need a copy, go to `http://get.adobe.com/reader/`.

- Adobe Flash Player for viewing the flashcards. If you need a copy, go to `http://get.adobe.com/flashplayer/`.

If you need more information on the basics, check out these books published by John Wiley & Sons, Inc.: *PCs For Dummies* by Dan Gookin; *Macs For Dummies* by Edward C. Baig; *iMac For Dummies* by Mark L. Chambers; and *Windows XP For Dummies* and *Windows Vista For Dummies*, both by Andy Rathbone.

What You'll Find Online and on the CD

The following sections provide a summary of the goodies you can find online and on the CD. *Note:* The CD will not open in maximized view. For optimal viewing, don't maximize.

Practice tests and question sets

To help you prepare for the ASVAB, *ASVAB For Dummies Online* includes the three full practice tests found in Part V of this book, as well as three additional full-length tests. These three new tests have the same number of questions as the computer version of the ASVAB, so they're a bit shorter than the pencil-and-paper tests from the book. If you want to sharpen your AFQT test-taking skills, you can take a practice AFQT either on the CD or online. (That test is the same as the one in Chapter 22.)

You can take the online tests only in a timed mode, which mimics how you'll probably take the actual ASVAB. At the MEPS (military entrance processing station), each test section has a rigid time requirement, and after you answer a question, your answer is set in stone.

Your results from these practice tests can't be saved. I recommend that after you complete a subtest, you write down the topics of the questions you missed so you can go back and review those areas.

If you want more practice on certain topics, you can create customized sets of questions within *ASVAB For Dummies Online*. You choose the difficulty level, the categories of questions, and number of questions you want to answer.

Vocabulary flashcards

A large part of your overall ASVAB score is determined by your knowledge of word definitions. To help you in this area, I include a set of digital vocabulary flashcards on the website. Use these flashcards to increase your knowledge of English words and their definitions. When you take the actual ASVAB, you'll be glad you did.

To use the flashcards, you can choose either random or sequential. Random allows you to view them in any order, while sequential starts at 1 and advances through all 300. While viewing the cards, use the Flip button to advance to the next card and the Back button to go back and review.

Articles

You can find links to the following online articles on the CD:

✔ **Breakdown of the ASVAB Subtests:** This article gives you a rundown of the subtests contained in the ASVAB and the AFQT. It shows you the number of questions you have to answer, how much time you have to answer them, and an overview of the content. (A similar table is included in Chapter 1.)

✔ **Matching ASVAB Scores to Military Jobs:** This document also appears as Appendix A in the book. You can reference this document to determine which jobs your ASVAB line score qualifies you for. If you want a certain job, you can determine what you need to score on the ASVAB.

✔ **A Detailed Look at Scoring the ASVAB:** This article explains how the ASVAB is scored (Chapter 1 already has the basics on scoring, but this document discusses scoring on a more technical level). Some of your ASVAB scores are used to determine your overall qualification for joining the military branch of your choice, and other scores are used to determine which military jobs you qualify for.

Hitting the Website

When you're ready to try your hand at a computer version of the ASVAB, head to `online practice.dummies.com`. On your first visit, you need to enter your *ASVAB For Dummies Online* PIN code. You can find your PIN in the back of the book, or you can get your PIN by registering your e-book at `dummies.com/go/getaccess`. (If you have trouble with the PIN or can't find it, please contact Wiley Product Technical Support at 800-762-2974 or `http://support.wiley.com`.) If you already have an account, log in and then enter your new PIN on the My Products page.

After you enter the PIN, you'll need to establish your own login information. When you want to return to *ASVAB For Dummies Online,* you'll simply need to log in with your personal information. No need to use the PIN a second time.

Your registration at *ASVAB For Dummies Online* is good for one year. After that time frame has passed, you can renew your registration for a fee. The website will give you all the important details about how to do so.

Using the CD

To use the CD, follow these steps:

1. **Insert the CD into your computer's CD-ROM drive. The license agreement appears.**

   Note to Windows users: The interface won't launch if you have autorun disabled. In that case, choose Start→Run. (For Windows Vista, choose Start→All Programs→ Accessories→Run.) In the dialog box that appears, type *D:***Start.exe**. (Replace *D* with the proper letter if your CD drive uses a different letter. If you don't know the letter, see how your CD drive is listed under My Computer or Computer.) Click OK.

Note to Mac Users: When the CD icon appears on your desktop, double-click the icon to open the CD and double-click the Start icon. Also, note that the content menus may not function as expected in newer versions of Safari and Firefox; however, the documents are available by navigating to the Contents folder.

2. **Read through the license agreement and then click the Accept button if you want to use the CD.**

   The CD interface appears. The interface allows you to browse the contents with just a click of a button (or two).

Troubleshooting and Customer Care

I tried my best to compile programs that work on most computers with the minimum system requirements. Alas, your computer may differ, and the CD may not work properly for some reason.

The two likeliest problems are that you don't have enough memory (RAM) for the CD, or you have other programs running that are affecting how the program runs. If you get an error message such as "Not enough memory" or "Setup cannot continue," try one or more of the following suggestions and then try using the CD again:

- ✔ **Turn off any antivirus software running on your computer.** External programs sometimes mimic virus activity and may make your computer incorrectly believe that it's being infected by a virus.

- ✔ **Close all running programs.** The more programs you have running, the less memory is available to other programs. If you have several other programs running, try closing a couple and then starting the CD again.

- ✔ **Have your local computer store add more RAM to your computer (or find out how to add RAM yourself).** This is, admittedly, a somewhat expensive step. However, adding more memory can really help the speed of your computer and allow more programs to run at the same time.

If you have trouble with the CD-ROM or website, please call the Wiley Product Technical Support phone number at 800-762-2974. Outside the United States, call 317-572-3994. You can also contact Wiley Product Technical Support at http://support.wiley.com. John Wiley & Sons will provide technical support only for installation and other general quality control items. For technical support on the applications themselves, consult the program's vendor or author.

To place additional orders or to request information about other Wiley products, please call 800-762-2974.

Index

John Wiley & Sons, Inc.
Online Test Software End-User
License Agreement

READ THIS. This Agreement is part of a package that includes one or more tests and certain electronic and/or written materials. You should carefully read these terms and conditions before downloading, installing, or using the Test Software Package(s). This is a license agreement "Agreement" between you and John Wiley & Sons, Inc. "Wiley". By downloading, installing, or using the Test Software Package(s), you acknowledge that you have read and accept the following terms and conditions. If you do not agree and do not want to be bound by such terms and conditions, promptly cease the download, installation, or use of the Test Software Package(s).

1. **License Grant.** Wiley grants to you (either an individual or entity) a nonexclusive license to download, access, install, and use the Test Software Package(s) (collectively, the "Software") solely for your own personal or business purposes on a single computer (whether a standard computer or a workstation component of a multi-user network). The Software is in use on a computer when it is loaded into temporary memory (RAM) or installed into permanent memory (hard disk, CD-ROM, or other storage device). Wiley reserves all rights not expressly granted herein.

2. **Ownership.** Wiley is the owner of all right, title, and interest, including copyright, in and to the compilation of the Software. Copyright to the individual programs of the Software is owned by the author or other authorized copyright owner of each program. Ownership of the Software and all proprietary rights relating thereto remain with Wiley and its licensers.

3. **Restrictions on Use and Transfer.**

   (a) You may only (i) make one copy of the Software for backup or archival purposes, or (ii) transfer the Software to a single hard disk, provided that you keep the original for backup or archival purposes. You may not (i) rent or lease the Software, (ii) copy or reproduce the Software through a LAN or other network system or through any computer subscriber system or bulletin-board system, or (iii) modify, adapt, or create derivative works based on the Software.

   (b) You may not reverse engineer, decompile, or disassemble the Software. You may transfer the Software and user documentation on a permanent basis, provided that the transferee agrees to accept the terms and conditions of this Agreement and you retain no copies. If the Software is an update or has been updated, any transfer must include the most recent update and all prior versions.

4. **Restrictions on Use of Individual Programs.** You must follow the individual requirements and restrictions detailed for each individual program on the Software. These limitations are also contained in the individual license agreements contained in the Software. These limitations may include a requirement that after using the program for a specified period of time, the user must pay a registration fee or discontinue use. By downloading the Software package(s), you will be agreeing to abide by the licenses and restrictions for these individual programs that are detailed in the Software. None of the material on this Software may ever be redistributed, in original or modified form, for commercial purposes.

5. **Limited Warranty.**

   (a) WILEY AND THE AUTHOR(S) DISCLAIM ALL WARRANTIES, EXPRESS OR IMPLIED, INCLUDING WITHOUT LIMITATION IMPLIED WARRANTIES OF MERCHANTABILITY AND FITNESS FOR A PARTICULAR PURPOSE, WITH RESPECT TO THE SOFTWARE, THE PROGRAMS, AND/OR THE SOURCE CODE CONTAINED THEREIN. WILEY DOES NOT WARRANT THAT THE FUNCTIONS CONTAINED IN THE SOFTWARE WILL MEET YOUR REQUIREMENTS OR THAT THE OPERATION OF THE SOFTWARE WILL BE ERROR FREE.

   (b) This limited warranty gives you specific legal rights, and you may have other rights that vary from jurisdiction to jurisdiction.

6. **Remedies.**

   (a) In no event shall Wiley or the author be liable for any damages whatsoever (including without limitation damages for loss of business profits, business interruption, loss of business information, or any other pecuniary loss) arising from the use of or inability to use the Software, even if Wiley has been advised of the possibility of such damages.

   (b) Because some jurisdictions do not allow the exclusion or limitation of liability for consequential or incidental damages, the above limitation or exclusion may not apply to you.

7. **U.S. Government Restricted Rights.** Use, duplication, or disclosure of the Software for or on behalf of the United States of America, its agencies and/or instrumentalities "U.S. Government" is subject to restrictions as stated in paragraph (c)(1)(ii) of the Rights in Technical Data and Computer Software clause of DFARS 252.227-7013, or subparagraphs (c) (1) and (2) of the Commercial Computer Software - Restricted Rights clause at FAR 52.227-19, and in similar clauses in the NASA FAR supplement, as applicable.

8. **General.** This Agreement constitutes the entire understanding of the parties and revokes and supersedes all prior agreements, oral or written, between them and may not be modified or amended except in a writing signed by both parties hereto that specifically refers to this Agreement. This Agreement shall take precedence over any other documents that may be in conflict herewith. If any one or more provisions contained in this Agreement are held by any court or tribunal to be invalid, illegal, or otherwise unenforceable, each and every other provision shall remain in full force and effect.

Apple & Mac

iPad For Dummies,
5th Edition
978-1-118-49823-1

iPhone 5 For Dummies,
6th Edition
978-1-118-35201-4

MacBook For Dummies,
4th Edition
978-1-118-20920-2

OS X Mountain Lion
For Dummies
978-1-118-39418-2

Blogging & Social Media

Facebook For Dummies,
4th Edition
978-1-118-09562-1

Mom Blogging
For Dummies
978-1-118-03843-7

Pinterest For Dummies
978-1-118-32800-2

WordPress For Dummies,
5th Edition
978-1-118-38318-6

Business

Commodities For Dummies,
2nd Edition
978-1-118-01687-9

Investing For Dummies,
6th Edition
978-0-470-90545-6

Personal Finance
For Dummies, 7th Edition
978-1-118-11785-9

QuickBooks 2013
For Dummies
978-1-118-35641-8

Small Business Marketing
Kit For Dummies,
3rd Edition
978-1-118-31183-7

Careers

Job Interviews
For Dummies, 4th Edition
978-1-118-11290-8

Job Searching with
Social Media
For Dummies
978-0-470-93072-4

Personal Branding
For Dummies
978-1-118-11792-7

Resumes For Dummies,
6th Edition
978-0-470-87361-8

Success as a Mediator
For Dummies
978-1-118-07862-4

Diet & Nutrition

Belly Fat Diet For Dummies
978-1-118-34585-6

Eating Clean For Dummies
978-1-118-00013-7

Nutrition For Dummies,
5th Edition
978-0-470-93231-5

Digital Photography

Digital Photography
For Dummies,
7th Edition
978-1-118-09203-3

Digital SLR Cameras &
Photography For Dummies,
4th Edition
978-1-118-14489-3

Photoshop Elements 11
For Dummies
978-1-118-40821-6

Gardening

Herb Gardening
For Dummies, 2nd Edition
978-0-470-61778-6

Vegetable Gardening
For Dummies, 2nd Edition
978-0-470-49870-5

Health

Anti-Inflammation Diet
For Dummies
978-1-118-02381-5

Diabetes For Dummies,
3rd Edition
978-0-470-27086-8

Living Paleo For Dummies
978-1-118-29405-5

Hobbies

Beekeeping
For Dummies
978-0-470-43065-1

eBay For Dummies,
7th Edition
978-1-118-09806-6

Raising Chickens
For Dummies
978-0-470-46544-8

Wine For Dummies,
5th Edition
978-1-118-28872-6

Writing Young Adult Fiction
For Dummies
978-0-470-94954-2

Language &
Foreign Language

500 Spanish Verbs
For Dummies
978-1-118-02382-2

English Grammar
For Dummies, 2nd Edition
978-0-470-54664-2

French All-in One
For Dummies
978-1-118-22815-9

German Essentials
For Dummies
978-1-118-18422-6

Italian For Dummies,
2nd Edition
978-1-118-00465-4

Available in print and e-book formats.

Available wherever books are sold. For more information or to order direct: U.S. customers visit www.Dummies.com or call 1-877-762-2974.
U.K. customers visit www.Wileyeurope.com or call (0) 1243 843291. Canadian customers visit www.Wiley.ca or call 1-800-567-4797.
Connect with us online at www.facebook.com/fordummies or @fordummies

Math & Science

Algebra I For Dummies,
2nd Edition
978-0-470-55964-2

Anatomy and Physiology
For Dummies,
2nd Edition
978-0-470-92326-9

Astronomy For Dummies,
3rd Edition
978-1-118-37697-3

Biology For Dummies,
2nd Edition
978-0-470-59875-7

Chemistry For Dummies,
2nd Edition
978-1-1180-0730-3

Pre-Algebra Essentials
For Dummies
978-0-470-61838-7

Microsoft Office

Excel 2013 For Dummies
978-1-118-51012-4

Office 2013 All-in-One
For Dummies
978-1-118-51636-2

PowerPoint 2013
For Dummies
978-1-118-50253-2

Word 2013 For Dummies
978-1-118-49123-2

Music

Blues Harmonica
For Dummies
978-1-118-25269-7

Guitar For Dummies,
3rd Edition
978-1-118-11554-1

iPod & iTunes
For Dummies,
10th Edition
978-1-118-50864-0

Programming

Android Application
Development For Dummies,
2nd Edition
978-1-118-38710-8

iOS 6 Application
Development For Dummies
978-1-118-50880-0

Java For Dummies,
5th Edition
978-0-470-37173-2

Religion & Inspiration

The Bible For Dummies
978-0-7645-5296-0

Buddhism For Dummies,
2nd Edition
978-1-118-02379-2

Catholicism For Dummies,
2nd Edition
978-1-118-07778-8

Self-Help & Relationships

Bipolar Disorder
For Dummies,
2nd Edition
978-1-118-33882-7

Meditation For Dummies,
3rd Edition
978-1-118-29144-3

Seniors

Computers For Seniors
For Dummies,
3rd Edition
978-1-118-11553-4

iPad For Seniors
For Dummies,
5th Edition
978-1-118-49708-1

Social Security
For Dummies
978-1-118-20573-0

Smartphones & Tablets

Android Phones
For Dummies
978-1-118-16952-0

Kindle Fire HD
For Dummies
978-1-118-42223-6

NOOK HD For Dummies,
Portable Edition
978-1-118-39498-4

Surface For Dummies
978-1-118-49634-3

Test Prep

ACT For Dummies,
5th Edition
978-1-118-01259-8

ASVAB For Dummies,
3rd Edition
978-0-470-63760-9

GRE For Dummies,
7th Edition
978-0-470-88921-3

Officer Candidate Tests,
For Dummies
978-0-470-59876-4

Physician's Assistant Exam
For Dummies
978-1-118-11556-5

Series 7 Exam
For Dummies
978-0-470-09932-2

Windows 8

Windows 8 For Dummies
978-1-118-13461-0

Windows 8 For Dummies,
Book + DVD Bundle
978-1-118-27167-4

Windows 8 All-in-One
For Dummies
978-1-118-11920-4

Available in print and e-book formats.

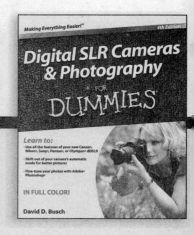

Take Dummies with you everywhere you go!

Whether you're excited about e-books, want more from the web, must have your mobile apps, or swept up in social media, Dummies makes everything easier .

Dummies products make life easier!

- DIY
- Consumer Electronics
- Crafts

- Software
- Cookware
- Hobbies

- Videos
- Music
- Games
- and More!

For more information, go to **Dummies.com**® and search the store by category.

FOR DUMMIES®

A Wiley Brand